EXTENDED PLAY

Sounding Off
from
John Cage
to
Dr. Funkenstein

●

JOHN CORBETT

DUKE UNIVERSITY PRESS

Durham/London 1994

© 1994 Duke University Press

All rights reserved

Printed in the United States of America on acid-free paper ∞

Typeset in Berkeley Medium

Library of Congress Cataloging-in-Publication Data
appear on the last printed page of this book.

Frontispiece on page vii Han Bennink (photo: Nick White)

"Blowtop Blues" by Jane and Leonard Feather copyright
© 1945 (renewed) by Embassy Music Corporation (BMI).
International copyright secured. All rights reserved.
Reprinted by permission.

"Just a Nuance" by Ivor Cutler from LARGE and Puffy, Arc
Publications, 17 Pudsey Rd., Cornholme, Todmorden, Lancs., UK.
Copyright © 1984 by Ivor Cutler. Reprinted by permission.

in
memory
of
John Cage
and
Hal Russell
and
Sun Ra

CONTENTS

●

PART THREE • MUSIC LIKE DIRT • *Interviews and Outerviews*

ACKNOWLEDGMENTS

●

Some of the essays, articles, and interviews in this book have appeared in various forms in other places. "Free, Single, and Disengaged" first appeared in *October* 54 (Fall 1990). "Spate of Flux" and "The Conversation Game: John Cage" were published in *New Art Examiner*. A number of the chapters appear courtesy of *Down Beat*, *The Wire*, *Option*, *Coda*, *Cadence*, *Butt Rag*, and *Victo Records*. I was fortunate to receive a grant from the Institute of Modern Communications at Northwestern University, which allowed me to videotape Lee "Scratch" Perry in Zurich. A preliminary interview with Derek Bailey was conducted at WGBH, Boston, thanks to John Voci. I am also grateful to have attended a number of music festivals, at which I was able to conduct various other interviews. Thanks to Michael Levasseur at Festival International Musique Actuelle de Victoriaville; Ken Pickering at the du Maurier International Jazz Festival, Vancouver; George Gruntz at Jazzfest Berlin; Ed Baxter at the London Musicians' Collective; and Huub van Riel at BIMhuis, Amsterdam.

As in any undertaking as varied as this, a great many people aided and abetted me. For things academic and otherwise, I would like to thank Mimi White, Jim Schwoch, Michael Hyde, Margaret Drewel, and James Webster at Northwestern University. Editors have helped in the process of preparing some of these texts for publication; I should especially thank Rosalind Krauss, Martha Buskirk, Mark Sinker, Pete Margasak, Robert Dulgarian, Mark Kemp, John Ephland, Dave Helland, Allison Gamble, Ann Weins, and Deb Wilk for their editorial suggestions. I extend my appreciation to the musicians who participated in the numerous interviews that went into the book; thanks to Steve Beresford and Derek Bailey, especially, for putting in editorial time as well.

I am fortunate to have friends who are also accomplices; muchos gracias Jalal Toufic, Tom "Sphere" Fry, Ben Portis, Mick Hurbis-Cherrier, Katherine Hurbis-Cherrier, Philip Kirk, Kevin Whitehead, Hal Rammel, Tim Fitzgerald, Jayne "AJ" Hyland, Russell Fine, Jim Macnie, Bob Snyder, Aaron Cohen, Allan Chase, Mark Wolff, Beth Rega, David Grubbs, J. P. Chill, Anna McCarthy, Rick Wajcik, the Chicago Music Reading Group, Anahid Kassabian, Art Lange, and Glenda, Andreas, and Effie Kapsalis. Ken Wissoker at Duke University Press was in on *Extended Play* at the ground level, and his editorial insight and personal attention were invaluable. For emergency computer assistance, I thank Rose and Max Corbett. For support, enthusiasm, and encouragement, I thank my parents, James and Joyce, and my sistahs, Jillian and Jennifer.

Finally, deepest thanks to my first editor, holistic partner, and inamorata, Terri Kapsalis. As Michael Hurley says, oh my stars how you undo me.

INTRODUCTION

Earmeals and

Expubedience

●

At last, I have a CD machine with shuffle mode. It's
a miraculous button, "shuffle." In an instant it does
away with the logic behind decades of music in-
dustry packaging, the kind of logic that works with A-sides and B-sides (the
soon-to-be-obscure domain of records and tapes), the same logic that sequences a release in a particular way so that cuts are preceded and followed
by appropriate others. For instance, think about how many hit singles are
positioned as the first cut on the second side of an album; that's well known
as the LP sweet-spot. In the place of this sequential logic, shuffle offers a
random number generator, an exciting turn of events. Now a disc can renew
itself virtually every time it's played, putting together unforeseeable combinations, segues, connections, and leaps of faith.

As I see it, this is one of the great possibilities of musical postmodernity.
In the process of shuffling, the activity of making connections and creating
meaning is somehow thrust back into the lap of the listener. Naturally,
shuffle mode doesn't eradicate the old logic; more often than not, a listener
will probably just press "play" and let the disc run its course. But that's part
and parcel of the postmodern: it makes a multitude of systems possible. At
its worst, postmodernism manifests itself as an empty form of eclecticism in
which, as Jean-François Lyotard suggests, the bottom line is still the buck.
At its best, the postmodern is about the opening up of options, the accep-
tance of incompatibility, the irreducibility of all forms of discourse to the
logic of one. Check it out—my aunt's got a player that shuffles between five
discs! Think of the possibilities . . .

Already, musicians have responded to the gauntlet thrown down by the
compact disc's programmability. Take Nicolas Collins's *100 of the World's
Most Beautiful Melodies*, a disc with forty-two miniature improvisations between Collins and fifteen different musicians. In the liner notes, Collins
encourages that "the listener now has the option of involving him or herself
in a further level of performance, by using the random access capabilities of
the CD player to rearrange the forty-two cuts." And the Canadian group Fat
has made a similar disc titled *Automat Hi-Life*. Pointing even more directly

to the variety of listener options, the Swiss group Karl ein Karl has an involved release called *Karl's Fest*, which contains instructions for programming the disc: (1) for a simple concert of improvised music by the trio; (2) for dinner music suitable for enjoying good food or wine; (3) for highly instructive statements; or (4) for songs. "But you can also combine these elements," they advise, "for instance dinner-music with songs—or you can create your own exclusive music-menu. And if you like surprises, select the shuttle-mode."

I like surprises. Perhaps someday, with the further development of electronic publishing, *Extended Play* will be subject to reprogramming via shuffle (or shuttle, or random) mode. That would please me immensely. While, in the end, I have chosen to organize the book into sections—to segregate the more academic and theoretically oriented chapters in "Dancing in Your Head" (title taken from the album by saxophonist Ornette Coleman) from the musician profiles in "An Ear to the Ground" and the dialogues in "Music Like Dirt" (title taken from the reggae songs by Desmond Dekker, referring to the amount of music in the world)—I would hope that a reader might take the opportunity to defy these categories, to bounce whimsically between sections or to use the index and discography in a creative way. This seems only fitting, given the vastly divergent contexts and modes in which knowledge about music is now generated—popular press, trade press, academic journals, radio, record stores, clubs, theaters, concert halls, liner notes, musicology departments, music television.

I encourage a randomized reading of *Extended Play* not simply to undermine my own careful sense of order and sequence, but because one of the impetuses behind the collection was the desire to get different kinds of music discourse to rub elbows. These different discourses, all centered on the same basic referent, approach and represent that object of study very differently from one another. But a theoretical tack on a particular musical issue is no less "authentic" than an experienced musician's tale, and, conversely, a musician's perspective is no less admissible or viable than a more critical approach. And the journalistic portrait presents yet another form of representation—and a widespread one, at that. The point is that by crossing these kinds of writing, by allowing them to butt up against one another, it is possible to create new connections, perhaps inspire unpredicted ways of thinking about music and the issues it raises, and simultaneously, denature the mythology that locates musical truth in one discourse rather than another.

There are a number of implicit and explicit polemics that figure in *Extended Play*, most of which I will leave either to speak for themselves or to remain in the shadows. But one deserves to be drawn out. Originally written in 1977, Jacques Attali's *Noise: The Political Economy of Music* was first translated into English in 1985. At that time, reading Attali's book seemed to open up a lot of things, many of which I was already thinking about, some of which were entirely new. It addressed questions of power, discourse, subjectivity, repetition, technology, economics, representation, and recording—issues mandatory for an adequate approach to music in today's society. I still think *Noise* is brilliant, epochal. It marks the beginning of a truly contemporary form of critical music theory. Indeed, since its publication, few music books or articles that attempt to deal with any social, political, or textual issues have escaped without citing Monsieur A.

Extended Play is perhaps a way of coming to terms with Attali, of taking what seems usable and necessary from *Noise* and adapting it to my own purposes. But this has also involved taking issue with Attali. The initial American publication of *Noise* was riddled with misspelled names, factual errors, and wrong dates, some of which were jumbled in translation and some of which were already there in the text. But it is specifically one section that I hope this collection of essays, articles, and interviews corrects forever: namely, Attali's death proclamation for free jazz. Or, as he so sweepingly titled it: " 'Uhuru'—The Failure of the Economy of Free Music."

What did it mean, in what by my reckoning was actually something of a banner year for improvisation, for a Parisian academic to suggest that free jazz (or free music) had "subsided, after being contained, repressed, limited, censored, expelled"? Why was this? Who says so? Was it because expatriate American musicians like Anthony Braxton and the Art Ensemble of Chicago left Paris in the early seventies? Moreover, what are the political consequences of the appearance of such a declaration in a paradigm-shifting book like *Noise*? What kinds of conservative bedfellows does Attali unknowingly snuggle up with when he says that because free jazz didn't change the entire economy of music production, it died? John McDonough puts forth a remarkably similar position in his diatribe called "Failed Experiment" (*Down Beat*, January 1992). "There comes a point in every *avant garde*," surmises McDonough, "when it must either put up or shut up." (For the proper response to this—and another exposed polemic—see "The Fires That Burn in Hal: Hal Russell" in Part Two.) Perhaps Attali should ask an American musician like Milford Graves or Fred Anderson or Mr. Braxton himself what it's been like to play dead music for these last fifteen years. Or, closer to home, how about asking someone from a group that is marginalized from almost all music discourse: European free improvisors like Derek Bailey, Sainkho Namtchylak, Peter Brötzmann, and Jon Rose. Doesn't Attali's death sentence ironically seem to implicate him in that very containing, repressing, limiting, censoring, expelling process that he regretfully sees in the popular (mis)treatment of free music?

Since 1977, in spite of Attali's proclamations (and in keeping with many of his predictions), the shapes, sizes, and colors of creative music—free and not—have grown expubediently (to borrow a term from Babs Gonzales). Working both as a music journalist and as an academic, I have time and again been startled to discover entire musical communities of whom I've never heard, often making a kind of music that I have a specific interest in and about which I like to think I know something. Take, for instance, Sweden's free improvised scene. In 1991, instrument inventor Hal Rammel told me about some happening Swedish stuff, gave me a tape, and suddenly I find I have a long list of fascinating players and groups with fully developed sound worlds of their own—Mats Gustafsson, Paul Pignon, Raymond Strid, Locomotiv Konkret, Sten Sandell, Johannes Bergmark, Per Henrik Wallin. From the other side of the Atlantic, it was precisely this kind of experience that writer Steve Lake says he had upon stumbling into the music of Hal Russell. And with any luck it might be the very feeling that someone reading *Extended Play* gets when listening to Lee "Scratch" Perry, The Ex, or Evan Parker for the first time.

In this sense, I see music as entertaining a complex, often antagonistic relationship with canonization. It constantly tweaks those who think they know it, it endlessly pushes back its own borders, it faithfully pledges to uphold the sneaking suspicion that, as harpist Zeena Parkins aptly put it in an album title, there's *Something Out There*. Indeed, something is out there, and it's waiting for you.

PART ONE
DANCING IN YOUR
HEAD

A man brought up on simple sounds   *Theoretical Jam*
and easy thoughts woke one night
with a nuance in his brain. Unable

●

to deal with it, he spoke it to a business associate with whom
he was sharing the room and who dabbled in semantics for a
hobby. Are you ill or something, Harry? he muttered, switch-
ing on the light. Let me fetch you a glass of water. It's all right.
Just a nuance, whispered Harry. Go back to sleep. I'll be all
right in the morning.—Ivor Cutler, "Just a Nuance"

BROTHERS FROM ANOTHER PLANET

The Space Madness
of Lee "Scratch" Perry,
Sun Ra, and George Clinton

●

I am the firmament computer, I am the sky computer, I am the orbit computer, I am the space computer. Inspector gadget Lee "Scratch" Perry, the upsetting upsetter, who make music better!—Lee Perry

It's more than avant-garde, because the "avant-garde" refers to, I suppose, advanced earth music. But this is not earth music.—Sun Ra

Funk upon a time, in the days of the Funkapuss, the concept of specially designed Afronauts, capable of funkatizing galaxies, was first laid on Man Child, but was later repossessed and placed among the secrets of the pyramids until a more positive attitude towards this most sacred phenomenon, Clone Funk, could be acquired. There in these terrestrial projects it would wait along with its co-inhabitants, the Kings and Pharaohs, like sleeping beauties, for the kiss that will release them to multiply in the image of the Chosen One, Dr. Funkenstein. And funk is its own reward. May I frighten you?
—George Clinton

Within the distinct worlds of reggae, jazz, and funk, Lee Perry, Sun Ra, and George Clinton have constructed worlds of their own, futuristic environs that subtly signify on the marginalization of black culture. These new discursive galaxies utilize a set of tropes and metaphors of space and alienation, linking their common diasporic African history to a notion of extraterrestriality. Ra worked with his free jazz big band, the Intergalactic Jet-Set Arkestra,[1] and asked "Have you heard the latest news from Neptune?" Perry helped invent "dub" reggae in his own Black Ark Studios and reminds us that "not all aliens come from outer space."[2] In his spectacular mid-seventies live concerts, funk-godfather Clinton staged an elaborate "mothership connection" and says "Starchild here! Citizens of the universe: it ain't nothin' but a party y'all!"

On the margin, all three have taken their production "one step beyond" into a zone in which, as Clinton puts it, "fantasy is reality in the world today." In doing so, they have all thrown their own identities into question, taking on a multitude of costumes and alter egos; each of them is a myth-making, alias-taking, self-styled postindustrial shaman. Such identity-invention is consistent with an ever-present issue in Afro-American and Afro-Caribbean music: the connection between madness and cultural production, exploration and innovation. The currency of terms like "crazy" and "way out" exposes this rhetorical figure, epitomized on the cover of an album by jazz bassist Curtis Counce from the 1950s called *Exploring the Future* on which Counce is pictured wearing a space suit, bass in hand. More recently—and less goofily—in an ode to her mother, Abbey Lincoln sings: "Evalina Coffey made the journey here / Traveled in her spaceship from some other sphere / Landed in St. Louis, Chicago and L.A. / A brilliant, shining mother ship / From six hundred trillion miles away."

Perry, Ra, and Clinton take space iconography seriously and turn it into a platform for playful subversion, imagining a productive zone largely exterior to dominant ideology. In this chapter, I will introduce these musicians and the issues that they manipulate, comparing and contrasting their use of science fiction (taken as fact), technology, industry relations (recording and distribution), eccentricity, insanity and the creative construction of alternative identities and renovated social possibilities.

Terrestrial ID

In his own way, each of these musicians presents himself as being extraterrestrial; Ra, Clinton, and Perry *live* as "brothers from another planet." This intergalactic identity may be meant literally, as in the case of Sun Ra, who, before he died in 1993, insisted that he was actually, physically from the planet Saturn. Or it may be more figurative, as in the outer-space (socio-) political party-ing of George Clinton, who adopts the explicability of the court jester: "Fool is neutral all the time, you know; I can be whatever comes through here without ever looking like I'm out of my bag." In either case, I want to suggest that an essential component of any serious consideration of their music and myth-making has to do with the acceptance of this impossible suggestion of outer-space origins, with believing, for a start, that Sun Ra was not of this world. I think this is true not only because they are great thinkers who deserve respect and suspended disbelief (though they are and do), but because while this E.T. metaphor—if it can be considered a metaphor—may indicate the *insanity* of its maker, it also cuts back the other direction, suggesting the fundamental *unreality* of existence for people imported into New World servitude and then disenfranchised into poverty. Thus Ra, Clinton, and Perry may force us not just to question *their* sanity, but to question our own. *Is it sane to believe them? Is it sane not to believe them? Is it "reasonable" to believe that they are from space? Is life on this planet not an unreasonable, otherworldly existence in itself?* It is a question of grappling with the African-American fight against what Cornel West calls "walking nihilism," a form of resistance waged with "demystifying criticism" or "critical prophecy."[3] Indeed, in their own separate ways, Ra, Clinton, and Perry are just such prophets, busily demystifying through remystifying—as Clinton puts it: "We're gonna blow the cobwebs out your mind." Thus, since their work must be dealt with on its own terms, I will spend just a brief time recounting the "real" history of each musician.

Sun Ra's earthly tenure is difficult to trace with any certainty, but he was born Herman Blount in Birmingham, Alabama, in the middle of the first decade of the twentieth century. He played piano and arranged for the bigbands of Fletcher Henderson and Eugene Wright before settling in Chicago in the early 1950s. There, the Arkestra took shape, eventually establishing a core membership some members of which are still in the group today. It was in Chicago, as well, in the mid-fifties, that Ra began experimenting with extraterrestriality in his stage show, sometimes playing regular cocktail lounges dressed in space suits.[4] In 1961 Ra left the Windy City, settling for nearly a decade in New York City, where he directly influenced a vast number of East Coast jazz musicians. At the start of the 1970s, Ra once again transplanted the Arkestra, this time basing the group in Philadelphia, where they continue to live, work, and record.

George Clinton was also born in the South, in Kannapolis, North Carolina, in 1941.[5] Moving up the coast with his family, in 1952 Clinton settled in Newark, New Jersey, where he formed the doo-wop group the Parliaments. From 1958 to 1967, the Parliaments recorded singles for various small record labels. Since many of these labels were located in Detroit, the musically adventurous Clinton learned about that city's psychedelic groups, especially MC5, Ted Nugent and the Amboy Dukes, and the Stooges,[6] and in 1968 he formed Funkadelic, an ensemble that innovated the combination of funk and psychedelic rock. In the same year, Clinton dropped the "s" from his more commercial outfit, making it Parliament. With these two groups and on his own, Clinton made hit records through the 1970s and into the 1980s, landing smash dance hits like "Give Up the Funk (Tear the Roof off the Sucker)," "Flashlight," "Knee Deep," and "Atomic Dog." Though persistent drug and money problems have substantially decreased his creative work over the last decade, Clinton has periodically revived the P-Funk All Stars, an amalgam of Parliament/Funkadelic members. With the support of Prince and Prince's Paisley Park record label, the last few years have seen a renewed flurry of P-Funk activity, including large-scale concerts and a couple of records.

Lee Perry is five years Clinton's senior, born Rainford Hugh Perry in Hanover, Jamaica, in 1936.[7] In the mid-1950s, at the same time that Clinton

Sun Ra (photo: Thomas Hunter)

was commuting between Newark and Detroit unsuccessfully trying to record for Motown and Ra was parading around Club DeLisa in flowing Cosmo-Egyptian robes playing "Magic Music of the Spheres," Lee Perry was working for Jamaica's preeminent producer Clement "Coxsone" Dodd, locating and recording new singers for Dodd's Studio One record label. Himself a singer, Perry recorded a number of singles for Dodd and others, and after a nasty fight he split from Studio One and formed his own Upsetter label. There, he was central in the evolution of reggae out of its predecessors ska and rock steady. Producing Bob Marley and many others, Perry was wildly successful, both in Jamaica and in the expanding British reggae market, and in the 1970s he opened his own recording facility, Black Ark Studios, where he continued to produce. Along with King Tubby, Perry invented the studio technique called "dub," and he recorded some of dub reggae's most outrageous discs. Perry had a turbulent period in the late seventies, fueled by the frustrations of the Jamaican music industry, substance abuse, and the loss (by fire) of Black Ark. He was institutionalized for a period, after which he left Jamaica for Europe. Settling in Switzerland, he has continued to put out records that chart the relationship between madness, space/time travel, the Old Testament, and African identity.

What is remarkable, uncanny perhaps, about the story of these three musicians, even in their merely mortal incarnation, is how they have independently developed such similar myths.[8] Coming from different backgrounds, working in different musical genres, based in different parts of the music industry, making music for almost exclusively separate audiences, with divergent political and commercial concerns, Ra, Clinton, and Perry have nonetheless created three compatible personal mythologies, each of which is premised on the connection between identity, madness, and outer space. These mythologies are materialized in three primary areas:

Aliases: Lee Perry, a.k.a. Scratch, the Upsetter, Little, King, Super Ape, Pipecock Jackxon, Inspector Gadget. Sun Ra, a.k.a. Herman Blount, Sonny, Le Sony'r Ra, Ambassador to the Emperor of the Omniverse. George Clinton (and various P-Funk bandmembers), a.k.a. Dr. Funkenstein, Sir Nose D'Voidoffunk, Mr. Wiggles, the Undisco Kid, Lollipop Man, Starchild, Bumpnoxious Rumpofsteelskin.

Costumes: Since abandoning the requisite big-band tuxedos in the 1950s, the Arkestra has become well known for its colorful gear, glittery suits, and outrageous hats, adorned with Egyptian hieroglyphics, stars, moons, and planets; for the last few years of his life, Sun Ra dyed his goatee red and wore an imitation tiger-skin robe and matching headpiece (among many other ostentatious outfits).[9] "Costumes are music," he said. "Colors throw out musical sounds." Since the beginning of the 1980s, Lee Perry's wardrobe has become an increasingly prominent part of his work, his personally crafted crowns, boots, and clothes a tremendous mixture of fetish objects (photos, mirrors, crystals, coins, postcards) and détourné commodities (such as suspenders emblazoned with "U.S.A."). During an interview, he turned around to display the image of an erect penis hand-painted onto his jacket, declaring: "This is Jesus Christ, giver of life." George Clinton's costuming started partly as a result of the high cost of dry-cleaning, as ex-P-Funk vocalist Fuzzy Haskins explains: "We were doing four or five shows a day, six days a week, and you had to have uniforms. We were wearing suits and ties and

Lee "Scratch" Perry
(photo: David Corio)

we'd sweat 'em up in one performance. Then you had to take them to the cleaners and it's a big mess . . . it all boils down to the fact we couldn't afford to get our clothes cleaned every day."[10] Clinton suggests that it also had to do with staking out an image separate from the prevailing Motown image: "The Temptations and the Pips had their type of thing wrapped up—the choreography, the outfits. . . . Instead of wearing the suits we'd just gotten pressed, we'd wear the bags they came back from the cleaners in. We'd just bust holes where the legs and arms would go. If we were on the road and we didn't have a costume, I'd take a sheet from the hotel and just dump whatever I had around on it."[11] From that point, in the 1960s, Clinton and crew built a huge wardrobe of outfits, from bedsheets covered in lipstick and ketchup to diapers and a pacifier to the Dr. Funkenstein persona as depicted on the poster from *Live P. Funk Earth Tour* LP—dressed head-to-toe in white fur pelts, white 10-inch heels, knee-high, rhinestone-studded boots and a phallic rocket/scepter resting on his thigh.

Wordplay: Central to the work of Perry, Clinton, and Ra is the reappropriation and manipulation of rational language. Perry commences his recent song "Welcome Aboard" with the invocation: "God the Holy Ghost, as He was in the beginning forever it shall be, *words* without end." In his poem "The Curtain Call," Ra writes: "The scenery must be cleared / For another day / Another kind of cosmo-play / A play on words."[12] Clinton directly relates his own, rather compulsive language twisting to audience empowerment: "I feel that words and word games is communications—like abstract paintings. But it is mainly designed to let you think about it and come to all the different things without preaching. It just make you come to some kind of conclusion yourself."[13]

Madness and (Black) Civilization

In African-American slang there is a longstanding constellation of terms that revolves around the interrogation of sanity. Subtle and supple, this group of words relies on a set of interrelated connotations—a certain fluidity of meaning—that links madness with excellence and innovation. For example: "crazy," "wild," "out of control," "nutty," "insane," "out." These terms have been most fully developed and deployed in relation to music, especially jazz and blues. Indeed, the first commercial blues record, released in 1921, was Mamie Smith's "Crazy Blues."[14] Initially, these terms carried two additional strong connotations: intoxication and love. On the Memphis Jug Band's 1934 record "Insane Crazy Blues," Charlie Burse sings: "I'm going insane, standing out in the rain, spend a thousand dollars, it don't mean a thing . . . Everybody calls it love, me and my little turtledove . . ." In 1954,

George Clinton
(photo: David Corio)

Dinah Washington sang her "New Blowtop Blues," a virtual topography of madness which connects it with both love and getting high:

> I've got bad news baby / and you're the first to know. (×2)
>   Well, I discovered this morning / that my wig is about to blow.
> I been rockin' on my feet / and I been talkin' all out of my head. (×2)
>   And when I get through talkin' / I can't remember a thing I've said.
> Now I used to be a sharpie / all dressed in the latest styles
>   But now I'm walkin' down Broadway / wearin' nothing but a smile.
> I see all kinds of little men / although they're never there
>   I tried to push a subway train / and poured whiskey in my hair.
> I'm a girl who blew a fuse / I've got those blowtop blues.
> Last night I was 5-feet tall / today I'm 8-feet 10
>   Every time I fall down stairs / I float right up again
> When someone turned the lights on me / it like to drove me blind
>   I woke up this morning in Bellvue / but I left my mind behind.
> I'm a gal you can't excuse / I've got those blowtop blues.
> Well, I got high last night / and I took my man to his wife's front door.
> Yes, I got juiced last night / and I took my man to his wife's front door.
>   She was a 45-packin' mama / and I ain't gonna try that no more.

While madness, on the one hand, is associated with the intoxicating effect of love and drug, it bears two further, more general connotations: passionate abandon and social oppression. It is a question of creating beauty in (or out of) a subjugating social system, the "madness" in which an African-American listener may lose her or his inhibition, but in which she or he is always inhibited. Hence, a complicated grid of historical, musical, and signi-fyin(g) strands connects Jelly Roll Morton's "Wild Man Blues" (1927), Jimmie Lunceford's "I'm Nuts about Screwy Music" (1935), Theolonious Monk's "Nutty" (1954), Ornette Coleman's "Focus on Sanity" (1959), Eric Dolphy's *Out To Lunch* (1964), the Last Poets' "This Is Madness" (1971), Prince's "Let's Go Crazy" (1984), and P. M. Dawn's "Reality Used To Be a Friend of Mine" (1991). Somewhere, in the midst of that mix, we could locate Sun Ra and the Arkestra's *Cosmic Tones for Mental Therapy* (1963), Funkadelic's "Back in Our Minds" (1970), and Lee "Scratch" Perry's "I Am a Madman" (1986).

Although the subtle shades of meaning that differentiate these various uses of craziness could fill a volume, what we are concerned with is the way that this discursive web sets the stage, in a fundamental sense, for the rhetorical and identificatory tactics of Ra, Clinton, and Perry, all of whom utilize the overarching idea of insanity liberally in their work.[15] Each of them doubles the intensity of this metaphor with a superimposed metaphor of outer space. In the tropology of madness, one is "close to the edge" or "out

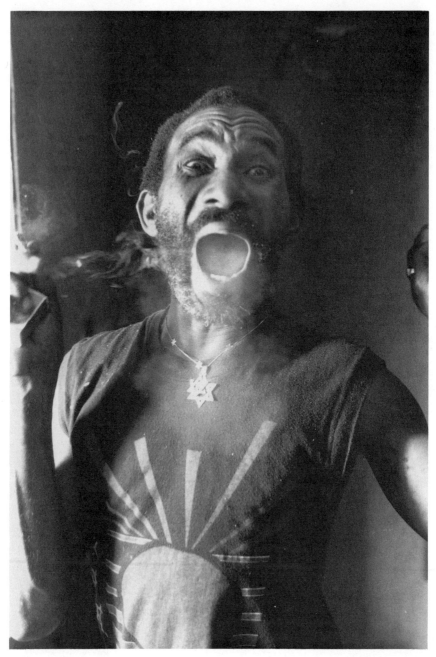

Lee "Scratch" Perry
(photo: David Corio)

of one's mind." The mind, and more specifically the *reasonable* mind, is configured as a terrestrial zone, as earth; sanity is the "ground," from which one departs in "flights" of fancy. Hence, the connection is established between "going way out" (a common phrase in jazz for a solo that transgresses a widely held musical code, such as the established harmonic framework),[16] and leaving earth. Tradition = earth; innovation = outer space. In the language of black music, madness and extraterrestriality go hand in hand.

In a phrase that suggestively supplements the sea-vessel image of Africans imported into "civilizing" slavery in the Western Hemisphere, Paul Virilio has called the imposition of *reason* "the boarding of the metabolic vehicles."[17] He discusses it as an "act of piracy" in which the dispossessed are made into "technical bodies or technological objects." What Ra, Clinton, and Perry do is to crazily reappropriate this image and retool it—transforming the sea-ship into a space-ship. In Ra's complex historiography, for instance, he gives accounts of travel in spacecraft as thinly veiled, sometimes explicit metaphors for the slave trade. Referring to the destruction of diverse, distinct African histories and their subsumption in the "melting pot" of miscegenation and history-without-genealogy, he suggests a creative alternative: "We came from nowhere here, why can't we go somewhere there?"

> You have to realize this planet is not only inhabited by humans, it's inhabited by aliens too . . . in mixed up among humans you have angels. The danger spot is the United States. You have more angels in the country than anywhere else. You see, it was planned . . . They say truth is stranger than fiction. Never in the history of the world has there been a case where you take a whole people and bring 'em into the country in the Commerce Department . . . It happened here . . . It was possible for aliens and angels and devils and demons to come in this country. They didn't need no passport. So then they'd come as displaced people. Perfect setup . . . They could come here and act like poor people, they could come here and act like slaves because they [the authorities] didn't keep up with what was happening.[18]

Thus Ra takes the disempowerment of slavery and turns it into a creative situation in which the absolute identity of African Americans—as people or as angels—is unknown to anyone but African Americans themselves. Similarly, in the 1970s George Clinton simultaneously developed two creative-identity projects: with Funkadelic he established "One Nation under a Groove," an earthly, politically grounded type of dancing-populism or a funky form of black nationalism; with Parliament, he staged the "mothership connection," a detailed myth-in-performance in which he emerged (replete with strong "birthing" imagery) onto stage from a space-pod, his mothership clearly conflating Africa (motherland) and space. Clinton's mothership, Perry's Black Ark, Ra's Arkestra—these are the new, unreasonable vessels for travel in discursive space.

In fact, the use of space as a metaphor is more involved than it might first appear. If metaphors basically work by taking something unfamiliar and substituting for it a known object or concept, then what happens when the metaphor chosen is, in itself, defined as the "unknown"? Granted, the word *space* conjures all sorts of associations, but one of its primary attributes is the notion of exploration—the very notion that links it with innovation in African-American music. Hence, one is left to define something by substituting for it the unknown, the unfathomable, terra incognita, "space"— the (endlessly deferred) final frontier. In their work on the "grounding" of metaphors, George Lakoff and Mark Johnson use a hypothetical outer space example as a critique of the idea of nonmetaphorized, directly experienced spatial reality: "Imagine a spherical being living outside any gravitational field, with no knowledge or imagination of any other kind of experience. What could UP possibly mean to such a being? The answer to this question would depend, not only on the physiology of this spherical being, but also on its culture."[19] Outer space becomes the testing ground for the limits of metaphor, a place where anthropomorphized spheres prove that metaphors, in the end, relate to no "absolute," but are always culturally determined.

What happens, then, in the case of Ra, Clinton, and Perry, is that they build their mythologies on an image of disorientation that becomes a metaphor for social marginalization, an experience familiar to many African Americans though alien to most of the terrestrial, dominant white "center."[20] Staking their claim on this ec-centric margin—a place that simultaneously eludes and frightens the oppressive, centered subjectivity—the three of them reconstitute it as a place of creation. It is a metaphor of *being elsewhere*, or perhaps of making *this elsewhere* your own. As bell hooks describes it: "I am located in the margin. I make a definite distinction between that marginality which is imposed by oppressive strutures and that marginality one chooses as site of resistance—as location of radical openness and possibility . . . We are transformed, individually, collectively, as we make radical creative space which affirms and sustains our subjectivity, which gives us a new location from which to articulate our sense of the world."[21] It is precisely this radical openness and relocation that Clinton, Perry, and Ra manifest in their elaboration of the insanity-outer space-marginality triad. For the three of them, as Donna Haraway puts it, "the boundary between science fiction and social reality is an optical illusion."[22] Or, as Ra prescribes: "Myth versus Reality (the Myth-Science Approach)."

From Cyber-Funk to Elephant Trunk: African Ghosts in the Machine

We have grown used to connecting MACHINES *and* FUNKINESS. *—Andrew Goodwin*

In 1990, discussing the logistics of a video documentary I was making on him, Lee "Scratch" Perry advised me not to worry about the contracts. "When you get home I'll tele-transport them to you," he said. He didn't mean facsimile, he meant telepathy. With Perry, Ra, and Clinton, technology plays a crucial role not only in their music—Perry pioneered many now-standard studio techniques, Clinton helped cultivate the creative use of drum machines and is a die-hard advocate of uninhibited sampling, and Ra was the first jazz musician to use synthesizers—but also in their mythologies, their black science fictions. In fact, each has played extensively with the cyborg image, the image of the human-machine. For example, consider Parliament's Clone Funk Afro-nauts, a mythological, mechanized-but-funky bunch also known as the "children of production." Or, for that matter, think of the title cut from Clinton's 1982 solo album *Computer Games* which directly links the cyborg image to the trope of madness: "I'm your funky dancing computer game / and of course I'm insane . . . May I invade your *space*?" Lee Perry calls himself the "firmament computer," and sings "I ain't got no money / but I got my Sony"—referring to his ever-handy camcorder. Back in the mid-seventies he sang of the need to "set super traps / to catch all those bionic rats," and more recently he has sung of destroying SDI and deprogramming the IMF computers. After suffering several severe strokes, Ra became increasingly dependent on a digital sampler, an easier-to-play keyboard triggered instrument that served as a sort of musical life-support system. In each case, the boundary between human and machine is blurred, and myths, electronics, defense weapons, and musical instruments conspire with people to produce the fuzzy image of the cyborg.

Donna Haraway sees cyborgs as "world-changing fictions" that in turn blur the boundaries between human and animal. This is particularly resonant with the mythologies of Clinton and Perry, both of whom have used, among others, the image of the human-elephant—on the album *Trombipulation* Clinton develops the myth of the "Cro-Nasal Sapiens," elephant-trunked ancient ancestors of his character Sir Nose;[23] on "The Groove" Perry sings: "I am an alien from outer space," and then slips in a variation: "I am an *elephant* from outer space, living in my suitcase" (the "trunk" pun remains unsung but implicit). Likewise, personified bats, apes, rats, and dogs make it into Perry's songs, as do other monsters—ghosts, vampires, werewolves, zombies—and attendant mad-scientists there to produce them. Clinton's

Dr. Funkenstein is also one of these monster-creators, making clones and reanimating the dead (the "Brides of Funkenstein"). As we have seen, Clinton, Ra, and Perry blur the lines between earth and space, a process that is mapped onto this cyborg/monster imagery, providing a wellspring of earth-cyborgs and space-monsters. As well, their mythologies deeply disrupt the division between urban and rural by suggesting a connection between ghetto, desert, and jungle. And yet another dichotomy is called into question in these fictions: namely, the line that separates the past from the future.[24] Ancient Egypt, ancient Ethiopia, Atlantis, the slums of Trenchtown, the Jamaican jungle, the D.C. ghetto, Maggotropolis, the Four Lands of Ellet, the Alter-Future—like the biblical apocalypse, these are at once now and then, simultaneously here and there. Hence in their work these three science fiction makers are dealing with a complex, mix-and-match set of categorical boundary transgressions that might break down like this:

Jungle	Urban
Primitive	Techno
Egypt	Modern
Maroon	Space
Tribal	SDI/Military Industrial Complex
Guerrilla	Future
Ghetto	Clones
Ancient	Angels
Monsters	Computers
Ghosts	Robots
Earth	Virtual

The blurring of these dichotomies suggests a whole range of new, impossible hybrids: ancient-human-machines, earth-angels, funk-robots, futuristic-techno-primitives, space-guerrillas. Indeed, in Ra's mythology it was the very mistaking of angels for beasts (Africans for animals) that allowed them to come into the U.S. unchecked. In "Blinkers," Lee Perry embraces inter-species bonds, declaring: "To whom it may concern: I'm defendin' human rights, an eye-for-an-eye and a tooth-for-a-tooth, jungle laws, animal laws, seabed laws, birds' laws. What are you defendin', mate?" Suggestively, George Clinton subtitled a song "(Endangered Species)."

Lee "Scratch" Perry's work in dub reggae is particularly interesting in its interrogation of the line between techno-world and spirit-world. When queried on the origin of dub's use of sound effects and various eccentric studio techniques, Perry responded that they were "the ghosts in me coming out." In fact, in a Jamaican context the word *dub* has etymological connections with "dup," or "dupe," patois for "ghost." Dub is about doubles, the *doppelgänger.* In 1969 Perry wrote and produced a hit single for Bob Marley called "Duppy Conqueror," which his rival Joe Gibbs followed up in 1971 with an instrumental called "Ghost Capturer." On "Super Ape," from the 1976 dub album of the same name, Perry's singers sing of the producer (who is, meanwhile, busy with his electronic ghosts): "This is the ape-man / driving to creation." Here, another pivotal word, *creation,* links the notion of innovation with the spiritual idea of origin—connecting dub with God—at the same time playing ironically on the racist association of blacks and apes.

Down to Earth: Tactical Landings, Surgical Strikes

This analysis has considered similarities between Ra, Perry, and Clinton in a variety of ways—through metaphor and myth, cyborgs and technology, through their creative reconstitution of African-American identity. There are, however, important differences between them, differences most clearly articulated in terms of their stance vis-à-vis the music industry. That is, to realize their black science fiction, and moreover, to disseminate it, they must position themselves in relation to—and be positioned by—the *business* of making and distributing recordings and playing concerts.

For Lee Perry, existence on the periphery was not simply a choice. For most of his career, he has worked in the Jamaican music industry, and therefore he has been on the margin (both geographically and economically) of the dominant American music industry and its British adjunct. This is a double-edged situation, in that he was able to produce and distribute music for a primarily black audience, with less regard for the centrist textual politics of large American labels. Given his isolation and relative obscurity, he could "version" American pop songs (producing Sharon Isaacs's cover of "Feelings" and Junior Byles's take on "Fever," to name but two) with little fear of retribution. On the other hand, although he has worked at times with large independent labels, like Island and Mango, Perry has also been ruthlessly victimized, by both black Jamaican and white American and European labels, who have taken advantage of Jamaica's ambiguous copyright laws in releasing compilations of stolen or pirated singles.

Sun Ra's isolationist production focused primarily on his record company, El Saturn Records. Controlling this label and all its production (along with Saturn president Alton Abraham) allowed Ra to regulate his mythology more effectively than he might if he had been, for example, signed exclusively to one (major *or* minor) label. It also gave him the opportunity to record and release at will; El Saturn has a catalog of over one hundred records, many of which were pressed in batches of a few hundred (or even fewer, made possible through a special arrangement with RCA Records, where Ra and Abraham had all the early releases pressed), given hand-painted covers, and sold at their shows. This served the important function of connecting the records to the Arkestra's live performances (only a tangential part of Perry's project), while eliminating the middle man, the usual recipient of revenue in the record industry. Ra retained the possibility of utilizing other labels, however; in the 1970s Impulse Records re-released a number of El Saturn records, a task that Evidence records rekindled in 1991, and Ra recorded for A&M, Black Saint, and many others as well.

Early on, George Clinton split his production into two bands: "Parliament was the glitter, the commercial, and Funkadelic was the loose, the harsh . . . Parliament was more vocal, more disco with horns, and a bit more conservative. Funkadelic was more guitars—no horns, more free-form feelings, and more harsh and wild."[25] Compared with either Perry or Ra, both Parliament and Funkadelic are located smack in the middle of the dominant American music industry, recording for Westbound, Casablanca, and Warner Brothers. But Clinton worked that system, pushing against its limits; for instance, the cover of Funkadelic's *Electric Spanking of War Babies* (which featured the image of a penile spanking-machine), was considered too much by Warner Brothers, who chose instead to half-cover the image, replete with peek-holes and the words: "The cover 'they' were too scared to print!"[26]

The point is that these three situate themselves differently. Perry works in a marginal industry, a local music industry that operates (to use another space metaphor) as a satellite to the dominant music industry. This allows him to cannibalize from that big business, but it also exposes him to its crushing force. Maintaining a flexible relation to the dominant music industry, Sun Ra situated himself outside of it, investing nothing substantial in it. Conversely, Clinton draws on the industry's power of distribution, struggling not to "dog out" his audience by "crossing over and never coming b(l)ack."

In 1970, at a concert in Germany, Sun Ra and his Intergalactic Research Arkestra ended a long medley with the chant—"It's after the end of the world, *don't you know that yet?*" Stanley Aronowitz suggests that where postmodernism is aligned with utopianism it "seeks to transform the present by articulating an alternative future" and that "its power lies in its lack of respect for politics as the art of the possible, in its insistence that realism consists in the demand for the impossible."[27] For Ra, as well as Perry and Clinton, the possibility of this impossible alternative futurity rests on re-configuring the past, on the construction of vast, transformative, science-fictional mythologies, on looking *back* at the end of history—not a romantic terminus, but the historical truncation endemic in the white "uprooting" of black African civilizations. Ra summarizes: "We are in the future." Lee Perry joins in, looking down on authority: "Hey FBI, I am the sky—who are you? Hey police, I am Christ—who are you I should be mindful'a?" Warning against black quietism ("placebo syndrome"), George Clinton deftly connects science fiction, gospel community, and self-defense: "En garde, protect yourself . . . there's spunk in the funk, we shall overcome, just shoot them with your bop gun."

Notes

1   The group is also known as: Astro Infinity Arkestra, Myth-Science Arkestra, Blue Universe Arkestra, Cosmo Discipline Arkestra, Solar Arkestra, Intergalactic Research Arkestra, Cosmo Love Adventure Arkestra. For more on the history of Ra and the band, see John Litweiler, *The Freedom Principle* (Morrow: New York, 1984), pp. 129–50; Graham Lock, *Forces in Motion* (Da Capo: New York, 1988), pp. 11–23; and Chris Cutler, *File under Popular* (London: November Books, 1985), pp. 35–79.

2   "With dub, Jamaican music spaced out completely. If reggae is Africa in the New World, then dub music must be Africa on the moon." Luke Ehrlich, "X-Ray Music: The Volatile History of Dub," in *Reggae International*, ed. Stephen Davis and Peter Simon (New York: R&B, 1982), p. 106.

3   Cornel West, "The New Cultural Politics of Difference," *October* 53 (Summer 1990): 105.

4   As early as 1953, Ra was using electronic keyboards, making him one of the first jazz musicians to do so. This interest continued, as moog synthesizers and digital technology became available.

5   For an excellent history of Clinton, Funkadelic, and Parliament, see Peter Jebsen, "The P. Funk Timeline," *Goldmine* 17, no. 2 (January 25, 1991): 42–46.

6   As a publicity stunt, it was at one point announced that Clinton and the Stooges' Iggy Pop (who shared the same management) would be married.

7   Though tough to find, the single issue of the fanzine *The Upsetter* (Issue No. 1, Winter 1989–1990) is an indispensable source of information on the notoriously difficult-to-pin-down Mr. Perry. Though I find it theoretically thin, Dick Hebdige's *Cut 'n' Mix: Culture, Identity, and Caribbean Music* (London: Comedia, 1987) contains some excellent information and a few great quotations from Perry as well.

8   Though he says he only recently heard the music of Sun Ra, George Clinton clearly knew something of his work and image, if for no other reason because MC5 (who used the same management as Clinton) recorded Ra's "Starship" on their biggest record, *Kick Out the Jams* in 1968.

9   See Jim Macnie, "Sun Ra Is the Heaviest Man in This Galaxy . . . But He's Just Passing Through," *Musician* 99 (January 1987): 60, for a marvelous description of Ra and band in full regalia.

10   "Giving Up the Funk: The Fuzzy Haskins Story," interview with Mike Danner, *Motorbooty* 4 (Summer 1989): 40–41.

11   "Stuffs and Things," interview with Danner, Danner, Henssler, and Rubin, *Motorbooty* 4, p. 20.

12   Sun Ra, *The Immeasurable Equation* (Philadelphia: El Saturn, 197?).

13   "The Doctor Is On," interview with Peter Jebsen, *Goldmine* 17, No. 2 (January 1991): 12.

14 Jeff Todd Titon, *Early Downhome Blues* (Urbana: University of Illinois Press, 1977), p. 204.

15 Take, as emblematic, the chorus to Perry's "Secret Laboratory (Scientific Dancehall)" from 1990: "Rockin' and reelin', havin' a ball / Singin' and swingin', straightjacket and all." After a 1990 concert of the P-Funk Allstars, a man in the parking lot proudly recounted the story of seeing George Clinton perform with Funkadelic in the early 1970s, at Northwestern University, nearly nude, crawling under the audience's chairs and licking the floor.

16 This harmonic framework, or a similarly transgressed rhythmic, formal, or melodic code could also be seen as a "ground" from which the solo has musically "taken off."

17 Paul Virilio, *Speed and Politics* (New York: Semiotext(e), 1986), pp. 75–95. Paul Gilroy has suggested that the ship be considered the chronotope for African Americans and members of the pan-Atlantic diasporic hemisphere.

18 Sun Ra, "Fallen Angel," in *Semiotext(e)* 12, vol. 4, number 3, "Oasis," 1984, pp. 115–16.

19 George Lakoff and Mark Johnson, *Metaphors We Live By* (Chicago: University of Chicago Press, 1980), p. 7.

20 Here, I think of Public Enemy's *Fear of a Black Planet*, the cover of which depicts earth from outer space, suggesting white anxiety at the thought of black terrestrial takeover.

21 bell hooks, *Yearnings: Race, Gender, and Cultural Politics* (Boston: South End Press, 1990), p. 153.

22 Donna Haraway, "A Cyborg Manifesto: Science, Technology, and Socialist-Feminism in the Late Twentieth Century," in *Simians, Cyborgs, and Women* (New York: Routledge, 1991), p. 149.

23 Of course, the prime allusion here is to cocaine.

24 The Art Ensemble of Chicago, a group that utilizes many of the same kinds of tropes, costumes, and myths as Clinton, Ra, and Perry, has taken as its motto: "Great Black Music: Ancient to the Future."

25 Clinton, *Motorbooty*, p. 20.

26 This executive decision was made largely on the basis of a threat from the feminist antiporn group Women Against Violence.

27 Stanley Aronowitz, "Postmodernism and Politics," in *Universal Abandon?*, ed. Andrew Ross (Minneapolis: University of Minnesota Press, 1988), p. 55.

SPATE OF FLUX

On the Unofficial Return
of the Fluxus Impetus

●

To those who look at the rich material provided by history,
and who are not intent on impoverishing it in order to
please their lower instincts, their craving for intellectual
security in the form of clarity, precision, "objectivity," "truth," it will become clear that
there is only ONE *principle that can be defended under* ALL *circumstances and in* ALL
stages of human development. It is the principle: ANYTHING GOES.—*Paul Feyerabend,*
AGAINST METHOD

Some old happenings don't go away, they just wait for an opportune moment to happen again. For instance, Al Roon's Health Club on New York's
Upper West Side was the scene of a happening on two nights in spring of
1965. Scored simply for "swimming pool," Claes Oldenberg's *Washes* constituted the sixth program in the First New York Theater Rally, a festival that
also included pieces by Robert Rauschenberg, Jim Dine, Trish Brown, and
Yvonne Rainer. In terms of form, the happening was a "composition in five
parts"—Fill, Soak, Spin, Rinse, and Dry. Although what actually "happened"
is unclear from the program notes (practically its only documentation),[1]
Washes seems to have involved water ballet, swimming, exercizing, floating,
and bathing. And it required a lifeguard.

Jump twenty-seven years to January of 1992, at the swimming pool of the
University of London, where a similarly situated event called "Fiume" was
cooked up by the London Musicians' Collective (LMC). A gala, gaga evening,
with unanticipatedly large attendance, the piece made use of a pool's unique
acoustic resonance, with singers bouncing songs across the water (then
diving in and swim-singing from *in* the waves), saxophonist Lol Coxhill
playing sax and a sub-aquatic horn, lights shimmering off the surface, and—
all the while—scuba divers filming the proceedings for future use on a
British children's television program. "It was something between an art installation and a sauna," summarized Jonathan Romney in the British music
magazine *The Wire*. "Open night at the dolphinarium or an invocation of the
demon Esther Williams."

In the world of performance, and moreover, in the *presentation* of perfor-

mance, a question lingers: Is the Fluxus flame burned out, or does it somehow continuously seem to reignite? At a certain level, the answer may simply come down to the question of "professionalism." Through the 1980s we
grew accustomed to the institutionalization of at least one end of the spectrum of performance art, which was mainstreamed in the same manner as
the plastic arts. Think of Sandra Bernhard's nightclub shtick, Laurie Anderson's high-tech narratives, Robert Wilson's stage extravaganzas, Ann Mag-
nuson's film and TV work, Spaulding Gray's seemingly endless round of talk
shows—even Karen Finley and Diamanda Galas are playing at rock clubs
and cabarets. As an extreme, consider the strange case of Blue Man Group,
the performance art trio that recently made its second appearance on Jay
Leno's *Tonight Show*. What is the first question we ask: *Who are they? Where
did they come from? What do they do?* No, instead we scratch our chins and
wonder: *Who the hell is their agent?* Of course, this group's appearances (and
subsequent mention on *Northern Exposure*), token as they may be, certainly
don't exemplify the "state of things" for performance-as-a-whole (and from
the other end of the spectrum, might not even be viewed as performance art
at all), but I think they indicate a shift in emphasis away from the totally unpresentable character of earlier performance work toward something more
reasonable, more *presentable*. Judging by the hoity-toity PR material that
passes through the offices of *New Art Examiner*, the performance art legacy
no longer harkens back to Dada, but to Las Vegas.

Indeed, in the intervening years since Fluxus and Happenings had their
heyday, a great number of artists and presenters have found it preferable to
feature the "cutting edge" on the big stage, to go upscale, to allow an audience to dabble in the dangerous from the shelter of a comfortable seat.
Probably this is a noble aspiration, but it is tempting nevertheless to wonder
how this generation of presenters would deal with the "anything goes" mixture of provocation, humor, and conceptualism that characterized Fluxus.
How, for example, would they handle an artist leaping from the stage to
wander through the crowd chopping off unsuspecting audience members'
neckties and dousing them with whipped cream, as Nam June Paik was
known to do in the 1960s? *Hardly professional manners, Mr. Paik—difficult to
sell tickets to them if they know they're going to be tarred and feathered.* Just
imagine the look on Leno's face . . .

Naturally, this shift derives from more than professionalization alone. It's
not 1965 anymore; in the nineties, audiences and artists alike are suspicious
about claims of spontaneity, chance, shock, and the unexpected. They're too
sophisticated to believe such modernist myths, too deep to place faith in
anything but the superficial. No one sitting in a darkened theater thinks that
what's happening onstage will *do* anything, that it might be "new," that it

could "change" anything. After all, it is arguable that Dada didn't prevent Vietnam and Hans Haacke didn't disrupt the way that art is funded. And if nothing's gonna change, why get so messy? From the standpoint of a cynical or ironized audience, any art or performance that seriously professes revolutionary or even milder forms of institutional change is little more than a joke. From this vantage, Fluxus was merely a failed experiment. Or more acutely, it was a demonstration of the futility of experimentation itself.

In spite of this, while the organizers of *Fiume* (Ed Baxter and John Grieve) might have known nothing of *Washes* (Baxter says he did), the same impulse seems to have been behind both events. This is true not simply because both events made creative use of a swimming pool, but because of the looseness of their presentation, the ragged forcing together of "spectacular" event and everyday occurrence. Indeed, without constituting a "movement," in the United States this sort of ground-up performance seems to be popping up in a few different places, particularly in the political work of groups like ACT-UP, Queer Nation, and Women's Action Coalition. It makes one wonder if the time for Flux-activity isn't upon us once again, not in mere name or as a museum piece, but as a valid artistic license to experiment with the unthought-of. The complacent seen-it-all-before excuse is growing thin, especially in the creepy, antagonistic, fundless environment into which art is now being forced. Fluxus was never really something in and of itself, it was perpetual motion. Or, better, it was an attempt to expand that delightful period *between* two fixed ideas, to try to maintain change. Perhaps, amid the growing orthodoxy and professionalization of performance art and the time arts, within the cynicism and irony of performance art audiences, the impulse to undermine is rising anew. Maybe, to use Paik's own floral metaphor for Fluxus, the seemingly dead plant is ready to come back into bloom. If so, the LMC would make a suitable window box.

The London Musicians' Collective is the product of a wave of British music, film, and arts collectives and cooperatives in the 1970s. Its precursor was the Musician's Cooperative, which was membered exclusively by free improvisors, like saxophonist Evan Parker, drummer John Stevens, and guitarist Derek Bailey. Entirely musician run, the Musician's Coop served as a safe zone for musicians who were creating relentlessly challenging music, uncompromised sounds that were in large part publicly ignored.

With the establishment of the LMC, the focus was broadened from improvised music into other genres, inviting participation from a variety of musical and performance areas (punk and poetry in particular) and increasing input from the Feminist Improvisors Group, as well. With the coming of the Thatcher Winter in Britain, the general cultural dole/drums of the late eighties threatened to do the LMC in for good, and through that decade its productions diminished. But *Fiume* was the wet-and-wild marker of the group's enthusiastic revival (replete, once again, with a regular newsletter) and a promise to continue that the LMC made good on with an extensive five-day festival in May 1992.

Of course, it may not be advisable to push the connection between the LMC's Festival of Experimental Music and Fluxus too far. After all, the festival coordinators made no such explicit connections, and as an institution the LMC is definitely *not* Fluxus. Indeed, founding exmember David Toop remembers that Fluxus was extremely stale and lifeless by the time LMC was formed. The LMC is a music collective, whereas Fluxus was—depending on which of the zillion definitions you choose—something like an art movement. But it is important to keep in mind that some of the earliest Fluxus events were concerts, that most of Fluxus's associates worked in music at one time or another (some, like Milan Knizak, John Cage, La Monte Young, and George Brecht, *primarily* worked in music), and, indeed, that improvisors like Cornelius Cardew, Misha Mengelberg, John Tilbury, Peter Brötzmann, and Takehisa Kosugi were involved more directly in Flux-events. Perhaps the very fluidity of music, its relaxed relationship with denotation, make it inherently Flux-ible.

Furthermore, the strong mixed-media (or "intermedia," to use the term coined by Flux artist Dick Higgins) orientation clearly audible and visible at the LMC fest was a trademark of Fluxus, where the walls that separated the various arts (and art from non-art) came under unflagging assault. Throughout the fest, visual artist Gina Southgate stood at the side of the auditorium, using mixed materials (colored paper and paints, mostly) to create scribbly images inspired by the music. There was a quiet, nonintrusive sound installation in the space's lobby by John Grieve; films and videos were screened on one afternoon. Onstage, there were dancers, electronics, television, tapes, and a staggering assortment of instruments, both electric and acoustic. In addition, the festival had an international roster, with performers hailing from Japan, Siberia, the United States, Italy, Germany, Belgium, and New Zealand. Mieko Shiomi suggests that Fluxus was "perhaps the first group of artists in art history to not only cross genres, but national boundaries as well." While this is unquestionably something of an overstatement, it is clear that Fluxus was one of the first groups *committed* to internationalism as a founding principle. While Gauguin and Debussy treated the world as their colonizable oyster, Flux artists from around the world found themselves sharing ideas in a telecommunications grass-roots global groove.

What places this festival in the Flux-lineage, or, if you prefer, in the "expanded arts" lineage (taking Flux master George Maciunas's much broader term), is more than its international music and mixed-media content. Indeed, you'd be hard pressed to find a contemporary performance festival ("performance" in the broadest sense) that didn't have those—they're part of the Fluxus legacy. Instead, it was the specific way that the festival was programmed that gave it its Flux flavor. It made use of players from dramatically different spheres, constituting a real polyglot of performers tied together in no particular way except that they were part of the festival—really ragtag, chance-determined programming. In this, it positioned itself outside of the professionalized performance mainstream. What is more, there was a standing invitation to join in for all who attended, with a small stage kept open throughout each day for unexpected musical (and theatrical, and poetical, and . . .) liaisons, an audience-participation dimension also typical of Flux events. This betrays another rare element in today's generation of music presentation: a strong social, political undertone. Under people's breath, I heard the fest described as "anarcho-politico" more than a few times, and, at least in terms of the politics of putting the fest together, it seems to fit. On the whole, perhaps due to the fact of programming-by-committee, there was no discernible overarching programmatic thread (it was, in this sense, an-arch-ic), be it generic, stylistic, or qualitative. The fest was, as one might rightly nutshell Fluxus, *all over the place.*

Even on the first night of the LMC's Festival of Experimental Music, the freewheeling contrast of jazz, electronics, invented instruments, and classical chamber music assured that things would be loose and interesting. New York's Ben Neill and Nicolas Collins played a set of intriguing duets. Neill plays his "mutantrumpet," designed with extra valves, mouthpieces, and slides. Meanwhile, Collins works on his "trombone-propelled electronics," a computer mounted on the body of a trombone built so that the slide lets him change various computer functions. Together, they used a combination of digital samples and acoustic horns in an often self-referential way, dismantling and reconstructing the performance, as on "Acid Rock," a meditation on going deaf in which it became increasingly difficult to make things out over a distortion-blur. Earlier in the evening, singer Phil Minton gargled, burped, and rasped along, while violinist Aleksander Kokowski's string-dominated group Media Luz mixed sweet chamber music with open improvisation. On the same bill, the LMC had bookended these two performances with two fiery free jazz trios, the better of which featured South African expatriate drummer Louis Moholo with fine pianist John Law and saxophonist Gary Curzon.

The week continued much in this vein—that is, without a vein. Bassist Barry Guy and vocalist Vanessa Mackness played a highly interactive, tactile set of duet improvisations. A trio of Clive Bell, Mark Sanders, and Steve

Beresford scavenged up a bounteous feast of sound; Beresford used trumpet to cut through his own Casio burble, Sanders found sensible points of entry for his engaging drumwork, and Clive Bell wheezed the anthill-like Chinese sheng and played whispery shakuhachi. The string trio ARC played while dance company No Mean Feat performed contact improvisations. Garden of Noise worked up a raucous, jazzy set that featured incredible drumming from Roger Turner and fanciful flights for piano and cheapo-electronics by Pat Thomas. Ikue Mori hooked up with vocalist Catherine Jauniaux in a startling wash of drum-machine sounds and Francophone sing-songs. Perhaps the weirdest moment came as Peter Blegvad took the stage to sing cynical folk-rock ballads; it was as if Bob Dylan had popped in on a Fluxus fest twenty-five years ago.

Tenuous as it was, the second night actually did have a through-line. In a long evening dress and her patented record-album hat, the avant-garde's newest diva, Sainkho Namtchylak was artist of the night. A Tuvan singer, she has an outrageous vocal range and has mastered a long list of difficult techniques that include the Buddhist practice of singing multiple notes at once. Namtchylak commenced with a breathtaking set of short solo pieces. Evan Parker then played a stellar soprano saxophone solo and Alan Tomlinson played a monstrous, technically superb (and very funny) trombone solo. After each of their solos, the lone men were joined by Namtchylak, who proved in both cases to be a highly inventive, responsive collaborator. Finally, as if she hadn't sung her share already, the vocalist accompanied violinist Sylvia Hallett, saxophonist/keyboardist Tim Hodgkinson, and drummer Ken Hyder for a nightcap that kicked off with Hyder singing multiphonics with the Siberian expert.

Though by no means my favorite event (in fact, one of my least liked), one performance stood out as being particularly armed with abrasive energy and conceptual nose-thumbing. Ghosts Before Breakfast, a young bass-drums-sax trio, organized a concert that was at once tedious and affronting. Musically, the three played de rigueur free jazz, ridden with clichés and lacking much to recommend it. At the same time, a video screen on the left side of the stage played a long loop of television commercials. And finally, beneath the fracas, a voice on the sound system read stock reports. Snide and unfriendly, the piece made manifest the group's brief manifesto, which stood in for a description in the program: "We endeavor at all times to provide the best possible service to our customers—if you like what we do, tell others; if you don't, then fuck you. We gratefully acknowledge the financial assistance of the London Arts Board." A sloppy, gimmicky speculation on the institutionalization and codification of expression, or perhaps on the plight of the vanguard in the face of commercialism, it was nevertheless the kind of slap-in-the-face-to-music that most music festivals, even "experimental" ones, refuse outright. In particular, its ironic poke at the naiveté of "freedom" was a direct attack on improvised music, the very foundation of the LMC.

The LMC will certainly never call itself Fluxus. It will no doubt continue to exist primarily as a much-needed, music-centered collective. But there are implicit connections, with member Nick Couldry scheming a series of site-specific performances called "London's Secret Spaces," and Baxter working with the performance/counterculture magazine *Variant*. In fact, there are even some explicit connections, as Couldry has been in contact with the XEBEC Corporation, a "sound arts" organization based in Kobe, Japan, that expresses an overt Flux interest. For what it's worth, 1992 was a special year for Fluxus; the New Museum, Franklin Furnace, Walker Art Center, and many other institutions marked the thirtieth anniversary of the first Flux-fest with a variety of shows and special events. Did any of it have anything to do with Fluxus as we've considered it here, or did these events pack up the ghosts of Fluxus past safely in mothballs? Who can say? In any case, events like the LMC's festival provide evidence that Fluxus, or the same counterinstitutional impetus that once called itself by that name, is not content to wither up and die.

There may, of course, come a time when it will be necessary to give reason a temporary advantage and when it will be wise to defend its rules to the exclusion of everything else. I do not think that we are living in such a time today.—Paul Feyerabend, AGAINST METHOD

Note

1 Oldenberg's script for this happening was reprinted in *Scenarios: Scripts to Perform*, ed. Richard Kostelanetz (Brooklyn: Assembling Press, 1980).

FREE, SINGLE, AND
DISENGAGED

Listening Pleasure and the
Popular Music Object

●

Rock and roll was scorned at first by the major record companies. They paid for their priggishness while base-ment labels like Chess and Sun made fortunes. Disco was discovered by alert independents like Casablanca. Once a bandwagon is under way the majors are happy to climb aboard—and elbow their way to the front—but they are rarely in the driver's seat. So it's silly to say of the listening public, as Adorno does, that "in this insistence on the fashionable standards it fancies itself in possession of a remnant of free choice." It is free—at least, its straitjacket is custom cut.—Evan Eisenberg, THE RECORD-ING ANGEL

Extending Eisenberg's sartorial metaphor, one can read the above quotation as articulating a line that divides skeptic from optimist in the evaluation of "popular music" as a cultural commodity. On the one hand: the custom-cut straitjacket. For the optimistic critic, this metaphorical body of the listening public constitutes an essential thing to which the music is tailored. In this paradigm the consumer is figured as the prime mover, the motivation be-hind production. Emphasizing as it does the selectivity of the populace, such a conception finds its greatest support within the network of (often contradictory) viewpoints of sociological heritage. These are not limited to the marketplace pluralism of quantitative research, but extend to the "bot-tom up" theories of many cultural studies scholars who conceptualize popu-lar culture as having inherent room for negotiation. Thus the major record labels follow smaller labels that, by virtue of their size, have their fingers on the prized "pulse" of the public, which is considered to be an *a priori* living, choosing, needing body.

On the other hand, clothes make the man. In this configuration "fashion-able standards" are not set by an essential popular body, but by the industry, which may choose at will to incorporate or disenfranchise smaller labels and artists, and these are in any case only seen as being judged in relation to industry standards. Here, the public body is contorted to squeeze it into ill-fitting pre-fab duds. This is Adorno's "fetishism" in which he likens the consumption of popular music to "the prisoner who loves his cell because he has been left nothing else to love."[1] Nothing custom cut about it. Clearly more skeptical, this camp is peopled by critics less interested in the barometric function of the "mass" and more concerned with the way that dominant ideology force-feeds its subjects, or the ways it more subtly controls the consumption and production of popular music.

Either/or. That the issue is entirely polarized should be of no particular surprise; two different analytic approaches to the question are represented. Actually, however, they involve far more than two methodological positions; each is borne of a different musical discourse—one deriving from the statistical, tabulatory, scientific irrefutability of the "top 40," the other charting the margins, groping for the project that was modernism (serialism/Adorno) or jettisoning the overt political questions in favor of a postmodern critical edge (punk/Baudrillard). In fact, one camp's skepticism is the other camp's optimism. For social scientists, the very "popularity" of pop music grounds and legitimizes it as an object of study, while, for critical theorists, popular currency provides the matrix for a critique of dominant industrial practice.

Once the antithetical positions have been defined and recognized as such, we are faced with an obvious, rational recourse: namely, to locate this text in the reasonable space that is neither/nor but both. I do not aim to synthesize this opposition, however, but to interdigitate its terms, to describe their compatibility, their simultaneity, and ultimately, the capital efficacy of their coexistence. To do so, in a sense, positions this text among those of skepticism, yet out of place there, with an important degree of optimism concerning the possibility of resistance.

To begin again, we should reframe the question, not in terms of fields, but in terms of pleasure. In short, how is aural desire constituted, charged, and inflected within the current social body? Posing this, we guardedly accept a provisional conception of the "mass public" as *a manifest thing*. This is cause to hesitate, not only because it is possible to conceive of *many publics*, but moreover because the very model of the "mass" may be an inappropriate way to understand the problematic given the specific way that commodity capitalism currently manifests itself.[2] Indeed, the recent reformulation within positivist communication studies of a more heterogeneous audience with any number of readings and uses of media (so-called "readership studies")— a move that sweeps the issue clean, rendering it neutral and apolitical—can itself be read as an effect of apparent changes in the economic discourse. Thus it is not that social science now better understands the way audiences work, but that fundamental changes have (or *seem* to have) occurred in the actual terms of consumption and the consumers' relation to mass-mediated objects. Jacques Attali identifies this change when he writes: "Contrary to currently fashionable notions, the triumph of capitalism, whether private or State, is not that it was able to trap the desire to be different in the commodity, but rather it went far beyond that, making people accept identity in mass production as a collective refuge from powerlessness and isolation."[3] The positing of a less monolithic mass audience, then, is correlated with an accompanying change in commodity relations, opening up two general modes of consumption, two types of fetishism—one individualizing ("the desire to be different") and one identificatory ("identity in mass production"). Rather than one superseding the other, as Attali would have it, let us suppose that these two modes coexist.

We can conjure many examples of both modes. First, the atomized, individualized commodity, such as the bumper sticker, the coffee mug, jewelry, sunglasses, sneakers. This mode exhibits a proclivity toward small objects that articulate a *measured distance* from identical others and are subject, amid a vast array of variations and mutations of a given form, to a relatively short life expectancy. Here the effectiveness of planned obsolescence is most deeply felt, personalized, and given a name: style. It is in this, what we might call "local" commodity mode, that collecting proper functions as people individualize their consumption and associate themselves with the singular, idiosyncratic object. This mode correlates with the type of "fragmentary" use of texts to which social science has turned: a heterogeneous media marketplace with its plethora of commodities is seen to provide anything for anyone. The problem, of course, is that the "measured distance" between personalized objects is just that; it works on the statistical probability (a promise) that two people, both wearing T-shirts bearing the motto "Foxy Lady," will not cross paths.

There exists, counter to the local mode, a species of commodity that works within what we might call a "systemic mode" of commodity association. In this case, there is no concealment of mass consumption, no measured distance. Rather, these commodities find their appeal in their "mass," in the proximity they share, in their simulation of a social body. A list of them might include now-useless examples: mood rings, pet rocks; perennial institutions, like Coca Cola and Pepsi; and new incarnations, such as the stuffed Garfields so ubiquitous in cars of late. Obviously, any local-mode form may well also be represented in the systemic mode, like Air Jordans or Ray-Ban glasses. And systemic mode commodities may also pretend to serve the local function, like Michelob Dry beer, which markets itself as "for those who thirst for something different," or Arby's Restaurant and their "different is good" television commercials. In any guise, systemic mode objects are beguiling. They represent the subsumption of heterogeneity, the unification of desire under the common flag of the commodity—as a clothing chain's recent advertising campaign makes absolutely clear: "United Colors of Benetton."

These two modes of commodity fetishism are not opposed to one another. On the contrary, the triumph of capitalism lies in its ability to incorporate both of these modes at once, to play them off one another in a form of reciprocal exchange. In the aural arena, it is the apparatus of the music industry that sets the basic terms of desire, pleasure, and interest that now encompass both the notion of free-choice/eclecticism/idiosyncrasy *and* the desire for "refuge" afforded by mutual consumption, and it has done this initially by conflating heretofore discrete definitions of "popular" as (1) statistical, (2) formal, and (3) technological.

Pure Pop: Clarifying the Object

All music is now popular. In a sense, this is true; there is virtually no music extant that has not been electronically colonized. Musical imperialism of this sort involves a complex treatment of the notion of "popularity" that cuts across three territories, blurring their boundaries.

1. *Popular music as a statistical region.* That which is popular is that which sells best, fares best in a poll, or in some other way "faithfully represents" a population. Clearly, some degree of recursivity is necessary to maintain this area. This is accounted for, for example, in *Billboard* magazine's use of record sales which mix pre-retail order shipments with actual retail sales to establish the "popularity" of a recording. On the fringe of this is music that doesn't "make it" and music that may have generic similarities to statistically popular music but operates in a different, "alternative" network of production and distribution.

2. *Popular music as a formal genre.* The preeminence of certain "types" of music that recur within the aforementioned category has produced a definition of popular music that aligns it with rock or rock-associated music, funk, soul—in short, music of American and British derivation—as a pop form. This allows, for example, a consideration of punk as popular music, regardless of its nonconsensual status.[4]

3. *Popular music as anything recorded.* In a certain respect, it is the medium that unites the previous two categories and blurs their distinctness, for the technology of recording has made it possible to consider any mediated music as popular. This idea has permeated the sphere of production, as is readily apparent in scratch, dub reggae, hip-hop, and rap (and British "acid house" and On-U Sound). In these musics, intertexts may include arcane pop music or classical music, spoken words, animal calls, music of "other cultures," and other sounds of known and unknown origin. Although an

analysis on these grounds is outside the scope of this essay, this is the bedrock on which deliberate postmodernism in music is founded.

The collapse of these meanings one upon the other has not been haphazard. It has progressively led to an all-encompassing usage of "popular" as that which represents popular *demand* and that which has been secreted along the edges of earlier need "gratification." Furthermore, it sets the stage for the appropriation of territory not yet sounded. The tremendous proliferation of both local and systemic mode sound objects corresponds to this slippage: any popular need can be sold; all music is popular; all music can be sold.

"You Won't See Me"—For Lack, a Better Term

Against traditional music history, which is constructed around the abstraction and idealization of music as art (or entertainment) and consists of musical periods, genres, movements, and styles, it is possible to elaborate another set of histories. These would focus attention on the material objects deliberately overlooked in the production of standard musical history. As a blatant instance of such "overlooking" we might invoke a scenario familiar to anyone who has studied music: imagine several partitioned cubicles, each of which contains a headphoned student who faces an amplifier and a turntable; on each platter spins a record of Beethoven's Ninth Symphony. One student lifts his needle to run to the bathroom; another listens twenty times to a difficult passage; a third is frustrated by a skip in the record and proceeds directly to the next movement of the symphony; at the same time another finds it difficult to concentrate due to the volume of her neighbor's headphones. Even as they do these things that are made possible only by the technology of recording, these students are required to develop a historico-theoretical interpretation as if the technical means through which the music is accessed—right there, staring them in the face—are of no significance whatsoever. This is disavowal, as in the Land of Oz: "Pay no attention to the man behind the curtain." Such idealization is not limited to classical musicology, though. In fact, the situation described could just as easily have taken place in the listening booths of a record store anywhere in Europe. The characterization of music as an abstract, autonomous entity is extremely pervasive, appearing as historical assertion in the popular music press from *Rolling Stone* to *Option*, as categorization in music guidebooks from the *Illustrated Encyclopedia of Rock* to the *Da Capo Guide to Contemporary African Music*, and in the form of "music cultures and subcultures" in academic music criticism by George Lipsitz and Larry Grossberg. All these sources base their analyses on recorded music, thereby accurately recognizing recording as the primary contemporary mode of musical exchange. Nevertheless, the question of the nature of the recorded music object remains relatively untheorized, its elements not yet sufficiently teased out.

As an initial step, we must therefore look *at*, rather than *past*, the material of music. In itself, the disavowal present in our scenario already isolates the basic condition produced by recording and reified in music objects: the audio-visual disjunction. What is elided in the construction of standard musical history is precisely the materiality of the apparatus, the status of music not as "immaterial production," as Attali would suggest, but as objects that produce their own visual lack. With these issues in mind, it is possible to draw the conceptualization of erotic fetishization into our consideration of musical fetishism as another form of commodity fetishism. Within feminist film studies, Laura Mulvey constructed a framework for the unveiling of the (male) gaze and its relation to and recuperation of visual pleasure as it is threatened by the image of the woman on film.[5] In the interest of providing a similar framework for better understanding popular music as an eroticized mass commodity, we shall now redirect that same gaze toward—not a representation of, but the empty space of—that which threatens it: nothing. Lack. The technology of reproduction specific to our experience of popular music, that of recording and playback, carries with it the mechanism for its insertion into the economics of compulsive consumerism. For it is lack of the visual, endemic to recorded sound, that initiates desire in relation to the popular music object.[6]

What makes Mulvey's model so appropriate for the study of music objects is that it does not rely on a single response to the threat of loss, but interrelates two "avenues of escape" for the unconscious in a reciprocal bind. In her formulation, the viewing subject occupies two primary positions with respect to the image of woman: voyeurism and fetishistic scopophilia. Although voyeurism in its usual sense has intriguing implications for a theory of listening pleasure (eavesdropping as it relates to radio broadcasting, for example), Mulvey's usage is more involved, linking voyeuristic pleasure with the sadistic narrative of the exposure of woman's guilt and her rectification and punishment. This is coupled with a complex fetishistic response, in which an eroticized object, even the object that produces threat of lack itself (woman), is overvalued and substituted for the missing phallus. As Mulvey puts it: "fetishistic scopophilia builds up the physical beauty of the object, transforming it into something satisfying in itself."[7] Recorded music, at once the site of intense pleasure and the producer of a similar threat of lack, is therefore constituted in its object-form as erotic-fetishistic, and the aural is mystified as "something satisfying in itself." Threat of absence, of loss, creates a nostalgia for the fullness of a mythical past; pleasure is inscribed in its memory—the gap.

If we modify those aspects of Mulvey's analysis that are specific to film, in particular the way that compulsive sadistic response to threat is rationalized via narrative, it becomes clear that a similar mechanism propels the commodification of music objects. Consumerist compulsion is rationalized in a narrative of trends and styles, the object's story of becoming obsolete. Through an intricate interweaving of disavowal and fascination, the music industry has succeeded in seizing a medium that optimizes both. Voyeuristic fascination is concentrated into issues of fidelity; "unfaithful" music objects (scratched records, obsolete technology) are diagnosed and controlled.[8] Fetishistic pleasure is organized around the reconstitution of the visual and the substitution of music objects for the impending loss that they trigger. Thus, in fetishistic audiophilia the scramble to negotiate the menacing void manifests itself in one of three ways: (1) the attempt to reconstitute the image of the disembodied voice; (2) the assertion of the autonomy of sound and the fetishization of audio equipment; and (3) the attempt to fill the void with recorded music objects. As these stages are crucial, they require individual attention.

Unseen Strategies

Since the second decade of the twentieth century, with the spread of commercial recording, the musical world has been driven by two conflicting quests: on the one hand, the direct attempt to disavow the cleavage of image/sound and to restore the visual to the disembodied voice; and on the other, the desire to complete the break absolutely, once and for all—and further, to naturalize the audio-visual split and interface the independence of recorded music with an already well established musicological construction of music as autonomous. Concomitant with these has been the ongoing commodification of music objects.

I. Replacing the Absent Image

Much of the work of the music industry has centered upon overcoming the absolutism of the all-sonic recorded music object. From this, we can produce our own historically specific account. First, recorded music objects in themselves have engendered more and more sophisticated graphic accompaniment. Thus, the album cover takes on tremendous significance as it provides a binding element for the aural/visual disarticulation. Bright colors, the image of the performer, the gatefold, the inside sleeve, as well as various more esoteric strategies, have become integral to the music commodity—something to look at while you listen. This can be read as the formative attempt to restore the visual, to stitch the cut that separates seeing from hearing in the contemporary listening scenario. The most extreme example of this, perhaps, is the "picture disc," in which the visual is inscribed directly upon the surface of that which produces its absence.

Concurrent with the general rise of visual advertising from the 1930s onward,[9] the image has thus assumed a particular and specialized role in relation to music. For evidence of its centrality to the industry, one need look no further than the fifth volume of *Album Cover Album*, the latest in a series of coffee-table books compiled by "album cover artist" Roger Dean.[10] While the record cover is the central focus of concentrated marketing techniques designed for its commodification (the true "billboard" of music objects), it is also an erotic surface, composed of the reckoning of audio/visual tension, rearticulated as lack.[11] In record shops, where these relations assume their most intense form, records are generally arranged to engage the consumer sensually: in order to find the desired object one does not just read the titles on their spines but must look through and touch many others. Records, CDs, and cassette tapes create a region in which economic and erotic fetishization coincide in visual objects on the market.

Of course, Music Television (MTV) is currently the most intensive strategy employed in the reconstitution of the visual in music. Indeed, since the beginning of record industrialization, the navigation of the audio/visual split has been accomplished in the context of moving pictures (an encounter that now often terminates in a purchase at the record store as well). Starting with musical accompaniment for silent films,[12] it is important to note the association of music, and more widely, recorded sound, with cinema and later with television. Synchrony, the assertion of a relationship between action that is seen and heard simultaneously, represents the filmic disavowal tactic: I know (that the sound is coming from a speaker and not the character's mouth), but I don't know (because they belong together). Lip-sync provides the effect of virtual plenitude, fusing the audio/visual fissure. In the filmic construct, as Mary Ann Doane summarizes, "all the signifying strategies for the deployment of the voice . . . are linked with . . . homogenizing effects: synchronization binds the voice to a body in a unity whose immediacy can only be perceived as a given."[13]

While they are both strategies for resolving the basic audio/visual tension, it is a mistake to use film (or commercial television) as the basis for an analysis of music video. In the first place, at base MTV is simply radio coming to grips with the overwhelming visuality of current music commodities; it exploits the association of vision with a medium long known to be merely auditory. It is therefore no great surprise that verisimilitude is not the basis for value in image/sound replenishment in music video, that the viewer need not "believe" that the singer is actually singing. As with extra-diegetic music in narrative film (MTV's closest cinema cousin, now available on soundtrack records), there is no assumption that the music emanates from within the profilmic space; the seen and the heard need not coincide in supposed unity. Rather, image and sound simply co-occur. As in the record sleeve, there is no assertion of a "real" identity linking what is looked at and what is listened to. Pointing to this condition in which "reality" and "fiction" are fused in the simulacrum, E. Ann Kaplan questions the applicability of psychoanalytic theory to MTV, asking: "Are 'fullness' and 'emptiness' still relevant terms?"[14] These are obviously no longer the criteria if we take them to mean that the effect-of-the-real is required to supersede (or "fill") fictive disbelief (the "emptiness" of the exposed means of production), as is accomplished through the linking of specific sounds with specific images in classical film. But if we look at MTV somewhat less dramatically as an adjunct to radio, this incomprehensible postmodern medium may make a bit more sense. If MTV is a "twenty-four-hour commercial," it builds on radio's dual construction of popular music as simultaneous instrument of pleasure and advertisement for itself. The visual is enlisted into this strategy, capitalizing on the audio/visual juncture in a way impossible for ordinary radio: by means of the cathode-ray tube. Rather than treat MTV as a radicalization of the codes of film and television, this allows us to recognize music video for what it is: a hybrid of radio and record jacket. Thus, working at the level of the basic music-reproduction apparatus, music video establishes a domain in which radio's visual lack can be "filled" with any set of images; the terms of psychoanalysis are therefore not bulk-erased. Between the seen and the heard, the plane of dislocation is a slippery one; the visual and the aural may be realigned imprecisely and still provide the erotic spark that drives the music industry motor.[15]

II. Gapping the Bridge

As a matter of fact, those who maintain that they only enjoy music to the full with their eyes shut do not hear better than when they have them open, but the absence of visual distractions enables them to abandon themselves to the reveries induced by the lullaby of its sounds, and that is really what they prefer to the music itself.—Igor Stravinsky, "LISTENING AND LOOKING AT MUSIC"

Various scholars have recently charted the construction of the concept of music as an autonomous sphere of creation.[16] The lineage that produced this conception, persistent in Western musicology, emanates from a precapitalist period in which music making was divided between those musicians outside the aristocratic system (ritual) and those fully under the ownership of the courts, whose production was dictated by them. Subsequently, money entered the scene, serving as a wedge that separated art from its social production. Standardization and widespread dissemination of music notation, coupled with new laws governing copyrights, enabled a valorization of the absolute value of music itself, apart from any material considerations. "End of the obliged sign, reign of the emancipated sign."[17] Musicology, as it now exists, remains a classical mode of analysis bound up in the defense of this independence, in the assertion of music as access to the "absolute," as timeless and apolitical. The situation of "art music" within the academic institution has served to reinforce this supposed autonomy—simultaneously allowing for the individualization[18] and transcendence[19] of music theory. Unencumbered by the social, political, or technological, Western art-music is seen to exist in a vacuous, theoretical space—the contemplative ether of the "great works."

It is no mere coincidence, then, that compact discs experienced their first wholesale takeover in classical music. The compact disc is the latest in a long line of audiophilic devices in the history of the attempt to eliminate the long-standing enemies of "fidelity" in playback: surface noise, scratch, hum, and hiss. To render music free of noise is to grant it its proper musical status as sonically autonomous. Such noise foregrounds the music object as such; it draws attention to the record's blackness, its roundness, its materiality—in short, to its visual presence. These defects, these idiosyncracies, the "grain" of the record, are vestiges of the image in sound. Adorno and Horkheimer explain: "Nature which has not been transformed through the channels of conceptual order into something purposeful, the grating sound of a stylus moving over a slate . . . has a penetrating effect; it arouses disgust."[20] Surface noise indicates the surface, a reminder of the visible topography of recorded music objects.

In order to temporarily alleviate (and capitalize on) the anxiety produced by the threat of visual loss audible in these imperfections, another strategy has developed: cultivation of lack itself; loving the gap; noise reduction; and consequently, fetishization of the technology that produces the lack. In Mulvey's voyeuristic formulation, this is "a preoccupation with the re-enactment of the original trauma."[21] The celebration of the liberation of audio from the vestigial visual is linked to the aforementioned musical autonomy with a naturalizing effect: of course we don't want noise, because it's not music! Just as a coughing cellist foregrounds the physicality—and potentially the social production—of orchestral music (a "mistake" that recording makes less and less frequent),[22] so does surface noise threaten to expose the visual lack—and potentially the industrial construction of musical autonomy—

produced by recorded music. Hence, the underlying significance of the American music industry's recent slogan: "Recorded Music Is a Sound Investment"—that is, it is an investment in the autonomy of sound.

This aspect of fetishistic audiophilia has provided for the curious possibility of larger economic investment in the playback apparatus than in the sound objects it is designed to feature. More significantly, the technology of the compact disc allows for a deeper disavowal of visual presence at the level of the mechanism. Turntables generally leave the record in plain view, while the disc machine consumes the CD, removing it visually and further concealing the playback process. Thus, a spatiality inherent in the technology of the record—a vestigial sense of materiality or depth—is absent in the playback of the compact disc, where the focus is turned to the issue of temporality (confirmed by the digital time display on most CD machines). It is, however, not only the disc that is taken in by the machine; the entire visual structure is supplanted by a prosthetic eye (the laser). No more analogy of material contact (tape/head; needle/groove), but a luminous reading—a *seeing*—internalized by the technology itself.

This reconfiguration in fact had precursors in several devices introduced toward the end of turntable technology. First, an oscilloscope is implanted in a bunker on the base of the table, casting a beam of light at a ring of dots around the rim of the platter. A listener fine tunes the speed of the disc until the dots seem to stand still, at which point the speed is correct. Denon Corporation produced an automatic turntable that relocates this beam on a cone just higher than the surface of the platter, which has four narrow pits in it. Each pit contains a tiny mirror. If there is no record covering the platter, the beam is bounced back to a receptor which shuts the table off, protecting the needle from damage. Finally, on "linear track" turntables, a laser beam positioned in the tone arm next to the stylus locates and guides the needle into the groove. These are steps toward a technology that looks at (and for) itself. With the oscilloscope the listener still participates in visual verification, but by the time the compact disc machine is fully deployed, the visual apparatus has been entirely reconstructed and tucked away in the machine itself, negating the issue of material and visual presence of the music object.

Paul Virilio links the loss of material space to the acquisition of speed and instantaneousness.[23] Material space still fully binds the magnetic tape, a non-random-access medium which requires that, to arrive at a given point, one must, in obedience to a spatial imperative, *pass through* everything between here and there. Phonograph records maintain their materiality in that, while they are random-access, to get to a given point the tone arm must *pass over* the vinyl between here and there. With the CD, there is no "here" or "there," no material space, only digits (track numbers, clock). As the increased speed of the spinning disc blurs its materiality (already concealed), so the instantaneousness of access erases the last metaphor of travel and territory. The technology that allows for the mass standardization of noise-free playback involves a shift in the status of the operative playback object, now immaterial and virtually invisible.

With the fetishization of audio equipment, the very sound of music has also acquired a noise-free standardization. Roland Barthes's essay "The Grain of the Voice" marks the transition to this universe of noiseless recorded music in the difference between the singing voices of Panzéra, as representative of the era *before* recording, and Fischer-Dieskau, as archetypical of the era *of* recording. Panzéra's voice sported the "grain" of his body, the trace of his visual presence, where Fischer-Dieskau's has been "flattened out . . . under the pressure of the mass long-playing record."[24] Wishing to resuscitate grain and implement it as an evaluative category by which a "different history of music" could be written (in a sense, the prototype for *our* reconceptualization of the current music-industrial formation), Barthes explains: "I shall not judge a performance according to the rules of interpretation, the constraints of style . . . (I shall not wax lyrical concerning the 'rigor', the 'brilliance', the 'warmth', the 'respect for what is written', etc. . . .), but according to the image of the body (the figure) given me."[25] Grain is thus explicitly visual, an *image*, in Barthes. While his critique centers on the loss of grain in performance technique, the last gasps of the visible body appear in recorded music as well. The flow of popular music production standards has worked to eliminate this image and to widen the gap between the bodies of performers and the sound of their music. It is now common knowledge that "voices have neither feet nor ears."[26]

Once again, the fetishization of autonomous sound enables an alternative history linked to this emergent conception, one that might otherwise be constructed strictly according to "musical content." In the late sixties, a music engineer named Manfred Eicher left Deutsche Grammophone and in 1969 he formed ECM Records. Its motto was: "The next best sound to silence." Over the subsequent decade, the label acquired notoriety for "the ECM sound," usually described as "ethereal" or "spacey." In the late seventies, ECM gained a distribution contract with Warner Brothers (later with Polygram, and most recently with BMG), spawned several "jazz" stars (Keith Jarrett, Pat Metheny), and set the stage for the introduction of an entirely new commodity genre: New Age Music. What set ECM apart was its use of several key production techniques: echo and compression. The combination of these, along with other studio methods, allows for the next step in the fetishization of autonomous sound—the elimination of the musician. The sound of fingers, lips, legs, and nose are all traces of the performer, the *absent* performer, and they foreground the visual. Echo, by doubling the sound upon itself, and compression, by doing away with unseemly transients, wrench the sound of music from the body of the performer and erase its trace. It is not surprising that ECM's records are of "audiophile quality." They appeal to a fantasy of absolutely independent music, where concerns of the image never enter the picture. Lullaby, close your eyes, and good night.

If the crux of this struggle, its battleground, is therefore the body, this is not to deny that the performer's body (or the body of the performer's instrument), is in itself a social construction; it is not to assert an essential biological body or a transcendence for the physical at an ontological level. On the contrary, the current conditions for the production of the music object work by removing the social body and replacing it with a homogeneous, universal absence: standardized lack. The sonic topography of the body is a partial product of, but not reducible to, its cultural context. This irreducibility is more than simple "individuality" in a romantic or preordained sense. Studio techniques such as echo and compression work to reduce such irreducibles, to make the individual body interchangeable and the sound of its contours more manageable. ECM and its brood (Windam Hill, Private Music, etc.) are not the only companies to use compression and echo. In fact, these techniques have been in development since early in the history of recorded music, with the ostensible function of providing "presence" for the recording space. Ironically, this inscription of "absence" (of the musician) has assumed a highly codified state, and now constitutes that which sounds like music in the popular domain.

Finally, just when it would seem to have perfected the construction of music as autonomous sound—production free from the body of the performer; reproduction free from its own noise—the industry enacts an apparent reversal. Visuality is reintroduced when, once again playing on the hot edge between seeing and not seeing, audiophile marketing coins a cryptic rhetoric around the notion of "audio imaging." Salespeople do not encourage consumers to visualize the musicians, however, but euphemistically to "see the sound." Given the erasure that is standard practice in contemporary recording techniques, it seems reasonable to wonder what one might look for. Such is the pinnacle of audio mystification: through an invisible apparatus the listener strains to evaluate the "realism" and "fidelity" of music on the basis of an image that has been systematically removed from view.[27]

III. Filling the Gap

Replenishment and autonomy are thus obviously not mutually exclusive. They work together as part of a coordinated effort to stave off the threat of lack within the framework of capitalism. The purchase of music commodities represents another strategy for the pleasurable mastery of objects of absence. Record collections register visual absence and offer to control it through ownership of the objects, proof in their display that they are visually present. For the record collector, though, there is no ultimate pleasure, no orgasmic release in ecstatic collecting. Pleasure is perpetuated, the moment of release constantly put off and translated into issues of record quality (there's always a better copy), the completion of series or sets, and the search for and establishment of "originals" (the jargon of authenticity is alive and well in record collecting). For the record collector, as they say, the thrill is in the hunt. Collections are described in terms of unities, continuity, a mythical plenitude—yet remain all the while staked in suspending completion. Thus, the "prior" lack—of the visual—is displaced onto and rationalized in a "later" lack—of records. Lack is the "always already" of the contemporary musical economy, there prior to its announcement. In fact, we might remember that lack is doubly articulated in the moment of economic enunciation: when a music object is purchased, it is visually complete *but lacks sound*. And the very composition of music objects expresses an eroticized form of play with this lack. In order to use them, the object must be disarticulated, the operative element (record, tape, or disc) taken out ("exposed") in order to be functional, and "slipped back in" in order to be complete. So lack is inescapable in collecting music. Even the ritual of playback is a fetish rite, a little *fort/da* game culminating in heightened fetishistic quality for the music object.

Walter Benjamin, himself a voracious book collector, explicated "a relationship to objects which does not emphasize their functional, utilitarian value—that is, their usefulness—but studies and loves them as the scene, the stage, of their fate."[28] This is also the drama of the accumulation of music objects; their actual use-time is stockpiled in the collection, as is their use-value, which is, at a basic level, their fetish quality. It is not that they are without utility, but that they create their own usefulness. One might insist that not everyone is a record collector, and that even record collectors have specific areas of interest. This is true, and it is the business of the music industry to protect against such dangerous excess, while ensuring the ongoing consumption of music objects.

Inflecting Demand

Fetishistic audiophilia addresses a term that John Mowitt has adapted from Adorno, the "listening structure" of the present discursive formation as it is dependent on a matrix of reinforcing and sublimating factors.[29] This construct provides us with a general hedge against the image of an autonomous consumer, but it is with the introduction of ideological charge that the recorded commodity enters either the local or systemic mode of relations. So far, the subject is polymorphously perverse—any record will do. It is the voice of the father, dominant ideology, that inflects the listening subject's desire and charges certain commodities; this is the entry of the subject into the symbolic. This has required the development of an elaborate apparatus: the music marketing industry. Attali addresses this question with a consideration of the "production of demand," a sphere no less *productive* in the most specific sense than that of supply. This is Adorno and Horkheimer's "circle of manipulation and retroactive need," though, as we have seen, the initial mechanism for fetishism is contained in the object of the current musical formation, diminishing the necessity for totalitarian connotation carried in the term "manipulation." According to Attali: "In an economy in which the production price of the supply is very low in relation to the production price of the demand, continuity of expansion depends largely on the improvement of commercialization techniques."[30] This is essentially correct, although "demand" in this case does not mean "need," as that is always constituted in the contemporary musical text. The production of demand consists of providing a particular erotic charge for certain commodities, a task managed by the music industry proper. Cheap Trick: "I want you to want me, I need you to need me."

To unpack this a bit, I offer two specific examples.

REM

In 1981 the tiny independent label Hib Tone Records released a single by the American rock quartet REM entitled "Radio Free Europe." Almost immediately the band was signed to a bigger label, IRS Records, and within months they released their first "mini-album" called *Chronic Town*. Between 1983 and 1988, they issued five albums of new material on IRS (with excellent distribution from A&M and MCA): *Murmur* (1983, which included a rerecording of "Radio Free Europe"), *Reckoning* (1984), . . . *Fables of the Reconstruction of the* . . . (1985), *Life's Rich Pageant* (1986), and *Document* (1987)—and two collections of old material—*Eponymous* (1988) and *Dead Letter Office* (1987). The latter is an assemblage of numerous "B-sides," that is, the unreleased flip sides of their popular singles. Late in 1988, REM released its first record on Warner Brothers Records, *Green*.

The ascendancy of REM is interesting in several respects. From the beginning they did not employ what is generally misconstrued as the fulcrum of popular music: clarity. The vocal track on early recordings is set back in the mix, and the lyrics are very difficult to distinguish. In addition, the audible parts are quite cryptic, resisting simple interpretation. The very title of their 1985 release is unfixed, as it can be read as either *Fables of the Reconstruction* or *Reconstruction of the Fables*, and this ambiguity makes listing the album, talking about it on the radio, or asking for it in the store somewhat more of a task. Perhaps most involved is their construction of their visual image—suggested by their very name, which implies the visuality of dream-state sleep. While they have made music videos from the very start, the band members have rarely appeared in them (more frequently, lately), and they have vocally opposed what they perceive as mindless star glorification apparent in many videos. Collaborating with avant-garde filmmaker James Herbert, they produced what might be called a visual soundtrack called *Left of Reckoning* as an adjunct to their 1984 album. Images from this film have been used as a backdrop for them in live appearances and on the jacket of *Document*. Elsewhere, the group's cover art is also relatively uncooperative, with graphics that make reference to various avant-gardes and express an informed and nuanced interest in contemporary issues of representation. Indeed, the inner sleeve of *Fables* may well provide the perfect icon of audio/visual lack: a disembodied ear is positioned at the crotch of a wooden doll, explicitly aligning the aural canal with the absent phallus. The back cover of *Eponymous* epitomizes REM's ironic attitude toward the production of its own promotional image, featuring a high-school photo of (unblemished) singer Michael Stipe with the inscription "They Airbrushed My Face."

In the old universe of the music commodity, these are all undesirable features. They seem to undermine the unity of the musical product, the unity of interpretation and subjective identification. In this way, they are like local mode commodities—but in fact they are not. They are simulations of local mode commodities, systemic mode commodities masquerading as heterotopia. Desire for them has been organized chiefly through the creation of demand—large-scale identification with the charged REM object. Through intense marketing pressure in terms of radio airplay, a profusion of visual accompaniment in the form of posters (both promotional and for retail sale), and an appearance on "Late Night with David Letterman," the industry has provided a reading of their resistant texts that *is* unified, but *gives the impression* of being fragmented. Eventually, according to a reciprocity commonplace in "alternative" music objects incorporated into the dominant network, the actual image and sound of the band have "cleared up"—airbrushed, no doubt, by the logic of capital.

Jackdaw with Crowbar

In 1987 a record appeared in a few stores specializing in "import" and "indie" records by a group calling itself Jackdaw with Crowbar. Distributed internationally by two firms, 9 Mile and The Cartel (both formed to disrupt the hegemony of big-label distribution), *Monarchy, Mayhem, and Fishpaste*, a four-song EP (extended play), listed Ron Johnson Records as its production company, gave no information about its participants (save a guest trombonist), and made a thinly concealed invective against MTV, claiming that: "Jackdaw with Crowbar still use live films. Here's to the end of the video-rodeo conspiracy." It also contained an open invitation to write to the musicians in London. Its cover features a Dadaesque collage, a portion of which is reproduced on the B-side record label. There are no photos of the band, or for that matter any music-related visuals. Musically, the record is varied: a song sung through a bull-horn ("Crow"), an accordion reggae-dub ("Fourth World"), a two-step featuring slide guitar reminiscent of Zoot Horn Rollo in Captain Beefheart's Magic Band ("The Night Albania Fell on Alabama"). The following year, another EP came forth, *Sink! Sank! Sunk!*, soon followed by a full-length album, *Hot Air*. The LP contains little more information, except for the names of band members and filmmakers who apparently work with the band on both its live show and in constructing the collages for their record jackets. Its music continues in the mode of others, alternating between drawn-out dub reggae jams and shorter songs with political and absurdist lyrics. Exposing a hesitancy over "finished products" (a common concern for dub reggae and Dada), the LP contains a completely reworked version of the song "Crow," with the vocals set back even further, the drums filtered through reverb, and a country guitar lick mixed in (accounting for its new name: "Travesty of C(ro)W"). After one inclusion on a compilation late in 1988, the group, with no promotional trail, no interviews, and no clear group "persona," has slipped away virtually without a trace. Now out of print (and Ron Johnson Records defunct), the brief appearance of Jackdaw's records exemplifies the local-mode commodity at both its most appealing and its most politically volatile.

It is interesting to compare these two bands in terms of their workings, the way that they are held separate by dominant ideology, despite bold similarities in their general approach. They share some basic concerns: making rich visual accompaniment for their records and live concerts, a general murkiness of vocal production, distrust of music video as it has been codified by MTV, and a playfulness with language. To be sure, the outrightness of Jackdaw's song "Fuck America" is more countercultural than the mild antiestablishmentary irony of REM's "It's the End of the World As We Know It (I Feel Fine)." But there is nothing essentially unmarketable about Jackdaw, just as REM did not skyrocket to success by virtue of their absolute gratification of *a priori* popular need. "To the extent that necessity is socially dreamed, the dream becomes necessary" (Guy Debord).³¹ Thus it is the activity of the industry that produces the charge and that inflects popular demand (already, in part, generated by the music object itself), compelling both the acquisition of individual identity through local-mode objects *and* acquiescence to conformity through systemic mode objects.

At the outset of this essay I expressed optimism concerning resistance. In a musical world devoid of experience *viva voce* (which is thankfully not yet completely the case), listening pleasure expresses a specific relation of consumers to commodities and of consumers to each other as articulated by commodities. Nonetheless, this does not entirely preclude the possibility of response or resistance on the part of either listener-consumers or musician-producers. There is room for counterattack, both using and opposing popular music as a form. Indeed, I think these sorts of negotiations are presently quite widespread in recorded music and may involve excorporation, mimicry, subversion, misreading, recontextualization, and a number of other tactics. Mayo Thompson wryly states that "capitalism still has progressive life in it,"³² and his work as a producer with Rough Trade Records and as a member of the band Red Crayola (or Red Krayola) supports him. Sharply political groups like Crass and the Ex have constructed alternative production and distribution routes consistent with their deployment of new, alternative lifestyles. In a more genteel manner, the Pacific Northwest's International Pop Underground and New Zealand's Flying Nun Records are but two examples of the innumerable grass-roots recording conspiracies currently in process on the periphery of the mainstream music conglomerate. Overlapping this is another important element that highlights the political valence of popular music: the ubiquitous smaller music industries in worldwide local markets, each of which continuously produces corresponding local-mode music objects. These in turn represent a potential wellspring for the dominant industry's exotic postcolonialist "World Music" category.³³ From within dominant industry, groups such as the Fall, the Pixies, Sonic Youth, Boogie Down Productions, Ice-T, Digital Underground, and Queen Latifah, have chosen to try to stretch the limits of the existing central industrial structure, making use of its tremendous power of dissemination and attempting to point out some of its internal contradictions—all the while playing on the edge of their own incorporation and potential diffusion and defusion.³⁴ And at the technological level, dub reggae has transgressed the standardized use of echo by pushing it beyond its naturalized limit. Likewise, rap sampling and scratch have reintroduced vinyl surface noise into the mainstream musical picture, even on CD.[35] Finally, the increased possibility for subversion provided by the ever-cheapening technology of cassette tape (the audiophile industry temporarily seeming to turn against the recording industry) opens up further opportunities for listeners to recontextualize pieces of music and thereby to bypass the proper course of capital through the industry by "home taping," and allows for underground producers to set up piecemeal local cassette networks.[36]

Material conditions do not entirely define or delimit the sound of popular music or its politics, but capitalist music production has seized upon, developed, and refined this industrial form of music—a pervasive, unfixed, highly flexible matrix through which potentially antagonistic texts of all sorts may be retrieved and recast. As we have noted, all musical forms are now latent expressions of "the popular," which leads Jean-François Lyotard to suggest that there is no "stable sound filtering system" in popular music.[37] The basic conditions of recording and playback do, however, constitute a strategically unstable system, a malleable (even reversible) structure through which all recorded music must pass. Given such a treacherous environment, the task at hand is to expose the danger of investing in the supposition that any resistance to or via this system will ever be permanent, that it will always be successful, or for that matter, that it is at every level possible. In other words, we must remind ourselves that opposition is not *inherent* in musical situations, but is subject to power shifts and the emergence of newer, more insidious strategies of institutionalization. These changes necessitate vigilant critique.

The context for our critique includes the recent awakening of a dangerous myth of "free, single, and disengaged" music consumers, a notion that has surfaced both within the academy (in the proliferating excitement over "popular culture" in general) and in a wider discourse that responds to recent developments in the music industry. In its current stand, this formulation positions audience members as "free" (to choose), "single" (that is, "individual"), and "disengaged" (from the influence of dominant ideology) by virtue of their access to a seemingly limitless variety of music objects and a corresponding multiplicity of readings. In scholarly circles, versions of this myth have arisen both under the sign of the pessimist (Arthur Kroker's "panic" mentality) and under the sign of the optimist (Andrew Ross's defense of popular pleasure as "autonomous").[38] In the music industry, the myth appears in the newly centralized "alternative music industry," which deploys a rhetoric thick with "independence." At the same time, it is also integral to the dominant industry's "new bohemianism," which plays on sexy notions of noncomformity and otherness, even as it engenders an implicit uniformity and consensuality.[39] As we have seen, local-mode objects are not impervious to being simulated or recuperated as systemic mode objects (REM, Talking Heads, U2, Laurie Anderson, Peter Gabriel, The The, The Cure), and even in their "post-Fordist" incarnation, legitimate local-mode music commodities are still fetish objects, always engaged in a complex way with issues of visual loss and reconstitution. These objects in turn entertain an ongoing relationship with a constantly changing audiophile industry, which creates new technical modes and sells equipment that is as centralized, stratified, and standardized as any systemic mode music commodity. As we have seen, the industry continues to invent subtle new ways to capitalize on this interplay, adapting to and creating more markets and mandating consumption of more music objects.

As a producer of local-mode commodities, the alternative music industry demonstrates the tenuousness of any opposition to the dominant industrial apparatus. This "independent syndicate"—within which Jackdaw constructed its considerably abrasive music and from which it obtained its pleasurably contrary status—must also be seen as a potential source for the industry; it is both a farm team and a cottage industry. Hüsker Dü's journey from SST Records to Warner Brothers, where it was commercially disenfranchised and eventually disbanded, is as much a part of this story as is Elvis Presley's move from Sun to RCA, where he was enshrined and for whom he made the true fortune. The alternative music industry, and local-mode commodities in general, must be seen not as merely antagonistic toward the dominant industry, but as its abeyant partner. To this end, the dominant music industry has at its disposal a radically exploded and blurred definition of "popular" and a medium that situates its basic mode of creation, exchange, and reception on both sides of the image line, in the oscillation between the renunciation of the visual in music and its resurrection as the site of its own highly eroticized visual advertisement. Recorded music has taken on a very specific kind of existence in this "culture of stimulation," consisting of objects, scenarios, and practices that produce the conditions for their own fetishization in the pleasurable mastery of their inherent audio/visual gap.

Any critique of this mechanism will have much in common with Adorno's analysis (however problematic in an American reading) of the adoption of a myth of spontaneism in the institutionalization of jazz in 1930s Germany.[40] For us, it is not the "taint" of popularity that drives this but the question of the music object as a multivalent fetish in a popular culture of commodity association. REM is interesting precisely because they seem so out of keeping with the traditional conception of what can function as popular. But rather than step back from the analysis and proclaim the inapplicability of critical theory due to the independence of the consumer ("See, people aren't misled into stupor—they *must* have chosen *this*!"), it is necessary to push the critique further, to explain how an industry can capitalize on a product that would seem to be so intent on impeding its own salability. Unlike Adorno's, then, what is needed is a critique that would not seek to impose on popular music the "silence of domination,"[41] guilty pleasure stifled by the hush of negative dialectics. Instead, it should be very noisy, a theoretical racket, the grating sound of Mulvey's "destruction of pleasure as a radical weapon." Most appropriate would be a *Katzenmusikritique*, a clamorous, disquieting analysis dissonant with the prevailing uncritical abandon, but also strident to those who would dismiss popular music out of hand; a wary, suspicious critique, it would do something like what Public Enemy calls for from its highly conflictual space deep within the belly of the industrial beast: it would "bring the noise!"

Notes

The title of this essay comes from a 1950s R&B song by Huey Piano Smith entitled "Free, Single, and Disengaged."

1   Theodor Adorno, "Fetish Character in Music and Regression of Listening," in *The Essential Frankfurt School Reader*, ed. Andrew Arato and Eike Gebhardt (New York: Continuum, 1982), p. 280.

2   See Jean Baudrillard, *In the Shadow of the Silent Majorities* (New York: Semiotext(e), 1983).

3   Jacques Attali, *Noise: The Political Economy of Music*, trans. Brian Massumi (Minneapolis: University of Minnesota Press, 1985), p. 121.

4   See Simon Frith, *Sound Effects: Youth, Leisure, and the Politics of Rock'n'Roll* (New York: Pantheon, 1978); Dick Hebdige, *Subculture: The Meaning of Style* (London: Methuen, 1979); and Chris Cutler, *File under Popular* (London: November, 1982).

5   Laura Mulvey, "Visual Pleasure and Narrative Cinema," in *Visual and Other Pleasures* (Bloomington and Indianapolis: Indiana University Press, 1989), pp. 14–26. As Mulvey makes clear in her follow-up article, "Afterthoughts on 'Visual Pleasure and Narrative Cinema' inspired by King Vidor's *Duel in the Sun* (1946)" (pp. 29–38), this form of visual pleasure is not exclusively male, but is predicated on a particularly "masculinized" subject position, available to both men and women. It seems to me that this is equally pronounced in relation to music objects and hi-fi equipment.

6   An extraordinary instance of castration and the recorded music object can be found on the cover of a record by the mid-seventies rock group Mom's Apple Pie. On it, a (conspicuously young) grandmother is pictured bearing a pie, from which a slice has been cut to reveal, not apples, but a gaping, dripping vagina. More recently, hear the Cramps' "What's Inside a Girl?" (Big Beat Records, 1986), and see the cover of Public Image Limited's *That What Is Not* (Elektra, 1992).

7   Mulvey, "Visual Pleasure and Narrative Cinema," p. 21.

8   For a discussion of the gendering of audio equipment and records, see Eisenberg, "The Cyrano Machine," in *The Recording Angel*, esp. pp. 90–91.

9   Roland Marchand, *Advertising the American Dream: Making Way for Modernity, 1920–1940* (Berkeley and Los Angeles: University of California Press, 1985), pp. 153–54.

10 *Album Cover Album 5,* compiled by Roger Dean and Storm Thorgerson (New York: Billboard Books, 1989). See also volumes 1–4.

11 In an argument suggesting that the function of commodity aesthetics is to "stimulate desire in every possible way," W. F. Haug specifically chooses an album cover as an example. Considering Andy Warhol's design for the Rolling Stones' *Sticky Fingers,* Haug writes: "Whoever buys the record, purchases with it a copy of a young man's fly, the package identified by the graphic trick which stresses the penis and highly stylizes the promised content. The buyer acquires the possibility of opening the package, and the zip and finds . . . nothing. It is a reversal of the tale of the Emperor's new clothes: the tale of the buyers' new bodies. They buy only packages which seem to be more than they are." *Critique of Commodity Aesthetics: Appearance, Sexuality, and Advertising in Capitalist Society,* trans. Robert Bock (Minneapolis: University of Minnesota Press, 1986), pp. 86–87. See also, W. F. Haug, *Commodity Aesthetics, Ideology, and Culture* (New York: International General, 1987).

12 Claudia Gorbman, *Unheard Melodies: Narrative Film Music* (Bloomington: Indiana University Press, 1987), pp. 31–52.

13 Mary Ann Doane, "The Voice in the Cinema: The Articulation of Body and Space," in *Narrative, Apparatus, Ideology,* ed. Philip Rosen (New York: Columbia University Press, 1986), p. 345.

14 E. Ann Kaplan, *Rocking around the Clock: Music Television, Postmodernism, and Consumer Culture* (New York and London: Methuen, 1987), p. 44.

15 The impulse to disavow lack need not be registered in media alone. The familiar mock or "air" guitar gesture which is a characteristic accompaniment to popular music listening— particularly among adolescent boys—conjures a strikingly literal example in the social field: the absent phallus is assertively replenished, its lack disavowed through visual mimicry, the missing organ gently caressed and metamorphosed into a longing for technical virtuosity and identification with the cult of the star.

16 See Attali, *Noise,* Janet Wolff, "The Ideology of Autonomous Art," and Susan McClary, "The Blasphemy of Talking Politics during Bach Year," in *Music and Society,* ed. Richard Leppart and Susan McClary (Cambridge: Cambridge University Press, 1987).

17 Jean Baudrillard, *Simulations* (New York: Semiotext(e), 1983), p. 85.

18 For example, Milton Babbitt, whose compositions are each based on individual mathematical theories. For a gloss of his music, see John Rockwell, *All American Music* (New York: Vintage, 1985).

19 Four-part harmony, à la Bach, is still taught as the foundation for students of music. See McClary, "The Blasphemy . . . ," for an alternative reading of Bach's academic appropriation.

20 Max Horkheimer and Theodor W. Adorno, *The Dialectic of Enlightenment* (New York: Continuum, 1989), p. 180. In its original context this "stylus" was clearly meant as a writing utensil, but it may be accurately misread as an audiophile "stylus."

21 Mulvey, "Visual Pleasure and Narrative Cinema," p. 21.

22 Attali, *Noise,* pp. 105–6.

23 Paul Virilio, *Speed and Politics* (New York: Semiotext(e), 1986).

24 Roland Barthes, *Image—Music—Text,* trans. Stephen Heath (London: Flamingo, 1977), p. 189.

25 Ibid., pp. 188–89.

26 Rudolph Arnheim, "In Praise of Blindness: Emancipation from the Body," in *Radio* (London, 1936), p. 191. This book foretold the coming institutionalization of the disembodied voice in audio production at a fairly early stage, valorizing the medium as the distiller of sound-art, free of the complications of the visual. In so doing, Arnheim succeeded in laying out (albeit from an antagonistic position to that of this paper) the major issues still at stake in the audio/visual problematic, as indicated by the section subtitles of this chapter: "The Bodiless Announcer," "Music without Musicians," "Voices without Bodies." Radio also represents the site for the deployment and dissemination of the standard practice of compression, a technique that is becoming obsolete with the expanded dynamic range of digital recording, but has left an indelible mark on popular music's sound.

27 Mick Taussig is currently developing a rich reevaluation of the RCA dog "Nipper" as the intersection of two meanings of "fidelity." An obvious meaning, "faithfulness or likeness to an original," is implied, but Taussig asserts the priority of another meaning stemming from relations of dominance and obedience inferred from the word's connotation of "loyalty." After all, "man's best friend" listens to "his master's voice." In Taussig's view, this is supported by the fact that many early music boxes and phonographs were adorned with images of women, animals, and "natives." "On the Mimetic Faculty," a lecture delivered at the Cultural Studies Conference, University of Illinois at Urbana-Champaign, April 5, 1990. A different version of this argument appears in Taussig's *Mimesis and Alterity: A Particular History of the Senses* (New York: Routledge, 1993).

28 Walter Benjamin, "Unpacking My Library," in *Illuminations* (New York: Schocken, 1969), p. 60.

29 John Mowitt, "The Sound of Music in the Era of Its Electronic Reproducibility," in *Music and Society*, pp. 173–97.

30 Attali, *Noise*, p. 109.

31 Guy Debord, *The Society of the Spectacle* (Detroit: Black and Red, 1977), p. 20.

32 Mayo Thompson, "What," *Durch* 3/4 (November 1987): 5.

33 See Roger Wallis and Krister Malm, *Big Sounds from Small Peoples: The Music Industry in Small Countries* (New York: Pendragon, 1984).

34 "You need only think of John Heartfield, whose technique made the book cover into a political instrument." Walter Benjamin, "The Author as Producer," in *Reflections*, trans. Edmund Jephcott (New York: Schocken, 1978), p. 229. For connections between Heartfield and the English punk band Crass, see Douglas Kahn, *John Heartfield: Art and Mass Media* (New York: Tanam, 1985), pp. 131–32.

35 For two glowing examples of recent music shaking the standardized technology of recording and playback to its epistemological roots, hear Mark Stewart and the Maffia's LP, *As the Veneer of Democracy Starts to Fade* (Mute Records, 1985) and Public Enemy's "Terminator X to the Edge of Panic," on *It Takes a Nation of Millions to Hold Us Back* (Columbia, 1988). Conceptual artists Milan Knízák and Christian Marclay have also created an important body of works that take the music object as their point of departure.

36 This so frightens the music industry that in the 1980s it took to printing a disclaimer on record sleeves (as if from the Surgeon General) featuring the silhouette of a skull and crossbones over a cassette tape, accompanied by the warning, "Home taping is *killing* music!" On the wall of a small, alternative record shop in New York City, a sarcastic response recently appeared: "Home fucking is *killing* pornography!" A forthcoming book promises to discuss cassette counterculture: *Cassette Mythos: Making Music at the Margins*, ed. Robin James (New York: Autonomedia, due 1994).

37 Jean-François Lyotard and Jean-Loup Thébaud, *Just Gaming*, trans. Brian Massumi (Minneapolis: University of Minnesota Press, 1985), p. 13.

38 Andrew Ross, *No Respect: Intellectuals and Popular Culture* (New York and London: Routledge, 1989), p. 193.

39 An A&R man on an episode of the short-lived record company sitcom *Throb* epitomized this in pitching a new group: "They're young, they're fresh . . . they're just like the Talking Heads!"

40 Adorno, "On Jazz" (originally published 1936). See Jamie Owen Daniel's new translation and her excellent introduction in *Discourse* 12, no. 1 (Fall–Winter 1989–90): 39–69.

41 Lyotard, "Several Silences," in *Driftworks* (New York: Semiotext(e), 1984), p. 108.

SIREN SONG TO BANSHEE WAIL

On the Status of the Background Vocalist

●

The Argo sped on in a fresh breeze, and soon they saw a beautiful island, green and flower-laden, the habitation of the beguiling sirens, who lure passers-by with their singing, but only to destroy them. Half bird and half maiden, they always lay in wait for new quarry, and no one who came near could escape them. Now they sang their sweetest airs to the Argonauts, who were just about to cast their rope ashore and make fast the ship, when Orpheus, the singer from Thrace, rose in his seat and began to strike such rich and ringing chords on the strings of his divine lyre that drowned out the voices decoying his friends to death.—Gustav Schwab, GODS AND HEROES

The Death Angels sing. Angels flap their wings. The Death Angel sing the sweetest song I ever heard.—Lee "Scratch" Perry, UPSETTER NEWS, No. 1

I

A technical device distinguishes the two realms—mortal and immortal—in Wim Wenders's *Wings of Desire*: the voice-over. At the start of the film, when point of view is strictly that of the spirit side, we experience a heterophony of disembodied voices, grounded nowhere, in flight. Angels, birds, airplanes—and voices: all are united by their ethereal quality, by their airborne ability, like the sirens, to take to the wing. Barthes claims that the grainless voice, the one not steeped in the body, is "all air, from the lungs . . . stupid organs."[1] If the body in narrative film is located in diegesis, then the extra-diegetic voice is precisely aligned with this ethereal substance.

But is the disembodied voice in the case of *Wings of Desire* extra-diegetic? Can it not be said that each of these voices corresponds to the thoughts of a specific character in the film? Even if the speaker is not shown, it is to be assumed that the voice relates to a Berliner. When the camera pans past a row of faces, the voice changes to relate to the on-screen face, to whom it belongs; the voice is thus actually related to the diegesis, but does not emanate from there. Hence, the difference between this (thought) voice and the depiction of spoken sound which is linked directly with moving lips is not only that of the mind/matter split, but concerns another fissure, one between interior and exterior. The disembodied voice, loosely reconnected with a specific body in this way, provides entry "into" that body; it "manifests its inner lining."[2] As the first shot passes over the city, floating voices open the port to the interiority of Berlin. The main characters of the film are Theognis's recording angels, in charge of impassively gathering and storing the events and thoughts of the world. Not coincidentally, it is the technology of recording, its disentangling of the visual from the aural and its ability to gain access to the characters' interiority, which provides the precondition for the film's construction of body/spirit worlds. The codes it plays on are not new, but are fully within the range of the vocabulary of mainstream film.

Indeed, the recorded voice is a major theme of the film. Synchronization of voices with bodies (as a reinforcement of the film's use of color) provides a locus for the spectator's transition between the two worlds: it locates the "fallen angel" initially in the spirit world, when the voices are not in sync, and in the corporeal at last, when they are. In service to this, the voice-off murmur serves to drown out any incidental environmental noise in the first half, whereas the main angel's first moments as a mortal are characterized by the clang of his armor and the crunch of pebbles underfoot. No more distracting, intoxicating voices draw attention from the sound of the street. And the voice figures explicitly at many other points in the film. For example, the angels are never seen "thinking" (*they* have have no interiority, only surface); no direct voice-over accompanies them. Only after he is fallen, at the very end, does the main angel, Damiel, have an interior monologue. The old storyteller recounts the tree-falls-in-the-woods tale of the "immortal singer who lost his mortal listeners and therefore lost his voice." When the female protagonist retires to her trailer to contemplate the eternal, she puts on a vocal record. As the suicidist jumps from the building, he is wearing a Walkman and voices(-over) engulf and seem to seduce him to "take the plunge." In the library, the hum of voices (in a place where one shouldn't speak) rises into a delirious epiphany, signaling the climax of the spiritual section "before the fall."

The strength of the film's use of voice lies in its treatment of a primary technical device as a theme. Taking the suicidist and the library scenario, for example, it can be said that the voice-over is coded as signifying the ethereal, flighty insubstantiality of thought; it is a filmic technique rationalized in the logic of a fantastic narrative as being diegetically related to the "extra-sensory" viewpoint of angels. But something exceeds this formal logic. To enhance the impression of ethereality, the disembodied diegetic voices are supplemented by an additional, truly extra-diegetic *woman's* voice, or in the case of the suicidist and library, *women's* voices. These belong to the sound-track proper; even in the expanded spiritual diegesis, they are inexplicable.

That they work to further the "unearthly" tone of these scenes exposes the structural importance of the disembodied woman's voice as *substantially* different from disembodied man's voice. Or, better yet, the woman's voice is constructed as *insubstantial*, as being different not simply in what substance it has—pitch, register, timbre—but different in that it is construed to have no substance whatsoever. This is, of course, a paradox, since woman's voice must be recognized for what it *is* before it can signify that it is *nothing*. Such is the profound inconsistency on which the construction of woman's recorded voice rests in patriarchy: it is grounded in the instability of insubstantiality. Therefore, as we shall see, it is either sweet or noxious, but the woman's voice is always constructed as a potentially dangerous vapor.

By looking at a film in which the voice-over is contrasted in various thematized and technical ways with the synchronous voice, we have set the stage for a consideration of a cultural arena which may be said to be entirely voice-over—that is, recorded music. To do this, it will be necessary to employ and adapt concepts that have been developed in feminist film theory's ongoing theorization of the female voice in cinema. In her book *The Acoustic Mirror* Kaja Silverman has expanded, debated, and revised ideas first put forth in articles by Mary Ann Doane, Guy Rosolato, Michel Chion, and Pascal Bonitzer, and her contribution has proved fundamental for the development of an adequate theory of the female voice in cinema (and recording in general). Before turning to recorded music, then, it may be helpful to briefly clarify a few of the precepts of this work.

First, as we have seen in relation to *Wings of Desire*, it is recognized that the voices of men and women are structurally different. Silverman writes: "It has gone largely unnoticed that like the visual *vraisemblable*, the sonic *vraisemblable* is sexually differentiated, working to identify even the *embodied* male voice with the attributes of the cinematic apparatus, but always situating the female voice within a hyperbolically diegetic context."[3] This can be seen as a refinement of the assertion by Pascal Bonitzer of "the arbitration and arbitrariness of the voice-off which, to the extent that it cannot be localized, can be criticized by nothing and no one."[4] If this is true, it would only hold for the male voice, since male and female voices are different not only in terms of what they sound like, but also with respect to how they function semiotically. Thus, where the disembodied male voice is generally identified as the voice of authority, such a status is normally unobtainable for the female voice-over/voice-off. Her voice, as Silverman explains, is subject to continual recuperation by the narrative, into the diegesis. It is required to "stand in" for a male voice that pretends to be self-knowledgeable and exterior to the "lure" of the narrative—it is made to speak a female interiority. Where this "expressive" voice might be seen in a positive way, Silverman cautions: "Interiority has a very different status in classic cinema from the one that it enjoys in the literary and philosophical tradition which Derrida critiques. Far from being a privileged condition, synonymous with soul, spirit, or consciousness, interiority in Hollywood films implies linguistic constraint and physical confinement—confinement of the body to claustral spaces, and to inner narratives."[5] Through readings of *Klute*, *Diva*, and *The Conversation*, Silverman shows that the female voice-off/voice-over is not, therefore, one of authorial intentionality, but one that is relentlessly brought back into the *telos* of the narrative and made to say things for the male listener, to be the "projection of all that is culturally debased and devalued,"[6] to feign the image of the insufficient man, to "sing someone else's song," as Mimi White puts it.[7]

The major theoretical dispute within the discussion of the status of woman's voice in film revolves around the concept of a voice that is taken as "pure sonorousness," a voice not recuperated into the narrative completely (not fully *diegested*, so to speak), but one that constitutes an "operatic and utopian enclosure."[8] Through Guy Rosolato, Doane links this to the maternal voice as a pre-Oedipal place of connection between mother and child, before the interdiction of the voice of the father, the external voice of authority. Like Kristeva's category of the "semiotic" as a feminine place of creation, this "sonorous envelope" is linked with a kind of exteriority to the ideological system. It is not the same exterior as the male voice's place of mastery and dominance, but an "image of corporeal unity" between the listener and the auditor. Such a voice is not reliant on being disembodied and may in fact gain from being synchronous—the sync binding the voice to the body in a reinforcement of the effect of plenitude. Furthermore, the voice, in this sense, does not communicate in comprehensible language, which is instituted by the structuring imposition of the father's command. Instead, this maternal voice is seen as essential and nonsensical, connecting the mother and child in "noise or babble." From Silverman's position, these notions are suspect and dangerous. She sees the interplay between the internal and external as being highly complicated, always working to disadvantage the woman's voice. She warns that the maternal voice

> must be understood not as an extension of its intrinsic nature, or of its acoustic function, but as part of a larger cultural disavowal of the mother's role both as an agent of discourse and as a model for linguistic (as well as visual) identification. The characterization of the mother's voice as babble or noise is also . . . one of the primary mechanisms through which the male subject seeks both to recover an imaginary infantile plenitude, and to extricated himself from the "afterbirth" of

perceptual and semiotic insufficiency. Last but not least, that character-ization contradicts the notion of exteriority which is implied by the metaphors of enclosure with which it is frequently linked—metaphors such as "envelope," "cobweb," or "bath"—and facilitates the alignment of femininity with an unpleasurable and disempowering interiority.[9]

For Silverman, the maternal voice is a myth that psychoanalysis shares with patriarchy in the construction of an inarticulate and helpless form of femininity.

Like Silverman, Mimi White disturbs this quiescent scenario by explain-ing the nostalgic "snare" it sets up by reinforcing a vision of "woman as exotic other." As White points out, this coincides (textually and histori-cally) with an equally overdetermined other: race.[10] We will return to this, but first we should move from this overview to the body of our text, where we will adapt this argument, replete with all its tensions, to the sphere of recorded music. In particular, we will address the category in which these tensions find an intense, condensed articulation: the background singer.[11]

II

Background singers: ask for them by name.—David Letterman

If, as was suggested earlier, the vocal record is entirely "voice-over"—voice always being disembodied by the act of recording—this is not to rule out the existence of a diegetic space in recorded song.[12] Specifically, the sound of the main vocalist can be said to articulate just such a diegetic space. And like the woman's choir which exceeds even the extended diegesis in *Wings of Desire*, the background singer occupies an extra-diegetic space, unlocaliz-able in the material *mise-en-scène* of the lead singer. Silverman insists on the compulsive circumscription of the woman's voice back into the diegesis. But we might point out that in her analysis of the film *Klute* she herself omits a set of women's voices. In her reading, Silverman concentrates on the role of prostitute Bree Daniels's voice—both "live" and recorded—as a mirror for her client, a site for the externalization and displacement of that which is abject to him, a "dumping ground for disowned desires."[13] Woman's voice is, in this account, a place onto which the debased is projected. But Silverman leaves out another important group of voices: the singing women that add an "eerie" ambience to several scenes, enhancing the lure and increasing the sense of danger at the point when John Klute investigates suspicious noises on the roof.[14] It is these singing voices, never fully accounted for in the economy of the filmic text, never avowed in critical readings, that exceed the practice of diegetic recuperation. These are the archetypical background vocals.

In what follows, I will be assuming that a bracketed term always precedes the construct "background vocalists," and that is, naturally, "(female)." Likewise, the lead singer is preceded by an unspoken "(male)." It is not insignificant that this gendering is most often disavowed; so strong is this construct that one need not utter its name to feel its presence. And such anonymity is one of the key features of the background vocalist herself. If we couple this with a strong fantasy of the return to the womb in the "sonorous envelope" of the disembodied female voice, we recognize two of the main (and most odious) aspects of the category of (female) background vocalist. Furthermore, there is another facet of the category whose disavowal is likewise constitutive of the (female) background singer. In front of the bracketed gender term there is a bracketed racial term: "(black)." Think, for example, of Lou Reed's description: "The colored girls go 'do, do-do, do-do, do, do-do.'" As White cautions against the championing of the maternal, uncovering its disavowal of race as a structuring absence, so is it necessary to acknowledge race as another index which must be cross-referenced with that of gender in the analysis of the (black)(female)background singer.[15]

Before moving to draw these various aspects out in greater detail, however, I would like to advance some additional thoughts on the disembodied woman's voice. First, it seems to me that the aural world offers a rich counterpart to the threat of castration theorized in visual terms by Freud. I believe it would be possible to suggest that castration anxiety may also be provoked by the female voice, in its very register. Central to this notion would be the castrato singer. Castration keeps the boy's voice as it is before it becomes a man's—that is, before it gains authority.[16] Historically, the castrati substituted for women's voices at a time when women did not sing from the stage.[17] It was largely under the influence of the castrato that opera developed in the seventeenth century, and this final link between women, opera, and death is pointed out by White (using Catherine Clément) in her reading of *Diva*: "Opera figures here as an overdetermined sign of women's romance, tragedy, demise and the voice as song foretelling of death."[18] Along with the more obvious generic influences of doo-wop and gospel choir music—both of which set up the racial overdetermination of the background vocalist— and the chorus girl, the castrati choir is thus one of the historical antecedents of the category of background vocalist.

A second addendum to the attributes of woman's voice deals with the dispute over the status of woman's voice as "babble or noise." The question is whether aural nonsense is threatening to male auditory mastery or whether it is merely another way that the possibility of female authorial position is foreclosed. Clément argues the former: "This language which has not yet reached verbal expression, but is held within the confines of the body, which signifies the body on all sides but does not transmit it in the form of thought-content, remains convulsive. Men watch, but do not understand."[19]

As we have seen, Silverman holds the contrary position, or more precisely, she adds to this notion that men do not only watch (or listen), but they *respond* by imagining a fantasy "bath" of prelinguistic babble into which they can immerse themselves and thereby forget the nagging truth that they are not, in fact, masters of all they survey. This fantasy functions at the expense of female vocal authority and linguistic mastery. Regardless of which argument we support, such a consideration contains particular significance for the background singer, given the prevalence of nonsense in the "ooh-oohs" and "hey-heys" frequently required of her. Even meaningful language is pummeled into incoherence, as Kate and Anna McGarrigle put it: "I could sing 'love' over and over and over / I could sing 'baby, baby, baby' till my tongue spirals out of my head / make you think it over / make you think I mean it . . . maybe."[20]

Finally, then, I would like to posit a vehicle that allows for the maintenance of this contradiction and its interminable shuffle back and forth between subjugation and subversion. Silverman suggests that one of the main forces driving the compulsion to contain the female voice within the narrative and associate the male voice with diegetic exteriority is the "possibility of leakage of those same [debased and devalued] attributes back onto the male voice . . . it must be understood as a defensive reaction against the migratory potential of the voice."[21] To use an image common to magnetic tape and menstrual taboo, I would like to figure this contagious potential as the fear of bleeding. Thus the incoherence associated with woman's disembodied voice, the "black hole where meaning drains out of the system,"[22] is threatening because it might bleed onto the male voice, and therefore it must be contained that much more strenuously.

Two primary attributes define the background singer in relation to the lead. These attributes are similar, but differ in important ways. First, the background singer produces (or cultivates) the fantasy of the womblike sonorous envelope, and in this its function is one of comfort. Second, the background singer is always nameless, and in this its function is one of support. Anonymous disavowing womb-crutch: this is the background vocalist assemblage.

We have already seen the tension in the issue of the concept of woman's voice as pure sonorousness between the notion that her voice provides access to a region of pre-Oedipal play and the notion that this is a treacherous myth that serves patriarchy. In popular music, the woman's voice indeed seems to be a mythical place, but one with a double function first of providing a haven for male subjectivity by "proving" his mastery in contrast to the immateriality of the background vocals, and second of potentially disembodying the very voice it is meant to clarify and support. First, the "ground" in the "back-" is just that: a place that situates the male voice. In this respect, a connection between gospel testimonial (can I get a witness?) and background vocalist is revealed: back me up, baby. As a comforter the background vocal is not so much extra-diegetic (in contrast to the diegetic space articulated by the lead vocalist), but it *constitutes* the diegesis. It becomes the very space for the lead vocals, blending in with the walls of the studio, becoming part of that larger instrument of the music industry. But the background vocalist becomes the diegesis solely to indulge the male lead in a fantasy of plenitude, to protect him from the danger of "going it alone," in which case *his* own status as disembodied voice might also be revealed, associating him with the status of woman's voice and diminishing his authority.

Contrary to this fear of isolation and disempowerment, which calls upon the myth of the maternal womb and calls forth the background singers, there is a second danger, this time inherent in the *presence* rather than the potential absence of the background vocalist. If the disavowal of "unpleasurable self-knowledge" makes the background singer necessary, then "what has been disowned returns in the guise of paranoid fantasies of enclosure, entrapment, and suffocation."[23] In other words, the sonorous envelope threatens to link the male voice to the woman's, this time by means of bleeding rather than isolation, comparison, and identification. The male voice is in a precarious position, where it might be dislodged and join the ranks of the disembodied women, swept away in the "sea of sound," smothered, suffocated, overwhelmed by the background voices. Think, for example, of the Bee Gees, who respond to the lure, *becoming* the background singers for Samantha Sang: "It's just emotion taking me over . . ." To keep this threat at bay while still facilitating the fantasy, an equation is drawn up, a special balance between pillowy, claustrophobic choir and piercing, self-confident soloist. Here, the image of the Argonauts holds sway; Orpheus's "rich and ringing" lead contrasted with the Sirens' seductive background represents just such a balance, simultaneously beckoning to the listener to join in the maternal fantasy even as it holds out an image of the triumphant and masterful male voice.

At the same time, there is the construct of background vocalist as "nameless support." By "support," I mean several things. On one hand it suggests the way that the female background singer equips the male voice with what it cannot achieve in terms of range and timbre; it *extends* the potential of the male singer. Emanating from the doubled world of the other (black woman), it also carries connotations of authenticity and exoticism that serve to "root" the lead vocalist. Moreover, by providing a harmonic "bed," it literally supports the singular voice, which is constructed as the central point around which the background vocals are laid as a foundation. And these vocals are commonly held to be an "expressive" supplement to the singular voice.

The ability of these voices to support in this way is based primarily on their namelessness. Of course, background singers aren't named (or appear only in fine print) for obvious economic and status reasons—though they have been known to "save" plenty of recordings. Since technique, authenticity, and expressivity are also criteria by which the male lead is judged, background vocalists must be kept in a special role so that the women never attain the status of named autonomous subjects (much less, artists), hence threatening to displace the male lead. But what happens if the bleed moves the other direction? If the background singer is named, is identified, this system is potentially disrupted. The possibility is always there that the background vocalists will not remain in tight harmony, but will individuate and exceed the delicate balance of expressivity and uniformity by which they support the lead. Instead, they may simply wail. In this vein, we might locate the historical developments of girl groups, from those of sixties soul (the Supremes, the Ronettes, the Chiffons),[24] or seventies punk (the Slits, Kleenex, the Raincoats), or eighties and nineties eclectic (Indigo Girls, the Roches, the Bangles, Bananarama, the Go-Gos, L7, Wilson Phillips, Akabu, the Breeders, Free Kitten). These women's voices are not part of the paradigm of the sirens' song, the seduction, per se, but mark the termination of the individual male lead as an exclusive subject position. Instead, they are better identified with the Banshee, the female Gaelic spirit whose wail forewarns of impending death. Of course, neither in the case of the siren-status of background vocalist nor in her Banshee sister is there an essentially positive figure. Thus what the siren accomplishes by enticing the lead vocalist and what the Banshee accomplishes by smiting the lead vocalist is not the establishment of a pure pre-Oedipal playground. We should remember that in questioning or taking on the role of the lead singer the background vocalist never leaves the realm of the music industry, a group of institutions that remains overflowing with sexist and racist overdeterminations just waiting in its patriarchal wings.

Notes

1 Roland Barthes, "The Grain of the Voice," in *Image/Music/Text* (London: Penguin, 1979), p. 183. Note that the "gas" metaphor (voice = air) is continued elsewhere in this essay; as we shall see, this relates to a cultural construction of the female voice as either "suffocating" or "intoxicating," both of which are notions consistent with the equation of voice with gas.

2 Mary Ann Doane, "The Voice in the Cinema: The Articulation of Body and Space," in *Narrative, Apparatus, Ideology*, ed. Philip Rosen (New York: Columbia University Press, 1986), p. 341.

3 Kaja Silverman, *The Acoustic Mirror: The Female Voice in Psychoanalysis and Film* (Bloomington: Indiana University Press, 1988), p. 45. Particularly important is the chapter "The Fantasy of the Maternal Voice: Paranoia and Compensation."

4 Pascal Bonitzer, "The Silences of the Voice," in *Narrative, Apparatus, Ideology*, p. 322.

5 Silverman, *The Acoustic Mirror*, p. 45.

6 Ibid., p. 84.

7 Mimi White, "They All Sing . . . : Voice, Body, and Representation in *Diva*," *Literature and Psychology* 34, no. 4 (1988): 33–43.

8 Silverman, *The Acoustic Mirror*, p. 87.

9 Ibid., p. 100. The debate between Silverman and Doane is most intensely expressed in relation to this idea, specifically as it occurs in music; Doane accepts the image of cohesion and plenitude associated with music, while Silverman emphasizes that this "harmony" between mother and child is only possible *after* sounds have been recognized as different from one another. In fact, both Doane and Silverman illustrate this point using the same quotation from Rosalato, translated in slightly different ways and given altogether different critical readings. I would like to point out that in both these cases it is taken for granted that what constitutes "music" is somehow predetermined and music exists primarily for the purposes of articulating this kind of primary relationship between mother and child. Music, as a fluid and nondenotative signifying system, has an essential identity that, for them, links it with nonsense-speak. That all music does not relate to the "tensions and releases" essentialized in Rosalato's original text seems to me to be the most important point—for example, consider the music of John Cage, which surely does not revolve around the *fort/da* of traditional Western classical music. And at the same time music can function as a denotative and strongly connotative signifying system completely out of keeping with this sort of pre-Oedipal concept. See Silverman, p. 85, and Doane, p. 343.

10 White, "They All Sing."

11 I use the term "background singer" exclusively in this paper, though "back-up singer" is also widely used. Each term carries a specific spatial connotation consistent with the staging of these singers: they are generally behind the lead, and they "ground" him or "back" him up.

12 To suggest a diegetic space removed from the issue of narrative, as I am here, may be problematic for dyed-in-the-wool film theorists. But given the fact that in audio recording space is constructed out of heterogeneous elements, often relying on the same sorts of temporal edits as film and calling on an equally complex set of spatial codes to naturalize it, I think that the analogy holds.

13 Silverman, *The Acoustic Mirror*, p. 81.

14 These voices appear after the tinkling "eerie" theme has already appeared in the film. Just as in *Wings of Desire* where the women's voices break through the already extended conditions of diegetic sound to signify the angel Damiel's epiphany in the library, so do the women's singing voices in *Klute* push one step beyond the music's ambiguous tonality (which already works to unsettle the listener) and seem to seduce Klute onto the roof and into danger.

15 Of course, there are counter-examples: black male background vocalists like the Pips and even white male background vocal groups such as the Jordanaires. These seem to me not only exceptions that prove the rule, but I think they gather much of their signifying power from a kind of aural and visual cross-dressing, the pleasure of seeing and hearing men masquerade in a position normally reserved for women.

16 In a number of places, Silverman directly addresses the connection between the female voice and castration, specifically in her discussion of Barthes's use in "The Death of the Author" of a quotation from Balzac concerning Zambinella, a castrato posing as a woman (pp. 191–93). She does not, however, suggest that castration anxiety and its ensuing projection and disavowal can be triggered by the sound of woman's voice. See Joke Dame, "Unveiled Voices: Sexual Difference and the Castrato," in *Queering the Pitch: The New Gay and Lesbian Musicology* (New York: Routledge, 1944), pp. 139–53.

17 In Brittany during the thirteenth and fourteenth centuries there were plain-chant and polyphonic women's choirs, recently performed and recorded on *Graduel d'Aliénor de Bretagne* (Harmonia Mundi HMC 901403), and a medieval mass to the Virgin, *An English Ladymass* (Harmonia Mundi HMC 907080) was re-created by a women's quartet that, not imprecisely, calls itself Anonymous 4. Robert Dulgarian notes that "the producton of castrati in the Papal States was for employment in ecclesiastical settings from which women were excluded, and the development of their vogue occurred on contemporaneous secular stages in other parts of Italy, thence to South Germany, etc., stages on which women *were* present."

18 White, "They All Sing," p. 39.

19 Catherine Clément, "Enslaved Enclave," in *New French Feminisms*, ed. Elaine Marks and Isabelle de Courtivron (New York: Schocken Books, 1981), pp. 133–34.

20 Kate and Anna McGarrigle, "Love Over and Over," on *Love Over and Over* (Polydor Records 810 042-1, 1982).

21 Silverman, *The Acoustic Mirror*, p. 84.

22 Ibid., p. 71.

23 Ibid.

24 For an analysis of girl groups in terms of what she calls a "structure of *feminine discourse*," see Barbara Bradley, "Do-Talk and Don't-Talk: The Division of the Subject in Girl-Group Music," in *On Record: Rock, Pop, and the Written Word*, ed. Simon Frith and Andrew Goodwin (New York: Pantheon, 1990), pp. 341–68. In "Rock and Sexuality," Simon Frith and Angela McRobbie make a point of differentiating between the 1950s (an era of "feminization" in the music industry) and the 1970s (an era of "masculinization" in the music industry). They stress the paradoxical use of background singers in the seemingly progressive arena of rock as opposed to the regressive (blatantly sexist) country, soul, and reggae: "Compare, for example, Bob Dylan's and Bob Marley's use of supporting women singers. Dylan is a sophisticated rock star . . . His most recent lyrics, at least, reflect a critical self-understanding that isn't obviously sexist. But musically and visually his backup trio are used only as a source of glamour, their traditional pop use. Marley is an orthodox Rastafarian, subscribes to a belief, an institution, a way of life in which women

have as subordinate a place as in any other sexually repressive religion. And yet Marley's I-Threes sing and present themselves with grace and dignity, with independence and power. In general, it seems that soul and country musics, blatantly sexist in their organization and presentation, in the themes and concerns of their lyrics, allow their female performers an autonomous musical power that is rarely achieved by women in rock." It is worth noting that Frith and McRobbie still refer to Rita Marley, Marcia Griffith, and Judy Mowatt as *Marley's* I-Threes. Ibid., p. 384. See also Charlotte Greig, *Will You Still Love Me Tomorrow?* (London: Virago, 1989).

BLEED THIS, MOTHERF*!#ER

The Semiotics of Profanity

in Popular Music

●

We've come to a strange point in U.S. cultural politics, where we're *lucky* to have voted into office a
Democratic vice-president whose wife also hap-
pens to have founded one of the most insidious and overt censorship cam-
paigns currently being waged. In a bipartisan movement, Tipper Gore,
Susan Baker (wife of James Baker), and their Parents Music Resource Center
(PMRC) can take much of the credit for the now-standard music industry
practice of "stickering," in which recordings that contain lyrics that *somebody, somewhere* might find offensive are marked with a generic "warning"
label. The text of this sticker or label directly addresses the PMRC: "Parental
Advisory: Explicit Lyrics." This practice was taken to its illogical extreme a
few years ago when, hopefully not without some irony, New Albion Records
stickered a CD which contained a single instance of the word *fucked.* The
disc was *Singing Through* by notorious music pornographer John Cage.

Stickers are not an end in themselves. The target for them is not solely, in
fact perhaps not primarily, the music consumer. They are, instead, part of a
larger strategy to inhibit the sale of obscene or profane music by impeding its
production and distribution. Marking certain discs takes away the excuse of
ignorance for record store clerks; marked products make it crystal clear
what can be sold to minors and what can't. And if store owners are ultimately
responsible, they can only eliminate the possibility that a counter person
will make a costly mistake by excluding obscene material from their stores
altogether. If there's no place to sell something, from the industry's perspective, there's no reason to produce it. As a result, many stores that have chosen
not to completely abandon stickered music objects have taken to keeping
the obscene material behind the counter, requiring proof of age for purchase;
buying music becomes an ID check. The fact is that the stickers have been
adopted by major record companies *voluntarily*, in the hope that this gesture
of self-regulation will sufficiently insure against outside, legislative regula-
tion. Hence, the warning sticker is part of a network of censorship, a prohibitory discourse that works solely through the chilling anticipation of
legal ramifications, without actual prohibition ever having to take place.

Much to the chagrin of the PMRC, the utility of warning stickers has in large part been undermined, reversed by consumers, particularly by fans of rap. Warning stickers have become a mark of authenticity; they are the prized assurance of *sufficient* profanity that makes some recordings desirable. In fact, contrary to their intended effect, it is clear that warning stickers *increase* the desirability of certain music objects, lending them the kind of transgressive appeal through which much commodity exchange now occurs. Profane music now wears its sticker proudly, defiantly, seductively. Not to have a warning label would be like a "mature" film with a G-rating. Indeed, rapper Ice-T and his record company, Sire/Warner Brothers, played on this when they placed a sticker on his 1989 release *Freedom of Speech . . . Just Watch What You Say.* The sticker follows normal warning label form, in big bold black and red letters: "ICE-T; X-Rated; Parents Strongly Cautioned." But beneath this, in small print it reads: "Some material may be X-tra hype and inappropriate for squares and suckers."

In lyrics to songs and in the writing on record and disc covers, the music industry and musicians themselves have developed a number of strategies and tactics for dealing with the issues of profanity and obscenity. The practice of "bleeping" or simply blanking out profane words—particularly on radio—was at one time the main means for censoring offensive lyrics out of songs. At one time this was done at the radio station, with time delay being the narrow margin-of-error window through which censors had to work their magic. Now, however, in the face of groups like the PMRC and changes in FCC "guidelines" (radio, too, *self*-censors voluntarily in fear of government intervention), the industry and musicians take a proactive attitude, employing a variety of complicated and semiotically tricky techniques to circumvent and, like Ice-T, often play on the prohibitory discourse. As a marker of the onset of these practices, recall that in 1967, MC5 issued their live album *Kick out the Jams*, the title cut of which included the rallying cry: "Now it's time to kick out the jams, motherfuckers!" Shortly after the record was released, executives at Elektra balked, recalling and destroying the copies already issued and sanctioning a second version, with a crudely overdubbed substitution: "Now it's time to kick out the jams, *brothers and sisters!*"

On a single record by Boogie Down Productions called *By All Means Necessary*, rapper KRS-1 makes clear the range of techniques now available for approaching the accursed curse: he swears uninhibitedly, bleeps out profanity, and even uses the old-fashioned synechdochial technique of substituting the first letter for the whole, such as saying "F-you" instead of "fuck you." In fact, especially in African-American music, there is a long tradition of evasive tactics for dealing with censorship. In songs from Lil Green's "In the Dark" where she sings "In the dark I get such a thrill, when he touch his fingertips against my Lil, and begs me to please keep still, in the dark" to Bo Carter's self-explanatory "Banana in Your Fruit Basket," early blues singers took double entendre to new levels and cultivated other techniques, such as humming in the place of obscenities, making an obscene word into part of another word ("Y'ass, Y'ass, Y'ass" was a favorite) or substituting a musical figure, such as a slide guitar riff, for the implied expletive.

The same cycle of restriction and reappropriation evident in the warning sticker's dual signification (as prohibition and mark of authenticity) has a counterpart in a process at work not simply in packaging and marketing, but directly within the music itself. In order to make rap radio-worthy, a new form of voluntary censorship has arisen in the record industry. In the place of a profane word, on radio versions (that is, recordings remixed specifically for airplay), the word itself is literally inverted. By digitally sampling the word and playing it backwards, the extremely concrete FCC guidelines governing airplay can be circumvented. For examples of this extremely widespread practice, listen to the radio mixes of NWA's "Straight Outta Compton," EPMD's "Head Banger," and Das Efx's "Straight out the Sewer."[1]

While this technique may seem simple and straightforward, it actually draws on a very intricate set of suppositions and has important consequences. First, it is clear that in most cases no one will mistake the profane connotation—or in many cases the exact meaning—of the reversed word. In fact, it might be correct to say that the *other* word substituting for the profanity—"tihs" replacing "shit" or "kuf" for "fuck" for instance—signifies exactly the same thing. (There are, in fact, a few cases, such as "cock" or "tit," which are audio palindromes and would be considered offensive either way you slice it, so to speak.) Of course, this backwards masking (like all euphemism and double entendre) confounds the steadfastly literal PMRC, whose stake is in prohibiting the word itself, the material signifier in all its positivity. For these groups, what is profane is absolutely profane; it is not open to interpretation. Fortunately, that's not how signification works.[2] What further complicates the situation, however, is that the replacement word was actually created in the same breath as the offensive word. Thus it is imprecise to say that it is not the same word just because it sounds different. As a digital sample, it is the same word, or at least it is derived from the same recorded source. For the PMRC this must be a very perturbing situation, since thanks to the technology of sampling (though it would be possible with analog tape, too) the material signifier can be there and not be there at the same time.

Backwards masking is an inherently convoluted subject; the very suggestion that backwards messages have some psychological impact relies on the implicit, if unformed, suggestion that people can read backwards, or better, can *hear* backwards. But in the case of rap's backwards swearing, the emphasis is decidedly on being able to overtly, consciously decipher the missing or mutated word. It must be there by not being there. In being present in its absence, a word is overdetermined by its context. The context in this case may be the semantics of a line, a rhyme, emphatic phrasing, or even just the jarring sound of the reversed word itself. In any case, for the curse to work, the mutated obscenity must bear the full weight of the original meaning without actually being sounded. It is a question of getting around a rigid prohibitory system by means of the signifying flexibility made possible, in part, by technology. Thus, if we consider that a sign is not defined or does not signify simply in terms of what it is—its positive value—but by confirming that it is not anything else, then we are led to ask what is the status of something that is not only "not anything else," but also *not what it is*. Legally, what is obscene about a word is what it sounds like, its material existence. So long as a word doesn't sound like what it means, it is acceptable. In the case of bleeping and backwards masking, contrary to the normal circuit of signification, I would suggest that it is in fact the meaning of the word that precedes its recognition. The word is suggested by its own profane meaning, and the meaning is implied, at least in part, by the fact that the word was mutilated or erased. An interesting connection could be made between this activity of mutating or mutilating words and Bakhtin's notion of the *grammatica jocosa*. As Peter Stallybrass and Allon White explain, this is the practice in which "grammatical order is transgressed to reveal erotic and obscene or merely materially satisfying counter-meaning."[3] Perhaps, here, we need a *semantica jocosa*, in which the meaning, the obscenity of a "bad word" is enhanced by the procedure that mutilates or transgresses it.

In a very interesting development, singer KRS-1 has adapted backwards masking for use in performance. In concert, recently, he has taken to *singing* curse words backwards, mimicking the technologically turned-around sounds. Thus what was initially a technique ostensibly designed to obfuscate profanity has given rise to a new set of profane signifiers; an artifact of technology has created new words. This is a similar but distinct process from the genealogy of the disco "handclap" that Andrew Goodwin has charted.[4] In Goodwin's analysis, the immediacy of the live handclap was the impetus for the recorded claps that became a regular feature of late-seventies pop. But the second generation of handclaps, when they were digitalized, were actually sampled from the same first-generation recordings, rather than new, live, clapping hands. The code of the clap had been set firmly in place. In the case of KRS-1, the technology of sampling permits a word to be mutated, and this mutation allows a new, different *live* profanity to emerge. It is, in this sense, a new generation of obscenity, a provisionally stabilized code of masked obscenity.

In a related way, the technique of turning words around has made its way from rap lyrics onto CD covers, as well. On the group NWA's breakthrough record *Niggaz 4 Life*, the disc's title was reversed, allowing the record to be displayed in stores without fear of retribution or boycott. At a local record store, this became fuel for a running joke, as clerks pondered the new NWA record *Efil Zaggin*. The point is that in strategies like bleeping, deletion, substitution, or backwards masking, mutilation and replacement act as viable methods for getting around censorship, be it legislatively explicit or economically controlled. For the PMRC the emphasis is on the material signifier, which must be complete and unadulterated in order to signify profanity. Herein lies the fundamental weakness, the poverty of this logic of prohibition, which, in a true sense lives by the letter of the law, or better, the law of the letter. This is perhaps most clearly illustrated in the album cover tactics of the punk bands the Cunts, who substitute an asterisk for the letter "u" (C*nts), allowing record stores to stock their records without having to, for all intents and purposes, hide their name.

For Jacques Derrida, it was likewise the substitution of a single letter that allowed him to express the provisionality of meaning, the "a" of *différance*. In his 1968 formulation, he stresses the twin keywords of Saussure: "arbitrary" and "different." In the mutilation of words to avoid the consequences of censorship, one clearly sees this arbitrary relationship between signifier and signified (mutilated curse words still signifying profanely) and it is also clear that this mutilation is allowed because the terms are part of a signifying ensemble of differences rather than by creating meaning in and of their own positivity. Derrida suggests two consequences of the operation *différance*:

> 1. One could no longer include différance in the concept of the sign, which always has meant the representation of a presence, and has been constituted as a system (thought or language) governed by and moving towards presence.
> 2. And thereby one puts into question the authority of presence, or of its simple symmetrical opposite, absence or lack.[5]

Hence, Derrida configures the "governing" role of presence, its "authority." And he suggests that the simple absence—or perhaps what we have looked at as bleeping—is likewise constrained. The kind of mutation or mutilation that we have examined in relation to rap lyrics, especially, suggests the fluidity of a contrary mode of signification.

As a final example, there is a practice which perhaps goes beyond all of the aforementioned tactics, and one that brings the question directly back into the domain of the community of listeners. In this technique, heard on Tim Dog's radio edit of "Fuck Compton" (retitled "Forget Compton"), the profane word is once again replaced with a sample. But this time it is a snippet of another rap song altogether. Thus, in Tim Dog's case, the only way to fully understand this form of substitution is to be familiar with the other rap songs, in other words, to be a member of the community of rap fans.

Notes

1 On the album version of Da Lench Mob's "You and Your Heroes," from *Guerrillas in tha Mist*, an unexpurgated, highly profane song contains a single instance of backwards masking when George Washington is called a "faggot." Clearly, there are certain things that the industry still will not tolerate in any form. A vast number of procedures are currently deployed by the music industry: plain old bleeping (hear Public Enemy's "Get the F＿＿＿ Outta Dodge"); drop-out, where the word is simply deleted (hear Shanté's "Dance to This"); the substitution of sound effects for curses (Boogie Down Productions' "Love's Gonna Getcha"). On House of Pain's radio version of "Get out Your Shit Kickers," called "Kick Out," a very sly method involves the replacement of the word *shit* with a lingering "shhhhh," hence imbedding a comment on the very "hush-hush" quality of self-censorship into the very act of self-censoring.

2 In *The American Heritage Dictionary of the English Language, Third Edition*, the definition of *fuck* offers an interesting early use: "The very first known occurrence in a poem entitled 'Flen flyys,' written sometime before 1500, is in code, illustrating the unacceptability of the word even then . . . 'Non sunt in coeli, quia gxddbov xxkxzt pg ifmk.' The latin words 'Non sunt in coeli, quia' mean 'they (the friars) are not in heaven, since.' The code 'gxddbov xxkxzt pg ifmk' is easly broken by simply writing the preceding letter in the alphabet. As we decode, we must watch for differences in the alphabet and in spelling between then and now. For *g* write *f*, for *x, z* (used for *u* and *v*); *d, c; b, a* . . . xx, vv (equals *w*). This yields 'fvccant vvicvys of helli.' The whole thus reads in translation: "They are not in heaven, because they fuck the wives of Ely (a town near Cambridge).' "

3 Peter Stallybrass and Allon White, *The Politics and Poetics of Transgression* (Ithaca: Cornell University Press, 1986), pp. 10–11.

4 Andrew Goodwin, "Sample and Hold: Pop Music in the Digital Age of Reproduction," in *On Record: Rock, Pop, and the Written Word*, ed. Simon Frith and Andrew Goodwin (New York: Pantheon, 1990), pp. 258–73.

5 Jacques Derrida, "Différance," in *Margins of Philosophy* (Chicago: University of Chicago Press, 1982), p. 10.

EX UNO PLURA

*Milford Graves, Evan Parker, and
the Schizoanalysis of Musical
Performance*

●

An Emblematic Anecdote

A friend tells the story of seeing percussionist Milford Graves perform a solo concert. Before the music commenced, Graves asked for someone from the audience to come up and help him with a demonstration. A young man volunteered, made his way onstage and stood facing the performer. Graves held out both wrists and asked the man to check his pulse, which was verified as normal. Then the drummer closed his eyes, concentrated, and halted his pulse—as the volunteer confirmed, in expectant delight. Relaxing, the regular pulse reappeared and the enlisted man released Graves's wrists. "No, no. Wait a minute," smiled Graves, holding his arms as they were, stock still. The assistant took ahold of Graves's wrists, once again feeling for a pulse. Once again, Graves closed his eyes and concentrated deeply. Some time passed, with the audience, volunteer, and Graves absolutely hushed in anticipation. Suddenly, the man jerked away in disbelief. "My God, they're not beating together!" he exclaimed. Graves quickly took a seat at his drum kit and began to play.

Subject to Change

That period we call modern . . . is defined by the fact that man becomes the center and measure of all things. Man is the subiectum, that which lies at the bottom of all beings, that is, in modern terms, at the bottom of all objectification and representation.

Because the essence of technology is nothing technological, essential reflection upon technology and decisive confrontation with it must happen in a realm that is, on the one hand, akin to the essence of technology, and on the other, fundamentally different from it. Such a realm is art.—Martin Heidegger

This chapter is largely a critique of subjectivity—or *subiectivity*, if you prefer—but it also assumes that such a critique of the centrality, the basicness of subjectivity may allow for a consideration of new forms of the relationship between people and instruments, between art and technology. In this, it works against the commonplace conception of technology that aligns it with control and prediction, and ultimately with science alone—in other words, with what Heidegger calls the "technical use of technology." This is an attempt to think about art and technology without grounding it in that sense of technique which draws a clear causal line between human subject, tool, and predicted outcome. It engages music—specifically solo improvisation—as a place for meditation, if not "decisive confrontation," with subjectivity and technology.

Divisible Subjects: Quite a Crowd

It is a central question, a questioning of center. Probably it is a question of possibilities, of the impossible, as well. The heart, in Milford Graves's case: is this not a unitary center? How is it possible that this central organ pulses differently in two like extremities? Thus in the anecdote it is a biological center that is tested. Inevitably, the issue of biology will come up again. But the core question initially has to do with another kind of testing, at the cultural level, which interrogates the necessity of individuation and unification at the level of the subject. The supposed "nature" of the word as ultimate unit of meaning has been deconstructed by structuralist and poststructuralist theory, interposing it instead in a *chain* of signification that relates it to parts other than itself. Likewise, we may ask the body why it is to be isolated at the level that it most commonly is (the "person," the "self"). In other words, why consider the subject so alone?

On the other hand, in the field of literary theory, analysis has broken up the supposed "natural unity" of canonical texts, whose plenitude had been taken as a given and which allowed a writer's works to be unhesitatingly considered as a "body" or *corpus*. Unifying discourse is that which seeks to systematize at a specific level, to make units of interchangeability and exclusivity, to em-body. In this vein, we are led to question the *subject's* body at the other extreme of isolation: why *unify* the various elements of the physical body at the level of the subject? Why does *this particular* combination of differences (hand-leg-eye-lip) and repetitions (hands/legs/eyes/lips) necessarily cohere at the individual level? Bilateral similitude, to be sure, but stand back-to-back with someone and likewise create another bilateral similitude: is this a unity, is this a "person"? Is the body not also an instance of colonialism, the trunk conjoining its limbs as roots and branches to a tree? And what form of organicism, what essentialism is founded on this unity? Taken for granted that the contrary questions—of the political consequences of positing this kind of subjective dispersal—are to be kept in mind. But such issues are not kept in mind just by being passively accepted.

Circulating around the central question of the body, then, are the twin issues of isolation and unification. At different points and in discreet ways, this falls into the general work of many theorists—Foucault, Derrida, and Deleuze especially—and may be hailed by the title the Politics of the Proper Name. "The proper name does not designate a subject, but something which happens."[1] Deleuze (in conjunction with Felix Guattari) has developed a form of analysis based on schizophrenia which will constitute the major theoretical touchstone for this investigation.

Where does one draw the line, or lines, that engender(s) the abstract subjective category, the indefinite third-person substitute for the first-person pronoun: "one"? How can one, rather, attend to concepts that allow the body to be configured in terms of discontinuity? Probably, it is a mistake to attempt to "solve" the problem of the unity/dispersion opposition, since such a solution would in itself be a discursive reunification. Instead, it will be better to use two examples that, in their musical activity, undermine the individual subject as absolute theoretical terminus for these lines of thought.[2]

Thus far we have seen two ways of conceptualizing the explosion of the notion of the subject. In one case, the subject becomes part of what Deleuze calls a "machinic assemblage." "The minimum real unit is not the word, the idea, the concept, or the signifier, but the *assemblage*."[3] The subject is no longer isolated from what might traditionally be called "context" (though this term secretly confirms the sanctity of the coherent "text" as separable from its "con-"). Instead, the subject is imbedded in a state of being between, as part of an individuation that is larger than the subject alone. "There is no subject of enunciation, every proper name is collective."[4] What this suggests is a trans-personality strikingly similar to group improvised music, in which different musicians with different agendas come together in the interest of constructing a new code, an in between, the guidelines of which may be continued or discarded thereafter. As Jacques Attali explains, this does not simply create a Tower of Babel situation, with players speaking past one another: "[Improvisation] does not prohibit communication. It changes the rules. It makes it a collective creation, rather than an exchange of coded messages. To express oneself is to create a code, or to plug into a code in the process of being elaborated by the other."[5] Improvising musicians create a genuine Deleuzian assemblage, a musical machine of desire—not binary, nor unitary, but multiple.

Thus, beyond the subject lies this area in between subject and others. But on the "near" side of the subject, *before* it encounters others, it is already multiple, "quite a crowd." It is in this sense that we will turn to the true object of our analysis, two musical assemblages that are arranged conveniently under proper names. In order to discuss them, however, we must first make a quick note on schizophrenic theory.

Schizoanalysis

Fredric Jameson and Jean-François Lyotard have both linked schizophrenia with postmodernism by means of an extension of the Lacanian psycho-analytic program. Schematically, the scenario goes something like this: identity is linked to linguistic development; through acquisition of language (the Father's "no" as Law/the meaning of language in general), the subject identifies with the phallus as center; language thus structures identity in an orderly way. Jameson explains: "Schizophrenia emerges from the failure of the infant to accede fully into the realm of speech and language . . . The schizophrenic thus does not know personal identity in our sense."[6] The salient point here is to envision schizophrenia as a mode of centerless production, not as "loss" of center or even "lack" of center, since these lead directly into psychoanalytic reconstitution that, for the duration of this study, I wish to avoid. Neither is it schizophrenia in the "multiple-personality" incarnation, Sybil-theory. Though I will speak of multiple voices, this is done in order to try to picture them as independent rather than split, realizing no past-wholeness-list, but a new, *multiple* assembly of parts resplendent in their distinctness.

Rhythmic Assemblage: Milford Graves

Early in the 1960s, a number of jazz percussionists began to shift the emphasis of their drumwork away from a time-keeping role to something different, something where meter was no longer the basis. Sunny Murray and Milford Graves are usually credited with this innovation, but many other drummers including Andrew Cyrille, Sunny Morgan, Rashied Ali, Jerome Cooper, Beaver Harris, Ronald Shannon Jackson, Steve McCall, Tony Oxley, Han Bennink, and Paul Lovens helped to reconsider the role of the percussionist in ensemble jazz.[7] At the same time, this move toward non-metrical drumming was accompanied by a drastic change in the basic size requirement for jazz groups. This provoked experiments in two directions: with gargantuan groups and with minimal, often solo performances.[8] For some players, like Milford Graves, the concurrence of these two options (unmeter and soloism) became the dedication of a lifetime of work.

Soloism—easy enough. But just what does lack of meter mean? For our purposes, let us assume that it means that the four basic jazz-drum voices (right arm/left arm/right leg/left leg) no longer *necessarily* refer to one consistent pulse (which is then distributed into a series of accents, which constitute its time "signature"). Instead, the limbs have been redisciplined to speak at different speeds, sometimes relating to each other (maybe even metrically, for some period), sometimes not.

In a certain respect, it is possible to consider that the various jazz-drum limbs have always had some degree of independence. The ride cymbal does not do exactly what the bass-pedal does, nor does the snare mimic the high-hat or tom-tom. To anyone who has tried to play the drums it is self-evident that they require a multiplicitous mind. The parts that the limbs play are not identical. But in traditional jazz drumming they refer to a single pulse, the point at which they periodically converge. This pulse becomes the "time" for the ensemble, which is in turn echoed and played with by the ensemble.

Time, tempo, meter: in these concepts we find a place of conjunction for schizoanalysis and music. Meter is the most "linguistic" element of music; it is shared by poetry. Implied by meter is the striation of time, the securing of temporal regularity. Jameson locates such a function in language: "It is because language has a past and a future, because the sentence moves in time, that we can have what seems to us a concrete or lived experience of time. But since the schizophrenic does not know language articulation in that way, he or she does not have our experience of temporal continuity either, but is condemned to live in a perpetual present with which the various moments of his or her past have little connection and for which there is no conceivable future on the horizon. In other words, schizophrenic experience is an experience of isolated, disconnected, discontinuous material signifiers which fail to link up into a coherent sequence."[9]

As usual, Jameson employs the rhetoric of noncompliance as *failure*. If time doesn't constitute itself in regularity, around a single center, it *fails*. So pervasive is this mode of thought that it renders inconceivable other ways of organizing temporality, even when they audibly manifest themselves. At the time when nonmetrical drumming was first presented as a technique, even to other "free" musicians, it was greeted with disbelief. As saxophonist John Tchicai relates, Graves produced just this response on first playing with the New York Art Quartet: "Bassist Don Moore became so frightened of this wizard of a percussionist that he decided that this couldn't be true or possible and, therefore, refused to play with us."[10]

Still today, the concept of true polymeter or unmeter is considered by some to be mythical, implying that these voices *must* cohere at some level, that the concept of independence of rhythm coming from the same proper name cannot be "true or possible."[11] This is understandable, as it threatens the concept of the body in a direct way. *How is it possible? He has the same heart, doesn't he?* Moreover: *he has the same brain, doesn't he?* It is objected: *"one" simply cannot do that!*

So what is at stake in this scenario is the status of the subject as invincible individuation, isolable and unitary. The "solo ensembling" of Graves represents another level of subjective organization, an assemblage of lines and times unto itself. Against a reading of multivoiced percussion that would seek to work it back into the general rhetoric of "liberation" associated with free jazz, it is possible to read Graves's solo work into a general social rubric, as Attali suggests: "Music effects a reappropriation of time and space. Time no longer flows in a linear fashion; sometimes it crystallizes in stable codes in which everyone's composition is compatible, sometimes in a multifaceted time in which rhythms, styles, and codes diverge, interdependencies become more burdensome, and rules dissolve."[12] To say that Graves's limbs are independent does not mean that they are incapable of cooperation. In fact, they frequently break away from their solo work, make secret pacts with the other limbs, complete joint exercises, and then part ways once again. For example, the right hand may be tapping an independent pattern on the open cymbal, then join the left hand for a press-roll on one of the tom toms. The two hands may then slip over to the high-hat, where they collaborate with the left foot, which opens and closes it. Meanwhile, the right foot is working a separate pulse on the bass drum. In a flash, the three conspirators split up, right hand moving to scrape a stick on a gong, left hand concentrating on irregular pops on the deeper tom, left foot kicking up a quick, constant beat on the high-hat.

It may be interesting to contrast Milford Graves as centerless rhythmic assemblage with a composition by Immanuel Ghent, in which several brass players each have parts written at different speeds. The score's tempi are sometimes so close, and the piece so dense and complex, that it is virtually impossible for the players to maintain their own beats. In order to perform the music, they must each wear headphones, through which they hear an individual "click track" which generates a rhythm to which they each independently relate.[13] Thus it is important for them to hear this regular pulse, but more importantly, they are prohibited from hearing the other players' parts, which might draw them toward unity of pulse. Ghent's piece works on the effect of lack of unity at the level of the ensemble (as a listener might experience it), even as it reasserts unity, with surreptitious cynicism, at the level of the body. The insinuation: noBody can resist the pull of the pulse.

In contrast, Graves's frequent use of difficult polymeter is characteristic of African drum ensemble rhythms, in which the point of reference is no longer determined by a downbeat, but by the position of a rhythm in an overall pattern. As ethnomusicologist John Miller Chernoff explains: "The establishment of multiple cross-rhythms as a background in almost all African music is what permits a stable base to seem fluid. Stable rhythmic patterns are broken up and seemingly rearranged by the shifting accents and emphases of other patterns . . . once you are playing the music properly, it becomes extremely difficult to play your part unless the whole ensemble is playing; you depend on the other rhythms for your time."[14] Graves does the same thing, except that by *positing the body as an ensemble in itself*, the organization of its activities becomes multivocal, relating limbs' time to one another rather than to an overarching bar line. This is completely different from the Jamesonean sense of time, which relates it to language structure as a meta-bar-line to which one looks for the "correct time."

Given these observations, it is now possible to see Milford Graves as more than a "free" drummer, but as an assemblage which refuses to accept the role of guardian of unitary jazz-time.[15] This role, in turn, participates in the construction of the abstract category "subject" and its equation with individuation at the level of the body. The suggestion is not that, in a "drive" sense, divisible parts of the body can "have" desire, but that they are part of an assemblage of desire, perhaps the same type of assemblage that prompts Otis Redding to sing of limbs, as if detached: "These arms of mine . . . *long* to hold you!"

Saxophone Assemblage: Evan Parker

Time keeping is not the only form of music making that reinforces unitary subjectivity. In jazz there is another, perhaps more pervasive individualizing concept: "expression." Expression, in jazz, is linked to the cultivation of a "voice," which, in instrumental jazz, is held to be representative of the individual who deploys the instrument. It is the jazz musician's primary form of self-identification. Thus the instrumentalist has "signature" elements of style unique to his or her playing, such as tone and phrasing. These are held to be the imprint of a singular subject; they mark off the jazz individual by means of a personal vocabulary. Here, again, we encounter the language metaphor as univocal structuring. For example, one might refer to "Coltrane's sound," as distinct from "Dex's sound." Of all instruments in jazz, the saxophone has acquired the primary position of the "voice" of jazz. Indeed, for black musicians it is obvious why the cultivation of such a voice has been politically significant. Progressively the saxophone became the primary expressive melodic vehicle for jazz, from the swing era of the 1930s (Lester Young, Coleman Hawkins, Ben Webster), to the bebop period starting in the mid-1940s. Charlie Parker initiated a time when the black saxophonist could be considered an artist, with the full force of the term. Until

Evan Parker
(photo: Val Wilmer)

then, jazz had been relegated to the status of "merely" entertainment genre. By 1965, on the other hand, it was possible for John Carter and Bobby Bradford to make a record called *Self Determination Music*. The title is suggestive of the reciprocal bind of jazz individuals: it is self-determined music—music made exclusively by black musicians—and at the same time it is music that determines a "self."

The ascendancy of the saxophone as a legitimate artistic voice also provided the ground for its separation from the rest of the ensemble. As bebop set in, saxophone solos grew increasingly longer. By the time of the mid-fifties, a hard-bop saxophone solo no longer had to concern itself exclusively with the "head" or composed material at the beginning and end of each piece. Bit by bit, the melodic line of the saxophone detached itself from its supposed relationship with the head; eventually, it became possible to separate the melody line from the harmonic context, the "changes," as well. By 1960 alto saxophonist Ornette Coleman had succeeded in extricating melody from harmony, creating a genuinely polytonal form of jazz.

By the mid-sixties the same soloistic developments that spurred Milford Graves to perform solo produced saxophone solo performances. Experiments by Coleman Hawkins, Eric Dolphy, and Lol Coxhill preceded the first full-length recording of unaccompanied alto sax, *For Alto* by Anthony Braxton, recorded in 1968.[16] At the same time, a group of European musicians, deeply influenced both by free jazz and by contemporary classical music, began to play what, for lack of a better term, they called "free improvisation."[17] One of the progenitors of this musical methodology was English saxophonist Evan Parker.[18] Since that time Parker has developed a way of playing the soprano saxophone, in a solo context, that is the melodic and harmonic analog to Graves's rhythmic divisibility.[19]

At the surface, it is easier to see how the percussionist's limbs represent another level of individuation: they are separate parts, physically and visually. Thus, while there may be some resistance to attributing them *identities*, Milford Graves's limbs are incontrovertibly separate. How, then, is it possible to picture the saxophonist as multiple? Isn't it true that melodic lines are the basic element of saxophone performance? And the saxophone is a single instrument, not four; a melody is *linear* after all, a single line. Historically, as we have seen, the manner of speech that links saxophone with voice, and voice with singularity of expression, gained hegemony. But the saxophone may be played in such a way that allows it to be fragmented as well, likewise at the level of the body of the performer. Fingers, mouth, tongue, teeth, lungs: these are the distinct members of the solo-saxophone ensemble. Joined together as the Evan Parker solo assemblage, they are constellated in such a way as to break the seeming unity of melodic expression. In an interview Parker charts the development of this mode of playing from the early-eighties *Saxophone Solos* to his 1987 recording *The Snake Decides*: "There's a more complex sense of linearity to the point where the line folds back on itself and assumes some of the proportions of vertical music, and some of the characteristics of polyphonic music, well, a pseudo-polyphonic music."[20]

The use of the term *polyphony* epitomizes the shift in saxophonist assemblage from a unity effect toward one of multiple voices. By combining techniques that are developed on separate parts of the body, like rhythmic biting of the reed (which produces high-pitched shrieks), rhythmic tonguing of the reed (which interrupts the sound in an intermittent way), and cross-fingering patterns that use the fingers on each hand as a micro-assemblage (playing patterns in opposition to the fingers of the other hand), Parker creates a solo sound that can truly claim multiplicity. He also uses a technique that was common in vaudeville and is also found in many reed musics in North Africa called "circular breathing." Just before running out of breath, Parker fills his cheeks with air, then forces it out with his facial muscles as he breathes more air into his lungs through his nose. This produces a continuous stream of sound.

With these separate but related techniques at his disposal, Parker can speak with more than one voice. As Richard Cook aptly exclaimed: "Hardly possible to believe these epically, epochally vast circumterrestrial processes are the product of a single mind, body and (rather small) instrument."[21] In fact, the melody line, which is usually considered a horizontal element of music, is exposed as already having vertical (harmonic) characteristics as well; in the sliver of time between when a tone is sounded and when it completely decays, Parker slips another in above or underneath it. Thus the melodic line is turned back on itself through a combination of speed, dexterity, and a multiplicity of focal points.

Parker summarizes his ongoing concerns as the combination of various techniques "to see what comes out of those combinations." "Sometimes," he says, "it's as predictable as addition, you get exactly what you expect, other times it's entirely unpredictable. For example, if . . . you have two basic rhythm patterns happening across the two hands—and then superimpose a related but different pattern of articulation from the tongue, you get a final result that is very hard to predict—because there's a three-layer process of filtering that might throw up patterns of accented notes which you couldn't think up."[22]

Derived in part from the explorations of harmony that John Coltrane, Albert Ayler, and other free jazz saxophonists undertook with ensembles in the 1960s, Parker's playing extends such explorations into the solo realm. During a given performance, he will cultivate several areas at a time: fully articulated note patterns at several levels, coupled with overblown harmonic squeaks, and growling vocal slurs at another level. Thus the music starts to separate, not always in direct association with a specific part of the body, but in association with some combination of body parts. Like blood in a centrifuge, the sheer velocity of Parker's blowing, coupled with "related but different patterns," gathers certain sounds into distinct regions, stratifying it. Multiple techniques that employ multiple parts of the Parker assemblage are *combined* not *united*; this combination then produces the effect of multiple voices. In contrast to Graves, where each body part makes a sound, each line in Parker's solo is created by the juxtaposition of body parts. One line is not, for example, connected directly with the tongue, one with the fingers. If the polyphony is "pseudo-polyphony," it is because there is always an element of horizontal linearity to the sound, and also because Parker is too modest to claim that he is really more than "one." But there is no longer a single player per se. In its place stands the figure of an assemblage, creating not a fugue (where voices *follow* one another) but music that—in its construction of various strata, to borrow a phrase from Deleuze and Guattari—"invents a kind of diagonal running between the harmonic vertical and the melodic horizon."[23] In Parker's music this diagonal, this pseudo-polyphony, serves as a musical critique of the inherent connection between technique and intentionality, and it points to the paradoxical status of "freedom" in solo improvisation:

> The freedom of the total music, if it has any sense of freedom, is only possible because some parts are very fixed. And by holding those fixed parts in a loop, by putting them on hold, you can look for other regions where variation is possible. But then I might discover a new loop in that new region which immediately loosens up the loop or loops that I've put on hold elsewhere. I'm shifting my attention from different parts of the total sound spectrum. If there's an illusion it will be confined to high, middle and low regions. I haven't yet really broken through to the level of having a loop across high, middle and low registers, which is obviously a challenge. That's where the use of repetition, although it appears to be a voluntary loss of freedom, actually opens up regions of the instrument which otherwise I wouldn't be aware of.[24]

In certain respects, Parker's work resembles early electronic music in that it has to do with interruption, with taking one system and using another interrupting system to create something new. For example, a common electronic music technique involves taking a wave signal and interposing another signal on top of it in order to produce a third pattern, a pattern that is often not always predictable. Parker does the same thing with his patterns,

interrupting rhythms with other rhythms. Indeed, in places he may completely interrupt his circular breathing, with a breathtaking effect.[25] Such
scrupulous unpredictability flies in the face of straightforward conceptions
of tool use, concepts that seek to align it with a single, univocal, intending
subject. Instead, in his music Parker articulates an alternative mode of
production in which—although the musician sets a group of variables in
motion and steers them in a general direction according to shifts in his
attention—the details of the music are as much determined by the interaction of chosen systems as the "desire" of the performer. It is in this sense
that Evan Parker is doing *research*, both on the possibilities of music for solo
soprano saxophone and on the possibilities of subjectivity.[26] In Deleuze and
Parnet's terms, "above all, it is objected that by releasing desire from lack and
law, the only thing we have left to refer to is a state of nature, a desire which
would be nature and spontaneist reality. We say quite the opposite: *desire
only exists when assembled or machined.* You cannot grasp or conceive of a
desire outside a determinate assemblage . . . each group or individual should
construct the plane of immanence on which they lead their life and carry
their business . . . *It is constructivist, not at all spontaneist.*"[27]

So much for the supposed self-expression of free music (improvisation is
so often predicated on the notion of the unitary, intending subject). In lieu
of the spontaneousness of improvisation, Parker and Graves suggest constructs of desire. Indeed, to push it one step further, in the place of the
individuals Evan Parker and Milford Graves we are left with conveniently
named musical machines. It is not that they have become automatons, but
quite to the contrary, they have accepted the challenge of experimenting on
their own identities; or better, they suspend identity indefinitely. In Lyotard's terms, they are obedient.[28]

Notes

1. Gilles Deleuze and Claire Parnet, *Dialogues* (New York: Columbia University Press, 1987),
   p. 51.
2. For a general treatment of the problematic of the subject, see the essays in *Who Comes
   after the Subject?*, ed. Eduardo Cadava, Peter Connor, and Jean-Luc Nancy (New York:
   Routledge, 1991).
3. Ibid.
4. Ibid., p. 143.
5. Jacques Attali, *Noise: The Political Economy of Music* (Minneapolis: University of Minnesota Press, 1987), p. 3.
6. Fredric Jameson, "Postmodernism and Consumer Society," in *The Anti-Aesthetic*, ed. Hal
   Foster (Port Townsend: Bay Press, 1983), pp. 118–19.
7. "How does this completely liberated drummer play? He interacts with soloists on the
   complex levels of Elvin Jones, without Jones' distracted timekeeping. Or he plays re-

sponses to horns, to horns' lines, so dense and intimate that he moves far away from the horns' directions. Or he plays pure sound, thus creating an essential element of ensemble atmosphere without motivating the performance rhythmically. From passage to passage, his playing is any of these. Whether it is rhythmic, arhythmic, or polyrhythmic, his mastery is thorough and complex even when seemingly simple. The entire mass of his playing is committed to impulsive abstraction, to moving away from surface engagement despite his many junctions with the main lines of the performances." John Litweiler, *The Freedom Principle: Jazz after 1958* (New York: William Morrow, 1984), p. 158.

8　Several decades in advance of the jazz avant-garde, Baby Dodds recorded drum solos for Folkways Records.

9　Jameson, "Postmodernism and Consumer Society," p. 119.

10　John Tchicai, in the liner notes to New York Art Quartet, *Mohawk* (Fontana Records, 1965).

11　John Mason, for example, who has played with Graves, says that he does not believe in polymeter because people "naturally" use a pulse. In his view, Graves's work is basically a trick, an audio-illusion.

12　Attali, *Noise*, p. 147.

13　Click tracks are very common in pop music studio production.

14　John Miller Chernoff, *African Rhythms and African Sensibility* (Chicago: University of Chicago Press, 1979), pp. 52–53.

15　See Elizabeth Deems Ermarth, *Sequel to History: Postmodernism and the Crisis of Representational Time* (Princeton: Princeton University Press, 1992), for a remarkable, nuanced reading of temporality in postmodern fiction. Ermarth frequently uses jazz as a metaphor for the subversion of historical time in contemporary narrative literature without reverting to a fixed definition of jazz rhythm. Rather, she appropriately leaves improvisation as an indefinite, experimental activity.

16　Graham Lock, *Forces in Motion: The Music and Thoughts of Anthony Braxton* (New York: Da Capo, 1988).

17　See John Corbett, "Writing around Improvisation," *Subjects/Objects* 4 (1986): 53–71; Nick Couldry, "Turning the Musical Table: Improvisation in Britain, 1965–1990," *Contemporary Music Review* (in preparation); Richard Scott, "Research and Method, Sociology and Music," unpublished manuscript, 1989; Derek Bailey, *Improvisation: Its Nature and Practice in Music* (London: The British Library, 1992); Bert Noglik, *Klangspuren: Wege Improviseirter Musik* (Berlin: Verlag Neue Musik, 1990).

18　For further biographical information on Parker, see Paul Keegan, "Evan Parker: The Breath and Breadth of the Saxophone," *Down Beat*, April, 1987.

19　Though Parker and Graves represent particularly strong, perhaps extreme examples, multivocal music is not a new concept—even for soloists. One need think only of Andrea Segovia's guitar transcriptions of Bach or Bach's own keyboard music. Indeed, the very ideas of fugue and counterpoint suggest independence of lines, and when accomplished on single instruments by single performers the motivation behind polyphonic music is clearly to produce the effect of multiplicity. In the history of reed and wind instruments alone, the impulse to develop techniques for performance with multiple voices goes back quite far. In the 1960s, John Coltrane honed the technique known as "split tone," in which a base tone is played and, by contorting the mouth, harmonics are simultaneously sounded, hence producing two notes at the same time. This technique was common in "bar honkers," forties and fifties R&B saxophonists like Big Jay McNeely and may also be heard in the recent work of saxophonists Ned Rothenberg, Luc Houtkamp, Charles

Gayle, and John Butcher, among many others. The method of playing with two (or more) saxophones at the same time also has a well-developed lineage; in the 1980s, Soviet saxophonist Vladimir Chekasin (among many others) used this technique, which is most widely associated with 1960s reedman Raashan Roland Kirk, but it also reaches back through hard-bop saxist George Braith deep into the trick bag of 1920s vaudeville. (See Leonard Feather's liner notes to Braith's record *Soul Stream* [Blue Note st-84161] for an excellent genealogy of the technique.) In fact, representations of such two-at-once reed-work are also found on Cycladic figures from the island of Keros, dated 2400–2200 B.C.

20 Evan Parker, interviewed by Biba Kopf in *Wire* 27 (May 1986): 48.

21 Richard Cook, *Wire* 100 (June 1992): 52.

22 Ibid.

23 Gilles Deleuze and Felix Guattari, *A Thousand Plateaus: Capitalism and Schizophrenia*, trans. Brian Massumi (Minneapolis: University of Minnesota Press, 1987), p. 296.

24 See "Saxophone Botany—Evan Parker" in part three.

25 This forces him to start from scratch: "After a while there's new information, but it's the same *kind* of new information, so a change is no longer a change. It's like looking at new ways to make changes that are really changes. In response to that sense in myself of it *going on a bit*, and then, yeah, wanting to open it out, to trick myself, to restart but to restart without stopping. As an interruption on a bigger scale than the usual interruptions. The usual interruptions are the substance of the music, the interference between two patterns, or the compatibility or lack of compatibility between two patterns."

26 On his latest recording, *Process and Reality*, Parker took the logical step implied by his solo ensembling: he recorded separate tracks of solo saxophone and superimposed them, multitracking his multivocal music. Two cuts on the CD are particularly interesting: on one he played the various parts without listening to the previous ones, hence making them fit together in an indeterminate way; on another, he played five separate times, listening each time to the previous track—then he removed the very first track, making it a ghost track, a track that is heard in its absence. This is not unlike György Ligeti's *Etudes pour Piano, Premier Livre* (Wergo wer 60134-50), which includes notes that are played but dampened (and thus left unheard). A similar effect appears frequently in dub reggae, where two tracks may be recorded simultaneously, then one removed, leaving a sort of shadow on the first track (compare Keith and Tex's "Stop That Train" (*Derrick Harriott and Friends: Step Softly*, Trojan trs 267), with Big Youth's talk-over dub version, "Cool Breeze" (*Creation Rockers Vol. 3*, Trojan trs 182), for an especially lucid example). Finally, Parker's music at times bears a striking resemblance to a skipping CD—hence another connection with unintended uses of technology and interruption. For an intriguing example of the artistic appropriation of this "faulty machinery," hear Nicolas Collins, "Broken Light (For String Quartet and Modified CD Player)" (*It Was a Dark and Stormy Night*, Trace Elements te-1019CD).

27 Deleuze and Parnet, *Dialogues*, p. 96.

28 Jean-François Lyotard, "Obedience," in *The Inhuman: Reflections on Time*, trans. Geoffrey Bennington and Rachel Bowlby (Stanford: Stanford University Press, 1988), pp. 165–81.

POSTMODERNISM—
GO, FIGURE

Smell, Sound, and Subliminal

Suggestion

●

*In conclusion, it is easy to see that a postmodernist culture
emerging from these political, social, and cultural constel-
lations will have to be a postmodernism of resistance, in-
cluding resistance to that easy postmodernism of the "anything goes" variety. Resistance
will always have to be specific and contingent upon the cultural field within which it
operates. It cannot be defined simply in terms of negativity or non-identity à la Adorno,
nor will the litanies of a totalizing, collective project suffice . . . At the same time, the very
notion of resistance may be problematic in its simple opposition to affirmation. After all,
there are affirmative forms of resistance and resisting forms of affirmation . . . No matter
how troubling it may be, the landscape of the postmodern surrounds us. It simultaneously delimits and opens our horizons. It's our problem and our hope.—Andreas Huyssen,* AFTER THE GREAT DIVIDE

For the sake of argument, postmodernism is often cast as cause for a choice:
one must take a position either "with" it or "against" it. This is particularly
the case for rhetorical studies, whose very existence is radically reconfig-
ured (its central "figure" called into question) by postmodernism. In the face
of postmodern theory, the traditional rhetorical project thus becomes one of
recovery, one of preserving the figure of the rhetor, literally *for the sake of
argument.* But this assumes that one has a choice, that the figure of the
autonomous, semiautonomous, or at least *evident* author is available for
questioning. If one agrees with Huyssen, however, this position itself is now
subsumed in the postmodern, which *constitutes* the contemporary "landscape" rather than being one of several particular theoretical and rhetorical
analyses of it. Postmodernism is therefore best seen as a set of practices that
respond to the condition of postmodernity.

What is striking about this is not that the rhetor and its instrumental use
of rhetoric are eliminated, but that what may count as rhetoric is wildly
expanded, that rhetoric functions discursively rather than instrumentally,
and that discourse takes a multitude of unimagined forms. Argumentation,
in its classic sense, is no longer the primary means of persuasion, but one of
many other forms. As we shall see, some of these are characterized by their

very transparency, by their lack of a clear and positioned figure. This may refer to what Vance Packard preliminarily named the "hidden persuaders"—subliminal discourse. It may also be observed in postmodern theory's turn from a concept of direct political contestatior, which rests on positional argumentation, to indirect forms of opposition, or even nonoppositional forms, facilitated by the adoption of a looser notion of "resistance." Thus, in both dystopian and utopian views of postmodernism, the issue of recognizing rhetorical strategies and tactics is made extremely complicated, but is never abandoned. The question is: how can one account for rhetorical situations in which there is no figure of the rhetor, or situations in which its position isn't easily identifiable? This essay considers these issues in terms of the reconfiguration of power that postmodern culture makes available, in both its most gloomy and its most promising senses.

The Terrorist Rhetoric of Smell:
A Nosedive into Nonsense

In short, the thesis proceeds like this: the end of the grand master narratives of the "civilized" world is precipitated initially by internal erosion of the legitimacy of knowledge within the domain of science. In this, Lyotard[1] locates the genesis of the postmodern situation differently from other theories, which would implicate either the march of consumer capitalism (Daniel Bell → David Harvey), or the inundation of information in mass media systems (Marshall McLuhan → Jean Baudrillard). Starting in the nineteenth century, the process of "delegitimation" that sparks the destabilization of science emanates from the inability of science to stand up to the rigor of its own language game, denotation, without recourse to another language game, namely narrative, which it presupposes. The significance of a scientific discovery or innovation is measured only in relation to those theories surpassed in the ongoing story of science-as-a-whole. The relation of science to what Lyotard variously calls "speculation," "the life of the mind," "the life of the Spirit," and "the realization of the Idea" is "rationalized," in Max Weber's terms, only in the discourse of scientific hermeneutics. This is exterior to (and plays by different rules—that is, legitimizes itself differently—from) the verification/falsification discourse of research. Even Weber, a die-hard progressivist totalizer, therefore concedes: "Science further presupposes that what is yielded by scientific work is important in the sense that it is 'worth being known.' In this, obviously, are contained all our problems. For this presupposition cannot be proved by scientific means. It can only be interpreted with reference to its ultimate meaning, which we must reject or accept according to our ultimate position towards life."[2]

Thus the certainty with which the "positivist" or "determinist" or "stable system" scientist once proceeded is now undermined by its reliance on a system it considers "unscientific." In Weber's consideration, we also find a hint of the delegitimizing agent that wrenches science from the other meta-narrative: emancipation of humanity. Without the presupposition of an ethical system into which scientific information will fall and be interpreted (its "ultimate meaning"), science proceeds by means of an ambivalent mechanism. It is "beyond good and evil." It is experimental. "There is nothing to prove that if a statement describing a real situation is true, it follows that a prescriptive statement based upon it . . . will be just."[3] Thus, as denotation it has no inherent role in the emancipation narrative. What is more, the practice of science is reliant on its use of "paralogy," that is: the "use of reasoning contrary to rules and formulas." Here it would seem opportune to turn to Paul Feyerabend as a model. But, ironically, Feyerabend legitimizes the disparate "anarchism" of science in precisely the two metanarratives that Lyotard claims it helps destroy. He says that his dadascience will "increase liberty," as it will contribute to "the development of our consciousness."[4] In Lyotard's terms, these are the lost narratives of liberation and speculation.

As a means by which to further elucidate the main argument of *The Postmodern Condition*, we may employ its afterward, "Answering the Question: What is Postmodernism?" Here we find Lyotard summarizing the reaction of artists to the disintegration of the grand metanarratives of speculation (the life of the Spirit) and emancipation (liberation of humanity) in terms of two possibilities: nostalgia and jubilation; "regret" and "assay."[5] The first of these corresponds to the modern, the second to the postmodern. This is an extremely important ingredient in Lyotard's position on postmodernism, which cannot be reduced to the "condition" that he attends to in the first essay, since that would imply a strict historical (and thus metanarrative) reading which he would be at pains to avoid. "Postmodern" is not coterminant with "postmodernity" (it is conceptual, not periodizing), but postmodernity *is* incapable of maintaining the discursive unity pretended by modernism.

If we read his "Report on Knowledge" through this distinction he makes between regret and assay, Lyotard's prescription of the latter postmodern reaction takes precedence over the former, nostalgic longing for totalism. In these terms, we may place his primary (ant)agonist, Jürgen Habermas, in the camp of the modernists (where he wouldn't squirm), nostalgic for the legitimizable consensus that the "diversity of discursive species"[6] precludes. On the contrary, Lyotard would proclaim of the postmodern condition: "It ain't perfect, but it's all we got." Thus, when Lyotard commences with a foreboding question: "Increasingly, the central question is becoming who will have access to the information these machines must have in storage to guarantee that the right decisions are made," he concludes on a cautious upbeat:

> We are finally in a position to understand how the computerization of society affects [the] problematic. It could become the "dream" instrument for controlling and regulating the market system, extended to include knowledge itself and governed exclusively by the performativity principle. In that case, it would inevitably involve the use of terror. But it could also aid groups discussing metaprescriptives by supplying them with the information they usually lack for making knowledgeable decisions. The line to follow for computerization to take the second of these two paths is, in principle, quite simple: give the public free access to the memory and data banks.[7]

The objection could be raised that there are pieces of computer information about you that you might not want publicly available. Perhaps Lyotard is stating the case in the extreme. But, on the other hand, consider the terrorist implications of *limited* access to data bank information: who gets it? who will know who gets it? for what purpose will it be used? legitimized in what way? in what form? with what check on its power? Mark Poster has applied Foucault's concept of the panopticon to this question, explaining that "'circuits of communication' and the databases they generate constitute a Superpanopticon, a system of surveillance without walls, windows, towers, or guards."

> The discourse of databases, the Superpanopticon, is a means of controlling masses in the postmodern, postindustrial mode of information. Foucault has taught us to read a new form of power by deciphering discourse/practice formations instead of intentions of a subject or instrumental actions. Such a discourse analysis when applied to the mode of information yields the uncomfortable discovery that the population participates in its own self-constitution as subjects of the normalizing gaze of the Superpanopticon.[8]

People submit to the collection, collation, and instrumentation of their information; they join the very databases that are used to keep tabs on them. By calling this form of Superpanoptical power "terror," I refer to Lyotard's definition of it in relation to language games:

> By terror I mean the efficiency gained by eliminating, or threatening to eliminate, a player from the language game one shares with him. He is silenced or consents, not because he has been refuted, but because his

ability to participate has been threatened (there are many ways to prevent someone from playing). The decision makers' arrogance, which in principle has no equivalent in the sciences, consists in the exercise of terror. It says: "Adapt your aspirations to our ends—or else."[9]

In fact, as Lyotard points out, the "multiplicity of finite meta-arguments"[10] that he favors is in itself dangerous, and open to misuse. As a concrete example of this, think of the terror associated with two current uses of data storage: credit and direct mail advertising. Both rely on selective and limited information access and data banks. Here I think of the utility of "demographics" in determining a "local" group of people to whom a certain product or program might appeal (this is the basis of direct mail): the recognition of heterogeneity is fundamental, but it is mobilized in order to organize, essentialize, and sell to the social fractal; the admission of multiplicity here simply enhances the performativity of the commodity. In a similar way, credit is established at the intersection of multiple types of information, drawn from a variety of places (banks, credit cards, loan institutions, utilities, real estate offices, work references, income) and manifested in a multiplicity of forms (quantities, statements, dates); these diverse utterances are pulled together to speak the unified, timeless truth of one's character. And we all know what kinds of "decisions" are made on the basis of such a determination. Such is the unreliable, fragmentary situation of the "state of knowledge" in postmodernity. But in contrast with this analysis there is no holistic alternative that is not an even more dangerous fiction.

As I see it, Lyotard presents us with two strategic options for approaching the postmodern as critics, somewhat at odds with one another. On the one hand, he supports the postmodern reaction to the sublime (the concept which is unpresentable, like infinity)—which is its demonstration. To produce sublime texts, one must turn to experimentation, a term which signals the strong affinity between science and art in Lyotard's pro-postmodern position. It should be emphasized, however, that this strategy is not anarchistic, or better, it is not at all levels unsystematic. As Lyotard says of catastrophe theory: "it is not without rules . . . but it is always locally determined."[11] There are no universal regulations, but rather the constant reevaluation and reinvention of the game. It is not a question of invention *sans* preservation. Instead, the model is that of the "temporary contract." No more grandiose narratives, but little ones to be sure.[12] In this, I think a positive role for the critic is retained even within a "go with the flow" reaction to postmodernism; what is jeopardized, or truncated, is rather the durability (timelessness) and generalizability (universality) of the critic's rhetoric. The question boils down to one of duration and reflection: how long is too short? how short is too long? Given science's prescription for performativity, its quest to achieve optimal efficiency, what is an appropriate interval for reflection? This brings us to the second reactive strategy.

As we have seen, Lyotard remarks on the "ambiguousness" of the postmodern situation.[13] If we recognize in him a jubilation toward certain aspects of the contemporary scene, such as the breakdown of the metanarratives, the emergence of multidisciplinarism, and nondeterminist tendencies in science (catastrophe theory, chaos theory, quantum physics, fractal geometry), there is at least one aspect of postmodernity that he approaches with palpable distrust: namely, performativity. Indeed, he advocates postmodern science as *opposed* to performativity. In *The Differend*, Lyotard writes against the reader who seeks to "gain time." Instead, the book is organized as a series of reflections, written in such a dense way as to make reading it unquestionably inefficient. Thus there is a quiet call in much of Lyotard's work, with no fanfare or absolute program, to yield to what Hans Blumenberg designates as one of the most important roles for rhetoric: "a consummate embodiment of retardation."[14] It is not, however, a reflection meant to stir up a nostalgia for the "reality" of the situation, but an impedance to a logic of performativity that would itself insist on a *real*, functional, well-oiled system.

In the split between the new methods of discourse which produce the paradoxical and paralogical sciences and the process of establishing proofs that take efficiency as their principle, we find the crux of the problem. Science, as a model of efficiency, develops a close bond with capitalism, which in turn uses the image of science-as-progress as a means to legitimate increasingly efficient means of production and consumption. For Lyotard, this is clearly the down-side. Even so, he does enumerate some of the "advantages" of performativity, most of which are related to the fact that it is a product of the same delegitimization of knowledge as is paralogic.[15] But his brief acknowledgment of the "up-side" of the performativity criterion leads directly to his discussion of the "arrogance of the decision makers." "What their 'arrogance' means is that they identify themselves with the social system conceived as a totality in quest of its most performative unity possible."[16]

Subsequent to *The Postmodern Condition*, Lyotard has abandoned Wittgenstein's terminology of "language games" as "too anthropocentric."[17] He summarizes the project of *The Differend*: "To refute the prejudice in the reader by centuries of humanism and of 'human sciences' that there is 'man,' that there is 'language,' and that the former makes use of the latter for his own ends,

SMELL & TASTE TREATMENT AND RESEARCH FOUNDATION, LTD.

PRELIMINARY RESULTS OF OLFACTORY NIKE STUDY
Alan R. Hirsch, M.D.
November 16, 1990

Thirty-five volunteer subjects were recruited to participate in a study evaluating sensory impact on common consumer goods. Subjects were not told prior to the study that the sensory modality being tested was that of olfaction.

None of these subjects were pregnant or breastfeeding. None had a significant upper respiratory infection at the time of the study. Upon completion of the study, four of the subjects were excluded secondary to form noncompliance. The age range of subjects was from 18 to 69 with an average of 32 years old. Thirty-one subjects in total completed this study. Sixteen percent (five) were male and 84 percent (26) were female.

Twenty-six percent (eight) of the participants were on medications. Nineteen percent (six) of the participants had an underlying medical disease. Twenty-nine percent (nine) of the participants were smokers.

The patients were alternately assigned into to identical room to examine a pair of Nike shoes. The rooms differed in regards to one variable: ambient air room was filtered such that purified (odor-free) air was in one room whereas another room was odorized with a mixed floral smell (which in prior studies has been shown to have positive hedonic impact upon subjects). The odor was dispensed in a metered fashion over one second prior to participant entering the room. The concentration of odorant was deemed to be suprathreshold and not of irritant nature based on consensus of expert panel at the Smell & Taste Treatment and Research Foundation.

Patients were asked to examine the consumer product present in the room for the duration of 30 seconds. At that point in time, the subjects were presented with an evaluation form discussing the hedonics, likelihood of purchase and monetary value of the consumer product (shoe). Between each period of examination, the subjects were placed in a neutral, odor-free room for three minutes to eliminate any impact of adaptation. Each subject served as their own control evaluating both shoes in both the ambient and odorized room in a random order.

After completing evaluation of both shoes, subjects underwent an exit evaluation of their perception of the odorized room in terms of the intensity of odorant and hedonics for the odorant.

Water Tower Place • 845 North Michigan Avenue, Suite 930W • Chicago, Illinois 60611 • 312/938-1047 • 800/45 TASTE

Figure 1

and if he does not succeed in attaining these ends, it is for want of good control over language 'by means' of a 'better' language."[18]

Rhetoric achieves a highly complex status in Lyotard's world, as we have already noted. But it might also be pointed out, post facto, that the linguistic tropes of *The Postmodern Condition* were also highly logocentric. To this, I pose the question: is there a set of nonlinguistic practices that constitute a rhetoric which might also conform to the basic contours (either rejoice-worthy or regrettable) of postmodernity outlined by Lyotard? Specifically, I

```
PRELIMINARY RESULTS OF OLFACTORY NIKE STUDY
Alan R. Hirsch, M.D.
November 16, 1990
Page Two


Finally, subjects underwent a detailed medical and olfactory
survey as well as 27 separate olfactory tests to assess their
olfactory ability.

Results of Study:  The odor affected the desirability of the
shoes in a positive way in 84 percent of the subjects.  Sixteen
percent of the subjects were affected adversely in regards to the
desirability of the shoe by the odorant.

This impact of odorant upon desirability had a greater affect on
women than men.  Smokers as a whole tended to evaluate the odor
in a negative fashion and tended to view the shoes that were
present in an odorized environment in a negative fashion.

Three subjects (10 percent) evaluated the shoes as having a
greater monetary value in the odorized environment than the shoes
in the nonodorized environment with an average increase in cost
of $10.33.  No one evaluated the shoes as being of lower monetary
value in the odorized air.

The likelihood to purchase the shoe and hedonic value for the
shoe were influenced by odor independent of the following:

1.   Odor strength
2.   Hedonics for odor
3.   Olfactory ability
4.   Hedonic rating of the shoes
5.   Purchasability of the shoes
6.   Age.

It is worth noting that the odor affected the desirability of the
shoes in a positive way in 84 percent of the people independent
of whether or not they entered the study liking the shoes or
entered the study willing to purchase the shoes.


ARH:MTS/k
```

wish to point out what I would call a terrorist olfactory rhetoric advocated by a market research study sent to the radio station whpk as (not coincidentally) a direct mail advertisement (see Figures 1 and 2).

The "Smell & Taste Treatment and Research Foundation, Ltd." is exactly the type of new institution for the practice of science that Lyotard sketches initially as the breaking up of the speculative function of the academy ("The old 'faculties' splinter into institutes and foundations of all kinds . . ."[19]) and then in the interweaving of science and capitalism:

> Capitalism solves the scientific problem of research funding in its own way: directly by financing research departments in private companies, in which demands for performativity and recommercialization orient research first and foremost toward technological 'applications'; and indirectly by creating private, state, or mixed sector research foundations . . . The prevailing norms of work management spread to the applied science laboratories . . . the development of saleable programs, market research, and so on.[20]

So this foundation fits the part of the scientific organ of the market capitalist apparatus; it is a market research group, that is, an independent scientific institute oriented around the application of social psychological "research" to the sphere of the commodity (the market). Its unit of measurement is "hedonics" from the same root as "hedonism"—a measure of the likelihood of consumption without reference to need. The study begins by stating the findings of the research, then asks: "What does this mean?" We know, of course, that it means increased performativity, another drop of oil on the machine. The institute's findings are based on "fragrances *proven to persuade* a certain market," and women (traditional victims of market terrorism) are isolated as a fragment group more susceptible to being, if you will, led by the nose.

The point is that this "proven persuasion" constitutes a *rhetoric* of smell. What is more, I would argue that it represents the same kind of "context control" by which, using computers as the model, Lyotard analyzes legitimation by power: "Power is not only good performativity, but also effective verification and good verdicts. It legitimates science and the law on the basis of their efficiency, and legitimates this efficiency on the basis of science and law . . . The growth of power, and its self-legitimation, are now taking the route of data storage and accessibility, and the operativity of information."[21] Like data in storage, smell can produce its effects without being detected, in absentia, as a subliminal, terrorist rhetoric. Like credit. A decision is made far from the other participant (whose "representatives" he/she does not know and cannot speak through), a decision that for some strange reason requires the opinion of Dr. Hirsh, a foundation, people at a radio station, and me—but not the consumer.

The arrogance of the decision makers thus lies in their identifying themselves with the social system as a totality in quest of its most performative unity possible. And just like credit, smell can effectively legitimate itself by means of the verdicts or decisions it pronounces. Who can say you shouldn't buy something because it (or the place you bought it) smells a certain way? Your very buying it legitimates the use of smell to sell. The purchase is the

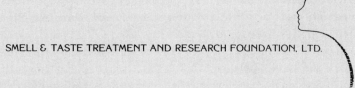

SMELL & TASTE TREATMENT AND RESEARCH FOUNDATION, LTD.

November 16, 1990

Mark Josephson
WHPK-FM, 88.5
5706 S. University Ave
Chicago, IL 60637

Dear Mr. Josephson:

Every year, Fortune 500 Companies spend millions of dollars on attractive packaging, something to attract the eye of a potential customer. Now preliminary results of a study by Alan Hirsch, M.D., shows that the sense of smell can be used as a powerful sales tool.

In Hirsch's study 35 people examined one Nike gym shoe in two identical rooms. The only difference between the rooms is that one was odor free, other odor controlled. Each person had thirty seconds to examine the shoe.

• Odor effected desirability of the Nike gym shoe 84% of the time;
• Odor effected women more than men;
• 10% of those who were effected by the odor, would pay an average of $10.33 more than list price for the gym shoes.

What this means is that Department stores, for example, could pump odors that appeal specifically to targeted audiences. Product manufacturers might scent packages with fragrances proven to persuade a certain market.

Enclosed are full details on this study.

Dr. Alan Hirsch, neurologist and psychiatrist, is the Director of the Smell and Taste Research Foundation in Chicago. His writings have appeared in the New York Times and Journal of American Medical Association. He has appeared on numerous television programs across the country, is quite an entertaining interview, and would be available to comment on this study.

Sincerely,

Vita

John Crane Vita

Water Tower Place • 845 North Michigan Avenue, Suite 930W • Chicago, Illinois 60611 • 312/938-1047 • 800/45 TASTE

Figure 2

verification of the good verdict, your nod of approval to the criterion of performativity. However, it is terrorist in that this language game is one of subliminality. You are never asked whether or not you want to play. Like the terror of estrangement, where, for example, one does not "know the language spoken here," there is a terror of familiarity, where the other player is silenced because the rhetoric is literally transparent (perfume), the game just too familiar and therefore not recognizable. Smells are everywhere; therefore, it can be argued that "environment control" is just a way of making the consumer "more comfortable."

The point is that the consumer's decision to purchase is influenced by factors that are calculated, but factors to which they have no access—subliminal discourse. This is a rhetorical situation with no clear figure of the rhetor, an argument with no one to refute. As they say: "No salesman will come to your door." In contradiction to Foucault's constitution of the subject at the crossroads of power and knowledge, Paul Virilio has argued that the postmodern situation works on pure performativity and speed. Assurance of purchase, in this case, is based on the *withholding* or *sublimation* of certain knowledge (in the name of efficiency), rather than its production: "The . . . logic of knowing-power, or power-knowledge is eliminated to the benefit of moving-power—in other words of tendencies, of flows."[22] Market research: producing knowledge about an audience, withholding knowledge from them, stacking the deck: what is at stake is the continuity of commodity flow; what is encouraged is the tendency to buy. Products need to be "moved." Lyotard suggests that in language-terror situations "there are many ways to prevent someone from playing,"[23] and subliminal discourse may well be the most insidious. It is a language game that you just don't *know* you are playing. Imagine a conversation with someone in which you thought they were dead serious, but really they were playing you for the fool. In the terrorist rhetoric of smell, 84 percent of the time they would be right.

Given Huyssen's agenda for a "resistant postmodernism," it is necessary to ask what might be an appropriate response by someone who wishes to undermine this terrorist use of smell. Perhaps the answer lies in a twist on Lyotard's key term, "sublime." Linking this concept—the presentation of the unpresentable—with the notion of "subliminality"—that which exists but is consciously imperceptible—the answer, both true to the postmodern condition and acceptable as a "resistant" displacement of power structures, is simply enough contained in the unveiling of these olfactory marketing techniques. David Carroll has called this process "sublime enthusiasm," to separate it from the politics of the sublime, which are only those of terror: "Sublime enthusiasm indicates that there is something more in the historical-political realm than the politics of interested parties . . . The distance (retreat) from the historical-political (which makes manifest the interested and partisan nature of the political) may be considered disinterested—but only in terms of what it cannot express, and not in terms of what it does express."[24]

To be sure, in subliminal discourses one is dealing with interested parties. But the contemplation of the limits of this exchange—namely the smell and its subliminal hovering between efficacy and perceptibility—"makes manifest" the partisan nature of smell's use. If we recognize that the terrorist deployment of smell is already an integral part of contemporary life (think, for example, of the smell of Karmel Korn, of freshly baked bread, cookies, or ribs, conveniently pumped into a consumer's path), then the possibilities of undermining this use of smell may seem obvious: gather information detailing the plans to influence purchasing power by intoxicating smells and literally *exorcise* this secret use of hedonics; tack up posters next to Karmel Korn stores; pump nauseating odors into shoe shops; give revealing speeches next to the tobacconist.

This assumes that an "informed consumer" is a critical consumer, that if people knew they were being influenced by factors they weren't conscious of they would naturally find this repugnant. As we shall see, the use of subliminal persuasion tapes suggests that there is at least a place in the lives of some consumers for hidden persuasion, purchased and self-administered voluntarily. But first, in order to more exactly understand the use of *smell* in this way, we need to distinguish between three types of subliminal olfactory marketing techniques, which should not be conflated. First, there is the type referred to in the study, which in fact differs from the examples above. The lightly scented air of the study's environment has no plausible relationship to the object being sold, except contiguity. A second type would include food, tobacco, and the enhanced smell of goods (leather shoes, for example) where the scent is directly related to the pleasure of consuming the product, perhaps even away from the site of purchase. The close ties between taste (in both senses) and smell are therefore marshaled together, and provide an airtight alibi for the retailer. In fact, it is quite possible that a consumer would recognize the connection between this species of smell and the desire it provokes, proud to purchase something that smells so good, thereby explicitly legitimizing the sales technique. Finally, perfume represents an extreme example of the internalization of subliminal persuasion. Think, for example, of the ferocity of salespeople at department stores, spraying the errant shopper and thereby employing the consumer's body as a mobile billboard. Perfume is a form of pure consumer code; it is what it sells. Thus there is no distance between the commodity and its smell; the commodity *is* smell. In this sense, the purchase of perfume can be seen as a take-home terrorist kit, designed to influence another person's perception of the consumer (perhaps making them more "marketable" as a love object) without being perceptible in itself. Thus the simple, agitational contestation of subliminal terrorism is obviously insufficient, since this form of "revealing" the persuasive use of smell is, in some forms, exactly the mechanism by which things are sold. This scenario locates the purchase as a part of a postmodern "mininarrative" of subliminal influence, recognition, and eventual consumption.

Dealing with exactly this form of micro-politics, Gilles Deleuze has echoed a question posed by Wilhelm Reich: "How can we come to desire our own repression?"[25] This seems to me to relate directly to the use of subliminal tapes, an outgrowth of the "self-help" recordings of the 1960s. Like Muzak, these tapes work on the concept that they inobtrusively effect one's behavior through imperceptible sound, just below the threshold of intelligibility. Muzak sets the general mood; subliminal tapes are more precise, more exacting. They attend to far more specific problems, such as weight loss, anxiety, sexual fitness, self-image, addiction, etc. The rationale for their subliminality is explicitly performative: they save time, they save money. Rather than take time out of a schedule to see an expensive psychiatrist or go to a weight clinic, they are used as a way of dealing with these dilemmas while asleep, while driving to or from work, or while *doing* work. Thus these tapes represent an important consideration in the use of subliminality. The postmodern predilection for performativity, for the well-oiled (nice-smelling and psychologically "together") machine, has created a situation in which, in commodified perfume and subliminal tapes, the use of hidden rhetoric may be dispersed from the centralized apparatus of power into the interstices of the space of personal lifestyle. Of course, this does not constitute a means of oppositional empowerment, but a more efficient form of domination.

Where Do You Stand?: Sophistic Resistance and Psychic Television

The first section of this chapter can be seen as an outline of some of the dystopian aspects of the postmodern condition. In postmodern culture, the political-rhetorical situation is confused (especially if judged through a modernist lens) to the point of virtual incomprehensibility. Who's right, what's left? On the other hand, there are utopian possibilities opened up by postmodernity, Huyssen's "hope." In this section, I will sketch out some of the possibilities of resistance inherent in the postmodern situation. At the same time, it will be necessary to remember the contingency and volatility of the postmodern arena: art is no longer good or bad, not only in the autonomo-aesthetic sense, but in the Marxist-realist sense as well.

We will now consider music, music that has a clear rhetor: Genesis P. Orridge. From 1969 to 1976, Orridge organized an extremist performance group called COUM Transmissions; from 1976 to 1981 he was the leader of a band called Throbbing Gristle; and since 1981 he has led a band called Psychic TV. Our interest will be trained on the transition between bands, from the oppositional counterculturalism of Throbbing Gristle to the postmodernist tactics of Psychic TV. Throbbing Gristle was a radical musical group, initiating a worldwide movement known as "industrial music" (their first record was released on their own label called "Industrial Records"). The music was generally noisy, brash, and loud, sometimes long and unchanging. But the group was not really generalizable. They varied their tactics, as Foucault would have it, "according to the questions put to them." To homogenize their work, then, would actually be unfair. As Orridge put it: "We just have a very simple philosophy, which is that we always think what we want to do next . . . And with the records that we do, usually we tend to—if we're not sure—contradict whatever we did last time, and it seems to work quite well. Most of us are quite good at predicting what people will expect, and then the four of us, between us, usually confuse that expectation."[26]

Obviously, to characterize such work as simply modernist would be incorrect. In Throbbing Gristle, there is an immediate attempt to "confuse" the audience, to break from one's previously established position. They had little staked in constructing a stable, individual style or vocabulary in the manner normally associated with a modernist artist like James Joyce or Edvard Munch. But the explicit philosophy of disturbing expectations links Throbbing Gristle with the politics of the avant-garde, and their recorded work and live performances at art galleries support this assertion. In this language game, it is still obvious who is on what side. The transition to Psychic TV, however, and the attendant Temple of Psychik Youth, an international organization established by Orridge, moves more fully into the postmodern alliance between deception, mimicry, and politics.

In this situation, the (now) traditional anti-art position is abandoned in favor of a politics of invisibility, mimesis, speed, and paganism. What unifies these subversive currents is not their form, nor their material, nor their "message," but their relationship to their antagonist; it is a question, to borrow a current film title, of "sleeping with the enemy." The range of issues raised by this maneuver may be brought together under one overarching concern: how can you tell what is subversive from what is dominant? In the case of Orridge's musical work, the contrast of methods is indicated in the very names of his bands. Throbbing Gristle: an organic metaphor, alive and pulsing, but grotesque and off-putting. Psychic TV: cybernetic, nonorganic, schizophrenic, cultish, and inviting. With TG, the modernist political positioning of the avant-garde is still at play, but Psychic TV employs a nonoppositional subversion, what Huyssen calls "affirmational resistance." They adopt the sound of dominant culture to "detourn" it, in the terms set out by the Situationists. What is subverted, in this case, is not the "expectation" of the audience (no "shock of the new") but the sign system that connects something that the audience *aligns itself with politically* to something the audience *recognizes*. If they recognize a type of music, do they unerringly recognize the politics of its author? If they don't, is it possible to "quietly corrupt their brain," as Orridge says he now intends? Ultimately, it comes down to a question of the position of Orridge-the-rhetor: where does he stand? "We are perhaps living the end of politics," suggests Michel Foucault. "For it's true that politics is a field which was opened by the existence of the revolution, and if the question of revolution can no longer be asked in these terms, then politics risks disappearing."[27] Foucault is precise in this formulation, since politics obviously doesn't "go away," it *vanishes*, becomes *transparent*, it *disappears*. It is this very recognition that facilitates Paul Virilio's study *The Aesthetics of Disappearance*.

Jean Baudrillard has argued that an antagonistic position necessarily confirms that which it opposes by granting it signifying legitimacy. His formula is: anti-x proves x. Contestatory positions constitute "operational negativity," mechanisms of "deterrence" that "try to regenerate a moribund principle by simulated scandal, phantasm, murder—a sort of hormonal treatment by negativity and crisis."[28] Watergate proves the legitimacy of party politics; Milli Vanilli proves the legitimacy of the music industry. The avant-garde, with its open oppositional politics, perpetuates dominant ideology by proving it the "norm." As Baudrillard puts it: "Power can stage its own murder to rediscover a glimmer of existence and legitimacy." Baudrillard's answer to this has been a form of affirmation, a theoretical mimicry of the forms of domination. His book called *The Ecstasy of Communication* can be seen as the philosophical twin of Psychic TV's newest album, *The Politics of Ecstasy*. In both, the disquieting question of whether the author is being genuine becomes paramount.

This notion is nothing novel. Indeed, practicing the very form of anoriginalism (no such thing as the new) as Baudrillard, we might quote Michael Newman quoting Gilles Deleuze quoting Plato quoting the stranger: "Once deception exists, images and likenesses and appearance will be everywhere rampant . . . And the sophist, we said, had taken refuge somewhere in that region, but then he had denied the very existence of falsity."[29] If one cannot tell the original from the copy, the genuine from the fake, there is little way to construct a modernist oppositional politics, which is founded on the stability of a political antagonist. Even within his very name Genesis P. Orridge plays on these notions: "genesis" and "orridg-inality." Of course we assume that this is not his "original" name, right?

In a retrospective, the Art and Language collective compare reading Guy Debord to a conversation with a fictitious character named Ralph: "The conversations are always the same, and it's them you fear: intricate unaccultured messes, empty but teleologically replete. Ralph is, as it were, a second-order aphasic. It is as if he gives an aphasic's account of the world in a second-order language which simulates the normal and the aphasic in one grammatical sequence."[30] Aphasia, the inability to communicate meaningfully, brought to a second order, with the ability to express the signs of language but a lack of meaningful depth, an "emptiness" attached to them: this is a perfect way to understand postmodern mimicry. It simulates the normal but is meaningless, thus throwing into question the meaning of the "original" that it supposedly simulates.

Psychic TV practice this form of second-order aphasia. Their music is based on repetitive, disco-inspired house music. Their investment is not in the "aesthetic" dimension of the music, in the sense of according it some "code breaking" or "transgressive" function. Instead, it is pap, inobtrusive, listless, unexceptional, boring. It is empty, but teleologically and semantically complete. It calls into question the very notion of falsity, of aesthetic intentionality, of positioned politics, of reasoned rhetoric. There are still signs that might divulge the politics of Psychic TV (pagan logos and graphics, even words like "politics" and "ecstasy" in titles), but they are not the bulk of its signifying surface. As Orridge has said about the group's live performance: "It is not something to sit and watch, but something to lose yourself in." It is not a distanced argument, nor detached "sublime enthusiasm," but a loaded concession, a dancing partner with dagger in hand. Douglas Kahn distinguishes such mimicry from the outright hoax.

> In stopping short of hoax, mimikry [sic] brings corresponding and contradictory aspects of both the original and mime to the fore, in the manner of modernist self-reflexivity. Unlike the bulk of artistic modernism, however, mimikry reflects back not only upon its own act but brings the social existence of the original, with which it is inseparable, into scrutiny. The complex resultant movements between original and mime (disguise, confusion, ambivalence, discovery, revelation, among others) constitute the true elements orchestrated within the tactic of mimikry.[31]

The move from Throbbing Gristle to Psychic TV has completed a development that was started in the transition from Coum Transmission to Throbbing Gristle, from a musical agenda that pitted itself against the popular to one that disguises itself *as* the popular. As Orridge explains:

> When we shifted from Coum Transmissions to TG, we were also stating that we wanted to go into popular culture, away from the art gallery context, and show that the same techniques that had been made to operate in that system could work. We wanted to test it out in the real world, or nearer to the real world, at a more street level—with young

kids who had no education in art perception, who came along and either empathized or didn't; either liked the noise or didn't. A little mini-Dada movement, eh?[32]

The ground covered in the move from Throbbing Gristle to Psychic TV did away with the last vestige of high art left in their work: noise, dada. These were left behind, perhaps to pick up again later, but decidedly not part of the Psychic TV arsenal. Instead of exposing people to affrontational art on their own turf, as they did when they were Throbbing Gristle, Orridge and crew now use a deceptive lure, one that draws you in but changes you. By playing pop music, they legitimate their products in relation to dominant industry. But their music also has a particularly partially coded message, perhaps subliminal, but some of which is available on the surface. Specifically, they advocate a turn to a form of paganism. Indeed, to take this quite literally, it may be interesting to note that Genesis and his wife Paula were married in Iceland according to a pagan wedding ritual. The Temple of Psychik Youth distributes propagandistic pamphlets and recruits members. But their party line is one of multiplicity, one that says: "Don't expect us to tell you what to do." This connects strikingly with Lyotard's own explicit call for neopaganism. In an essay called "Lessons on Paganism," he says: "When I say 'pagan' I mean godless. And the reason why we (you, not me) need to be taught a lesson is that we still want justice. That is the point of my instructive story: justice in a godless society."[33]

Psychic TV is now played in dance clubs around the world. Like the subliminal use of smell or sound, they have taken their research public, put it to work. Their "sophistic resistance" is similarly imperceptible, not because it has no discernible rhetor, but because Genesis P. Orridge refuses to ground his politics in a particular agenda, rather opting to ride the wave of postmodern fluidity, capitalizing on its variety of language games. An acquaintance of mine left school to join Orridge and Psychic TV several years ago. If they are using subliminal messages, they seem to be working. Let's hope, in Lyotard's sense, that they're just.

Notes

1   The title of this section is taken from Jean-François Lyotard, *The Postmodern Condition: A Report on Knowledge*, trans. Geoff Bennington and Brian Massumi (Minneapolis: University of Minnesota Press, 1984), p. 39.

2   Max Weber, "Science as a Vocation," in *Essays in Sociology*, eds. H. H. Gerth and C. Wright Mills (New York: Oxford University Press, 1946), p. 143.

3   Lyotard, *The Postmodern Condition*, p. 40.

4   Paul Feyerabend, *Against Method* (London: New Left Books, 1975), pp. 20, 30.

5   Lyotard, *The Postmodern Condition*, p. 80.

6   Ibid., p. 26.

7   Ibid., pp. 14, 66–67.

8   Mark Poster, *The Mode of Information: Poststructuralism and Social Context* (Chicago: University of Chicago Press, 1990), p. 93.

9   Lyotard, *The Postmodern Condition*, pp. 63–64.

10 Ibid., p. 66.

11 Ibid., p. 61.

12 See ibid., p. 60, on the *petit reçit*.

13 Ibid., p. 66.

14 Hans Blumenberg, "An Anthropological Approach to the Contemporary Significance of Rhetoric," in *After Philosophy: End or Transformation?*, eds. K. Baynes, J. Bahman, and T. McCarthy, trans. R. M. Wallace (Cambridge: MIT Press, 1987), p. 445.

15 Lyotard, *The Postmodern Condition*, pp. 62–63.

16 Ibid., p. 63.

17 See Geoff Bennington, "Introduction: The Question of Postmodernism," in *Postmodernism: The ICA Documents*, ed. Lisa Appignanesi (London: Free Association Books, 1989), pp. 3–6.

18 Lyotard, *The Differend: Phrases in Dispute*, trans. Georges Van Den Abbeele (Minneapolis: University of Minnesota Press, 1988), p. xiii.

19 Lyotard, *The Postmodern Condition*, p. 39.

20 Ibid., pp. 45–46.

21 Ibid., p. 47.

22 Paul Virilio, *Speed and Politics*, trans. Mark Polizzotti (New York: Semiotext(e), 1986), p. 47.

23 Lyotard, *The Postmodern Condition*, p. 64.

24 David Carroll, *Paraesthetics: Foucault, Lyotard, Derrida* (New York: Methuen, 1987), p. 180.

25 See Gilles Deleuze and Felix Guattari, *Anti-Oedipus: Capitalism and Schizophrenia*, trans. Robert Hurley, Mark Seem, and Helen R. Lane (Minneapolis: University of Minnesota Press), 1983.

26 Genesis P. Orridge, interview on KPFA in *Re/Search #4/5: William S. Burroughs, Brion Gysin, Throbbing Gristle*, ed. Vale V. and Andrea Juno (San Francisco: Research Publications, 1982), p. 66. Indeed, in this interview Orridge discusses Throbbing Gristle in terms of becoming invisible, a concept brought to fruition with Psychic TV.

27 Michel Foucault, "End of the Monarchy of Sex," in *Foucault Live* (New York: Semiotext(e), 1989), p. 152. In many places, Foucault opposes polemics and direct confrontation, and he admits to having used Marx without citation. "There is a sort of game I play with this. I often quote concepts, texts and phrases from Marx, but without feeling the obligation to add the authenticating label of a footnote to accompany the quotation. As long as one does that, one is regarded as someone who knows and reveres Marx, and will be suitably honoured in the so-called Marxist journals. But I quote Marx without saying so, without quotation marks, and because people are incapable of recognizing Marx's texts I am thought to be someone who doesn't quote Marx." ("Prison Talk," in *Power/ Knowledge* [New York: Pantheon, 1980], p. 52). In this respect, in his own writing I believe Foucault moves into a discursive form of politics as disappearance. This is clearly what Deleuze means when he calls Foucault "a man without references."

28 Jean Baudrillard, *Simulations*, trans. Paul Foss, Paul Patton, and Philip Beitchman (New York: Semiotext(e), 1983), p. 36.

29 Michael Newman, "Revising Modernism, Representing Postmodernism: Critical Discourses in the Visual Arts," in *Postmodernism: The* ICA *Documents*, p. 139.

30 Art and Language, "Ralph the Situationist," in *An endless adventure . . .* (Longon: Verso Press, 1989), p. 93.

31 Douglas Kahn, *John Heartfield: Art and Mass-media* (New York: Tanam Press, 1985), pp. 120–21.

32 Genesis P. Orridge, interview in *Re/Search #6/7: Industrial Culture Handbook*, ed. V. Vale and Andrea Juno (San Francisco: Research Publications, 1983), pp. 15–16.

33 Lyotard, "Lessons on Paganism," in *The Lyotard Reader*, ed. Andrew Benjamin (Oxford: Basil Blackwell, 1989), p. 123.

PART TWO
AN EAR TO THE
GROUND

I can't help thinking of the critic
who would not try to judge, but
bring into existence a work, a book,

Profiles in Sound

●

a phrase, an idea. He would light the fires, watch the grass
grow, listen to the wind, snatch the passing dregs in order to
scatter them. He would multiply, not the number of judge-
ments, but the signs of existence; he would call out to them, he
would draw them from their sleep. Would he sometimes invent
them? So much the better. The sentencious critic puts me to
sleep. I would prefer a critic of imaginative scintillations. He
would not be sovereign, nor dressed in red. He would bear
the lightning flashes of possible storms.—Michel Foucault,
"The Masked Philosopher"

HAL RUSSELL

The Fires That Burn in Hal

●

"Thank you, ladies and gentlemen," quips a grey-haired man in nasal monotone. "For our next number, we would like to play something you're sure to enjoy . . . if that is at all possible." Whether in the spotlight of a big festival in Berlin or in the intimate darkness of Chicago's Club Lower Links, Hal Russell is always disarmingly humorous, ironic without being condescending, self-effacing but never morose. "I want to keep from becoming so deadly serious," he explains. "That kills me when people get up there and pretend they're doing some fucking very serious thing. Man, they should be thinking about having some fun. To me, that's what jazz has always meant!"

For Russell, always is a long time. He's been involved in music for most of his sixty-six years, having picked up drums at age four. "I would set up a small band of lead soldiers in front of the radio," he recalls, "pretending that they were the members of an orchestra." At Riverside-Brookfield High School, outside Chicago, he had a quartet ("a funny band: tenor saxophone, valve trombone, drums, and piano") which played original charts. A scholarship took him to the University of Illinois for college. "I had a big band there," he says. "Hal Russell and his Orchestra . . . a Lionel Hampton style band. Big, raucous; we used to play at fraternity houses and blow out the walls."

Summers were spent on the road with various big bands. "At the time there was a shortage of musicians due to the war, so I played with people like Woody Herman, Claude Thornhill, and Boyd Raeburn. They were mainly doing vaudeville, playing five or six shows a day; then you got a break during the movie, and came back after. As a stage band we would have to back tap dancers, singers, magicians, various acts—I was undoubtedly influenced by the show business aspect of it."

As with many young players in the mid-1940s, Russell's life was irreversibly changed by bebop; Parker and Gillespie's Guild recordings shifted his musical perception completely. "The thing that fascinated me most was the freedom allowed the drummer," he remembers. "Up to then we used to keep

Mars Williams, Hal Russell, and Kent Kessler
(photo: W. Patrick Hinely, Work/Play)

time on the bass drum; everything was pretty straight. Then we heard these little fills that Kenny Clarke and Max Roach did. That changed my entire concept overnight."

The decade of the fifties drew Russell completely into the bebop life, both musically and personally. Based in Chicago, gigging around the Midwest, tripping to New York, he worked constantly with an incredible chain of players. "I played with a lot of now-famous people. At that time they were just other musicians; they hadn't reached stardom. When I played with Miles in 1950, he was about on par with me in terms of musical knowledge. *The Birth of the Cool* had come out, but there weren't too many people buying that."

With Davis, he backed Billie Holiday at the Regal, and he worked with a veritable who's-who of famous jazz musicians: Sonny Rollins, John Coltrane, Stan Getz, Mildred Bailey, Duke Ellington, Erroll Garner. "This is hard to remember, because drugs seemed to take over my life," says Russell, who was a dedicated heroin addict for ten years. At the end of the fifties, he got the monkey off his back, started doing commercial jingles (". . . a drag, man.") and playing lounges. "It wasn't too bad," he admits of the lounge work. "Some of the acts I played with were really good, like Tony Bennett, June Christy, Jonathan Winters, Woody Allen, Kingston Trio, Barbra Streisand. There were a thousand people. Name some people—I probably played their show!"

Perhaps unique to American jazz, Hal Russell has spiritual kin in various British musicians who have used session experience as fuel for experimentation with open form. Guitarist Derek Bailey backed pop singers, reedman Tony Coe soloed for Henry Mancini, saxist Lol Coxhill played with Rufus Thomas and ska bands; nevertheless, each has been drawn to the possibilities of free music and extended jazz. When it is suggested that avant-garde jazz should "put up or shut up," Russell grows impatient. "Why? What does that statement mean? It doesn't mean a goddamned thing to me. The first time I heard Monk, I hated it. The same is true of Duke, I couldn't stand it. This is the same, it just takes a certain amount of concentration and listening, and you will like free music. What we have to do is produce a music that satisfies us. If we please ourselves we stand a pretty good chance of pleasing the audience, or at least attacting some new people."

Russell's stance on free music is seasoned. In 1959 he had a regular gig at the Rumpus Room with Gene Esposito on piano, Russell Thorne on bass, and Joe Daley on tenor saxophone. "Joe, Russell, and I said: 'Wouldn't it be fun if we didn't have to do all the things that we'd done up to now, if I didn't always have to keep time, or if the horn player could play off different changes or no changes?' So we started with 'Nica's Dream,' took that and went out. We told Gene to stop playing because we didn't want a piano putting down any chords. Immediately, we discovered that it was no good to take other people's tunes, that we write our own stuff. That was how the Joe Daley Trio was formed."

More or less concurrently, in L.A., pianist Paul Bley's days with Ornette Coleman were also numbered. "As a matter of fact, we didn't know about Ornette until after we started experimenting," assures Russell. After a few years, an RCA scout heard the trio and signed them on for a hugely unsuccessful record, *Newport '63*, which was mostly studio material. "People didn't play like that," Russell remembers. "At the time it was way out." Thorne soon left the group, and eventually Daley drifted back to bop.

But Hal Russell had been bitten by the free jazz bug, and he persisted in playing it. Moving to Florida for a year, he led a band at a black hotel, on the beach, and at the Playboy club. A mysterious sickness overcame him ("I was allergic to something in Florida, *mold spores*"), and he returned to Chicago. With the encouragement of his wife, the better part of the seventies was spent auditioning band members. "We went through a thousand different personnel changes, people who didn't work, people who showed some promise. I tried a singer, I tried commercial gimmicks, but mainly they weren't good enough. Then I came across the right personnel."

With some modifications, this "right" bunch forms Russell's core corps, the NRG (as in "En-er-gy") Ensemble. In 1979 Russell started playing tenor saxophone (now his main axe), soprano saxophone, and trumpet—in addition to drums and vibes. "This throws me into a completely different improvising scene," he explains. "When I change from tenor to trumpet, I cease to think like a tenor player and I start thinking . . . trumpet! My ideas are not the same. The benefit in changing instruments is the different train of thought it will set off in me."

With this change, Steve Hunt, an incredibly versatile percussionist, took over the main drum duties. Muscular bassist Kent Kessler and bassist/guitarist/trumpeter Brian Sandstrom now flank Russell along with reed cowboy Mars Williams, who left the group briefly to tour with the pop group Psychedelic Furs. After ten years of struggle—"terrible gigs for nothing, loft concerts at my home, just a hobby"—NRG has had a big break, touring Europe and releasing *The Finnish/Swiss Tour* on (of all unlikely places) ECM Records. "The whole success thing has been the story of our relationship with [writer/producer] Steve Lake," says the ever-humble Russell. "Starting with the Moers festival of 1990."

Through its tough formative years, the group was anything but stagnant. It amassed a giant original repertoire with contributions by all members, and it put out several self-bankrolled records, one with saxist Charles Tyler. "I prefer the way ECM does it," smiles Russell. "They send you a check, a big check. I think the guys in the band prefer that, too." Along with NRG classics like "Hal the Weenie" and "Raining Violets," the group has worked on a number of longer suites. *Fred*, dedicated to Fred Astaire, won over the audience at the 1986 Chicago Jazz Festival. There's also *Time Is All You've Got* for Artie Shaw, *St. Valentine's Day Massacre*, *The Sound of Music* (imagine the full soundtrack as rendered by Albert Ayler circa *New York Eye and Ear*), and *The Hal Russell Story*.

In addition to the NRG Ensemble, Russell always maintains several auxiliary bands. "Things happen that change it all, make you wonder what you might be into next. I keep all these groups because each one shows me something a bit different." Currently, he's very excited about a nascent partnership with pianist Joel Futterman ("makes me wonder if I missed the piano thing entirely!"), with whom he has played in Berlin. He has a rock-oriented trio called NRG 3, with Ed Ludwig on drums and Noel Kupersmith on bass. Named for Hal (née Harold Luttenbacher), the Flying Luttenbachers are yet another group. Presently looking for a bassist, they feature Chad Organ on tenor and Weasel Walter on drums and "other things . . . like screaming. Weasel has a really nice, high-pitched scream," agree Russell and his wife Barbara.

Audience in 3-D masks, Hal Russell memorial, Southend
Musicworks, Halloween 1992 (photo: James F. Quinn)

Of late, the NRG Ensemble has started to use a new method of composition. Hal dredges an old tune from his bottomless pit ("It's crazy, I just know millions of them!") and the band finds a way of playing along, composing on the spot. For Russell, there is no great divide between free and pre-free; kookiness, swing, and experimentation go hand in hand. "This is where my vaudeville experience comes in," he suggests. "See, at the time people seemed to be having a lot more fun playing. That's what I want to re-create. I want to make sure that people have a good time playing with me. And consequently, I want the audience to have a good time, too. I'm just trying to get them to enjoy it as much as I do."

"I keep finding new ways of doing things," says the sexagenarian saxophonist. "One should keep striving for new experiences, new ways of playing. That's why I don't think they'll be any end to it. We haven't exhausted free jazz by any means!"

Elegy: Heaven and Hal

Halloween night. Ghosts, witches, and devils swirled in the smoke of cigarettes as a crew of musical hobgoblins came out trick-or-treating in memory of free jazz mischievist Hal Russell, whose sudden death in September 1992 shocked and saddened the Chicago music world. Russell had just finished recording his third record for ECM, a suite called *The Hal Russell Story* that charted his life from beginning to end. Never at a loss for a twisted joke, he took this one too far.

Hal loved Halloween—he called one of his pieces "Hal the Weenie" in homage to the prankster's holiday. Couldn't have been a more appropriate send-off for him than this festival of black-and-orange looniness. Between sets, live concert footage and music videos were screened, and a slide show culminated in color images that the gigantic audience viewed through 3-D glasses that were affixed to Hal Russell masks. Looking around, it was like being caught in a psychotropic version of *Life* magazine's famous photo of bespectacled theatergoers. For the peckish, Southend Musicworks roasted weenies, from which protrudings toothpicks bore tiny xeroxed Hal-heads. Without a doubt, in spirit it was all Hal's eve.

The music started bizarrely enough with two groups of Russell's students: the All Nations Mission Orchestra (a south side Baptist church band) and the Anointed Ones (their gospel group). And what to our wondering ears should they play, but a version of "Chariots of Fire." The NRG Ensemble played a set of riveting Hal-tunes, with guest ex-members like Chuck Burdelik and the terrific Ken Vandermark. The NRG 3 worked with various people taking Hal's chair (Mars Williams played a lovely tenor piece with them), and the Flying Luttenbachers spewed a set of snarly stuff, with Vandermark on tenor and bass clarinet.

Everyone played their asses off. Even the huge group-grope that closed things came off well. Like so much of Russell's music, the memorial was a conglomeration of elation and expurgation, simultaneously a surreal celebration and a tearful wave goodbye. Maybe it was the only way for us to wean ourselves of Hal.

IKUE MORI &
CATHERINE JAUNIAUX

When the Twain Meet

●

"We first met two years ago," recalls Japanese percussionist Ikue Mori on the day following her duo
concert with Belgian singer Catherine Jauniaux at
the London Musicians Collective's first Festival of Experimental Music.
"That was the very beginning. We each had a solo performance in New York.
People saw us, somehow imagined it together, and mentioned that maybe it
could be interesting."

Brow slightly knotted, Jauniaux hunches forward from a reclining position on the couch. "But this day we also played *together.*"

"Oh, that's right, we did!" Mori stands corrected. "Those five-minute
things together."

Jauniaux adds: "And people said that was the best part."

Could be that this duo is indeed the best part. Until seeing them, Mori's
electronic percussion was a source of some bafflement to me. Earlier she'd
seemed a trifler, a hunt-and-pecker dabbling at her drum machine's stock
sounds without conviction or expertise; now she's synthesized her oddball
sense of time with a rich range of timbres, textures, and even tonalities, all at
the touch of a finger. And where Jauniaux's voice has sometimes served as an
exotic accessory (she likes playing and recording as an invited guest), with
this duo her singing is substantive, the basal stuff.

In principle, they make a well-suited pair, two small women interested in
equally—as they put it—"compact" improvisations, with a noted bent toward song-form. Two autodidacts, each with a strong "Eastern" inclination,
from rock backgrounds, relocated from their native lands to New York City.
Two such compatible musicians . . . totally unfamiliar with one another
despite a number of key in-common colleagues like Fred Frith and Tom
Cora. Inevitable encounter maybe, but when the right partner comes along
the best part can't be far behind.

In all fairness, for Mori and Jauniaux the respective roads to get to this
meeting point were both full of varied, exciting sound making. Hardly the
"worst part" by any measure. Jauniaux's was a journey that began in Brussels
in the mid-seventies as an actress taking lessons in classical voice that she

began to find repugnant. "I felt really in jail," she remembers. "I mean, you can't do anything but just one kind of voice. I couldn't express myself, except in the interpretation. And that was not enough." In fact, Jauniaux traces her interest in improvising back to a much earlier, primal period. "I think I improvise because I *need* to. I always did, when I was a little child. I would go into my room with my books of poems and sing them. And I always invented languages. I think it's because it's a need. I need to do that!"

Her improvising didn't come completely out of thin air, though. Dagmar Krause's chilly vocal work with Art Bears was an inspiration that Jauniaux followed up by joining Marc Hollander's Belgian vanguard rock band Aqsak Maboul. Fidgety, skitterish, at times birdlike, Jauniaux's voice burbles above the Bo Diddley beat on the classic "A Modern Lesson" from their *Un Peu de l'ame des bandits*, where her remarkable imitative abilities are used to trade lines with guitar, percussion, and reeds. At a concert with the short-lived Maboul, English out-rock group The Work asked her to join their merry band. She obliged, touring and recording with them in the early-eighties, and proved herself to be a truly distinctive emergent voice.

Since that time, she's sung with most of the Recommended/Woof Records eclectic crew, guested with numerous other groups like Test Department, and led her own multimedia band Jonio. Cellist Tom Cora, who played on *Fluvial* (the record she made in collaboration with ex-Henry Cow saxophonist/keyboardist Tim Hodgkinson), in turn invited her to sing on his collaboration with Dutch anarchist punkers the Ex. Cora and Jauniaux have an ongoing duo as well, and she also appears on the debut of Third Person, a fill-in-the-blank trio with Cora, percussionist Samm Bennett, and a third . . . well, you got it. Most recently, she has participated in Heiner Goebbels's opera *Romanische Hunde*, a "patchwork" piece featuring "a rapper, two classical singers, one Spanish more theatrical guy, and one Italian professor," voicing texts from Heiner Müller, Brecht, and ancient Roman sources.

"I think I like every kind of *sad* music," she says, laughing. "It's like the only thing I can do. I need to sing the sadness of life." The last few years have seen her explore the bottom end of her range—she prefers her low voice to what I identify as her stratospheric highness. Likewise, time has brought out the more overtly "folk" (in Jauniaux's case Gypsy) element in her singing. "I am very sensitive to Eastern music," she muses, "because my grandmother is from Romania and she was a singer. I have a kind of relationship with her without knowing her. It was very obvious when I started to improvise that I had this impression that I was improvising *for* her, or *by* her, or *by* these people who died in my Romanian family." Together with a newfound interest in Skip James, Jauniaux directly attributes this tendency to her 1989 relocation to the Big Apple. "I'm out of my culture in New York. The fact that

Catherine Jauniaux and Ikue Mori
(photo: Jayne Wexler)

I'm far from this culture makes me desire it. It makes me come back to these kind of roots."

Mori concurs: "There's always nostalgia, an interest for Asian or Japanese music when I come to New York. And I also like to write dark songs from the dark side of your mind. It's more easy to express than a sort of gay feeling. Just more naturally comes out . . . a terrible thought." Perhaps that same dark drive prompted Mori to move from Tokyo to New York in 1977 and start playing drums in a no wave band. Yes, that's her amid the mug-shot lineup on the back of *No New York* with the ID-tag "Ikue Ile, DNA, Drums"! "I never played drums before or anything," she admits in still-choppy English. "But also Arto Lindsay never played guitar before. It was very easy to make our music. Three of us never played before, but everybody just starting at that point, just pick up guitar, bass, singing. Very exciting time."

As DNA unwound its five-year-strand, Mori became friends with improv-punk Japanophile John Zorn, who promptly introduced her to the downtown NY scene and its cast of shady characters. Before long, she was a regular on the improvising circuit. I first saw her in a drum duet with someone who no longer plays at the now-defunct Tin Pan Alley. She spent some years going back and forth to Japan, playing and recording in ad hoc improvising settings as well as with bands. But she's finally given up all attempts to start an ongoing rock group, now that Toh Ban Djan, her rock duo with bassist Luli Shioi, has broken up.

Partly due to apartment problems (nowhere to practice) and because she was feeling the inhibition of being a technically limited drummer, Mori bought a small, very basic drum machine in 1986. Thereafter, she has devoted most of her energies to putting together the fresh, three-drum-machined sound she now uses. "Of course, you can work on melody," she explains. "And you can pull out more music from your head. With drums, it's just drums because I have no technique." She now has a colossal palette of tuned percussion, metallic scrapes, brushes, and echoey, whispery inexplicables, all mixed into a live-dub potpourri, with panoramic stereo and a very visual sensibility to boot. For first evidence of the full effect on record, check out her contribution to harpist Zeena Parkins's *Ursa's Door.*

Apart from her relationship with Jauniaux, Mori has a few other fave projects. She works as often as possible in a quartet with guitarist Frith, vocalist Shelly Hirsch, and bassist Mark Dresser. And she has hooked up with Joey Baron, the most in-demand drummer in NYC. "I really enjoy playing with him," says Mori. "He is like my drum hero." Of late, she's also been cultivating a strong interest in visual media, mixing songs with film and video.

What makes two musicians like Mori and Jauniaux decide to work together? Some magical combination of affinities and differences, no doubt. "We matched," offered Mori. "We had the same timing, the same harmony." At the time of this writing the duo has recorded its first release for RecRec, which includes the songs featured on their European tour. After a few early freely improvised performances, Jauniaux and Mori chose to skeletally determine the repertoire in advance, a working method they continue to use. Now one of them initiates a song and the other helps flesh it out. "When I heard the cassette, it was so like pieces," says Jauniaux, looking back at their first encounter. "For me it was interesting how the improvisation could be just a piece, like a written piece."

With Mori and Jauniaux, in spite of any basic similarities, it is actually the space they reserve for each other that makes working as a duo particularly special. In the end, that independence may help explain the fuzziness over their initial gig two years back. After all, if playing with someone brings out the "you" in you, maybe it's possible to forget they're there at all. "I can be in my own world and she can be in her own world," explains the percussionist. "And mixed in a really strange way."

"That's maybe why you can feel our cultural roots," adds the singer. "Because we can really be ourselves."

ED WILKERSON, JR.

One Bold Soul

●

A big-shouldered wind-man in the city of big
shoulders, the Windy City—from the outset there
are clear connections between tenor saxophonist
Ed Wilkerson, Jr. and his hometown, Chicago. And the parallel goes well
beyond the surface. Since the mid-1960s the central task for Chicago jazz
musicians has been the construction and maintenance of a community, a
protective network fostering experimentation with an attitude of trust and
respect. By its rightful name, this is the Association for the Advancement of
Creative Musicians, and such values are likewise at the heart of Ed Wilkerson's music. He embodies several subtle contradictions: a band leader bent
on emphasizing ensemble, a record producer whose true love is live, and a
composer primarily concerned with making the score invisible. In each
case, the issue revolves around reconciliation of individual expression and
community interchange. Wilkerson relates this to an ongoing theme: "It's a
tradition in black music that it has certain social implications, purposes
beyond 'good music.' It has function in people's lives. The loft thing in New
York came about because people needed some place to go to be stimulated
intellectually that wouldn't cost $50 per person per night. That's always
going to be the case, whether it's the AACM, musicians in New York, or a rent
party in the thirties."

It was an encounter with the AACM that drew Wilkerson more deeply into
the Chicago scene. Born in Indiana, raised in Cleveland ("mainly in the
Midwest, that's the important thing"), Wilkerson in 1971 entered the University of Chicago, where he was exposed to two distinct musical communities,
one historical and one contemporary: "Studying Renaissance music showed
me the value of association, that the way things change is not through one
person sitting down and coming up with an idea. It's through interaction
between people. The Florentine Camerata wanted to provide a forum for
making certain things happen, so they made an association the same way
the AACM did. That was a way of having people to perform your music,
people to bounce ideas off of." The Art Ensemble of Chicago's legendary
Mandel Hall performance inspired Wilkerson to begin studying in the AACM
school, and in 1975 he fulfilled the group's membership requirements.

The 1970s saw the settling-in and eventual dispersion of the first wave of AACMers. Early in the decade, the Art Ensemble returned to Chicago from Paris; already, Braxton did not come home again. Fred Anderson led power-house groups, Henry Threadgill broke ground with Air, and later in the period grand-père Muhal Richard Abrams had a working big-band that included a young tenor player named Wilkerson. "Muhal's band had an ability to go through so many different areas seamlessly," he reflects. "That group performed every Monday night for three years and it never released a record." In fact, many important groups from that period went undocumented, including Quadrisect, an all-wind group that included Wilkerson.

Received knowledge has it that Abrams and Threadgill found the city stagnant and left for the greener pastures of New York, but Wilkerson reads this move with characteristic optimism. "I don't see it as deserting ship. I think the AACM has always had a spirit of pioneering and proselytizing in certain ways, and I think guys look at it as a missionary project, going out into the wilderness and carrying a message in music." A more hospitable place to spread said gospel was Europe. With its rapidly developing independent record industry and friendly jazz-club infrastructure, it welcomed the American avant-garde. In the face of U.S. labels' blank indifference, European labels like Red Records, Black Saint/Soul Note, Moers, and others attracted many of the best and brightest, among them Kahil El Zabar's Ethnic Heritage Ensemble. A 1978 tour of Europe cemented Wilkerson's position in this group, one of the three ensembles that form the nucleus of his current activity.

Shrunk-down from a sextet to a quartet and finally trio ("I think Kahil and I have both settled on the idea of a trio format for the group, with that triangular type of exchange"), the Ethnic Heritage Ensemble is the environment in which Wilkerson's considerable improvising skill is given the longest leash. "A lot of things we do will be based on rhythmic things, things in meter, or a poem, and won't necessarily be a composed line," he explains. Cutting a broad tone, his tenor work comes out of Coleman Hawkins via Archie Shepp, a well-developed, highly vocal sound. Wilkerson doubles on clarinet, which opens up a range of coloristic possibilities, and the group will often graze a riff, reveling in the combination of timbres inherent in a two-horn/percussion lineup. Four records (all on European labels) span a decade of shifting third members, including saxophonists "Light" Henry Huff, Kalaparusha Maurice McIntyre, and Hannah John Taylor, trumpeter Rasul Siddik, and now trombonist/Defunkt-leader Joseph Bowie. Wilkerson clearly likes the present group, and its record, *Ancestral Song* (Silkheart Records). "That's a killer-diller! This group is so heavy-hitting, moves so fluently and has such good rapport, it's like the music is automatic. And playing with Joe is like getting in the ring with Mike Tyson. I feel like I've been getting body-punches after a concert is over, and after a tour with them I'm in great shape!" Pugilistics aside, Ethnic Heritage Ensemble's concept is still communal, albeit intimate and loose—a great talk between close friends.

Contrary to the paring-down of the Ethnics, in 1981 Wilkerson conjured his own big-band out of a trio, Shadow Vignettes. Or, as he puts it, "I got a little carried away with adding people." Performing to "Honky Tonk Bud," a poem written by John Toles-Bey, the trio turned into a nonet, then eleven pieces, and eventually an enormous twenty-five-strong ensemble, with a string section and several percussionists. After composing for and conducting the group over several years, Wilkerson decided to take recording matters into his own hands, and, AACM self-determination firmly in mind, in 1986, Wilkerson's own Sessoms Records released the Shadow Vignettes LP *Birth of a Notion*. On the record, we hear nothing directly from him (he conducts, doesn't play), but his compositional sense, which centers on a buoyant treatment of section interplay and brassy forthrightness, betrays its heritage in the big-bands of Lunceford and Gillespie as much as in the open-ended work for larger ensembles of Abrams or Roscoe Mitchell. For Wilkerson, these represent distinct strategies for mediating player contributions, located along a stylistic continuum. "I'm moving away from saying 'this is bebop' or 'this is blues,' cause there were some cats, Leo Parker in the 1950s, and Sidney Bechet, man he was doing multiphonics, playing outside the changes. What Ornette does is important, but what Stanley Turrentine does is also important. And Hank Crawford. I played with the Temptations last summer and it was an honor, you know. I'd do it again."

Wilkerson has fashioned his big-band out of the rich variety of black culture, both musical and personal. "Shadow Vignettes is like traveling with a little village. All different types of people, different religions. In the bus, I just sit and listen, and it's never dull. I've tried to model the music on that." Citing film shorts of Cab Calloway and acknowledging the opportunities opening up in the world of visual production, Wilkerson conceives of the band as a performance troupe, more theatrical and multimedia oriented than his other groups. Already, the Vignettes have released a videotape version of "Honky Tonk Bud," and they are at work on a film with Floyd Webb. They played at Brooklyn Academy of Music and they have toured Japan. Undaunted, Wilkerson sets sights for the band even bigger: "I want to do a whole revue, a Regal type show, with singers and dancers. One of these days . . . it'll take a lot of bucks."

Cultivating the Vignettes also gave Wilkerson a birds-eye view on virtually all of the Chicago players, from whom he could hand-pick a smaller group. In 1985 he organized an ensemble to do a one-shot series of concerts of music he had been writing for mid-sized group. "It was a way of getting to know people better," he explains, "people who I didn't have a chance to play with much in a small group setting where we'd have that kind of musical interaction." Calling the series "New Music for Eight Bold Souls," Wilkerson was hardly ready the response it received. "I had no idea of keeping the group together at the time. When we finished the last concert, I said 'Okay, that's it.' But people kept calling me up, 'Why don't you play for this?' I said 'Dag, people kind of like this!' So we just kept playing by virtue of the fact that people kept calling. I started thinking about it, and I really enjoyed the fact that it was the same eight people. I heard the pieces growing and being reinterpreted; people were challenging themselves with how they played the music."

Hence the birth of Eight Bold Souls, the group that most clearly demonstrates Wilkerson's integration of self-effacing sociality with compositional and instrumental virtuosity. Like Threadgill's Sextett ("We share a common love for Ellington"), the Souls' instrumentation is extraordinary, with a tuba-bass-drum bottom-end linked by cello to the front line of two reeds, trumpet, and trombone. This allows them to split up into unusual subgroups, matching bass-to-tuba, tuba-to-'bone, cello-to-bass, and so on. Wilkerson attributes this emphasis on timbral overlap to his study with composer Hale Smith: "He reinforced things that I was feeling, that you can make one sound, but after a while you want to write music that is made up of combinations of sounds. Like using a box of crayons, using the primary colors after a while you begin to mix them together. More and more I'm mixing the colors."

Originally including the late, great Steve McCall on drums and Richard Brown on bass, the lineup has otherwise remained the same, Dushun Mosley taking over percussive duties at an early date and Harrison Bankhead filling the tough shoes of Mr. Brown. Unlike the rest of the group, most of whom studied at one time or another with Abrams, Mosley comes by way of Detroit, bringing the popular punch of Motown and the stinging precision of Roscoe Mitchell's Creative Arts Collective. A wellspring of experience, Bankhead has spent years playing in Fred Anderson's groups. Clarinetist and multi-reedman Mwata Bowden was the most familiar member to Wilkerson, due to their concurrent enrollment in the AACM and apprenticeship with Muhal. On tuba, Wilkerson writes specifically for "Chicago legend" Aaron Dodd, a stalwart session-man for seventies soul stars like Donny Hathaway and Roberta Flack and a mainstay of the AACM. "He's not the kind that would sit and play whole notes all night. He likes to get up-front himself and play." From his experience with them in the Vignettes, Wilkerson selected trombonist Isaiah Jackson and trumpeter Robert Griffin, with whom he had also played in a few smaller settings. Cellist Naomi Millender is the only non-Chicago resident, breezing in from Gary, Indiana, where she is a section leader in the symphony. "Having a woman in the group, it really makes a difference," says Wilkerson. "She adds another kind of spirit to the group, and her solos are like that: relaxed, patient. That's the type of person she is." Jackson adds: "It changes how we react to the audience, which is mostly male. Instead of proving how hard and fast we are, we have to pace ourselves and adjust to a different kind of energy."

Two years ago, with Brown still on bass, Wilkerson decided to appease the mounting curiosity of the non-Chicago world by releasing an Eight Bold Souls record. Still unable to garner the interest of other labels, Wilkerson again adopted the DIY approach, putting out *8 Bold Souls* on Sessoms. Critical praise was virtually univocal. The record has things in common with the group of jazz composers writing "architecturally" for chamber-sized ensembles, like David Murray, John Carter, Anthony Davis, and especially Threadgill. But it is unique, both in Wilkerson's singular compositional style and in its evidence of the developing group dynamic. Evocative textures float elegantly through shifting meters, easily slipping into another funky world. Since the record, the ensemble's sense of cohesion has grown, as has its repertoire (which now includes an arrangement of Ornette's "Lonely Woman"). "For an eight piece, I think we have a *oneness*," says Wilkerson. "I'm interested in having the group take predominance over the individual players. The only way you can get that is by playing together a lot, and I think we have that now." Nonetheless, the individual players have grown immensely as well, and Wilkerson's soloing seems to bloom in the Bold Souls' greenhouse. "I've come to like having the same people. There's a certain newness about playing with people you've never played with before, but there can also be this other kind of knowing. We've become very comfortable with each other and confident about things on stage. As people become more relaxed, they'll take more chances." Perhaps Dodd put it best, "There's no ego-trippin' in this group—just a lot of love."

Letting the ensemble grow together is part of the sound Wilkerson is looking for. For instance, in rehearsing a new composition the horns are encouraged to "add something, it doesn't need to be a run, it can be a shape." Anywhere else, such a phrase might be ambiguous, but in this context it is loaded with meaning—and lo-and-behold the Souls draw it out successfully. Wilkerson focuses on transitions, choosing difficult passages and then, with the help of the group, finding ways to navigate them. "Everybody can write great episodes or moments, but going from one moment to another moment, that separates the good from the great. Threadgill's groups do that effortlessly. In writing, that's where I spend the most time: how do I get from *here* to *there*?"

Wilkerson doesn't see records as the ends, but the means of music. "I look at them as a promotional device, a thumb-nail sketch of what the band can do. The experience is to sit in front of the group and be at the concert, and everything else is an attempt to get that to happen." In keeping, conversation with Wilkerson is scattered with recollections—his and others'—of live music. Seeing Monk. Seeing Coltrane. Missing Ellington. As he puts it: "It begins to take on those legendary aspects. Pretty soon, 'Sun Ra stood up, raised his arm and lightning came across the sky.' Or, 'We went to a concert and Mingus and Juan Tizol were fighting with a knife.' It begins to take on bigger than life proportions. And it begins to communicate things beyond the music." One of his favorites is about Bird: "I was talking with a guy who said 'I would sit in the first row and listen to him play and it was like someone dropping little drops of wisdom on your forehead.' Such a nice way of thinking about it, just absorbing it." To the suggestion that people don't have the time to be social anymore, he nods "Like you say. But I don't know—what *do* we make time for?"

LEE PERRY

Tabula Rasta: The Upsetter

Starts from Scratch

●

It is a day like any other day. Like any other Fourth
of July. In Zurich, Switzerland. In front of the
American Hospitality Center. With a cheesy band
playing "Blue Moon" in the background, Swiss and U.S. flags flapping in the
summer wind, a small Jamaican man emerges from a van. He is dressed in
black, covered from head to toe in gold and silver rings and medallions,
topped off with a homemade crown built from a hodgepodge of postcards,
playing cards, coins, snapshot photographs, and a toy SST jet protruding
like a feather from the back of his head. Nonchalant, he unpacks a bag filled
with an assortment of essential Independence Day items: iron crucifix, batman doll, plastic laser gun. As I said, a day like any other.

Call him what you will—"Little," "King," "Pipecock Jakxson," "Upsetter,"
"Super Ape," or just plain "Scratch"—Lee Perry would stand out in a mum-
mer's parade, let alone on the quiescent banks of Lake Zurich. Nonetheless,
it is here and now, July 4, 1990, that I have chosen to commence a video documentary on the legendary reggae musician and producer. To kick things off:
a nice stroll by the water to feed the ducks and have what Perry terms an
"outerview on outdependence day." Indeed, he's one to turn an interrogation
back on itself, to turn an inquirer inside-out.

"Lee Scratch Perry ready!" Cross in one hand, pistol in the other, he
slowly turns around, displaying himself to the small disbelieving crowd.
"Me and my space laser goin' on, ridin' in from San Juan, to United States of
America, with lightnin' and thunder, yessir brimstone and fire. Countdown
10, 9, 8, 7, 6, 5, 4, 3, 2, 1, zero, blastoff! Answer! . . ." Rhyming, punning,
tongue-tripping, spoonerizing, neologizing: Scratch is zip-lipped. He ex-
temporizes at a mind-boggling rate, squeezing every available ounce of juice
out of a phrase or just a word. This linguistic play constantly makes use of a
vast, complicated set of references of varied origin—personal, biblical, rastafarian, obeah, cabbalistic, conspiratorial, musical, megalomaniacal, sexual,
and scatalogical. More often than not, these references are enmeshed in
some subtle social subtext or deep double entendre.

Bending down to buckle his heavy black boots, he explains some adorning
coins and decals: "Switzerland on top of Britain. And on my heel, Switzer-

land good-lucky horseshoe. St. Michael on my boot. And a little king inside on boot tongue." At this, he points at a publicity shot of himself in full regal attire affixed inside, and laughs proudly: "The king of tongue!"

After shaking hands with two old Swiss women who are certain that Perry is a medicine man, we set off along the lake. Right away, he instructs me to zoom in on a radio tower atop a hill on the opposite bank. "Pick up everything," he says flatly. "And look at those streaks," he adds, directing my attention to two jet exhaust streams crossing the blue sky. "Them pick up the whole of Switzerland over there." In Perry's world everything is imbued with meaning; later in the day he hoists a huge stone onto his shoulder, traces a perpendicular angle on it with his finger and whispers cryptically: "See what I told you—seven!"

Like game-show Jeopardy, Perry's answers precede any questions; actually posing them somehow seems extraneous. "This is it!" he exclaims, picking up the pace. "I present the cool Swiss air. I am the Emperor of Switzerland and I own the Continental Bank and the Swiss Bank. All the Swiss banks and all the Swiss francs, all the French banks and all the French francs, I own. I own all American currencies, all the dollars, all the English pounds and all the sterling . . . by the power of breeze, whirlwind! Catch good air and fair's-fair! So y'havin' an outerview wi'Lee Scratch Perry, n'interview. An outerview catchin' fresh air, speaking from inside through air, breeze. Music breeze. To tell the United States of America that I am the gome of Switzerland."

"Gome?" I ask, edgewise. Mirelle Campbell, Perry's manager and wife, pipes up: "Gnome, you mean." Without a pause, Perry picks up the ball: "I spell different. I am the g-n-o-m-e, *gome*. I don't use bad spells, I make good spells. I make evil spell good spell. I am the gome that come to rob the gnomes with my big black comb in Switzerland!" He laughs hysterically. We are walking through a populated picnic area, but I am totally captivated and he is oblivious and on a roll. "With my laser space gun in hand and my iron cross in hand, I am the luckiest one under the sun. All I have to do is shake a leg and a lot of money come. Money come out of my jump, money come out of my bass, money come out of my briefcase, and money come out of my suitcase. Briefcase of money. Suitcase of money. Carload of money. Shiploads of money. Plane loads of money. I am the money maker, and I am the money taker. I am the money conqueror and I am the money bankerer. I am the music skankerer and I come to skank all the wankerers . . . like the popes and bishops and deacons and elders. Time for them to quit because I'm taking over! 'Achtung, achtung!' mean 'Attention, attention!' I am taking over eart'! I am an alien from outer space, with my space gun and my iron cross, I don't make fun."

Passing a couple reclining on a bench, my gome guide points them out, insisting that I film them: "C'mon, lovers in the park!" Drawing up under a beautiful, sprawling old tree, Scratch instantly names it his "Switzerland money tree." He touches it with his iron cross, and we move on to the stony beach at the end of the park. Here he stops and gazes out at the water. "Look at all those ships. All those little boats belong to me, President Abraham Lincoln His Imperial Majesty. Power through the Trinity of life, water. I am the conqueror of life and death. I am both. I am life and I am death. I am the same. If you want me good, I can be good. If you want me evil, I could be terrible evil. I am good and evil. And those are my holy stones." He gestures into the water. "Stones like peas. I won't turn these stones into bread, I will turn them into Swiss francs!"

"The money messiah," I suggest.

"Yes! The money messiah. I the money messiah!" He pauses, gathering words to end with. "By power of my throat, deep throat from deep sea. Atlantis. From my planet under the water . . . Record!" The last word—spoken as he walks towards me—is a direction to press the red button on my video camera that takes the interview over-and-out.

Entering a discussion with Lee Perry puts you in his domain: language. At his home the next day, he pulls out a notebook full of wild scrawl (a truer "scratch" pad there never was): "Words make up the world. By saving the words, we'll save the world." Perry's is a discursive kingdom, a creative world of hidden connections and secret pacts exposed in language. He is nuts, undoubtedly, admittedly. "I am permanently mad. I can't be cured!" he assures. His madness is not without calculation, however; it is a craziness that he takes quite seriously. Some think it's a lunacy of his own design, that he's crazy like a fox. Or, as the chief of Heartbeat Records, Chris Wilson suggests, Perry "plays fool to catch wise."

Maybe so. But a short trip through his memory banks would certainly demonstrate sufficient cause for plain old "crazy." At fifty-five, Perry's checkered relationship with the reggae music biz—and of bizzes, there is none sleazier—has pushed him to the periphery of sanity, and from the shores of the Island to the heart of Europe. Starting out at Clement Coxsone Dodd's Studio One, Perry spent the first half of the sixties producing and singing on ska records. I asked him what music he was listening to at the time, and his answer was unequivocal: "American music! What do you think I am, stupid?! Blues, soul. And I'm a rock man, can't change that."

After breaking from Dodd, Perry worked briefly with Wirl Records, Prince Buster, and Joe Gibbs. In fact, Gibbs became the first of a long line of Perry antagonists; the sparring "People Funny Boy" was a direct attack on Gibbs and a smash-hit single for Perry's new "Upsetter" label. Inspired by ecstatic singing at an Afro-Christian Pocomanian church (*poco mania*—"a little insanity"), Perry is credited with inventing the newer, groggier beat called "reggae," which is said to have started in 1968 with that very single. His reputation for weirdness already firmly established, Perry was superproductive for the duration of the sixties and seventies, cranking out a massive load of his own flipped discs with his killer house band, the Upsetters (previously known as the Hippy Boys) and producing virtually everyone involved in the music. With the Upsetters, Perry nurtured his love of American pop culture, cutting singles like "Kimble" (named for David Janssen's character in *The Fugitive*), "Guns of Navarone," "The French Connection," and a string of instrumentals named for Clint Eastwood/Sergio Leone westerns ("The Good, the Bad, and the Ugly," "A Few Dollars More").

At the start of the seventies, influenced by stripped-down, bass-and-drum heavy instrumental records by the Meters and Booker T. & the MG's, Perry joined King Tubby in inventing "dub" reggae, a more extreme form of the earlier "versioning" (using the same rhythm track for different songs) and a crucial step on the road to rap. "The origin of dub is coming from a clear vision that if you want to make music and have a good clean bass and drum, you take them into the studio that day. And if you want a piano you take them in later, like that. Instead of puttin' them all in and making rubbish. The *funny* stuff, that's what's inside comin' out, so you put it down on a record. That's what it is, the ghost in me coming out." To work more constantly and independently, Perry opened Black Ark Studios at his Kingston home in the early seventies. There his dub work stewed and his mixes got thicker and further out.

Riding high, Perry had started working with Bob Marley, gathering a monster band with the Upsetters' bassist Aston "Familyman" Barrett and brother drummer Carlton "Carly" Barrett, teaming them with Marley, Bunny Wailer, and Peter Tosh. Thus configured, the Wailers cut some of their most ferocious music, nailing big hits with "Duppy Conqueror" and "Small Axe" for the Upsetter label. "I did it all," Perry told me off-camera, bitterly. "Everything. It was all my idea. I wrote it, recorded it, told them what to do." But after a fractious tour of the U.K., during which Perry sold Wailers tapes to Trojan Records and apparently kept the change, Island Records' mogul Chris Blackwell signed the band to a lasting contract, thus usurping the heart of the Upsetters, taking a band with the sound that Perry had personally tailored, the same sound that would go on to make reggae an international business.

Though he has worked on and off with Island since, putting out some excellent recordings with them, Perry openly despises Blackwell, and he con-

Lee "Scratch" Perry's *Judgment in a Babylon*
(Lion of Judah Records)

siders the English company another cultural imperialist enterprise (". . . he wants to steal Africa"). In 1985 Perry went so far as to release a twelve-inch called *Judgment in a Babylon*, the chorus of which went: "Chris Blackwell is a vampire, sucking the blood of the sufferer." But four years later he was back in the studio cutting another record for Island, the excellent *Secret Laboratory*. On "Vibrate On," he took a sharp jab at the label, starting the song by hollering to Blackwell's right-hand man: "So, Jambo, your master send ya to face the fire, eh? Okay, Okay, no hard feelings!" This struck close enough to the bone that the first line was mysteriously dropped from the final mix. Perry's attitude about the late Bob Marley is similarly unrestrained. "The cowardly lion. He was a coward because he didn't believe in the black monarchy and he didn't believe in the imperial government. He never believed in black supremacy. He didn't believe in nothin' but politicians and quick money. He didn't believe in me."

Late into the seventies, Perry persisted, experimenting with increasingly daring dub work, putting together a giant catalog of cuts, pressing his four-track studio way past conceivable limits. But the trials of time had taken a toll, and at the end of the decade the reggae pioneer, dub inventor, and Marley-maker was precariously close to the edge. Events are cloudy, but Perry was temporarily hospitalized for a breakdown and Black Ark caught fire and burned down. Rumor has it that Perry grew fed up with the Jamaican music industry and torched the studio himself, but he insists that it was faulty wiring. In any case, Perry chose to leave Jamaica—with stops in Amsterdam and London: "I am a black male on my side, and I'm mostly cooperatin' with the white side. I am a traitor and a blackmailer. I blackmail my color. Because they want to compete with me and I don't like competitors. They have no patience for me. I am a loner and I choose to be with the people who love me." Eventually he met Mirelle, who whisked him away to Switzerland. She convinced him to "put down the bottle," though ganja remains high-priority for Scratch.

Through it all, Perry remains a friendly kind of crazy. On an upbeat, he applauds grass-roots musics: "Congratulations to the hip-hoppers, punk-rockers, and rappers for advertising *their* words!" On the other hand, he calls Blackwell an "energy pirate," Dodd a "cold, slimy snail," Gibbs a "toad from the mountain," and Mad Professor a "false image." He accepts his reputation for negativity with a sly grin: "Everybody say they are positive. I am the negative man, come to spoil all the positive people's plans. I make pictures. Can't make pictures without negative. I am extremely negative. I don't want to be what somebody else is." Anybody else like Scratch? I just can't picture it.

Spiral Scratch—A Guide for the Upsetter Collector

Judging from the staggering amount of his music finding its way into stores, it would seem reasonable to conclude that Lee Scratch Perry regularly receives a fat wad of royalty checks. Truth is, he hardly knows about any of it, and is remunerated for even less. Could it be that some respectable looking record companies are little more than bootleggers? Right after King Tubby was murdered in 1989, his studio was robbed and many of Perry's valuable tapes were stolen. Strangely enough, many of the missing songs started showing up on Rohit Records, with licensing credits to rival producer Bunny

Lee. Mad as this makes him, Perry has words for such backstabbers: "Bob Marley dead, eh? Peter Tosh, I finish with him. So save your breath for the last scream, 'cause here I am the living dream!'"

As for buying Perry product, your conscience should be your ultimate guide, but these are some tips. Apart from scattered cuts on compilations, the only taste of Perry's earliest records is the fabulous *Chicken Scratch* (Heartbeat), which documents his extensive work with Studio One. From the Upsetter period, there are several excellent reissues, including the poorly remastered but musically fantastic *All the Hits* (Rohit) and a mighty cross-section called *Some of the Best* (Heartbeat), which includes "People Funny Boy" and "Duppy Conqueror." *Give Me Power* (Trojan) collects a number of older pieces, but also includes the original version of Junior Byles's "Rasta No Pickpocket" and the smash "Babylon's Burning." Trojan's *The Upsetter Collection* and their three-record (two CD) *Upsetter Box Set* are both brilliant, essential Scratchy listening.

Once Perry started making records out of Black Ark Studios, they came fast and furious and many of the original twelve-inch disco plates have found their way back onto wax. In the eighties, Seven Leaves Records released two volumes of *The Heart of the Ark*, both electrifying compilations of rootsy rockers and love songs. *Roast Fish Collie Weed & Corn Bread* is still available (just issued on CD), though the label listed is Upsetter, which actually no longer exists. Likewise, the enigmatic Anachron label put out a stunning collection of Ark material called *Magnetic Mirror Master Mix*, which includes Leo Graham singing "Voodooism" and Perry's own amazing "Bafflin' Smoke Signal." Trojan subsidiary Attack Records issued *Public Jestering*, a fine release compiling "verbal attacks and commentaries" launched from the Ark. Trojan has put out two double CDs, *Open the Gate* and *Build the Ark*. The first of these is the better, though *Build the Ark* contains Junior Murvin's unbelievable "Cross Over," with perhaps my favorite mix of all time. Anyone who thinks PiL's *Metal Box* was a major innovation has simply never heard this.

Plenty of Perry's dub work is still obtainable. Two ground-breaking LPs, *Scratch and Company* and *Blackboard Jungle Dub*, originally issued on the New York-based Clocktower label, are out again on Ras. *Super Ape* (Mango) is a tornado of sound, but *Return of the Super Ape* (Upsetter) is muddy and less interesting. Two volumes of *Megaton Dub* (Seven Leaves) are great, with echo, magnified percussion, funky filtration, and flange drum effects. Somewhat dubious but also highly enjoyable are *Black Ark in Dub* (Lagoon) and the extremely short *Blood Vapour* (LA Records), both of which reflect the dubwise genius of Perry, sound sculptor extraordinaire.

As a producer, Perry has crafted some of the most crucial music ever cut.

Lee "Scratch" Perry
(photo: David Corio)

Trojan has kept Perry's Wailers' records in print; there's *African Herbsman*, *Soul Revolution* (*Pts. I & II*), *Soul Rebels*, and the best, *Rasta Revolution*, which has "Mr. Brown," my pick for the best thing Marley ever recorded. Junior Byles's extraordinary collection *Beat Down Babylon* (Trojan) demonstrates the Afro-consciousness Perry was instrumental in cultivating. *Police and Thieves*, by lilting vocalist Junior Murvin, and the irresistible *Party Time*, by the Heptones are available as Mango CDs, and Jah Lion and Prince Jazzbo also made excellent albums under Perry's watchful eye.

Since the mid-eighties, Scratch has made a series of increasingly screwy vocal records, (often working collaboratively) with his own rapping, chanting, and ranting superimposed layer-upon-layer, like a churchical Ken Nordine. The least successful of these, like his collaboration with Mad Professor, *Mystic Warrior* (Ariwa), the so-so *Satan Kicked the Bucket* (Rohit), and the positively dreadful *Message from Yard* (Rohit), are marred by uninspired rhythms and lackluster mixes. Two stunning collaborations with Adrian Sherwood, *Time Boom X De Devil Dead* (On-U) and *Secret Laboratory* (Mango) are quite the contrary, however, with batty beats, carnivorous mixing, and Perry's brainsick invocations. Also check out *Battle of Armagideon* (*Millionaire Liquidator*) (Trojan) and *Mystic Miracle Star* (Heartbeat). A similar vein is tapped on *Spiritual Healing* (Black Cat), the wild recording he was finishing when I met up with him. Two powerful releases on Heartbeat extend this mode of activity; *Lord God Muzick* rests on potent dancehall grooves by Winston Niney Holness, and *The Upsetter and the Beat* unexpectedly reunites Perry with Coxsone Dodd at Studio One, laying wacky new words over time-honored old tracks.

FRANZ KOGLMANN

Meister of Melancholy

•

The year is 1969. You are in an Austrian nightclub, in the city of Vienna, seated at a table sipping cappuccino and munching on Sacher torte. After a while, the club owner appears onstage to announce the evening's performers: "Damen und Herren, tonight we are proud to present the finest free jazz group in all of Vienna: the Masters of Unorthodox Jazz. Please put your hands together for tonight's special guest, on trumpet and flugelhorn . . . Frrrranz Koglmann!"

Okay, so it sounds more like superheroes lost in a film noir fantasy than an entry in the jazz archives. But this plausible jazz moment was embellished straight from the casebooks of Herr Koglmann himself, a living testament to the existence of free music in Austria. "I was never a member of the Masters, just played as a guest," says Koglmann. "But I liked them. They were painters and only dilettantish musicians, but in an interesting way. It was the opposite of all that I learned in the conservatory, completely free and really . . . unorthodox!"

Twenty-odd years later, it is clear that this Viennese unorthodoxy might well have faded into complete oblivion if not for the tenacity of Franz Koglmann. Hardly clear-cut, the path that took him first into free jazz and subsequently into his now-fomenting cross between European classical music, free improvisation, and older American jazz is marked by the decisions and reconsiderations of a reflective mind. Trumpet studies from age fourteen pointed young Koglmann in the direction of classical performance and composition, but a live concert by Miles Davis abruptly changed his line of sight. As he recalls: "I realized it would be really stupid to be a trumpet player in symphony orchestra playing Beethoven, on one hand, and on the other to compose so-called contemporary classical scores for *nobody* to play. Jazz musicians compose their own music and they play it. That's the real thing."

As one of the first students of the jazz faculty at the State Conservatory in Vienna, Koglmann studied bebop and traditional jazz, but before long he became ensconced in the free scene. Although he didn't hang up his trumpet completely, around this time he also began to concentrate more on flugel-horn. After seeing Steve Lacy live in Paris in 1971, he asked the soprano saxophonist to join him on his first record. "I loved his introspection," remembers Koglmann. "When I first heard him I thought: 'Here's the Chet Baker of free jazz!'" In 1973 they recorded *Flaps* for Koglmann's new label, Pipe Records, supported by two members of the Masters of Unorthodox Jazz (bassist Toni Michlmayr and drummer Walter M. Malli) and a computer engineer (Gerd Geier) that Koglmann had met on a student job as a night porter for an electronics firm.

Emboldened by the artistic success of this record, he sent a copy to one of his favorite musicians, the similarly soft-toned and concise trumpet player Bill Dixon. "I thought maybe he'd be impressed," laughs Koglmann. He was impressed. And Koglmann was surprised to receive an unsolicited accep-tance from Dixon to play in Vienna. Seizing the opportunity, Koglmann featured the trumpeter on his second record, *Opium for Franz*, which also employed free-luminaries Aldo Romano on drums and Alan Silva on bass.

Both of these early recordings are straightforward, skillfully realized free jazz. Composition is minimal, consisting mainly of short themes, the blow-ing ranges from meditative to hot and heavy, and there is a hint of the plain-tive element, the melancholic undertone, that has become a central feature of his later work. But by the end of the seventies the free thing had started to lose its appeal for Koglmann, its brand of unorthodoxy seeming increas-ingly orthodox. "I can't say that I broke with the free improvisers," he spec-ifies. "Because there are some that I like so much, like guitarist Derek Bailey. But the typical kind of expressive free jazz became more and more boring for me. I mean, I respect the energy of Peter Brötzmann, but it's not my way."

The eight years between *Opium* and his next record, *Schlaf Schlemmer, Schlaf Magritte*, presented Koglmann with a creative impasse that resulted in yet another rethinking of his musical direction. As a special project for a late-seventies festival, Koglmann chose to unite jazz and classical musicians in a performance of original music. This notion has since germinated into the variable group he calls the Pipetet. "For me it was very organic," he remembers. "The different lines of my life came together at this one point, and this mixture of chamber music and jazz interested me. But I'm not a child of third stream. I never really heard it, just knew it by name. Later I heard Bob Graettinger and all the Gunther Schuller records." With this reorientation, Koglmann's identity gradually shifted from player to com-poser and arranger, from jazz musician to composite conceptualist. Soon thereafter, he began a fruitful relationship with the Swiss hat ART label, whose ongoing support and sympathetic production values have proved ideal for him—he, in turn, being the exemplary omnibus hat-artist.

In a strange way, the pipes and mixtures that dot Koglmann's lexicon may serve as the best clue to his music. He is a compositional tobacconist, uncovering commonalities between classical music and jazz and more broadly between music, visual art, film, poetry, and philosophy, and binding them in a Euro-blend that is entirely new, not derivative or imitative. "Even the earliest European music, Gregorian chant, is not pure," he muses. "It is a mixture of Byzantine, Jewish, Greek, and Italian influences. And jazz is a mixture of African music and European instruments and harmonies. In a typical bebop tune you hear the same chords as in a Wagner opera. If you think about the diminished chords at the beginning of *Tristan und Isolde*, you can hear 'All the Things You Are.' Both cultures are great mixtures, and for me it is a normal idea that these cultures should come together as a new mixture."

Although he is an avowed musical elitist, Koglmann tows an otherwise conventional postmodern party line. As he sees it, the classical and modernist movements of America and Europe—from bebop, cool jazz, and romanticism to free jazz, free improvisation, chance, and serial composition—have played themselves out, their pioneers having explored all the options inherent in their various musical languages. For him, it is crucial to be able to choose from any of these forms, not to adhere to one alone. "It is a wrong idea to stay in one system," he insists. "That was necessary for Schönberg and Webern, for example, because they had to find out all the possibilities of the system. But now we know the possibilities. And free jazz and free improvisation found the end of their ways the same as twelve-tone music did. It is absolutely necessary in our time to use all the systems we have and use them together."

Koglmann puts his dogmatic antidogmatism to work by combining compositional methods. Listen to the innovative quintet arrangements of standards with Lacy and the astounding Swiss drummer Fritz Hauser on *About Yesterday's Aesthetics*. Or the droll citation collages of *A White Line* (which caused quite a negative reaction with liner notes by Koglmann concerning the differences between black and white jazz that Koglmann now calls "an overstatement"). Or, take "Constantine's Dream," from *The Use of Memory*, which was inspired by Renaissance painter Piero della Francesca. Afraid that it might become a mere period piece, Koglmann decided to use a tone row "to stay in this century." On the same release, "Chateau de Bouges" attempts to apply the film editing technique of Alain Resnais to music. "He has a special way of cutting," explains Koglmann. "It is the opposite of flashback, a flashforward. I tried the same in composition. You hear an element and don't know why. And five minutes later you remember all the elements, you have them all together and then you know why they were there."

For another example of his methodological flexibility, listen to the Pipetet's ". . . Flüchtig, Ach! Wie Die Jahre" on *Ich*. In the middle of writing a waltz theme, he was seized with the need to insert a fugue for trombone and tuba. "But the fugue is always broken up, so you hear part of the fugue, then part of the waltz," he grins. "Theoretically, you could separate them and make a complete fugue and waltz." At the same time, Koglmann is quite open to suggestion, as is evidenced on four duets with Dutch pianist Misha Mengelberg on his latest release, *L'Heure Bleue*. "We didn't rehearse," says Koglmann. "I wrote him parts, but he said 'No, forget the parts. I'll just listen to your line.' So I played it solo, he said 'Okay we play now,' and we recorded. I really liked it because he immediately checked out the best way to do everything. He has an incredibly good ear and he played much better than I could write it for him!"

Koglmann calls his artistic nonallegiance "contemporary mannerism," an embrace of artificiality and rejection of naturalism in art. Indeed, the episodic, often kaleidophonic combinations of jazz, free, and classical forms on his hat ART releases support his claim that the only way to create something new is to delve into the past. To "start again," as he puts it, "to find a way not to come back to the same end point." He defies his father's generation: "Yesterday's revolutions are today's academicism." But he adds: "The revolutions of the day-before-yesterday have a stimulation effect like mellow wine. For that reason, Schönberg is telling me more than Cage, Tristano more than Taylor."

For Koglmann, choices of musical material largely revolve around an overarching concern to strike a balance between the two poles of his interest: melancholy and rationality. He sees the latter of these as a feature of his involvement in "Latin" (i.e., French and Italian) culture—Jean Cocteau, Paul Valéry, Marcel Proust, Igor Stravinsky, and more recently Olivier Messiaen, whom he calls "a French expressionist." As for melancholy, it is clearly in his blood, as well as his music. "Vienna is a melancholy city," he reports. "I think it has to do with the Slavic influences . . . they are extremely melancholy people."

Turning away from his preoccupation with dedications and pastiches, Koglmann is now trying to distill melancholy, and he is at work on an abstract suite for an eighteen-piece version of the Pipetet which will somehow relate to Vienna. Asked whether his understanding of melancholy has anything to do with the blues, he suggests: "Well, the blues is always major and minor at the same time. You have the major third in the chord and in the melody you have the blue note. Maybe this gives it an affinity to Viennese music, like Berg." But then he hesitates: "I'm not sure. I mean, what is the blues for a man from Vienna?"

PINETOP PERKINS

Boogie + Woogie

●

When he was nine years old, Joe Willie Perkins rigged a one-stringed instrument between a standing wall and the side of his house in Belzona, Mississippi. With a bottle for a slide, he played the standard Delta blues tune known as "Rollin' and Tumblin'," a musical figure that Hambone Willie Newbern would lay on shellac seven years later, in 1929. Versions followed by Little Brother Montgomery, Robert Johnson, Sleepy John Estes, and Baby Face Leroy, before Muddy Waters committed the tune to vinyl on two occasions in 1950. That was just nineteen years before Joe Willie—by then known as "Pinetop"—joined Muddy's band.

Pinetop is one of those capsule embodiments of music history; his career spans virtually the entire expanse of recorded blues. And yet, one listen to his latest release, *On Top* (Deluge), lets you know that he's a hefty trek from the preservation society. His firm, rambunctious style sounds as fresh now as it did when he started recording.

"Started out on guitar," says the seventy-eight-year-old Perkins, referring to advances made on less ad-hoc instruments. "I started working with a piano man, tunin' pianos. Learned one key from the other and then taught myself to play, listening to records. I started playing piano around 1930, doublin' on guitar. If I hear somebody play something once or twice, I can get it. I have a good ear; I can hear changes comin' before they get to me."

What he didn't hear coming was an angry woman with a knife, who, in the mid-forties, chose his main axe for him by severing muscles in his left arm. "I couldn't chord like I used to, so I stuck to the piano," he recounts, undramatically. "Before I got this muscle cut," he kneads his upper arm and fondly recalls his left hand of yore, "I had bass rollin' like thunder, man! Now I have to play straight bass, more like bass guitar." At the time of the injury, Perkins had been working for several years with Sonny Boy Williamson on KFFA's *King Biscuit Time* radio program, broadcasting from Helena, Arkansas.

In the mid-fifties, Perkins decided to move north to Chicago, like Williamson had, but he first stopped in Houston to make a couple of recordings for Sun Records with guitar great Earl Hooker. These included a remake of Clarence "Pine Top" Smith's original "Pine Top's Boogie Woogie," the very song that introduced the term "boogie woogie" into the blues and jazz lexicons back in 1929. "I didn't play it just like Smith," says Perkins. "I loved it when he played it, and I *couldn't* play just like it, but I wound up with a style of my own."

When he finally settled in the Windy City in 1954, Perkins had indeed developed his own chugging, boogie-infused style, replete with a darker side and jazz shadings. This made him hot property, even in a city full of monster pianists the likes of Lafayette Leake, Sunnyland Slim, Big Moose Walker, and Otis Spann. In fact, Spann was to play a decisive part in the next chapter of Perkins's musical story, which was interrupted by a hiatus, during which he worked as a mechanic. At the end of the 1960s, Perkins went back into the studios and recorded a batch of sensational sides with Hooker, recently reissued as *Two Bugs and a Roach* (Arhoolie). "That boy could play some guitar. Whooo! He played off and on with me from when he was about fourteen years old till he was about forty."

In 1969 Muddy Waters came to see Perkins and Hooker, telling the pianist: "Anytime you want another job, I got one for ya." Otis Spann had left Muddy, opting to start a new group with his wife, Lucille, and Hooker grew increasingly sick ("two bugs" = tuberculosis). So, Pinetop took up Waters's offer. After surviving a terrible car accident that put Waters in the hospital for several months, Perkins spent the next eleven years playing piano (and organ, and even harpsichord) around the world as a member of the Muddy Waters Blues Band, recording for Chess and then Blue Sky. In 1976, while on tour with Waters, Pinetop and guitarist Luther Johnson, Jr., each cut sessions for the French Black and Blue label, *Boogie Woogie King* and *Luther's Blues* (reissued on Evidence Records).

In the early eighties, the Waters band seceded and became the Legendary Blues Band, and Perkins played on a couple of records with them. After a few years of low profile, he once again emerged in 1988, with a Blind Pig record called *After Hours*. The nineties have already been extremely productive for Pinetop, with *On Top*, *Pinetop's Boogie Woogie* (Antone's), a live record with the Fabulous Thunderbirds recorded at Antone's, a CD with Diniu Dóra (an Icelandic blues band), not to mention session work, like his crankin' contribution to Zora Young's *Travelin' Light* (Deluge).

"I tried to play jazz, but my fingers were too slow," Pinetop admits. "I love Count Basie, Erskine Hawkins, Joe Liggins. But I was in a rut—got in some blues and couldn't get out of it." Then he raises his eyebrows and says: "But the way I play, I play like horn style." He sings "Salt Peanuts" and jabs at an air-piano. "See, I don't make turnarounds like nobody else. Other people, like Sunnyland, got them old-time turnarounds. But I really make it turn around!"

BARRY GUY/LONDON
JAZZ COMPOSERS
ORCHESTRA

"If I was a bass player," intoned Cecil Taylor a few years ago, "I would want to be Barry Guy." Jazz transubstantiation—heavier praise just does not exist. "What I'm trying to break down is the barrier between the instrument and the person," explains Guy. "To try to divert energy through the body and the arms actually *into* the fingerboard and strings." Indeed, to see Guy perform is to experience the alchemy of a consummate improvising bassist. Concentrating on textural minutia, at once he may shoot to another zone, perhaps threading a mallet between three strings, thwacking it and simultaneously tending to a lovely harmonic line on the final string. This compound of energy and craftsmanship is carried from his solo work into various ongoing and ad hoc duos and small groups, including his long-standing trio with saxophonist Evan Parker and percussionist Paul Lytton and his new trio with pianist Irene Schweizer and drummer Paul Motian.

LJCO 2 U

●

For twelve of the years that he was free improvising, Guy was also high-class moonlighting as principal bassist in Christopher Hogwood's Academy of Ancient Music, the pioneering early-music ensemble. "It was a hugely interesting experimental research project," he demurs. "Just like many of the jazz experiences, it was a question of exploration and opening up musical areas that I was aware of but in detail I had a lot to learn—working with early articulations, early instruments." Guy's decision to split from the group was in part internal. "From my point of view it actually got taken over by the record companies," he says, flying in the face of the typical image of "autonomous" classical music. "In the end, we were making records and not making music. I thought it was going in a fairly negative direction. Musically we were being steered by the record companies rather than by the artistic direction."

In the period since leaving Hogwood, Guy has had more time to devote to his hugest project, the London Jazz Composers Orchestra (LJCO). This, Guy's top-rank free jazz big band is set to release *Portraits*, its fifth recording for the Swiss Intakt label. In 1970 LJCO grew out of Guy's wish to explore the intersection of large-scale free improvised music and contemporary classical composition. "I was dissatisfied with big-band music where things were

Barry Guy
(photo: Marcel Meier)

still based around regular patterns, regular riffs, repeated chord sequences. Mingus's big bands were very inspirational to me in the way he could shift time and shift the space in which people worked. But I had the feeling that there was something that I could do—not with the black American music, but reflecting the move in Europe. Somehow, I thought there was something compatible between the rigors of, if you like, European music and the research that was going on in improvised music, that there would be a symbiotic, compatible area where we could meet."

Nevertheless, the Jazz Composer's Orchestra Association (JCOA), started by Michael Mantler and Carla Bley in New York in 1964 out of the remains of Mingus's Jazz Composers Guild, was an important influence. "One was very clearly aware of the JCOA's activities in America," says Guy. "I suppose the title of the London Jazz Composers Orchestra actually reflects that knowledge. Of course, I'd never been to America then, and I didn't know many Americans. I was kind of a greenhorn, really. When I got a copy of the first JCOA record, I was very interested to see the score that Michael Mantler did for Cecil Taylor. It was interesting because he was using proportional notation, and so was I. I had got my proportional notation ideas from Krzysztof Penderecki and Luciano Berio."

Working with an orchestra of improvisors contained certain challenges, especially considering the inch-and-a-half-thick scores that Guy was composing. "It was hard for the guys to adjust from complete freedom to iron barlines. Wisdom is to learn how to free everything up and actually retain structure, invent structure, have a kind of progression in the music. At the same time, to make everybody reasonably happy and give everybody a chance to really play, and to have an individual sound." The group's first record, *Ode*, recorded for BBC radio and released on Incus, was what Guy calls "a celebration" of his newfound friendships within the improvised music world, an attempt to draw together some of the strands of his interest.

"It must be emphasized," insists the composer, "that this is not the idea of 'third-streaming' the music, trying to get a synthesis. The idea was actually to do with structure and compatibility with improvised music, rather than trying to get classical music and jazz to meet. It's about the sound areas of improvisation and the structural activities of composition." Guy breaks up the LJCO's history into three phases, starting with his celebratory initiation and a period of increasingly difficult, abstract scores, moving into a second phase in which he opened up the task of composing for the group to other members (and in which they also played a Penderecki piece written for Alexander von Schlippenbach's Globe Unity Orchestra—the only band remotely like LJCO at the time). Phase three began when the group dropped its conductor, Buxton Orr. "Because one had a conductor, it almost made you write scores which needed a conductor. I wanted a looser arrangement, where I could actually give a couple of signals and the guys could be responsible for the initiatives."

Against the grain of festival novelty-need, Guy has maintained the group as a long-term endeavor. "That's the only way we can work out the problems of the music. You can't solve some of the problems in a year or two . . . or three." In its more than twenty-year existence, the group's personnel has remained remarkably consistent, spotlighting some of the premier players in European improvised music. The LJCO's seventeen members now include bassist Barre Phillips, saxophonists Evan Parker and Trevor Watts, trombonist Paul Rutherford, and pianist Howard Riley. "It's a soloist band, and as such everybody's playing for their life. There are no passengers."

Over the last few years, as the "third phase" has taken more definite shape, the group has moved away from exclusively "abstract and difficult music" to embrace an expressive paintbox that includes sonorous and melodious material it might have shunned at an earlier date. "It's not a turning back, not a retrogressive thing, but a wisdom about the totality of the music we're dealing with," Guy muses. "It's like visiting other planets and bringing back the good news from each."

GEORGE CLINTON

Every Dog Has His Day

●

Alone in the sound booth, George Clinton presses
the headphones hard against his ears and bears
down, squinting as he leans into a sensuous line:
"To-ooo tight for light . . . !" On the final word he falters and steps back from
the microphone. "Hey, that's a *human* playing that drum," he says to the
engineer. They're putting the final touches on what was originally designed
to be the follow-up to Funkadelic's smash dance hit "(Not Just) Knee Deep."
Almost fifteen years later, Clinton is gettin' down with a dig, an archaeologi-
cal dig, unearthing supergroovalistic booty in dusty tape boxes, covered in
half-scribbled names, dates, and numbers.

"Drum machine's always right there," explains the godfather of funk,
adjusting to the older track and readying himself for the next take. "You
know, it's: Ba! Ba! Ba! But a human decides to *laaaay* on that groove. I'll
have to pretend like I'm singing live." The engineer fiddles with a knob.
Suddenly, a nasty jolt of feedback zaps Dr. Funkenstein. Instantly, he pushes
the phones up onto his blueberry-blue knit rasta-beret, which squeezes his
voluminous hair together like a second head. "Uh-oh! Nosebleed!" he blurts.
A profusion of apologies follows from the sound man, but moments later the
mixing board once again undergoes a feedback seizure, this time much
worse. The engineer kills the screeching sound and looks in worriedly to
assess the carnage. But Clinton is grinning, the phones already back up on
his hat. "I'm cool, I'm cool," he assures. "I could see it coming—I read that
mo'fucker's lips!"

Purveyor of the P-Funk, main-man of caucasoid funkateers like the Red
Hot Chili Peppers and Royal Crescent Mob and black rockers like Living
Color and Fishbone, prime sample-mine for rappers and hip-hoppers like
De La Soul, Digital Underground, and Redman, and a continuingly funky
monster all on his own, the fifty-two-year-old Atomic Dog is also a grandfather. "Fourteen grandchildren, I *think*," says Steph, Clinton's partner for
sixteen years and wife since 1990. She is currently raising George's son
Tracey's—aka Trey Lewd's—two kids. "Anyway, a lot," she sighs. Known as
the maniacal wild-man of funky music, the same Star Child whose appetite
for drugs and lunacy caused even as committed a doo-doo chaser as bassist

Bootsy Collins to sit it out for a year in 1973, in person grampa George is affable and well-spoken, his fuzzy face shot through with white hairs and his fluorescent extensions curled atop his head like a neon medusa. Outfitted with a deep, bubbly speaking voice, it is hard to describe how many ways he has of inflecting a word, emphasizing a phrase, and most of all of laughing. He giggles, he snorts, he chortles, he snickers, he yowls, he hee-hees, he ho-hos, he ha-has. No megastar attitude clogs Clinton's laughing canal, even when a well-meaning engineer accidentally sizzles his earholes.

We retire downstairs to a stark lounge. Clinton sinks back into the sofa, comfortable and clearly at home in the studio ecosystem. Outside, the un-assuming concrete structure called The Disc, Inc. sits on a heavily trafficked street. It is fronted by a big white sign announcing the amalgam of studios associated with the Recording Institute of Detroit—though one corner of the sign is reserved for Motor City Collision, an adjunct body shop. The Disc, the branch of the Institute we are in, is in fact the very same East Detroit studio where, in 1970, Clinton and Funkadelic collided funk and acid rock head-on, with *Free Your Mind and Your Ass Will Follow*, the legendary LSD-basted record that has recently come back into vogue since being reissued on CD. "They think that's the best," chuckles Clinton bemusedly. "I'm so embarrassed. We did that entire record in one day, mixed it and walked outta here."

Clearly one of the bravest innovations in studio mixology, *Free Your Mind* was, for Clinton, the result of naive experimentation. "I had just learned about *panning*," he admits. "I still don't know about the board. I don't *wanna* know nothin' about the board. It's bad enough with one ego who writes the songs or sing 'em; you get all your different egos involved—your producing ego knows better than your singin' ego that you singin' shouldn't be that fuckin' loud! But your singin' ego wants your voice all the way up there. Your engineer ego knows that you ain't supposed to dub the shit on more than one blah, blah, blah . . . You know what I'm saying?" Putting down the piece of chicken he's wolfing for dinner, Clinton reduces his point to a saying from Sly Stone. "Sly say: 'Hey, man, don't learn no better.' I say: 'What you mean?' He say: 'If you knew better, you wouldn't do that!' It take you a long time to think about what that mean: if you knew better you wouldn't make those *nice mistakes*."

Capitalizing on those kinds of mistakes is one of Clinton's specialties, a skill he displayed when producing Funkadelic's 1971 record *Maggot Brain*, the title cut of which included a golden guitar solo from the late-great Eddie Hazel. "I learned to make a record out of any two minutes of noise I got," says Clinton. "I had four baby junkies; they settled to go to sleep right there on the session. So I had to make a record out of whatever I got. Once I

George Clinton
(photo: Mick Hurbis Cherrier)

learned to do that, fuck it, give me two minutes of *anything* I'll make a record out of it. Forget sampling; sampling wasn't even invented yet. 'Maggot Brain' was an excellent piece of guitar work, but the rest of the band sounded like shit! So I faded they ass right the fuck out and just let him play by hisself the whole fuckin' track."

The George Clinton saga goes back far beyond the proto-hardcorefunk that Funkadelic pioneered in early-seventies Detroit. He was born in an outhouse (aqua-boogie way back when) in North Carolina, and spent his early days in Washington, D.C., his earliest memories of which contain a couple of images (atomic bombs, flashlights) that, along with his famed canine imagery, he would later develop into an elaborate P-Funk lexis. "The first thing I can remember I was about five years old. My father had just come back from the service. The war was over, everybody was talking about atomic bomb. I can remember the blackouts, big searchlights all over the sky at night. And in the daytime you couldn't see the sky for rows and rows and rows of planes. I mean, it literally had a *top* on it, all day, everyday." As he passed his first decade, Clinton moved to Newark, New Jersey, where his cousin Ruth gave him a bunch of records. "I was right away into music," he emphasizes. "Then Frankie Lymon popped up with his little hit record 'Why Do Fools Fall in Love?' and that was it."

At fourteen years old, Clinton formed the Parliaments, a Garden State doo-wop group that stayed together through junior high school and in various incarnations for the next twenty years. "We performed all around town, dances, cabarets, and things like that. We'd go over to the Apollo and win, go back and change names, put on another wig and win again!" he bellows. "We did that two or three times." Parliaments personnel shifted as the group started recording for little labels like Apt and Flipp. Then, in 1964, Clinton began working for Jobete Records, the Motown publishing company based in New York, and the Parliaments auditioned and cut demos for Motown as well. In fact, even though Motown never put the Parliaments on their first string, founder Barry Gordy remains one of Clinton's idols. "I wish I could be like him," he says, dreamily. "You know, I like groups and business and family and all that shit. I think that inspired me to do this whole thing."

Clinton also worked professionally in a Jersey barbershop, doing the doo in doo-wop. "Uptown Tonsorial Parlor," he says, savoring the name in his mouth. "That's where we all used to work. And I had one called Silk Palace." Hair—and style in general—is a through-line in the story of Dr. Funkenstein. "After you've done other people's hair for so long you know the concept of doin' hair," he says, wrapping a bright braid around his index finger. "The garbage man looked just as cool as the pimp and the singer when they left the barbershop. Really, style is just a bunch of bullshit, it's just how you carry it. If you is safe with that concept, then you can be ugly as you wanna be or as cool as you wanna be and know that neither one of 'em mean shit! No matter how cool you are, you can go someplace where you look corny as hell to somebody. They thought that to have your doo was the corniest stuff in the world when you got around hippies. And then a few years later, the afros came out and then the black people started lookin' silly. So it means that styles just go 'round and 'round and ain't nothin' permanently cool or corny."

As it so happened, early encounters with the budding hippy counterculture were to prove a turning point for Clinton and Co. "Psychedelic *down*! I was in New York when it broke," he recalls. "I was there when the Cheetah opened up, the first one. They did *Hair* right there on the dance floor. We were all like: 'What the hell, what'd y'all stop the music for?' They went through the whole play, people stand up right next to you and sing 'Aquarius'": he looks around quizzically. "We was like: 'Damn, they sound good!

How did you know these songs?' The Cheetah was the hot-spot, with strobe lights and tinfoil, which would *knock your head off*! You didn't need no drugs! That was the cheapest high I've ever seen." Later, the Parliaments spent time in Boston and Toronto, drawn increasingly out of an exclusively black music scene and into psychedelia.

"We were still over in the ghetto in Plainfield, New Jersey, trying to sing for Motown. We got to Boston and the Sugar Shack—the teachers, the parents, and everyone was walking around hippified, half-dressed. You went over to Harvard, you could get the drugs right from the campus, be a test student and everything. We didn't know anything about it, we just knew about marijuana, 'cause from Jersey you be afraid of heroin, it was so much the big thing that anything that sounded like drugs was scary. Then you found out that people was runnin' from the war and understood why, and mainly us we were just chasin' young girls. You know, flower-child sounded like free-love, and we were dead on that! But after a while you start being ashamed of your whole ghetto scene, because you were able to travel. And me for one, I would get pissed at my wife 'cause she was jealous at the drop of a hat. Traveling around, you realize how people get trapped into that. I felt a *big* relief just being into that whole scene. It straightened our life out, made it much easier to survive out here. I used to make $700, $800 a week doin' hair, but always spent everything on cuttin' records. We got to Boston and realized that we didn't need suits no more, that the hip thing was jeans with holes in 'em. We said *damn*, we could easily do that. I grew up down South, I know how to be a bum! You mean that's cool? Sheeeet. So we were immediately out to lunch with it."

Those experiences with psychedelia would make their indelible mark on the group's style as well as its music by the time the 1970s rolled around. Along with new outfits that included bedsheets, Indian headdresses and loincloths, prison stripes, musketeer coats, three-cornered hats and wigs, street-clothes, and birthday suits, they experimented mixing gospel music, R & B, and soul with high-volume on amps they borrowed one evening from Vanilla Fudge. Right away, they went out and bought some of their own. "We had Marshalls all over the place!" exclaims Clinton, now dressed conservatively in a T-shirt, unbuttoned overshirt, jeans, and brand new running shoes. "So we became the loudest black band in the world, Temptations on acid."

By the mid-sixties, Clinton had taken his slowly emerging new sound and sartorial approach to Detroit and started working for Motown rival Golden World Records, producing songs for the label's owner Ed Wingate (whom Clinton still dutifully calls "Mr. Wingate"), and eventually recording the Parliaments for the smaller Revilot label. Just as Wingate sold out to Motown and Revilot closed down, Clinton took the Parliaments back into the studio one last time, recording three more songs. Out of a job, he returned to New Jersey and the barbershop, but in his absence one of those final songs, "(I Wanna) Testify," hit it huge, and he immediately found himself back in Detroit, this time leaving the hair-biz for good. A beautifully crafted, fairly straightforward soul song, "Testify" also had a downright lascivious element ("Oooh, luscious, sure been delicious to me . . .") that would later culminate in songs like "Ick a Prick," songs that made Prince's dirtier moments sound like New Kids on the Block. A revived Revilot took the group back into the studio several times, cutting among others a version of "Sergeant Pepper's Lonely Hearts Club Band." "Beatles?" says Clinton, furrowing the deep groove in his brow. "*Goddamn*, that shit is unbelievable! Like, what I do is read a little bit, find out what's goin' on, who said what, where it's headed. And it's a matter of ingredients that's past and current, mixed together. I may have an *intuition* for which ingredients, but it still can be done trial and error. But that shit Sly and the Beatles did, I don't care how many trial and errors, you can't get that shit back like it was."

Clinton's final single for Revilot, whose label owner Lebaron Taylor left town with the money from the very first Funkadelic concert, set the stage for Uncle Jam's next development. "Good Old Music," a mid-sized hit, listed a new group called the Funkadelics as co-authors. Rather than try to grab at another hit soul single after "Testify," a definite crap-shoot in a town with Motown's martial law, Clinton decided to go another direction. "We just went off into the psychedelic thing to be different," he explains. "We already had a little cult following because we'd already started lookin' silly. And it was such a different sound than everything else out there that we just went for that. We started treatin' it like a band, like a rock 'n' roll band. At the same time the guy at Revilot had skipped town and we couldn't use the name Parliaments, so we just recorded the band. They were our backup band, but then we switched it—we became their backup singers. And once we realized that worked and then we *did* get a chance to use the name Parliament again, we did. So we had two bands."

Thus was born the Parliament-Funkadelic Thang, a giant extended family that bounced back and forth between names over the course of dozens of records, numerous record labels, new sounds, new gimmicks, new members, and an ever-expanding legion of fans. Indeed, what P-Funk has since achieved is a version of Gordy's Motown, a crossover that didn't have to "blanche" black music, but extracted the meanest, downest, dopest parts of white music for its own designs. In fact, Motown's Temptations copped a good bit of P-Funkiness—"Norman Whitfield should have stayed out of our shows with his tape recorder, recording our shit!" says Clinton, good-naturedly. "More white people like the blackest of music than black people do," he suggests. "Public Enemy, white people like them. I found them to be the same as the Last Poets—I used to be *scared* to play with them. I'm thinkin' the white people are gonna go nuts! I'd get there and the white people came to see *them*." Around Motor City, in the late sixties and early seventies, the various madmen of pre-punk shared the stage and management with George Clinton. In the group of bands collectively known as the "Bad Boys of Ann Arbor," Clinton swapped licks with MC5, Ted Nugent and the Amboy Dukes, and Iggy and the Stooges. In fact, management cooked up a special marital publicity stunt for George and Iggy. "He could have been my wife," titters Clinton, glancing cagily at Steph. Proof of their racial nether-status, Funkadelic actually graced the cover of the second issue of *Creem* magazine.

By the time Funkadelic was through with its first few albums, Clinton, always looking ahead of the project at hand, had decided it was time for something else. "We felt that the early shit was over, the cool doos, and the hippy thing was done, with sheets and things. So we went right on to *America Eats Its Young*. That's when we started saying: 'Okay, let me see if I got any brain cells left.' Black was still popular, but if you're gonna do something you gotta do it better than the black groups *and* better than the white groups. And *Tommy* and *Sergeant Pepper's*, to me, was the classiest two pieces of music that I had ever seen where everything related to each other. So I wanted to do one of those kind of things." What came out of this was a series of loosely conceived concept albums that sunk Parliament deep into the hearts and minds of a fanatical audience, marked their place for good in the history of popular music, and instigated one of the most audacious tours of all time. "Black was it, so first it was *Chocolate City*," prescribes Dr. Funkenstein, referencing the album that renamed the nation's capital "C.C. and Its Vanilla Suburbs." Clinton boils down the overarching concept: "Put niggers in places that you don't usually see 'em. And *nobody* had seen 'em on no spaceships! Once you seen 'em sittin' on spaceship like it was a Cadillac, then it was funny, cool."

Chocolate City's follow-up, eventually titled *Mothership Connection*, is the one Parliament record to own if you're (foolishly) owning only one. The late Neil Bogart of Casablanca Records tried to convince Clinton to call it *Landing in the Ghetto*. "I said: 'No, no, ghetto is a cool place by now. You're late with that shit! People ready to build up the ghettos and *keep* 'em! So that ain't gonna shock nobody.' It was Parliament again, so if we're gonna go back to costumes we got to go way deeper, couldn't come back looking like Earth, Wind, & Fire or Ohio Players. We got to come back lookin' like we're *steppin'*." Out of their own pocket, spending nearly half a million dollars garnered from the smash hit "Give up the Funk (Tear the Roof off the Sucker)," Parliament mounted an unprecedented "earth tour" far exceeding any Spinal Tap fantasy, replete with motorized spaceships, pimp costumes, a huge publicity machine, and a motherload of sound. "We bought . . . whose equipment was that?" Clinton looks at Bob Dedeckere, the long-time P-Funk road manager who has serendipitously just stepped into the room with a handful of Clinton's dry-cleaning. "Aerosmith's," replies Dedeckere deadpan. "Yeah, everything was *huge*," grins Clinton.

In the sixteen years since mothership mania took funk to heaven in '77, Clinton has had his share of hits and misses, scoring big with ParliaFunkadelic pieces like "One Nation under a Groove," "Knee Deep," "Bop Gun," and "Flashlight," and, since 1982, with solo shots such as "Atomic Dog" and "Do Fries Go with That Shake." Still, in the brine behind his boat Clinton is said to have left a wake full of disgruntled partners: ex-Parliament drummer Jerome Brailey recorded *Mutiny on the Mamaship*, a record-length invective; ex-Funkadelics Fuzzy Haskins, Calvin Simon, and Grady Thomas claimed partial ownership of the Funkadelic name and recorded *Connections and Disconnections* under that moniker; Warner Brothers grew impatient when Clinton started his own label, Uncle Jam Records, while signed with them ("I didn't realize it bothered them that much . . . they never *said* nothin' to me"). In 1984 Clinton filed for bankruptcy; Prince, who signed Clinton to his Paisley Park label in 1989, allegedly paid Clinton's insurmountable tax bill at the same time. Indeed, over the course of the two-and-a-half-hour interview, calls from lawyers punctuate our conversation, and in the end Steph holds a hefty pile of legal faxes, some of which clearly have to do with the *One Nation under a Groove* album, as of yet unreissued, but owned by Clinton. "We're tryin' to get all these people outta the pot, outta the kitchen," he jokes, jovially. Clinton takes it all in stride, suggesting that Brailey should have released his record on Uncle Jam and speaking lovingly of Fuzzy Haskins: "Crazy, funky motherfucker. He's a preacher, now; got a hip-hop rap church song—he should put it out!"

Clinton may be laughing, but the other members haven't completely gotten over the sour deals that went down toward the end of Funkadelic's Westbound years. In the liner notes to *Music for Your Mother*, a two-disc collection of Funkadelic singles, Calvin Simon suggests that Clinton had taken too much control over their lives. "We didn't want to leave [Westbound]," he says. "It was George's idea, more or less. He said Armen [Boladian, the label's owner] couldn't afford to do what we wanted to have done. Warner Brothers would spend the money—that's basically what it came down to. At least that's what George was telling us." P-Funk is currently undergoing reissue madness. Westbound has put out their Funkadelic catalog; Casablanca's Parliament records are all available on CD; even the first Parliament record on Invictus has been reissued, in a remastered, fantastically cleaned-up edition called *First Thangs*. And, legal or not, the Warner Brothers records have now been reissued by Charly. Only the Revilot singles remain in the vinyl graveyard.

Dedeckere hands Clinton a couple of cassettes. "One has the rehearsal on it," he says. "Oh wow, that should be very interesting," Clinton replies. "Lots of sampleable shit there." He turns to me and cracks a shrewd smile through slightly in-turned front teeth. "We're sampling *everything* these days." Clinton has taken seriously the task of keeping up with rap and hip-hop samples, hoping to avoid the money-draining snare that caught James Brown. To counter the record company hegemony on copyrights, Clinton has bought a tremendous cache of his own funk, reportedly five hundred to seven hundred cuts, including live material, studio outtakes, and unreleased tracks some of which, like the brilliant "Too Tight for Light," were left just shy of completion. In addition to five CDs of full-length songs coming out as *George Clinton's Family Series*, there are five CDs scheduled to be called *Sample Some Disc, Sample Some DAT*, veritable samples samplers, with around a hundred eminently loopable snippets on each disc and simple, four-point instructions for obtaining permissions. "The idea is to make it easier for them to sample," explains Clinton. "When samples came out I realized it was a good way to be on the radio anyway and I could still make some money off it. Ordinarily, the stuff's been outta print so long that everybody just takes for granted that you ain't s'posed to get paid for it no more. Now they have to rethink all the things they been doin' to people. The record companies do send people to us now, to ask us can they do it. They didn't do that at first."

In fact, Clinton doesn't put his seal of approval on every sample that walks through the sound gate. In the notes to *Spice-1*'s debut album, a disclaimer on the one P-Funkified song reads: "Because of our beliefs, expressed in 'One Nation under a Groove,' it would be hypocritical to deny use of the sample, but we are not in agreement with the thoughts and ideology expressed in 'Peace to My Nine.'—George Clinton." He expands the thought: "Even though artists have the right to write and sing about whatever they write and sing about and you recognize that they're mirroring the streets, a lot of people don't understand speakin' in the third person. I mean, the way they jumped all over Ice-T was ridiculous, you know I know that. But at the same time we give them the right to do it, we make sure that we say that we don't agree with . . . *whoever said this.*"

A ceaseless entertainer and fonkin' educator who puts a premium on teachers ("They should be paid more than anyone in the fuckin' world!"),

George Clinton
(photo: David Corio)

George Clinton continues to take it to the stage. In each of the three shows I managed to catch at Chicago's China Club over the last six months, he put out over four hours of uncut funk before letting us drag our dead asses home. Truth is, he confesses that the recent influx of older, metallic Funka-delic material they've been featuring is the result of the Red Hot Chili Peppers reteaching them their own songs. And those present at recent live shows have also been introduced to his strangest current project, a sort-of "I can make anyone funky" magic act starring Clinton's Syrian chauffeur, Louis "Babblin'" Kabbabie, the most unlikely microphone commando you could picture: balding, white, paunchy, middle-aged, and a touch on the dim side, he nevertheless manages to rap a blue flame, while George's hand palms his egglike head as if telepathically transmitting some funky powers. Soon to be released—Babblin's debut CD, penned by Tracey Lewis, produced by Uncle Jam himself. Title? *Clueless*, of course. Clinton sings on keyboardist Bernie Worrell's finest solo record, the new *Blacktronic Science*, and he produced Trey Lewd's unfortunately underpublicized, deeply funky *Drop the Line*. Also on the agenda, there's George's long-awaited second Paisley Park re-lease, *Hey, Man, Smell My Finger*, and "Dope Dog (CIA I Owe)," a single that Clinton is putting out on his own One Nation label, for obvious content-related reasons.

"The business?" says Clinton, leaning forward on the sofa, reflecting on four decades in the music industry. "The vibe of people isn't there no more where the muther say, 'I *got* one, Frank!' It's a commodity now, for the most part. But everytime they try to make it a commodity, you get a bunch of independents like hip-hop and alternative music. To me, it's good whenever they try to make it like that 'cause it makes brand new music come out. That's the way rock 'n' roll was. So, I guess it's changed, but that same mentality of trying to get that buck and beat your ass out of everything is still there. Of course, it's a slave concept: they can loan you the money to make a record, you pay the money back, and they still own the tapes and records. Any other business, the product would be a fifty/fifty joint venture." He pulls down his jet-set glasses, giving himself an appropriately space-aged look. "But it's gettin' deep, I mean you had rock 'n' roll which kinda snitched on every-thing; now you got rap which kinda snitches on everything. If they keep mixing together, like Public Enemy and Anthrax and Run DMC and Aero-smith, record business is gonna have a *real* problem." Picture it: George Clinton, doggest of them all, rapping shotgun in some inter-genre, miscege-nist convoy of speedcore-death-thrash-jazz-funk, all the way right up to tattle on the major labels' big, fat, monopolizing asses. Sounds like snitch-and-a-half to me.

FRED ANDERSON/
VON FREEMAN

On the Radical Lounge Tip

●

Choose the pair of words most likely to evince
groans from a discriminating jazz fan. Did "jam
session" or "local musicians" come to mind? Two
of the faintest praises in marquee-ville. Isn't it strange, then, that two of the
toughest tenors in Chicago, Fred Anderson and Von Freeman, would both
actively embrace their *local* status? Big fish in a big pond? Stranger still, why
would these world-class musicians consider jam sessions to be among their
favorite possible gigs? Taking lemons and making lemonade? What gives?

In the first place, Freeman and Anderson share a regional perspective
born out of practical circumstances and life choices. Uneasy with terms like
"neglected" or "overlooked" (Freeman has called himself a "very popular
unknown musician"), each takes responsibility for his own low-ish profile.
Says Von: "I guess Fred thinks like I do: you just let the chips fall wherever
they fall. My son Chico's been trying to get me out of Chicago for ten years.
But I feel comfortable here. I'm busy trying to learn this horn and learn
music. If fame comes it comes, if it doesn't it doesn't. I've never sought it and
I don't think Fred has either. My calling is to keep trying to grow."

Anderson elaborates on the nitty-gritty: "I'm so busy out here just tryin' to
survive, you know? Keep the bread coming, keep my health going, pay the
rent. I never really think about the lights. I mean, that's cool. But I don't have
time to think about being a star. So, basically it's my own fault. I haven't
done a lot of traveling for the simple reason that I had a family and bought a
house. That was my priority and I was realistic about it. I knew the kind of
music we were playing, and there was no way I could have sacrificed them
for that. I love the music, don't get me wrong. But that was the way it was. I
said: 'I can do it right here in Chicago.' After my kids got grown, I thought
maybe I'd have a chance to do it. And then I got hooked up with *this* . . ."

This is a jam session that Anderson arranges every other Sunday afternoon at the Velvet Lounge, the small bar he owns and tends on the near-
south side. Further south, Von (or Vonski, as he prefers) oversees a jam
session late into every Tuesday night, as he has for the last ten years, at the
New Apartment Lounge, a two-room club (one red room, one blue room)

replete with shag rug, a stage that obstructs the entrance, and an amoebic bar. "I think Von put it this way," explains Anderson. "He said: 'Jam sessions can be very good or they can be very bad.' But even the bad times, you can probably get some positive things out of, you know? It gives a person a chance to deal with themselves. That's there whether they play well or not. The thing about it is that they were doin' *something*!"

More than just an indication of their beneficent, easy-going personalities, the local, open-mike orientation of these jazzmen indicates a broader current in the music. In fact, it suggests the existence of a vital and largely unrecognized movement, an underground lounge scene. Chicago jazz used to thrive in the high-class hotel ballrooms and dinner theaters—the Regal, Savoy Ballroom, Beehive—located downtown on 47th, 55th, and 63rd streets, where local jobbers would often set up house to play behind a constantly rotating cast of national and international stars. With the virtual elimination of those outlets in the 1960s (Joe Segal's Jazz Showcase in the Blackstone Hotel is a faint echo), jazz was pushed into the ubiquitous lounges that dot the Chicago map. It's the school of the Windy City streets, graduating an alter-roster of shadowy luminaries like pianists John Wright, John Young, King Fleming, Brad Williams, and Jodie Christian, tenor saxophonists E. Parker McDougal, Eric Alexander, and Lin Halliday, drummer Wilbur Campbell, bassists Larry Gray and Brian Sandstrom, and trumpeter Brad Goode, to name but a few. And the music isn't cocktail-tinkling fair. Indeed, it runs the stylistic gambit from the street-smart bop 'n' ballads of Von Freeman to the post-Ornette-ology of Fred Anderson.

Freeman is the quintessence of Chicago jazz. He has lived his entire seventy years in Chicago, starting on piano as a toddler and moving to reeds when he turned seven. Self-taught until adolescence, he attended DuSable High, where, like so many of Chicago's greats, he fell under the tutelage of the great educator Captain Walter Dyett. For a year, just before he was drafted into the U.S. Navy, Freeman was in the big-band of Horace Henderson, Fletcher's younger brother. "Henderson knew how to rehearse a band," he remembers. "I was only goin' on seventeen at the time, so I was the young kid on the block. He had all the pros in the band—I was old enough to know that I was way over my head!"

After a four-year stint in the Navy band, Von returned to civilian life and formed a group with his brothers, guitarist George and drummer Bruz. With the help of McKeefe Fitch, the famous Chicago booking agent, they landed a permanent spot at the Pershing Ballroom that lasted until the end of the forties. "We were lucky enough to play behind Charlie Parker, Dizzy Gillespie, Billie Holiday, everybody of note from that era. That happened and changed my life, really. Changed my direction, hearing Bird. 'Cause I was always out of Lester Young and Coleman Hawkins . . ." Freeman catches himself, then adds: ". . . still am! still am!"

Early in its development, Freeman also played with Sun Ra's Arkestra. "The band was in its formative stages," says Freeman. "Sun Ra's just a great man. I learned a lot from him and his group: Pat Patrick, who just passed, and John Gilmore." In fact, it was with Patrick on baritone sax that Freeman first recorded, on a single on the tiny Ping label, with the Andrew Hill Combo in the early fifties. From then until 1976, when he first toured Europe, the energetic saxophonist played continuously in his hometown.

Still today, on most nights Vonski is playing somewhere in Chicago. He's a shameless ham who loves to emcee events, talking on endlessly about nothing in particular. When he puts the reed in his mouth, though, things acquire a point. His rich, sometimes stinging tone took years to develop, and he has absolutely pinpoint phrasing. Most relaxed as a live performer, Freeman has had a spotty recording career, with a session for Atlantic and two LPS for Nessa in the 1970s, collaborations with Chico on Black Saint and India Navigation in the 1980s, and a more recent CD called *Walkin' Tuff*, made for Chicago's small Southport label. As a guest, he appears on numerous records with people like Willis Jackson and Milt Trenier, and he takes some nasty solos on a funky Groove Merchant record (*New Improved Funk*) with his brother George Freeman.

Though he legitimately claims the Prez-Hawk-Bird lineage, Von has remained open to newer developments. In this, he freely admits a debt to his saxophonist son: "I learned a lot from Chico. He keeps me current and he says I've helped him a lot. I listen to all of the young guys and I came up with almost all of the old guys, so I try to find a middle ground—not get too far out and not get too far in." Likewise, he credits the younger musicians who come out to jam with him: "See, the main thing is just to *hang*! It's so hard just to stay in there. And sometimes you say: 'Aw shucks, I think I'll retire.' But there's still so much to learn. That's the way I look at music. Guys say 'Man, you can play the horn *backwards*! What is there to learn?" I say there's plenty to learn, always. I'm up on the bandstand with cats half my age, [drummer] Michael Raynor's a third my age. But I've learned a lot from him. He's young, vibrant, stays into it. This way you get older, but you don't get *old*!"

The impetus behind Freeman's jam session work is not selfish, however. He offers it as an opportunity for younger players to learn from a master. Freeman acknowledges: "I was helped like that, so I never forgot it. A lot of people took me under their wings. So I try to perpetuate the same. It's no big deal, just somebody's gotta do it, y'know. It's relatively easy for me to do it, because I'm just a local musician. So we just talk, we're on the same level. I try to encourage them best as I can. I encourage them through example more than any teaching or anything. Try to play well, try to dress well, treat the audience well, and have people watch. Through example. This music, if it's not perpetuated, it will die out."

"I remember Von was playing in the 1950s with Lefty Bates, left-hand guitar player," says Fred Anderson. "I was practicing like mad in the fifties, but I wasn't playing professionally. I used to go sit and listen to him, I'd just be absorbing things. One day he had a chance to hear me. He told me: 'Keep on working on what you're working on, man!' One thing about Von, he encouraged me, never did discourage me. Always had something positive to say, whether he meant it or not."

Seven years Freeman's junior, Anderson was born in Louisiana and moved up to Chicago just before the U.S. entered World War Two. He too played piano as a child. At twelve he started playing tenor saxophone, and after the war was over a Navy friend turned him on to Charlie Parker. For the duration of the 1950s, Anderson was a dedicated music-sponge, practicing but never playing out. "I had a lot of respect for the music and I was determined to see what was going on, sit back, listen, and sort out the things that I thought were important to play. I'd listen to the guys talk and they would tell me about the chord changes and different things."

After working diligently on the fundamentals, Anderson finally began playing professionally in the early 1960s. An early concert came about when Sun Ra took the Arkestra to Canada, on to New York, and permanently out of Chicago. "They left here around 1961, and John Gilmore had a gig down here somewhere on Michigan Avenue. He called me up and gave the gig to me." Anderson soon started working with a bunch of musicians who would form the Association for the Advancement of Creative Musicians (AACM). Doggedly independent and strongly under the influence of Ornette Coleman, they played and presented their own music. With Anderson on tenor, Joseph Jarman on reeds, Billy Brimfield (who would become to Anderson what Bobby Bradford was to John Carter) on trumpet, the late Charles Clark on bass, and New Orleans drummer Arthur Reed, the first official AACM concert took place in 1964 at a rented space on 79th Street. Soon thereafter Anderson recorded with Jarman for Delmark. Still gigging around, he acquired a reputation that occasionally got him kicked off bandstands. "We took the music out a little ways. On sessions, we wouldn't play the licks that the people were used to hearing. Eddie Harris started telling people: 'Man, there's this guy in Chicago, Fred Anderson. You guys talk about *yourselves* playin' out, jack!'" All of this earned Anderson a moniker, bestowed on him by Kalaparusha Maurice McIntyre: "Lone Prophet of the Prairie." Anderson laughs: "Ain't that somethin'! But it's right. I was alone; nobody listening."

In fact, a younger generation of players *was* listening, and the 1970s were very productive for Anderson. Fresh out of Yale, trombonist George Lewis returned to Chicago and asked to play with Anderson. Groups featuring Lewis, multiple reedman Douglas Ewart, powerful drummer Hamid Drake, and twisted trumpeter Brimfield played as regularly as a free jazz band can. Over this period, Anderson's sound changed somewhat as well. After experimenting extensively with extended techniques, he came to prefer a direct intonation. "Clarity is very important. Being able to play each note and have each note be distinct. It's all right to do all these effects; Trane did a lot of them. But I play with a full sound, I don't subtone anything. Trane, early he had this sound. And I think Coltrane got that from Chu Berry, hitting everything right on the button. But you gotta have air, some lungs, to support it. So I quit smoking. And most cats are scared of the bottom of the saxophone. But I play the bottom just like the top. That's what I mean by a full sound, all over the saxophone." As with Freeman, recording has been little more than a side activity for Anderson, and the majority of his releases have been on European labels.

In the late seventies Anderson opened a north-side club, the Birdhouse, which he replaced in 1982 with the Velvet Lounge. "We used to get up on stage at 12:00 and play till 4:00 in the morning," he recalls. "That was important for those guys, gave them a chance to come out and play. You've got to remember, jam sessions were just about over. The young guys didn't have anywhere to go and play. When they play with me, they have a chance to really express themselves freely. That's what playing here every other Sunday is about. I let them do pretty much whatever they want, so they see what's really happening. Some come and play, and then I don't see them for a while—that's cool. They go home and woodshed. And that's what I used to do!"

Where Von Freeman insists that "the name of the game is to grow," Fred Anderson breaks down the jazz credo one step further: "You try to be an extension and some kind of contribution." In definition, the word *lounge* carries a strong connotation of laziness and loafing. In practice, Von and Fred know better.

SAINKHO NAMTCHYLAK

Madame Butterfly Knows

Only Enough

●

Sainkho Namtchylak is sitting in the front seat, zipping down one of London's narrow streets. She's telling me that she's not limited to improvised music. "You what?!!" I say, straining to turn around, crammed in the back of Ken Hyder's tiny car, sucking petrol, trying hard not to vomit, Hyder's drum kit jabbing me in the ribs. "That's right," she says, with a testy grimace, "I made a record with Andreas Vollenweider! Why not? Why does everyone think that improvisors should only play improvised? I like to try every kind of music!"

Later, in the less volatile environs of saxophonist/keyboardist Tim Hodgkinson's flat, the singer unearths the logic behind this seemingly impossible encounter between vanguard singer and new age harpist. "Okay, I'm living in the West, but I have Oriental eyes," she says, touching the outer corners of her lids. "I am looking out of my windows, my Oriental eyes, and I have Oriental mind. Western philosophy says: this is good and this is bad; this is allowed to be and this is not allowed to be. I don't even trust my own feelings when I see things that are ugly. So maybe it's not true."

Namtchylak is a self-searcher whose introspection has led her on a journey from traditional music into the avant-garde. She has enjoyed the kind of meteoric ascent that rarely occurs in the at times insular world of improvisation. But her insatiable desire to create new, deep, *moving* music also makes her a fickle partner and a ruthless critic of even her own music—a point she makes explicit when discussing the limitations of free music. "Sometimes I'm playing and I have this flash that it's empty music," she says. "So beautiful, powerful, and all, but it's empty."

Born in 1957 in the region of Siberia called Tuva, a site known worldwide for its rich and varied music traditions, Namtchylak became enamored of the ritual singing she heard on records. She taught herself to sing the extreme, exacting vocal techniques of two Buddhist sects: "Overtone singing is from Lamaism," she explains, "the other sounds—copying of animals, birds, wind, all sounds from nature—belong to Shamanism." She joined the U.S.S.R.'s Siberian folkloric ensemble and traveled extensively, demonstrating Tuvan vocal techniques for audiences in Australia, Western Europe, Canada, and

Sainkho Namtchylak
(photo: Pius Knüsel)

the United States. But she was not completely satisfied in that musical milieu. "With the folk program, I was a bit lost," she admits, in her dramatic, slightly pouty voice. "My voice was much bigger, and the emotion I wanted to express really free. But they're so limited, these pieces. Even if it's a ritual piece, ballad or something, it was too fixed for me."

After playing with the ensemble for five years, the restless singer heard a record by Vladimir Tarasov, then percussionist with the U.S.S.R.'s best-known free jazz group, the Ganelin Trio. She quit the Tuvan folk troupe and in 1989 began working with the now-disbanded Tri-O horn ensemble. "I'd *found* my freedom," she says with a tinge of irony. Yet after six months, she stopped playing with the group because, she says, "it was again not enough for me." In the midst of perestroika, Namtchylak moved to Austria and married wind player Georg Graf. Around that time, the improvising community started taking notice of her multiphonic abilities, her boundless range, and most of all, her knack for instant composition.

Since 1990 she's worked with many of the best European improvisors. She recorded a miniopera called *Tunguska-Guska*. The Berlin-based Free Music Productions (FMP) has taken such a liking to her that it has released two CDs, one solo outing called *Lost Rivers* and a quartet disc called *When the*

Sun Is Out You Don't See Stars, featuring German bassist (and Sainkho adulator) Peter Kowald, Swiss sax-maniac Werner Lüdi, and American cornetist Butch Morris. With such sudden attention, it would be easy to forget that she comes from a land in which culture was (until not long ago) centrally controlled; in fact, Namtchylak only recently heard her closest counterpart female vocal innovators. "In one night I heard tapes by Diamanda Galas, Laurie Anderson, Cathy Berberian. I was shocked. I was sure that I was the first to do these things. I said, 'It's *mine*, I found it!' I stopped singing and lay in bed saying, 'Should I suicide?'"

Fortunately, her depression passed, and Namtchylak continues to experiment both alone and with various ensembles. "I have no fixed group, no fixed program," she says. "I'm just a nomad in music." Such constant change jibes nicely with the free-music ethic, but she expresses some reservations about the improvisational status quo. For instance, in contrast to what she sees as the "olympic games" mentality of Western improvising, Namtchylak has formed a quartet called the Oriental Contemporary Music Project, a group whose motto is: *I know only enough.* "It is from Zen, written on hieroglyphs," she explains. "It means to study just enough that you can carry, to know really deep, to take small things, maybe, but to know it one hundred percent." In her solo show, wearing her trademark record album headpiece, she avoids the trap of becoming an ethnographic curiosity, singing brief, intense pieces that make sparing use of her spectacular throat sing. "It's important not always to have a kind of *circus*, going from one thing to another," she says, making prancing movements with her hands. "Sometimes it's necessary to have something very slow, very *few*."

Gearing down for the end of our interview, Namtchylak returns to her interest in commercial music. Contrary to the usual improvisor's dilemma— wanting to improvise but having to gig for dough—Sainkho says she would like to improvise more infrequently. "It's important not to play too often, but I have no other job. I'm looking for something else so I can play maybe only one improvised concert a month." She stops and begins to remove her severe eye makeup. "They ask me 'Are you a free-jazz singer or what?' I don't know who I am. I'm just a woman on stage"—by now she's talking to herself—"I'm just a painted lady on stage."

SUN RA

Eulogy and Light

●

A cruel twist on a worst-case scenario: I'd arranged
to meet Sun Ra at Chicago's O'Hare Airport at noon.
My timing would have been impeccable had the
plane not arrived egregiously early. Now Ra sits waiting in his wheelchair in
front of baggage claim, next to him saxophonist Noel Scott, his assistant. Ra
is silent and motionless as I approach, a purple cape wrapped around his
shoulders and a cheetah cap on his head. Suddenly, I am seized with fear:
maybe he's much sicker than I'd thought; maybe he can't talk; maybe he's
furious.

It's a cold Chicago morning in spring of 1991, and Ra is on tour with his
Arkestra for the first time since two massive strokes took him briefly out of
commission. When the deafening silence is broken, I help Scott hoist the
jazz legend into a limousine. It's a lesson in humility, a confusing jumble of
spirit and flesh: here is one of the great jazz bandleaders, one of the world's
most profound musical mystics, and for me a genuine hero, in terrible pain
and incapable of self-locomotion. As we settle into the back of the limo, its
forced proximity gives everything a fish-eye feel. Ra remains silent as Scott
makes small talk. Then Sun Ra's demeanor shifts abruptly.

"It's nice to be back in Chicago," he says. "You know, I've been to Europe
several times, Egypt, all over the world. Sometimes it gets so I don't know
where I am or what time it is." As he opens up and starts to bubble, the cab
grows perceptibly warmer, less claustrophobic and paranoid, more regal;
the experience is instantaneously transformed into an encounter with intergalactic royalty as Ra recalls the circumstances surrounding the Arkestra's
relocation from Chicago to New York in 1961: "First we went to Montreal.
Then we came down to New York, but we got into an accident. Totally
demolished the car. We had no money, and Sonny Rollins and Charles
Mingus asked me to stay in New York. So I did."

This fateful transplant was a turning point in the public history of Ra.
Chicago had been an excellent place to nurture the young Arkestra; Ra
expanded a trio into a smallish big-band with a cohesive core, an unmistak-
able identity, and around a dozen records. Chicago's booming jazz scene
provided regular working engagements, and the band drew enthusiastic

audiences, surprisingly tolerant of his mix of allusions to the space age and ancient Egypt and his use of unusual harmonies, timbres, and early deployment of electric pianos and proto-synthesizers. I wonder if the band ever got any negative response while based in Chicago. "Only from musicians," he says pointedly. "Nobody else. Audiences always came to see us."

To synchronize music-history chronometers, consider that Ra was recording with a synthetic sound source ten years before it was commonplace in avant-garde classical music, fifteen years before fusion brought it into pop jazz, nearly twenty years before the debut Tangerine Dream LP, and at the same time as Elvis Presley was crooning "That's All Right" for Sun Records. Ra's first synth recording was a duo version of the standard "Deep Purple," recorded with violinist Stuff Smith around 1953 (now available on *Sound Sun Pleasure*). "We recorded that in my apartment in Chicago," he recalls. "It was the first time Stuff Smith heard a Solovox. That was the mother of synthesizers; it came first. I played it for him, and then we made that recording on his home recorder."

The introverted Sun Ra was never arrogant about his innovations. "Most innovators don't belong to a time," recalls gritty tenor saxophonist Von Freeman, who worked with Ra for a couple of years during the Arkestra's nascence. "And like most innovators, Sun Ra had little to say; he let the band find its own way." Ornette Coleman's controversial eastward journey a few years earlier took New York by surprise; Ra's move likewise gave him greater exposure and direct contact with the multitude of players on the Eastern Seaboard. As our limo jets down Kennedy expressway, I ask him about his connection with fellow pianist Thelonious Monk, then a resident of NYC. "I never heard Thelonious in person," he says. "I met him, though, when I first got to New York. I met him before I had been listenin' to him. John Gilmore listened a lot to Thelonious and all the bop people. When I first met John that's all he really cared about. Then I began to show him some other things, like I did Coltrane."

The stretch pulls into Chicago's Marriott and empties us into the lobby. As Scott and Ra proceed to check-in, they wheel past P-Funk/James Brown saxophonist Maceo Parker, who is checking out, accompanied by his organist. I stop to thank them for their exuberant show the night before, and Parker's sideman nudges him: "Hey, that's Sun Ra!" Maceo, perhaps numbed to such outer-space spectacle from his years with George Clinton, points at Scott, who is dressed in plain clothes, and Ra, in his cape, cap, and rhinestone-studded sunglasses, then whispers: "Which one?"

Backstage, just before an Arkestra appearance in May of 1992, soft-spoken tenor saxophonist John Gilmore elucidates an epochal moment: "What

Trane heard that night was the rhythm approach," he recalls, struggling to be heard over a horrible prog-rock opening band. It's an oft told jazz-tale: Coltrane stands at the back of New York's Birdland, listening to newcomer Gilmore blow. At the end of a solo, Trane runs up to the stage yelling: "You've got the concept, you've got the concept!" In a flash, Coltrane's playing and the history of jazz are changed indelibly. As Gilmore tells it, this bemusing situation was the direct result of a clash between Windy City and Big Apple styles. "I was playing with guys I'd never worked with before," he explains. "They played differently than I did. Ronnie Matthews was on piano, Willie Bobo was on drums; it was kind of rigid. Chicago musicians play loose, you know, laid back. Musicians from New York don't play the laid back style. They play . . ." he beats out a quick, regular pattern ". . . right up on the beat. Chicago musicians, they be . . ." he taps out a slower, more fluid rhythm. "That was the way I was used to playing, and it was difficult for me to jump in there and get with them playing like that. So I tried another approach in order to make it sound right. And whatever I did, Trane liked it."

"We started out workin' in the Village," he continues, mapping the influence of Ra and the New York-era Arkestra. "That's where they started calling us the outer-space men. And that's when people started changin' their clothes and wearin' different kind of shit, after they saw us. That's when the afro came out, everybody started getting diversified dress." By most accounts, the Arkestra had started wearing costumes while in Chicago. "We had space vehicles, robots—just little toys, with lights and shit. We were doin' all that kind of space stuff, way back then."

In the early fifties, Gilmore was a hard bop saxophonist extraordinaire. Blue Note's *Blowin' in from Chicago*, which couples him with Clifford Jordan, is testament to his potential as an independent reedman; since then, Gilmore has made a valuable handful of non-Arkestra recordings with pianist Paul Bley and drummers Pete LaRoca and Art Blakey. "I think I could have struggled on through," he laughs a sweet, humble laugh. But in 1953, after replacing Pat Patrick in the bassless trio by then known as the Arkestra (which Patrick soon rejoined), Gilmore affixed himself to Ra and relinquished his solo voice to the will of the group. He says that Ra's composition "Saturn" was his revelation. "It was the jumps and leaps; so unusual, I'd never heard anybody write like that before. It took me a long time to *hear*, you know, to hear the beauty of it. And he's got so many others like that: 'Shadow World,' 'Cosmic Co-ordinator.' He's got some rough numbers, man! They equal anything you'd find on the symphonic level, and they will rival any horn player to try to play them."

The challenge of playing the material that flowed freely from Ra's pen hooked Gilmore for good. "There was never any boredom. No limitations, always new, fresh music. Half of the music we've played at rehearsal has never been heard, and maybe never will be heard. Some of the most beautiful stuff that we've ever done has never been played in public. I've got drawers full of music. Sometimes I feel for the public who will never hear it. For a period of time we'd go to different towns and he'd write something special for the town. Like Silver Springs, Maryland—he'd write maybe seven compositions about Silver Springs. And man, the stuff was so beautiful, but we only played it when we played in Silver Springs, you know? We'd go back over tapes and say 'Wow, what is *that* and what is *this*?' We even forgot the names of some of them, because we only played them that one time. You could never get bored with a repertoire like that, constantly changing all the time."

At another level, Gilmore admits that his loyalty also had to do with his relationship with Ra, with Ra's reliance on him. "You don't want to leave a vacuum with a person you've been with for so long, even though you can be replaced and things will go on. But you know after a person is dependent on you being there, if you drop out it's gonna take a while to train somebody else, nobody is gonna be able to get *everything* you had. No one person can knock the music off its course. Even though I know this, I wouldn't do anything to make it harder on Sun Ra, and I know it would be harder for him if I were to go. I can sorta hold it all together on the horns. He's on piano and doesn't have direct contact, and I know exactly what he wants most of the time. If I left, there would be nobody there to interpret what he wants and give it to the rest of the members. So I stay to do my share and help him. Not to burden him, that's why I stay around. It's not about us, it's about the overall thing. The unity, not the individuals.

"We just gotta bring him back to his full strength." Gilmore wrinkles his placid forehead in concern. "If we can do that, he's gonna be greater than ever. But we gotta bring him back to his full mental powers and physical powers. He's playing some different ideas now. He's got a lot of rebuilding to do, but if he's able to do that, he's gonna come out with some new stuff, I'm sure of it."

Winter 1992, Sun Ra experiences a third stroke. It's been a very hard year for jazz and the avant-garde: John Cage, Miles Davis, Hal Russell, Ed Blackwell, Phillip Wilson, Beaver Harris, and the Arkestra's own Pat Patrick have all passed. Rumors are that longtime Arkestra altoist Marshall Allen is not in great shape, and John Gilmore—very short of breath during our interview six months back—is absent on an Arkestra record for the first time in more than twenty years; *Destination Unknown* (enja) was recorded while Gilmore was busy rebuilding his own physical powers. I phone the Morton Street house in Philadelphia where Ra and various Arkestra members have lived since moving down the East Coast around 1971. Gilmore answers and explains that Ra is in rehabilitation. "Did you hear about our singer?" he asks. "June Tyson died last week. Breast cancer."

Immediately I think of the first interview I did with Ra, in 1985. Ra had pontificated beautifully, rummaging around beloved topics from the possibility of impossibility to his "nerve-music"—"See, on the earth plane they got nerve-gas and all that," he'd said, sweeping his hand majestically. Gilmore was sitting behind him, eyes shut tight, nodding appreciatively. "Well actually I've got some nerve-music. I play my nerve-music and get these folks on the planet in order." At this, the child-faced Tyson, standing at his side, started giggling uncontrollably. At first I wondered whether she was laughing at him, but then I thought about it: it was *funny*, that's all. The last time I saw Tyson, in May, she looked as ageless and healthy as ever, scraping madly on an unmiked violin and singing: "We travel the spaceways, from planet to planet . . ." She was fifty-six when she died.

Sun Ra's civilization is in rough shape. In 1986 the Arkestra played at alto saxophonist Jimmy Lyons's benefit, while he lay dying of lung cancer. Sun Ra was resplendent, in a tiger cape which he held in each hand as he conducted the band in his own, inimitable way, alternately pounding out epileptic barrelhouse solos on a concert grand piano. Now, with Ra in the hospital, a few benefits are being arranged for him. Arkestra trumpeter Michael Ray will play a tribute with his Cosmic Krewe at the New Orleans Jazz and Heritage Festival, and fellow trumpeter Ahmed Abdullah has formed Satellites of the Sun, a Sun Ra repertory band. Another project consists of a real estate deal aiming to purchase a house in the crescent city—a sort of Arkestra retirement home, privately bankrolled by a concerned patron.

Dizzy Gillespie slips away on the same day I reach Ra. "I'm also thinking about a house in France," says the Ambassador to the Omniverse, in typically grandiose terms. On the phone from his Philly rehab center, Ra's speech is mildly impeded, and, to his frustration, he forgets a few names. He is still in fine form, loading his answers with meaning. But where he once rambled, constructing elaborate double-entendres and brilliant wordplay, Ra now answers directly and offers little more than he is asked; he's more inclined to talk about music and less about cosmic equations. I wonder if Gilmore will move with him. "Yes," he says, confidently, then chuckling: "He doesn't know 'bout it yet, though."

To start, I ask how space became a central feature of his work. "Introducing the space age—I been singing about space all this time." Then, in unusually down-to-earth terms, he explains: "I had dreams about space. That's

June Tyson and Sun Ra
(photo: David Corio)

why I named the record company Saturn." I continue by inquiring about the period in New York when the Arkestra worked very little, rehearsals constituting most of their playing as a unit. "I didn't really want to work," offers Ra. "I always like the low profile." I suggest that his profile had grown pretty high, and he counters with a characteristic paradox: "That's because that's the way life is. It gives you things you don't want. So therefore I didn't care about the profile. I didn't care about the money." Two things that he *didn't* want and therefore *might* get. "I cared about the music," he says. "And that made a lot of musicians afraid of me." Perhaps this betrays a slight paranoid streak, but there clearly were musicians and jazz aficionados alike who perceived—and continue to perceive—Ra's unconventional music as a direct threat.

In a booklet enclosed with the Arkestra's first record, *Jazz by Sun Ra* (now reissued as *Sun Song* on Delmark Records), Ra expressed disappointment at Duke Ellington's statement that he was not interested in educating people; indeed, Ra has taken on the task of global pedagogy—as a supersonic cosmo-science sermonist. I ask if in the age of edutainment—in a period when Ra has expressed frustration with the seeming indifference of the black community to his music and philosophy—he still feels so strongly about education. "As long as a person holds his spirit together, I'm interested in them," he says. "I'm not interested in the *wrong kind* of education."

He continues by reinforcing his admiration for various pianists, including Ellington. "Duke Ellington was greater than people realize. Playing the piano, too. They didn't notice his piano playin' much, but he was really great." Ra also expresses a love of Art Tatum. "He played so lyrical," says Ra. "Another piano player I used to like was called Herman Chittison. Round the same time I used to listen to Tatum. Don't seem to be too many people know about him, but he was a wonderful pianist. Another pianist, Avery Parrish: one of my favorites. We went to school together. He used to play with Erskine Hawkins." In the 1940s, Ra spent time playing piano and arranging for Fletcher Henderson's band, which for him was quite a treat. "Unbelievable," Ra blurts in recollected exhilaration. "I always did like Fletcher. As a little child . . ." he continues, projecting himself into another identity, as young Herman "Sonny" Blount, in Birmingham, Alabama, in the late 1920s, ". . . I listened to Fletcher Henderson, Coleman Hawkins, Red Allen, people like that."

At this point, back in his childhood, Ra stops the interview; either he's tired or it's dinner time. As we hang up, I wonder to myself whether I'll ever see him play again. When Sun Ra does finally move on to other planes of there, he will have left a deep impression on this meager, often thankless and inhospitable planet, as a prophet, as a musician, and as a person who has held his spirit together. Space may be the place, but we are fortunate he joined us down here on the ground. Or, as saxophonist and composer Anthony Braxton—who has learned much about both musical and verbal creativity from Mr. Ra—puts it: "I view the work of Sun Ra as *essential*, as an essential component that must be experienced as part of moving into the constructs of the next thousand years."

Doo Wop Coda

Lower than it oughtta be, a baritone voice "oohs" its way through a bass, drums, bongo, piano intro: "Ooooh . . . Dreaming, dreaming / Here I am dreaming again / Dreaming, dreaming / I'm in a daydream again / Sleeping, sleeping / It's time for me to wake up / For no matter how I dree-eam / It always makes me cry . . ." The four voices change key for the bridge: "If you live in fables then you'll know what I mean / For that is a world where things aren't what they seem / Dreaming . . ."

First of all, there's the almost imperceptible, lurching piano, a Sun Ra trademark. And then there are the just off-center lyrics, which in retrospect seem like Ra deciding whether or not to make the trip over into his myth-science fable-world for good. Were it not for these factors, one could easily mistake it and its Rudy Valeeish flip-side for a normal, middle-of-the-road fifties vocal track. As it is, it's caught somewhere between a sock-hop and the outer limits. "I had two vocal groups at the same time," says Ra. "One was called the Cosmic Echoes. And the Cosmic Rays, too." Not destined for the Top 10, the Cosmic Rays' "Dreaming" (b/w "Daddy's Gonna Tell You No Lie"), a seven-inch single released on Saturn Records, is nonetheless a fascinating blip in the histories of Ra and doo-wop. It's now available only as a bootleg, and good luck finding one. "I met them through a friend," remembers Ra. "It was at the same time that John Gilmore joined the band. I saw the possibility they could really be great. So I began to teach them, to coach them. They were connected with a barber shop, but I taught them other things."

"Some of them were barbers," recalls John Gilmore. "We'd go down to the barber shop and rehearse them. Sun Ra had them singin' some beautiful stuff." Early as this was, around 1953, it was probably a part of Ra's attempt at community building, the same notion that would eventually turn the Arkestra into a communal living arrangement. "I think he probably was saving them from themselves," says Gilmore. "They were around and weren't doing anything. He heard them, heard their potential, snatched them off the street, and started making them do something constructive. As it was, all of them wound up tragically, except for one. He was the only one to last for a while, then he went through some tragic experiences in '88 or '89. But the rest of them, they were *wild*, you know. Wild young cats. He did the best he could with them."

The Cosmic Rays, a quartet of anonymous bad-ass kids, singing with Ra in the mid-fifties. Just think, a year or so later a different bunch of wild youngsters start working in a Newark, New Jersey, barber shop called the Uptown Tonsorial Parlor and rehearsing doo-wop at night. They are led by fourteen-year-old George Clinton and call themselves the Parliaments; later they will lose the "s" and, twenty years on, mount a tour premised on the landing of an Afrocentric spaceship. A bizarre coincidence, perhaps. Then again, maybe it exposes the hidden cosmic interconnectedness, the mystical barbershop/doo-wop link in the Sun Ra–Dr. Funkenstein chain. Or am I just dreaming, dreaming . . .

Inherit the Sun—Sun Ra's Sunset

> . . . They are the chosen ones
> . . . The begottened begardened
> Restin' in their place of berth . . . .
> . . . . they were borne
> > To their place of rest.
> > > It is a backward version of birth
> > > > Which is better stated as a re-birth.
> A rebirth is being born again . . . .
> . . . . A cryptic word of crypt-intent . . . .
> —Sun Ra, "The Garden Of Eden,"
> from *The Immeasurable Equation*

The funeral program reads: "Graveside Obsequies Celebration of the Homegoing of Sun Ra, Elmwood Cemetery, Birmingham, Alabama, Saturday, June 5, 1993, 12:00 Noon." Le Sony'r Ra died on May 30, 1993, after the series of strokes that started in 1991. Ra came to this earth via Birmingham, the city of his sad and lonely childhood and a humanoid family he vigorously disavowed, and it was from Birmingham that he returned to outer space, to travel the spaceways from planet to planet, to sprinkle the Milky Way with his own mad musical pixie dust. Not a homecoming, but a home-*going*—Birmingham was both Ra's landing spot and his launching pad. Buried in full space regalia, with appropriate music chosen by Arkestra bassist and trumpeter Jothan Callins, the headstone proudly decrees his rightful name: "Sun Ra."

In a just world, the musical significance of Sun Ra and his Arkestra would be beyond refute. Synthesizer pioneer, piano avatar, brilliant orchestrator and arranger, master craftsman of the large-scale open jam, and the single most important big-band composer and bandleader since the swing era, Ra was finally elected into the *Down Beat* Hall of Fame by the critics in 1984. A question as insulting and ignorant as "Sun Ra: Visionary or Con Artist?"—the very headline that ran on the cover of *Jazz Times* just a month before Ra died—would be embarrassing if it wasn't so hurtful. Indeed, Ra was deeply affected by a disbelieving article that ran in an Atlanta newspaper in 1992. Of course, anyone claiming to be from the planet Saturn will be the subject of continuing ridicule, no matter how irrefutably out of this world and truly prophetic their music is. In that respect, Ra's outlandish image and philosophy of the impossible may threaten to overshadow his musical achievements as he goes down in the annals of jazz history.

But more imminent and pressing threats now face Ra's widowed band: staying together and procuring work. The first question is whether people will book the Arkestra without Sun Ra, and furthermore whether the band will be able to continue to work at as high a level as they did when Ra was alive. After refusing the job for some time, tenor saxophonist John Gilmore has finally accepted the daunting task of leading the Arkestra, which will be known as Sun Ra's Arkestra directed by John Gilmore. Trumpeter Michael Ray also has his own band, Cosmic Krewe, which features half-Ra/half-Ray material and attempts to "keep the cosmic pageantry alive, with a costumier, banners, and the like." As for the Arkestra, they have only just started thinking about a new keyboardist; Dave Burrell has contacted them, Gilmore is considering Jaki Byard and Muhal Richard Abrams as well, and rumors are circulating that Cecil Taylor might want to take over the band. "I'm gonna knock them into shape," says Gilmore from the Morton Street abode where many Arkestra members have hung their hats over the last two decades. "Ra would try something once, maybe twice, and if everybody wasn't with it he'd just move on. Me, I'm gonna straighten them out! The funny thing is that we have so much music that we never even played, beautiful music, that we don't even need anyone writing for us. We're a repertory band, but we've got a lot of new music. No problem there!"

After the first series of strokes debilitated Ra, clubs started to cancel dates. Gilmore hopes that this will change now that there's no chance of waiting for Ra to recover, though with his severe emphysema there are legitimate questions about Gilmore's own capacity to lead the band. Indeed, Gilmore now doubles Kenny Williams on tenor for nights when he finds it particularly hard to breathe. Taking the frontline in booking the Ra-less Arkestra, New York's Bottom Line was the site of a post-funeral extravaganza. Many of the band members flew to Birmingham and then returned that night for the gig, which featured guest appearances by poet Amiri Baraka, violinist Billy Bang, Arkestra-alum (and ex-Monk-) bassist John Ore, and—weirdly enough—guitarist Stanley Jordan, who played with the Arkestra once at Sweet Basil, years ago. "Jordan was *cookin'*, jack!" exclaims Gilmore, sensing my skepticism. "He was playing space guitar, unbelievable!" Is it a turning point in Jordan's career, or a symbolic death knell for the Arkestra? I can't help wondering.

Lurking beneath these immediate worries are a host of deeper concerns about the state of Ra's estate. As you might expect, Ra had no last will and testament. This means that all his belongings—including the house, which saxophonist Marshall Allen's father signed over to Ra years ago—are now liable to be claimed by the next of kin, that is, by Ra's sister Mary Jenkins. "Sparks are definitely gonna start flying," says Gilmore. "But the band doesn't have anything. We were broke when he was here and we're broke now that he's gone." What hangs in the balance, among other things, is any income for the band from future royalties on past recordings. The family, which had virtually no connection with Ra or his career, has already laid claim to Ra's entire wardrobe and personal effects, and lawyers are working on the rest. But when it comes to the sheet music, which is in various states of condition, some extensively copied and existing in multiple editions, some limited to one crumbling page, Gilmore grows animated: "Man, they can't touch that! There's so many arrangers other than Sun Ra, like Hobart Dotson, Pat Patrick, Julian Priester. They can't know *whose* it is."

"I'm not gonna mess with his things till everything gets straightened out," says Jenkins, though in truth she has turned all legal duties over to her niece Marie Holsten. Asked about her relationship with her brother, Jenkins reaches back to a trip to visit in-laws in Chicago three years after Sonny had vanished from Birmingham without trace. "Someone said, 'Hey, Mary, you got some kin here. He's the one makin' all that music!'" she recalls. The siblings then lost touch for some thirty-five years before Ra phoned to say he was being inducted (at the same time as Jo Jones) into the Birmingham Jazz Hall of Fame. "He told me to get all the kinfolk together," says Jenkins, with a sprig of pride. "We got our pictures taken with him." After this, the two maintained limited contact, Jenkins calling the house from time to time until Ra's first strokes, at which time she traveled to his Philadelphia hospital. "Everything was fine," she says. "Then they sent him down here and it just about ruined my life."

"They"—the Arkestra—sent Ra to Birmingham for good reason. "We had no central heat," explains Gilmore. "And his room was right next to the front door." After suffering a third stroke, Ra recovered in a Germantown rehabilitation center, but when he was discharged, in the middle of cold

Philadelphia winter, it was decided that he should stay with his sister. Jothan Callins, who is also from Birmingham, took Ra on the long train ride south. So began the grim last days of Sun Ra, who promptly caught pneumonia on the train. He stayed only briefly at Jenkins's house before medical care was needed, at which time it was discovered that Ra had a long-untreated hernia. Five days after treatment for pneumonia, reputedly without consent or consultation with his Philadelphia physicians, Ra was operated on, and never recovered. Gilmore says that a major malpractice suit is now being looked into.

The "sparks" that Gilmore mentions are thus not the Arkestra's. Though a certain portion of the group is attempting to set up an "Arkestra Foundation," in fact, the Arkestra is currently at the mercy of other powers in the fallout controversy now developing in the wake of Ra's death. Those powers are, on one hand, Ra's relatives and variously potentially malevolent forces within the band itself (items have been disappearing from the house, including tapes), and, on the other hand, various academic institutions who have expressed interest in housing the Sun Ra archives, and Sun Ra's longtime patron, friend, business partner, and co-mystic, Alton Abraham.

"The story can now be told," says Abraham across a café table at the beginning of a rare interview. He reaches into a large briefcase and extracts a bundle of documents. Sifting through them, he selects one and instructs me to read it. It is the original legal paperwork from October 20, 1952, that changed Herman Poole Blount into Le Sony'r Ra. It is a magic document, we both know, and he spreads a broad smile and hands me another piece. This time it's a booklet from the American Federation of Musicians, the original registration papers for Saturn Records, from 1956, with Alton Abraham signing in as president. "I wanted to establish who I am, my credentials," he says. "You see, I own the name Sun Ra. We always shared everything; he always said *we* were his family. And you don't need any Arkestra Foundation—our company, Ihnfinity Inc., that's the foundation." Among other papers that he produces upon request are the original contracts that he negotiated with ABC for the Impulse series (two sets of releases in the mid-seventies, extremely important in Ra's career) and a rough draft of the paperwork for Blue Thumb Records' *Space Is the Place*. Scanning this contract, I pick out a clause with an "x" through it that reads "Concerning copyright on planets other than earth . . ." Abraham nods: "Yeah, I guess we decided to take that out."

Herman Blount (pronounced "blunt"), probably born on May 22, 1917, first played in Chicago in 1934. He was just out of high school, but returned for college at Alabama A & M, known at the time as the State Agricultural and Mechanical Institute for Negroes. Blount and Alton Abraham

Sun Ra's name change documentation
(courtesy: Alton Abraham/El Saturn Records)

met around 1951, well after Blount had settled in Chicago. On the South Side, Abraham was part of a group of people, a sort of open-secret society, researching ancient civilizations, astrology, German philosophy, and outer space, spreading their findings through soapbox lectures in Washington Park; this group eventually included James Bryant, another early Ra supporter who joined Abraham and me at the café. Abraham and Blount (who was working behind a curtain at whites-only strip joints in Calumet City) struck up a friendship, and over the next few years Abraham forcibly convinced Ra to change his name, paid his rent, bought him food and instruments, booked him in clubs, helped build the Arkestra to a seven- and finally eleven-piece band, and took Ra from being a reclusive misanthrope ("'I hate black people,' said Sun Ra," recounts Abraham. "'I don't know about white people, I don't know any. But I know I hate black people.'") to the spotlit kid he became.

When Ra left Chicago and moved to New York in 1961, the Arkestra worked only sporadically, and some members did very unusual studio jobs; Pat Patrick played sax and Ra played organ on a popular version of "The Batman Theme," for instance. Throughout this time, Abraham supported them, sending money constantly, and when the group settled in Philly, Abraham gave them vans, station wagons, recording gear, and more money. "I gotta deal with Abraham," says Gilmore. "I don't have any clout, no lawyers. He's been here for forty years, a friend, gave plenty of money, plenty! He and Sun Ra may not have seen eye to eye all the time, particularly towards the end, but Alton's been there for us the whole time." In fact, Saturn Research has maintained the same post office box since the early fifties, and Abraham owns a huge archive of historical materials, numerous tapes (which he claims ownership of as continuing president of Saturn), several vintage Ra pianos, early synthesizers, and other odds and ends that could probably fill a warehouse. Since Ra's first stroke, Saturn has experienced a series of thefts—probably by musicians or musicians' friends. Abraham leaves the door open for anyone wanting to return stolen items, report bootlegs, or fink on the thieves (Saturn Research, P.O. Box 7124, Chicago, Illinois, 60680).

For the record-buying public, there is a seemingly bottomless Ra archive already available and more on the way. Evidence Records is busy reissuing a number of the Impulse records (*Atlantis, Magic City, Angels and Demons at Play with Nubians of Plutonia, Fate in a Pleasant Mood*) as well as an important collection of long-obscure Saturn singles. Leo Records has just put out an unusual 1990 collaboration between the Arkestra and a Parisian symphony orchestra; there are Black Saints, A&Ms, Leos, Delmarks, DIWs, hat ARTS, and much more. And for those who never saw Ra live, the public estate contains at least four full-length films—the mediocre French *Mystery,*

Mr. Ra, Robert Mugge's fantastic *A Joyful Noise* (both of these are available on video), the newly discovered narrative film *Space Is the Place*, and Edward O. Bland's fascinating *The Cry of Jazz*, which features the Chicago Arkestra, circa 1959, with plenty of hot blowing by an uncredited John Gilmore, a demonstration of jazz rhythm by Ra on piano, and a bizarre trek through jazz history with the Arkestra. Of course, whatever the outcome of the custody battle over Ra's rights and rewards, the real inheritors of Sun Ra's wealth of wisdom and knowledge will be future generations of jazz listeners.

PART THREE
MUSIC LIKE DIRT

Interviews and Outerviews

●

LYOTARD: *Generally speaking, writing is irresponsible, in the strict sense of the term, because it does not come in response to a question. It proceeds of its own pace . . . Writing marches to its own beat and it has no debts. Whereas in the style of the conversation we are having, I feel indebted in relation to the questions you are asking of me. The result is that what I say is always finalized by a question.*

THÉBAUD: *Yes. I believe that in writing there is a surfeit of artifices that, contrarily to what one may think, makes for more vivaciousness than is possible in speech. The latter may appear vivacious at first but actually is not that much.*

LYOTARD: *Yes, I agree wholeheartedly. Orality is not vivaciousness. This is the danger of this oral work.*

—*Jean-Loup Thébaud and Jean-François Lyotard, from* JUST
GAMING

JOHN CAGE

The Conversation Game

●

In 1989 I managed to tentatively schedule an interview with John Cage when he was invited to present a
group of readings, performances, and workshops at
the School of the Art Institute of Chicago. But as I began to prepare questions
and look over past interviews with the composer—so summarily compiled in
Richard Kostelanetz's 1988 Conversing with Cage—something seemed out of
order. Not that the interviews weren't good: Cage was a magnet for interesting
inquiry, often aimed (usually unsuccessfully) at tripping him up. And Cage
always gave fascinating, loaded answers. What bothered me was that the whole
process of interviewing seemed inherently un-Cagean.

In his work, Cage endeavored to minimize intention and ego-investment, two
of the staples of interviewing. Normally, the interviewer attempts to get an artist
to say what he or she "really means" by imparting penetrating, complete, and
satisfying questions in a well laid-out, logical order. In other words, interviews
generally encourage formal conservatism. What's more, an interview is always a
bit of a meta-event: the artist steps back from his/her work and deciphers it
while the informed interviewer looks on, asks provocative questions, nods, and
comprehends. For an artist like Cage, who long sought to diminish such art/life
barriers and put the responsibility for comprehension in the ear of the behearer,
it seemed particularly strange to treat the interview as some sort of sacrosanct
ringside seat.

With this in mind, I decided to try to construct an interview that was conceptually consistent with Cage. Inspired by the concert he and Marcel Duchamp had
given in Toronto in 1968, in which acoustic signals were produced by the individual moves of a game of chess, I chose to make the interview into a game in which
the questions would be selected by chance operations. As it so happened, after I
had designed the game, gathered and composed most of the questions, it became
clear that time would not permit the interview as planned.

The interview finally took place in March 1992. The game involved a two-step
chance operations procedure. Kings and aces were removed from a deck of cards,
which was then divided into suits, making four piles of eleven cards each.
Questions were gathered from four sources, each of which was assigned a pile. I

wrote half of the total questions: half of these concerned his work in general, while the other half focused on his visual art. Another quarter of the questions were quotations from various artists and theorists on which he was asked to comment. The final set was taken from the "Keirsey Temperament Sorter,"[1] a psychological personality test designed to decode one's character and temperament type. Questions from each group were printed on the backs of cards from a given suit, so that:

> *clubs = general conceptual questions*
> *spades = artist/theorist quotations*
> *diamonds = questions about his visual art*
> *hearts = personality-test questions*

To decide which suit he drew from, Cage threw two coins. He then tossed dice to choose which of the eleven corresponding possibilities he would answer. If he rolled a twelve, he took any card from that suit. The result was an interview that was composed by me, but performed by him. The exact course of the interview (which questions were asked, in what order, which questions were left unanswered) was determined entirely by chance. He flipped the coins, rolled the dice, chose the questions, and asked them of himself. With the exception of a few explanatory notes and a couple of brief follow-up questions, I remained virtually uninvolved.

On a warm March morning thick with fog, Terri Kapsalis, who photographed the interview, and I joined Cage at his bed-and-breakfast in Evanston. He offered us whole-grain bread and tea, and after pouring the tea he left the pot whistling at a low boil. Thinking that he had meant to turn it off, Terri told him that the flame was still burning. "Oh, I know," he replied. For the duration of the interview (a little over an hour), that pot provided ambience, a lovely, brittle, unforgettable background music.

GAME. [six of diamonds] *Specifically in terms of process, what is the relationship between your composition and your visual work?*

CAGE. You mean composition of music, is that right? The relationship between the work that has to do with the eyes and the work that has to do with the ears is naturally not the same because the eye isn't an ear. And the eye, for instance, is used to looking at the world and so sees the horizon and is concerned largely with horizontals. Whereas the ear is interested in time and the succession of events, and so is interested in the vertical.

GAME. [nine of spades] *"The very definition of the real becomes that of which it is possible to give an equivalent reproduction."—Jean Baudrillard*

CAGE. It reminds me of Wittgenstein's discussion of color. That when you say "blue" you don't know what it means because it isn't real. But the moment you give a sample of the blue that you're talking about then it means something. And as he says here, it is then possible to either repeat or vary that blue, once you know what blue it is. [laughs]

GAME. [eight of clubs] *Does the word "serendipity" describe a salient part of your work? How does one measure serendipity, except in relation to norms? That is, if I discover a serendipitous co-occurrence in a piece scored independently for two instruments, a note or rhythm in common, is my enjoyment of that event not measured in terms of its coherence, rather than its chaos?*

CAGE. I never use the word "serendipity," so that I have trouble knowing what it means. Does it mean, for instance, "a rose is a rose"?

CORBETT. *When I use* serendipity *here I mean the pleasurable co-occurrence by chance of some things. So, two players playing together might come across a rhythm that they both play at the same time by chance.*

CAGE. But what is serendipity?

CORBETT. *Fortunate luck.*

CAGE. So the question is: If I discover a fortunate co-occurrence in a piece scored independently . . . what does that mean?

CORBETT. *In a piece like* Ryoanji,[2] *where two players might be playing it who have scores that were written independently, if they're playing it at the same time and something happens that connects them in a certain obvious way . . .*

CAGE. . . . then is your enjoyment . . . I have no idea what your enjoyment is. Because one could enjoy noticing the same thing happening in another place, or one could be annoyed by that. Different people react in different ways, hmm? It's irrelevant whether the thing you notice is its coherence or its chaotic character, because that might have to do with the enjoyment or it might not. It could vary certainly from person to person, don't you think?

CORBETT. *Yeah, I do. My interest was in that listening sometimes to some pieces, people often remark on how things co-occur, and there happen to be things that occur . . .*

CAGE. . . . and give the impression of being composed. Those are the things that we don't "discover," but which hit us over the head, as it were. [laughs] So that it's really more interesting to discover things that you're not aware of than that you know. I'm more and more suspicious of repetitions and of variations. And those are the two things that Schönberg taught. In fact he said everything was repetition. So that what he's saying is that a squirrel is a repetition of a cow, hmm?

KAPSALIS. Or a variation.

CAGE. Or a variation. Obviously it's a variation. Some things are similar: both have eyes, etc. . . . But they are shaped differently. So it's a variation.

GAME. [eight of spades] *"Despite these appearances, the musician has never been so deprived of initiative, so anonymous. The only freedom left is that of*

John Cage plays the interview game
(photo: Terri Kapsalis)

the synthesizer to combine pre-established programs. A simulacrum of self-management, this form of interpretation is a foreshadowing of a new manipulation by power. Since the work lacks meaning, the interpreter has no autonomy whatsoever in his actions. There is no operation of his that does not originate in the composer's manipulation of chance. Managing chance, drawing lots, doing anything at all consigns the interpreter to a powerlessness, a transparency never before achieved. He is an executor bound by laws of probability like the administrator in a repetitive society."—Jacques Attali

CAGE. That's what I thought also when I wrote the *Music of Changes*.[3] That I had reduced the performer to what you might call an automaton. So I changed what I was doing and introduced what is called indeterminacy. At present, for instance in the *Europera*, which you heard, each performer performs what he chooses, and he can choose either as we're choosing now by chance operations, or he can choose with his own will. It makes no difference. As in a Rauschenberg painting, it makes no difference whether the face is that of J.F.K. or A.M.L., you know? It leaves the performer free to choose in whatever way he wishes. It gives him a sense of doing what it is he's doing originally. In the case of the cello concerto, which you didn't hear, the time brackets overlap in a flexible way, so that the sounds can be either long or short, according to the decision of the performer. And there's no automatic pressure, one way or the other by the composition.

CORBETT. *It works the same way in the composition* Two?

CAGE. Yes. Performances of all these pieces can be extraordinarily various. They remain recognizable, though. But they're also not predictable by reference to the score. So, if you're obliged to hear, say, twelve performances in a row, you don't have to look forward to boredom because they'll all be different. You might fall asleep, but it would be for some other reason. [laughs] It would be because you were tired! Music in the past has—performance not only of music, but theater and so forth, even our critical thinking, all of that—has moved toward an invisible but knowable goal, a single center, so that one has tried to do the best, rather than the worst. If you were doing anything. In my own experience—say thinking of the criticism of Mozart—the criticism in all my experience that I like the most of Mozart is Kierkegaard's "Either/Or," where he praises *Don Giovanni*. He finds it to be, of all works of art graphic or audible or anything, the most beautiful thing that the human race has produced. It's a magnificent text. When you read it you're carried as Kierkegaard was, to an excess of praise, you know? Or as so many educators now feel that Black Mountain College was just magnificent. They have no idea what it was, [laughs] but that there couldn't possibly be a better college. It was a marvelous college, but it's impractical to think of repeating it!

GAME. [eight of diamonds] *Do you consider words to be visual objects, a poem to be a visual art experience on the order of a print or painting?*

CAGE. I think I do, and this is one of the pleasures of the current technology. Not so long ago I still had a typewriter, and I moved to the IBM Selectric typewriter. I had something like seventeen spheres with which I could change the look of the printing. That was curiously complicated compared with the word processor. Now we can make the most beautiful pages. I myself don't do it as well as Andrew Culver, who helps me with my computer work. I haven't learned to program, and I am aware of the fact that the computer belongs to the person who programs it, I mean each individual computer. So that even if I learned how to program the computer, it would be better for me to have my own, rather than to have a computer that had been programmed by someone else. Because I'm constantly running into the simplest impasses, where I simply can't get the machine to do anything. Because I haven't been told what the secret is, you know, the open sesame. But if you know *that*, the possibilities are great. And even in my ignorant state I can take advantage of some. I can't yet take advantage of all the different type faces. But Andrew Culver can do it for me. But I prefer the idea of a life without an assistant to the life with an assistant. I think each person should be able to do his work. That's in contrast with another contemporary idea that I think developed in China under Mao. It was the idea that work should not be done by individuals, but by groups. I still feel very strongly that individual work is preferable to group work. I think that's one of the very interesting questions, though, as we continue, is what is our attitude toward doing something, whether it should be done by one person: with others, or not. And I think not. Whereas many people think it would be nice to work together. But I think in working together you make everything really impossible.

That is what Thoreau said, he said "If I go with anyone else than myself into the woods, I do not go into the woods." In other words, being with someone else means that it takes precedence over whatever else you're doing. You're concerned with the other person. It can go in a thousand different directions. And those thousand are interacting with another thousand in the other person, so that you have a vast set of circumstances between one person and another that bring about a complexity that you can't describe and which most people find utterly confusing. I no sooner come here to Chicago and discover that people who I thought of as married are no longer married. You know what I mean. So we don't know how to solve the problems of being together. And if we do solve them, I believe— which my friend Norman Brown does not believe—that each person should leave space around himself and the other person. An emptiness between two. So that if you do go with another person into the woods, and succeed in being in the woods, it will only be because you think of yourself as independent of the going into the woods of the second person. And then you have a situation that neither one of you can possibly deal with because your inclination the moment you see something that attracts your interest is to point out to the other person that it's interesting. But that person is meanwhile seeing something else that is interesting. And you get a confusion. And then you run into the problem of sharing or not sharing, hmm?

CORBETT. *And then walks take as long as your walk with Mark Tobey.*

CAGE. Well that was a great experience, of course, for me. And I think . . . well that makes me question all that I'm saying. [pause] But he's no longer living, so I can't talk with him anymore. But there are very few people whose talk you can . . . *use*. Norman Brown, for me, was one of those. Lately, in recent years we haven't been able to talk, largely because he became interested in Islamic thought, which is very complex. It has many divisions. Sufi is one thing and some other form of Islamic thought is another. And I didn't even know the ABC's of it. So we couldn't really converse, because the things that interested him were unknown to me. Now I hear from his wife Beth that he's interested in other things generally, as he used to be. And that we probably could talk. He was a person I loved to talk with.

GAME. [ten of spades] *"The disaster: stress upon minutia, sovereignty of the accidental. This causes us to acknowledge that forgetfulness is not negative or that the negative does not come after affirmation (affirmation negated), but exists in relation to the most ancient, to what would seem to come from furthest back in time immemorial without ever having been given."—Maurice Blanchot*

CAGE. I'm not sure what that means, but it seems to have to do with the opposites: affirmation/negation, disaster or not disaster, accidental or not, forgetting and so forth. Yes, and he says it comes from furthest back in time immemorial, so that the presence of the opposites together is basic. It's part of what we're involved with . . . [long pause] . . . or *is* what we're involved with.

GAME. [four of hearts] *Does it bother you more having things:*
- *a) incomplete*
- *b) completed*

CAGE. The question is: What am I doing? [laughs] If I'm in the business of making something, then I just go on making it. And if I'm finished then I go do something else. So I don't see the presence of bother.

GAME. [four of clubs] *Could Muzak be considered a kind of "furniture music"? If so, what distinguishes it from the kind of furniture in your music or Satie's?*

CAGE. Exactly. It doesn't have to be considered as furniture music; it should be considered as Muzak. [laughs] It seems to me to be like ambient sound. And it's not very imposing. Those big boxes that young people carry through the streets with the radio or some other thing on, those are very imposing, and the Muzak is at the opposite end of the dynamic range. The question that this brings to me now is: What's the nature of furniture? Here we have a number of chairs, but this is not where I live, really. I wouldn't have those chairs at home. [laughs] What the furniture music is is an ostinato, it's a passage which is repeated. And the ostinato itself is a single line or a few notes that you can hear being repeated. And that's not what Muzak is. Muzak is more like . . . I haven't experienced it much lately. But it's like the fog for instance. A change of the environment. And it's very polite, as it were. It doesn't want to disturb you. Whereas the car alarms do. But I don't think that there's furniture in Satie's furniture music, for instance. It's something which is repeated over and over.

GAME. [three of spades] *"Writing is fifty years behind painting. I propose to apply the painters' techniques to writing; things as simple and immediate as collage and montage. Cut right through the pages of any book or newsprint, lengthwise for example, and shuffle the columns of text. Put them together at hazard and read the newly constituted message. Do it for yourself. Use any method which suggests itself to you. Take your own words or the words said to be the 'very own words of anyone living or dead.' You'll soon see that words don't belong to anyone."—Brion Gysin*

CAGE. Yes, it's a very useful statement. And it's a suggestion that could lead other people to think of their own way of doing something with words, so as to bring about a fresh experience of them.

GAME. [ten of clubs] *Do you prefer city sounds or country sounds? City sights or country sights?*

CAGE. Well, another way to put it would be: are you in the city or are you in the country? [laughs] One nice thing about going to a strange or unfamiliar place, either in the country or the city, is to notice the architecture, which is true certainly of coming to Evanston from New York City. And, well just going from the East Coast to the West the trees and everything change in the country. [rolls dice] This is an amusing game, I must say.

GAME. [five of diamonds] *Conceptually, how does your visual work relate to your composition?*

CAGE. They both are related through the common use in each of chance operations. And I try also to become engaged in something that I don't think, or don't remember, that I was engaged in before. That doesn't always prove to be true. Thinking I'm doing something I've never done, I often repeat myself. My back isn't so good as it used to be, so that when I travel I must travel lightly. I used to be able to take a basket that I have with me on a trip. It fits under the seat in front of you on an airplane. And I could carry rocks in that basket, or food, for instance, but I no longer can. So that I didn't take the rocks that I ordinarily take to the Crown Point Press in San Francisco, to make etchings this year.[4] However, I had left some very large rocks, or larger than the ones I would have taken, that came from the Rocky Mountains, and which I used in prints before. So that not having the rocks that I might have brought and having also small paper that was made for me—not at my request, but as a gift—I used the big rocks, but instead of using them to draw around completely I used them just to make lines along the side, and so made an interesting change in the work of the previous years. And the reason it was interesting was that one side of a rock is less like an object than the whole rock. So that the containedness of the rock disappeared and something that relates to horizon came into use. And then when you put several of these lines superimposed in an indeterminate way the work became very suggestive, but in relation to horizon. And so we call it *Without Horizon*.

GAME. [five of hearts] *Are visionaries:*

    a) somewhat annoying

    b) rather fascinating

CAGE. I'm thinking of Bucky Fuller. And I don't find those questions ones that I would ask about him. I didn't find him annoying in any way. And I wouldn't say that he was *rather* fascinating, I would say that he was amazingly engrossing. I've talked about this with several people, but one could be in a large audience listening to him speak, and he gave each person the feeling that he was talking to only that person. Quite amazing.

GAME. [jack of spades] *"To extend the principle of dissonance universally is to stop misleading the ear."—Jean-François Lyotard*

CAGE. That's a very good statement! I'm taking for granted that we love dissonance. [laughs]

CORBETT. *We're among friends.*

CAGE. Yes.

GAME. [jack of clubs] *There's not really a school or movement of aleatory composition as there was, for example, with serialism after Schönberg. Since your project has larger societal implications, would you like to see others working in the same territory? Should there be . . .*

CAGE. . . . well you say "should there be other John Cages?" But it seems to me the proper question is: Should there be other people working with chance operations? I think so, yes. There's so many ways to do it, and I've only been able to do the ones that I noticed. Whereas the thing that makes us all so difficult for each other is that we notice different things. [laughs] So, I think that more things would be noticed if many people did it.

GAME. [four of diamonds] *It is well known that you are not fond of records, that they seem too static and immovable to accommodate the change inherent in your music. How is a painting or print unlike a record in terms of this stasis? Is it not fixed?*

CAGE. Well, it's because it's to do with the eye and the reproduction of a print or a painting has the quality that a record has of music, and we don't generally like such reproductions. I mean we don't really enjoy them. I don't know of anyone who would prefer a reproduction to an original print. Of course in a print, in an edition . . . maybe that's what's meant here. No, how is a painting or print . . . it's simply something to look at, and so it has to be fixed. It has to stay what it is in a way that music doesn't do. One of the problems associated with prints and things we put on the wall is the glass that we put in front of them. And that brings them to a point where we can't see them without seeing other things at the same time. So that you see reflections of the room when you look at anything you have on the wall, if you have glass in front of it. And this becomes very clear if circumstances arise where you need a photograph of a work in your collection. You actually have to take the glass off, take the print or work out of the frame, put it in a circumstance where it won't have too many reflections when you make a copy which will later have glass over it! [laughs] Sometimes I use records as instruments that can change in a combination with other instruments.

GAME. [three of diamonds] *Given your recent interest in the use of timbre, tone color, do you find that your discoveries in musical color are applicable to your visual work? How do you make color and combination choice without resorting to intention or taste?*

CAGE. I think I do that by listing all the possibilities, or as many as I can envision, and then accepting the answer when I find, say out of forty-nine possibilities, which one I am to use, say it's forty-two. Recently in connection with prints at the Crown Point Press, having used in the past a maximum of four colors in combination, I extended the number of colors to be mixed to six. It wouldn't always have to be six, but could be six and a minimum of course would be one. I always have heard that mixing colors tends toward grey, and I haven't seen that happen. It seems to me that when you mix colors you get a mixed color, and it isn't grey. And in fact it's very, very colorful to do that. Jasper Johns speaks of mixed colors as polluted colors. Norman O. Brown speaks of [how] the addition of pollution to our environment has improved the effect of our sunsets. In the case of musical instruments and their combination, I use, of course, chance operations. If I'm working with parts for orchestra then I don't carry them to the extremes of range that I would for a virtuoso. But I make the parts less difficult to play.

GAME. [two of spades] *"A day will come when by means of similitude relayed indefinitely along the length of the series, the image itself along with the name it bears will lose its identity: Campbell, Campbell, Campbell, Campbell, Campbell."—Michel Foucault*

CAGE. Yes, that's very true. That idea which is in this case from French philosophy is familiar in Zen. Where you think something's boring after two times, try it for four, try it for eight, try it for sixteen. Eventually it becomes interesting.

GAME. [six of spades] *"What did dadaism do? It held that it doesn't matter whether one simply bats the breeze or recites a sonnet by Petrarch, Shakespeare or Rilke, or whether one polishes bootheels or paints madonnas. There will still be shootings, still be profiteering, still be hunger. What is art for? Is it not the height of deception to pretend that high art creates spiritual values?"—George Grosz and Wieland Herzfelde*

CAGE. I don't find that remark interesting. It's rather floundering thought I think. [laughs]

GAME. [three of hearts] *Which appeals to you more:*
a) consistency of thought
b) harmonious human relationships

CAGE. Well I think harmonious human relationships don't come from harmony or consistency between two people, but rather from space, emptiness between them, around them. And as far as consistency of thought goes, I prefer inconsistency.

Notes

1 David Keirsey and Marylin Bates, *Please Understand Me* (Del Mar, Calif.: Prometheus Nemesis Books, 1984).
2 *Ryoanji* is a set of musical compositions that started as a series of drawings and etchings centered on the number 15 (the number of stones in the Ryoanji garden in Kyoto, Japan). Each composition was written as a solo, but in performance any number of them may be played simultaneously, with an indeterminate relationship between them. For example, hear the voice and percussion version by mezzo-soprano Isabelle Ganz and percussionist Michael Pugliese (*Etudes Borealis/Ryoanji*, mode records, 1/2).
3 *Music of Changes, Books I–IV*, Herbert Henk, piano (Wergo Records, WER 60099-50).
4 Every year after 1977, Cage made an annual visit to Crown Point Press to make prints. They also served as his gallery and agent. See *John Cage Etchings 1978–1982* (San Francisco: Point Publications, 1982).

STEVE BERESFORD

M.O.R. and More

●

JOHN CORBETT. *Do you ever think about a general musical philosophy?*

STEVE BERESFORD. No, never.

What if you were forced to?

I'd probably run out the door and throw myself under a bus.

You do have this remarkable ability to switch between different kinds of music.

Well, I don't know if it's an ability, but I'm interested in that. The last two projects I've done sort of demonstrate that. They were both projects for TV: a series with Paul Morley called *The Thing Is*. We've done: "The Thing Is Motorways," "The Thing Is Boredom," and "The Thing Is Prisons." The latest one is an hour-long thing called "The Thing Is Entertainment" [they eventually called it: "A Paul Morley Show"], which is set in a pseudo-entertainment variety show context. I was asked to do the studio band; it's a kinda Paul Shaffer thing. But I decided I didn't want to use an organ, I would just use a white grand piano and use [saxist/clarinetist] Tony Coe, [bassist] Chris Laurence, and [percussionist] Mark Sanders. We did quite a lot of free improvisation as well as doing things like "Bewitched," "Top Cat," a Neil Young tune—you know, different stuff. With huge pink foam rubber sets, Paul Morley comes down and there's a bunch of dancers in plus-fours with spangly golf clubs. Very silly indeed. I don't know how it's gonna look, but it's like Paul's fantasy: he's dreaming that he's got his own chat show. I wanted the music to be *wrong* for that context, but also to make reference to M.O.R. [Middle of the Road] music. Which, of course, is Tony's roots. He played with Henry Mancini. It's not like none of us know anything about it and are saying, "Ha, ha. This is funny music." Some of us have actually done M.O.R. music quite well. The other project is with Louis Moholo, these tiny, five-second stings [i.e., "bumpers"], putting sound effects and tiny pieces of music, maybe bits of dialogue together for little flashes. Little idents for an art program on Channel 4. They have to work in-themselves, and you only have five seconds to make them work. Louis looks great; he's ideal for TV because he uses very small gestures but everything he does is very intense.

How do you know when this kind of music works or doesn't work? Are there general criteria?

I think I'm pretty clear and quick. Some pop stars end up spending three years making an album—they can afford to make decisions and then go back on them all the time. We can't. Given an improvised music background, you make very quick decisions about what's working or you just say "No, no, no, that's horrible. Throw it out." Obviously, I want to enjoy the music as much as possible, but sometimes you do get a very fast impression of what's going on in somebody's music and you just don't like it. And maybe later on you work out why. And that's true of your own music, if you listen back and think, "That was horrible; I wonder why." No, there aren't any general criteria.

Would you link this instant decision making and switching positions to communications culture, the existence of big record collections, etc.?

Of course it's related to that. Just around this area [Portobello Road, London], there's loads of music going on. If you were living in the middle of nowhere, with people sending you records of Tibetan music and electronic music, etc., you'd have a different way of absorbing that music than if you saw how it *related*. Seeing how people play music is very important in understanding how they hear it. The first time you hear Han Bennink, suddenly all those records fall into some kind of context that they weren't in before. It all makes total sense. Evan Parker's said: "My roots are in my record player." But he hangs out with other virtuoso saxophone players; it's not simply records that he's listening to.

The compulsion to cross over from genre to genre is clearly related to recordings, don't you think? Like hip-hop culture—I'm thinking of Ice-T and his turn to hardcore, the interesting racial dynamics of recent groups fusing rap, acid jazz, heavy metal, and punk.

It got confused early on. I mean, if you listen to those early Paul Winley break-beat records, people like DJ Kool Herc were using white rock records as break-beats. There was a Thin Lizzy tune they used a lot. Grandmaster Flash on "Wheels of Steel" used Queen. (Partially because it was a rip-off of "Good Times.") Obviously it gets confusing because I don't think Run DMC thought, "Oh, let's do a record with Aerosmith and that will cross us over." I think they did it because they liked the break-beat.

Very often, the best curveballs are the ones you don't know you've thrown. I remember a guitarist really putting me through it one night. All I had was a tiny, tiny, tiny amp, a euphonium, a ukelele, and a really out of tune piano. And he played fantastically loudly all the time, like a wall of noise. I could do nothing against this; it was like Godzilla. I was almost in tears, thinking "How could he be so completely, impersonally horrible to me." Forty-five minutes of him deafening me . . . and everybody else. Then, just recently, somebody else said to me, "I loved the way you took the piss out of him in

Steve Beresford and cat
(photo: Caroline Forbes)

that show. You really completely destroyed him. You picked up the ukelele and did this rock 'n' roll gesture and he was so upset!" I didn't remember anything about this at all. He'd obviously set out with the idea of somehow subverting *me*. I think in improvised music what's very nice is that you can set out with one intention and end up doing something completely different.

I suppose the sort of things I *don't* like I always associate with that performance-art aesthetic which I always thought was some sort of middle-class violence, where you say, "I am going to hang myself upside down for twenty-four hours, whatever happens, and it *is* interesting because *I'm* doing it." I think that might be a good way to start, but maybe after a few hours you think it's not such a good idea, so maybe you can do something more interesting. But the aesthetic of that kind of art says you must never do anything else, even if you're completely bored. I remember Charlotte Moorman playing an ice cello in '72 in London. It was quite obvious that the idea was that it would melt. But it was going to take all night to melt: it was a solid piece of ice in the shape of a cello. Plus, it made no noise at all. So, it's like, "Jesus, what am I doing here?" You know that kind of art . . .

The art of conceptual consistency, like John Cage's embrace of boredom.

But we also know that John Cage has written some beautiful pieces that are really listenable, and he's also a very funny performer. There's some great stuff by him, and there's stuff that's kinda boring but also great, and then there's stuff that's boring and not great at all. So what does that mean? What's happened now is that conceptual consistency has come to this idea of *rigor*, and the bourgeois intellectuals (or supposed intellectuals) have turned the whole idea of listening to music around to the point where rigor is the most important thing. It's like, if I start off beating my knee with my fist, I'm not rigorous if I don't do it for a specific amount of time. The fact that it makes no sense . . . what's the word "rigor"? It's not like an argument where you go from A to B to C. Does the word "rigor" come into it? I don't think so. It's just a word that people put on that music. We all know who we're talking about here. The fact that you could actually start enjoying the music for its sensual qualities or for its surprises or because it frightens you or because it seduces you . . . all these things are thrown out the window. And everybody's so pleased that they're thrown out the window, 'cause they don't have to think about it anymore. They can reduce music to this idea of repeated images and say it's Andy Warhol. But, again, Andy Warhol was a great performer. When English people import stuff from North America, they forget about the show-biz, they forget nearly all North Americans are, first and foremost, performers. Whatever they're doing. That's what is enjoyable about most of those people, ultimately, is the fact that they do it and they're great and they charm you. And when *we* do it, we're charmless.

I was really excited when I heard Astor Piazzolla for the first time, because I suddenly realized that he was playing music at one point that sounded like Elton John. And I *hate* Elton John. But it had just *got there*, I don't know how. And then suddenly he's playing music that sounds like English improvised music. I can't work out how it occurs, but somehow the music just gets there. I love that. He allows it to get where it needs to go. That's not to say it's like winding up a clockwork toy, holding it until it runs down. We're talking about some kind of dialectic.

What are the dangers associated with that kind of thing?

You can become self-conscious about what you're doing and then you have to take it somewhere else. That's why most punk groups couldn't get out of that trap. When I was in the Slits they started saying to me, "I think our strong point is that we're really naive." If somebody starts telling you they're naive, they're *not* naive. But you get to that point that you're a bit less spontaneous about it and you still aren't questioning other things. What starts off being really spontaneous and seems to come from nowhere, inevitably it's gonna become self-conscious, and you have to confront that head on. I mean, you make a reference to a Dusty Springfield song, and then maybe you do a bit more, and then you start collecting Dusty Springfield pictures, and then you start thinking "What is going on with this Dusty Springfield thing?" You have to work through this stuff, it's part of development. Sometimes what you come up with is not so interesting, sure. But something might be going on underneath, like an interest in Sandy Shaw or in chess. I don't know. The human brain: if it gets stuck then you go balmy.

You went through a period where you weren't playing so much free improvised music. Why was that?

Nobody offered me a gig, I don't know why. The fact that I was in the Flying Lizards, on Top of the Pops one night and at the LMC playing to three people and a dog the next night, certain people really didn't like that. They thought it was somehow betraying improvised music. I thought it was *great* that I got to play in front of ten million people and then in front of three people. That's interesting to me, it's exciting.

Like other aspects of your music, you revel in extreme differences—genre, audiences, different approaches to pop stardom . . .

Of course, you don't make the determination, "I will be a pop star." It's not as deterministic as that. It just so happened that I did this and this, met this person . . .

But you could do things that would say "I'm not going to do things that would jeopardize my becoming a pop star." Like play in front of three people.

That's true. That's the interesting bit, isn't it?

You also use many different instruments.

I suppose that's because I think it's what I would like to watch if I was in the audience.

Do you feel institutional pressure to choose an instrument and to choose between all these other differences? Is there a compulsion to define yourself?

Absolutely! Somebody (who will remain nameless) was quoted as saying that Han Bennink could have been the world's greatest drummer if he had just chosen to play the drums. I love Han, everything he does. And I think if Han hadn't played all those other instruments I don't think he would have understood other things as much as he does *because he plays them*. The fact that he plays bass clarinet, violin, and trombone maybe means that he can play better with a bass clarinetist or violinist or trombonist. Or that he understands the *drums* better.

The one consistent thing about virtually every career move I've made is that it's enraged the English critics. When I did that record with Han [*Directly to Pyjamas*] I thought, "Maybe I'll finally get a good review for this." I think it shows that I play the piano, somehow. Nobody ever noticed that record. It was very strange. But then people need devils, a dartboard. It's perfect because whatever they've decided you're doing, you go and do something else. They hate that.

It's something you share with the Dutch improvisors.

Oh yeah, I think Amsterdam and New York. We first went there in '79, when [the club] Zu was running. Zorn was doing stuff, Polly Bradfield, [Eugene] Chadbourne. Chadbourne, Charlie Noyes, and [Toshinori] Kondo came over here—[Henry] Kaiser as well. I always felt I had a lot in common with these people. 'Cause everything they did was very powerful, and it immediately communicated something.

When did you first get involved in playing music?

Started playing piano when I was eight. My dad had been a guitarist and singer in a semi-pro dance band. My maternal grandfather, it turned out later, played cornet in a really early jazz band. He'd been to Chicago during prohibition. I knew nothing of this. He seemed a bit embarrassed of his jazz background. My great uncle played piano with a society orchestra and was resident accordionist for Gaumont British Films.

I was brought up in a musical environment. Mom and Dad were big-band enthusiasts. Dad had lots of Glenn Miller records, Count Basie. Mom brought home a Spike Jones 78 and her dad wouldn't let her have it in the house. It was assumed that I would take up the piano when I was old enough. I had classical piano lessons, took up the trumpet at fifteen. Actually, I wanted to play the saxophone, because by that time there were these Coltrane and Ornette Coleman people. I just expanded out; I wanted to hear the weirdest music in the world. I was trying to find out about Sun Ra, just picking up information in a tiny market town in Midlands. In fact, Philip Larkin had been the librarian at the local library. (Larkin was a poet and rather reactionary jazz critic.) That library had things like *Witches and Devils* by Albert Ayler, *Rip Rig and Panic* by Roland Kirk. Also, the popular music press was writing about these people. You could read perfectly intelligent reviews of Albert Ayler in *Melody Maker.* I mean, that stuff's pretty frightening even now—we all remember the first time we heard Ayler, I think.

Then I heard the Spontaneous Music Ensemble on the radio. It was weirder than anything I'd heard and I thought, "I'll have to find out about these people." I ordered *Karyobin*—and I was very confused because there seemed to be two guitarists who played very similarly, Derek and Dennis Bailey [Derek Bailey is incorrectly listed as "Dennis" on *Karyobin*]. It was understood I'd go to university to do music. I was interviewed by Wilfrid Mellers, and I mentioned Ornette and I think that was what got me in. I didn't know anything, I was just a hayseed. I'd never heard of Luciano Berio . . . thought Berio was Berlioz. I never had that much interest in classical music, *really*. I got interested in Webern and Schönberg and Debussy. Had a horrible time at university, hated it, never knew what I was supposed to be doing. Then I met a guitarist named Neil Lamb. He had this idea, listening to these country guitarists and then hearing Derek. He wrote a piece for Derek, who was very cruel to composers in those days; he'd say he was going to play the piece and then never play anything quite like it. Anyway, we started booking. We had Derek and Han at York University. I didn't learn anything at university, but I stayed three years afterwards, and that's when Neil and I formed this improvising group with a drummer called Dave Herzfeld from New York. We had a group called Bread and Cheese. Derek heard it and booked us. At that time, the Musician's Co-op had Sunday nights at Ronnie Scott's. Our first London gig was at Ronnie Scott's. I mean, you go into the Bar Italia, over the road from Ronnie's, and they're watching big-screen Italian football, you have your first espresso *ever.* Pretty exciting stuff! That's how I got to know Derek.

There was lots of vocal improvisation. I was playing the piano, but I had trumpets and toys. It was very influenced by Berio. Neil was studying with Bernard Rands. Over that three-year period I had lots of bands with a saxophone player named Jan Steele, who's now known mostly for working with Indian pop groups. We did one side of a record for Brian Eno's Obscure label. Also, there was the Portsmouth Sinfonia. That's how I met Gavin Bryars, Michael Nyman, Nigel Coombes. I started commuting, working with Derek a bit at the Little Theatre Club. I was commuting on the midnight coach from York to play with them and sometimes with the Sinfonia. So, in '74 I moved to London. I had a circle of people—especially Evan and Derek, both of whom were extremely encouraging. By that time I had worked out what I was doing in music a bit more.

A particular style, which included toy pianos, toys . . .

That grew out of a group we had called the Four Pullovers, which was Nigel, Roger Smith (who I still think is an absolute genius), Terry Day, and me. The idea, partially, was we could play places that didn't have a piano. I'd just have toy pianos and stuff. The music was very, very stridulatory—scraping noise, unvoiced noise. I always really liked that band. Pullovers had a real direction to it, a special sound.

Was Hugh Davies an important influence in terms of your coming to electronics?

Yeah. I'd always really liked what Jamie [Muir] was doing in Music Improvisation Company [which also had Davies]. Maybe AMM. But maybe when Alterations came up that was maybe more of an AMM thing, to me.

How so? Seems like fine hairs to be splitting.

What was interesting about Alterations was that we would choose a direction individually and just take it. It didn't fucking matter what else was going on, so you could get real Charles Ives things. Or one person would do things that were really slow and the others would do things that were really fast. It was a shock when we started using drum machines and bass guitars. But Evan and Derek had such worked-out approaches to their instruments. Either of those is like a whole world, you could do that your whole life. It was almost a deliberate policy, saying, "I'm not going to go into it deeply in that way—they've done it so well."

The other thing about Alterations that was like AMM was that we knew what we were doing but we had a feeling that very few other musicians did. The balance could be easily upset in that band. It was a very strong group, but if someone came in and walked all over it with clod-hopping boots, you could very easily end up with horrible music.

It seems you must have become impatient with the hermeticism of the improvised music world, bringing in punks and others . . .

We did this thing called the "Jazz Punk Bonanza" at the LMC. A group called the Door and the Window. Post-punk. And then I replaced Gareth in the Slits. Viv Albertine used to come and check out improvised music gigs a lot.

How did the Melody Four start?

I'd played with Lol in lots of contexts. Jean Rochard [owner of Nato Records] had a festival in a tiny village called Chantenay. His father has a group called La Chantenaysienne, a fanfare band. Tony Coe was on the festival. They wanted to make a record with Lol, Tony, Jean Rochard's father . . . and I was asked to play piano. I was terrified of playing with Tony Coe because I'd only met him very briefly and it was obvious that he was the most amazing musician *ever* and could do anything. I said "I don't know if I can do this stuff, I'm sorry Tony." Anyway, it was all right. That was the only time I've ever had alcohol for breakfast in my whole life. Monsieur Rochard cracked open a bottle and said, "This is the last bottle of this sort of Eau De Vie in the whole world, you must have some."

So, we've done these ten-inch records, theme records, love songs, TV tunes, a Latin album. It exorcised our interest in middle-of-the-road music. As a performing band, we're very interesting because we have this tradition of having arguments. I think Lol and I started that tradition of having arguments on stage. Some people take them quite seriously. We have discussions about the texts of the songs. Sometimes we really have to persuade Tony to sing his song about teddy bears. Some of it is real, some of it isn't real. And it's not all M.O.R.; we do Ellington.

Is it taking M.O.R. material and pushing it?

No, it's just doing it. Charles Armirkanian said it's to do with deconstruction, and I said no, it's to do with liking the tunes. Sometimes we do songs because we think they're crap . . . and we're not gonna tell you which! [he makes a snide face] I mean, we do Ellington because they're great and because Tony Coe plays them so well. That's why I started playing changes. I'm not a jazz pianist at all, but it's silly not to do them with him. It just seemed to make sense.

It's yet again another difference—between doing a tune because you like it or because it's terrible and there's some kitsch value.

I love it as a listener, that's why I do it. I think of myself as an audient.

What have been your most recent projects?

Doing a half-hour video based around the life of cartoonist George Herriman; the trio with Clive Bell and Mark Sanders; and a piece with a Finnish animator that involves little men that look like penises being smashed against roadsigns.

Whew!

[London, May 1992]

EVAN PARKER

Saxophone Botany

●

Evan Parker likes to give me a hard time about being a
knee-jerk structuralist, or poststructuralist, or post-
modernist, or something like that. Whatever it is that
I am, he knows I'm a Continental-philosophy kinda guy, which is something he's
certain that he isn't. Between us lies the gulf—or better, the channel—that sepa-
rates the Parisian pulsebeat and Frankfurt forefolk from the rationalist thought
of A. N. Whitehead et al. Nonetheless, when I told him that I was preparing a
theoretical article based on his solo saxophone work, one in which I would use
poststructuralism to analyze him and vice versa, he showed great interest.

In May of 1992, I spent a week in London, at which time we had a chance to get
more deeply into certain common interests and overall differences. It was the
same month during which Oxford University was debating whether it could, in
good conscience, give Jacques Derrida an emeritus degree. Evan delightedly
brought me a running cartoon strip by Steve Bell that he'd clipped which fea-
tured Derrida in the Oxford toilet, asking what is, perhaps, the ultimate textual
question: "Où est le papier?" At the same time, he brought me a hand-written
page transcribed from E. P. Thompson's eloquent but vicious critique of Al-
thusser, The Poverty of Theory.[1] *A few days later, the college botany major*
(philosophy minor, I think) showed me around some extremely strange architec-
ture while we talked about various other things, ranging from his interest in
science to new projects.

EVAN PARKER. Gardening yesterday, I was amazed that effectively a robin
had me working for it, digging worms. Pretty clever that they know when
you're digging—the bird came from somewhere else, probably by smell.
Then its timing is brilliant, just waits for you to move off a bit, nips down,
grabs the worm. As you start to dig again it's up in a tree, watching. It just
paces your work, according to its appetite. When it's had enough, it veers
off. Very good.

JOHN CORBETT. *Do you read a lot about cognitive science? About thought*
processes, how the brain works and the like?

I don't go to the library and read original papers or anything like that. I read the popular science versions of it. But usually, yeah, in a fairly up-to-date way. I try to keep abreast of what's happening. Usually, with pop science, that means you're probably about fifteen years behind, aren't you? By the time it gets written up in that form. There's that quite interesting book by Betty Edwards, *Drawing on the Right Side of the Brain*, which had a big impact, finally, here [in Britain]. Because, well, I was already interested in left-brain/right-brain studies. When I saw the title of that book I knew immediately that it might be interesting.

I was intrigued by a comment that John Cage made, that he found he needed to "make a change" in his music at one point. It seemed to suggest a fundamental difference between people who follow what it is they're doing—who treat their development as an "organic" or "evolutionary" unfolding—and some who more intentionally "make a change" and let what they do follow that. I'm wondering what you think about that, for example, in relation to switching from one instrument to another.

I think when you talk about switching instruments you finger an important rule of thumb for which camp people are likely to be in. If they play an instrument, they're likely to be in the camp where the work follows the work. If they write or conceptualize away from the instrument, into notation forms or the structuring of computer programs or the building of electronic instruments, then they're likely to say, "I must rethink this between pieces." Because that's the whole nature of how they express their creativity: the ability to rethink. I wouldn't say that can't be in some sense "following the work." I mean, in other words, that's what you expect from John Cage. That's what you expect from a composer in that idiom . . . "idiom," ha! That's what you expect from a composer using that approach or using those techniques. Each may be expressing certain limitations or responding to a certain set of limitations, but they're different limitations in either case.

I was prompted to ask that question because of the changes that have been taking place in your work. Your recent experiment with sound engineer Walter Prati and your record with overdubs both surprised me, delighted me. Particularly interesting was the last piece on Process and Reality, *where you took Steve Lacy's recording "The Cryptosphere"—on which he plays along with a Ruby Braff record—and you re-recorded it with the microphone in the middle of your soprano saxophone. Something like that certainly required conceptualization away from the scene of the crime.*

That's true, definitely. But then again, the sleeve notes don't make it clear enough how long ago that piece was conceived. I mean it was conceived almost as long ago as I first heard *Lapis*, the Steve Lacy record that it comes from. It must have been back at the time when Steve was over to do the

Emanem recordings. Maybe 1975. In fact, I've got early versions recorded at home with the Revox which are in some ways more successful. Because the precise delay between the two channels has a very important influence on the atmosphere that you generate. I also used feedback, in addition to the drumming sounds. The early versions sound quite different. Using a simpler system with the microphone jammed into the instrument and the bell sealed off, if you have the tape recorder playing back in the same room that you're recording in, then you can set the playback level to the point where it can induce feedback, if you've got enough keys open. So controlled feedback became part of the piece as well. Well, semi-controlled feedback.

When I think about it, in the late sixties I did a performance where I played with a tape that I'd put together myself. I haven't actually had the courage to get the tape out and play it again since then, but I will one day just to find what it was I did—at least the fixed part. Everybody was trying things quicker then, with not exactly a throw-away attitude, but with almost a greed for the experience. Then, after a point—you can either characterize it as complacency or certainty about what it is you want to do (depending on whether you like the results or not)—I got interested in the specifics of the instruments, what they could do, and I settled on that for a long time. And now, maybe, I'm just opening up to other possibilities, having got a kind of firm base, in the sense of instrumental technique and approach and language (or however you want to put it—they used to call it "vocabulary"). So there's something there now that I feel is mine, which is up for adjustments in other circumstances. But for me that is essentially no different from improvising with other people, with the same openness to modification by external forces that characterizes the difference between solo work and group work. You're throwing your thing into a process of collective decision making. If it's your band, you might be able to use one or two other bits of emotional blackmail and economic blackmail to get what you want, as well . . .

. . . scare tactics.

Scare tactics, brow beating. You know, the usual. [laughs] Anyway, however much of that you try, in a group situation what comes out is *group music* and some of what comes out was not your idea, but your response to somebody else's idea. Especially in the trio with Barry [Guy] and Paul [Lytton], the mechanism of what is provocation and what is response—the music is based on such fast interplay, such fast reactions that it's arbitrary to say, "Did you do that because I did that? Or did I do that because you did that?" And anyway the whole thing seems to be operating at a level that involves . . . certainly intuition, and maybe faculties of a more paranormal nature. I don't know. You develop an understanding about timings in terms of speed and dynamics which helps to give a sense of coherence to the performance. It may be interesting for the listener to be able to see why everything happens; that the process be listenable has a use. But I think that what is even more interesting is when the process is *lost* and things happen that are clearly the basis for an understanding, but the understanding is no longer worked through at the overt, explicit level. That's an important qualitative transition in improvised music. You have improvised music where it's pretty clear what kinds of things can happen and why and when. And then you have improvised music where the fact that there's an understanding is clear, but quite how it works is moved to a level of mystery again.

There are connections evident here between your solo and group playing. In a sense, you are like a solo-group, trying to invent or produce a way of playing as a soloist that's like playing as a group: coordinating things in a way that may be controllable, but not predictable. That seems strikingly similar to the group processes you've been speaking about.

Well, that's very interesting that you say that. Because I hadn't thought of it quite like that. And if it's true, it pleases me because then there's a kind of coherence. It must be a kind of appetite for the way things fit together, a certain pleasure . . . it's almost like a watchmaker's pleasure, but all the cogs are the right size and they turn at the right rate, and at the end of it the piece tells the time accurately or something.

But it's about an unpredictable time, a time that speeds up and slows down, where there's some range of possibilities that includes something like a group dynamic where you and the relationship between the subset of techniques that you might be using at a given time and the instrument are all three interacting, in a way that's like different performers. In that sense, there's a level at which it's not a solo performance. So, to say "I'm doing what I want to at this moment," isn't exactly what it's about. It's about trying to set things up so that when you're finished you can step back from it and judge what happened. And to literally have been in some sense separate from it. It's setting a process in motion.

In some ways, in some situations, the freedom of the total music, if it has any sense of freedom, is only possible because some parts are very fixed. And by holding those fixed parts in a loop, putting them on hold for a while, then you can look for other regions where variation is possible. But then I might discover a new loop in that new region which immediately loosens up the loop or loops that I've put on hold elsewhere. That's what I'm trying to do: I'm shifting my attention from different parts of the total sound spectrum, which you could analyze in terms of high, middle, low. Let's say, if there is an illusion it will be confined to one of those regions. I haven't yet *really* broken through to the level of having a loop across high, middle, and low, which is obviously a challenge.

That would be really incredible.

There's no reason it can't be done. It's just a question of confidence and ease with the material. That's where the use of repetition, although it appears to be a voluntary loss of freedom, actually opens up regions of the instrument which otherwise I wouldn't be aware of. So, a lot of the time that "pure research" aspect of what can be done, paradoxically, is based on the fact of doing the same thing, or setting out with the goal of doing the same thing again. Partly because that's not really what I want to do, but it's a means to an end. Then the other, newer possibilities come clear to me. That's why it's easier to see progress by looking backwards and seeing where the solo music is now in relation to where it was twenty years ago. At the time it feels like you keep returning to the same thing over and over, but in fact the music has that organic, evolutionary quality that you referred to at the outset of our little discussion.

It's interesting to hear you speak of a goal.

But it remains theoretical until it's happened. It's not like somebody doing rigorous scientific research, where you set out to determine *is this true?* then link together the outcome of those smaller experiments to test some bigger hypothesis. It's not really like that. Could be dressed up like that, but what's really going on is a nonverbal, largely nonconceptual kind of activity, once called "play." You know, "playing" the saxophone.

There's the sensual dimension keeping it from being that abstracted experience.

Hearing; sound in the room; the movement of the sound of the room.

That's the only material sound has to speak of. Listening to you play solo last night, in what was I think a superb concert, I was thinking about the question of "interruption"—repeated patterns and interruptions. But also interruptions that I'd never heard you make before, long tones that stop everything at a bigger, formal level.

Yeah. That's a nice way of, let's say, having everything make sense, which I hope of course it does. So I hope it could be true, what you're saying. But what makes me do those things is an awareness that when you've been playing complex music for longer than a certain amount of time, you're in danger of losing the audience's attention. They just oversaturate with the detail, the information. After a while, it's like there's new information but it's the same *kind* of new information. So the change is no longer a change. It's like looking at new ways to make changes that are really changes. Also, to give myself a chance of restarting. In this schizophrenic context, it's almost as if there are two people, one of whom is playing the saxophone and one of whom is talking to the guy who plays the saxophone. And when it comes to it, the guy playing the saxophone actually gets the final say, and the one telling him what to do stands there and says "I tried, fellas. There he goes again. This kinda goes on a bit, doesn't it?" It was in response to that sense in myself of it "going on a bit," and wanting to open it out. Just for myself, to trick myself, to restart but to restart without stopping. To characterize it the way you have is exactly right: an interruption on a bigger scale than the usual interruptions. The usual interruptions are the substance of the music—the interference between the two patterns or the compatibility or lack of compatibility between two patterns. That's the usual stuff of the detailed music, so to impose a break on that you need to do something different, with long notes or whatever.

If records are yet again another step out in that process, both the Prati project and overdub project might also be an interruption—for the listener, it's like saying "you've come to expect something, and this is different."

Also, it's a way of dealing with making records a bit more often. In the sequence leading up to those two recordings, there were between any two of the solo records at least three years. So if you haven't got enough for forty minutes' fresh music after three years, maybe you should leave it for four years, five years, six years, or whatever. And if you're gonna make records more often than that, where the evolution of the pure material doesn't warrant further—dare I say it—documentation, then you need to think about other ways of structuring the music in order to give it some fresh perspective. Not only for yourself, but also for the people that you're hoping might listen to it.

Then again, some listeners will be rabid collectors who would also want a record of Evan Parker's farts.

Well, I doubt that, you know that's going too far. I'm very, very, very humble in the face of even the possibility that such people exist. On the other hand, it's a constant balance between egomania on the one hand and . . . My solo output is quite extensive; there's a lot of stuff. It's spread over a long period, not quite twenty years. I just hope that it strikes some sort of balance that makes sense. That's one of the things that I do when I'm in the editing phase of a record, I go back to earlier things and say "Is there really enough substantially different?" Maybe the biggest revelation for me was when I fished out the old tapes from what was left over of the sessions that I did with Jost Gebers in Berlin when I needed extra material for the first solo record. I did a bit more than an hours' music in Berlin, just looking for the extra five minutes I needed for the record. A lot of the other material, apart from what I used on the record, seemed very extreme to me at the time. But listening back to it, when I included it on the collected solos, I realized that they were the germs, however rough and crude, of most of the things that I later became interested in. At the time they'd seemed too extreme to use, but later they became polished up and more under control, but essentially the same material. So I don't know how much of it is really new in some fundamental sense. The question of technical control is the one that interests the player. For a lot of players, the question is not *what concept does this seem to represent?* but *how well do I play it?*

You've said before that if craft-musicianship isn't part of the game, you don't want to play . . . or something to that effect.

[laughs] Yeah, I think so. But it's just that on one hand I'm saying that I go back to earlier material with a view to evaluating the sense of *need*—and "need" is already a very grand word—the *sense* of any new release or the *place* of it. Then, as long as certain things are there and they're well done, that might be the criterion. On the other hand, if you want to look for traces of those things in earlier works, they're already there but less well done. They're buried, hidden, they haven't been pulled out into the light. I wouldn't say it's like flower arranging, but it may be that all I've got is this one bunch of flowers and I just turn the vase around, or change the vase, or change the lighting, give a little more fertilizer to the red ones. I don't know, it's a bit like that.

This marks you as different from the category of improvisors who think that everything they do turns to gold and everything they do will be different from the last thing. That attitude influences how people listen, it comes from a mode of listening that isn't always very careful or thoughtful. There's a collector attitude that goes along with it—things, not the music they contain.

Well I am very much a collector myself, not of my own material—I'm not terribly good at that—but I do collect, say John Coltrane music quite fanatically. Na, fanatic's too strong, but you know: *avidly.* I like listening to small changes, and I don't care if it's three different recordings from the same tour. In fact, that's what a lot of the possibilities for Coltrane collectors now consist of: one night on a tour that you didn't have before, or one half of a concert. And there's always the possibility of being *totally* surprised by something. And there's also the possibility of being reassured by the material. You never quite know what you're gonna get.

I think nowadays more or less everything you do is gonna be recorded by somebody in the audience with a Walkman or maybe even a DAT. People have got a way of hooking up with one another and exchanging tapes. I know that for the people who are really interested in every detail they have their own network which functions quite well without my active collusion. The people that I really like I put in touch with one another anyway. It's already difficult enough to juggle with being ready for any given concert. If you then start to worry about making sure it's accurately recorded and then accurately archived, the work would be endless. I don't take it all seriously.

What I do take seriously is when a certain feeling comes to me: "Okay, now you should record something." Having just done three—for me—quite important solo concerts together, and being reasonably happy with all of them and very happy with the best one, it makes me feel like next week I might try and do some recording. Even if it's not edited down and packaged for release. I've got a few things like that on the shelf. I don't know what will become of them, but that's how I work.

Note

1   The section he transcribed reads: "The difference between 'playing' a game and being gamed illustrates the difference between rule-governed structuration of historical eventuation (within which men and women remain as subjects of their own history) and structural*ism*. As always, Althusser has simply taken over a reigning fashion of bourgeois ideology and named it 'Marxism.' In the old days vulgar Political Economy saw men's economic behaviour as being *lawed* (although workers were obtuse and refractory in obeying these laws), but allowed to the autonomous individual an area of freedom in his intellectual, aesthetic or moral choices. Today, structuralisms engross this from every side; we are *structured* by social relations, *spoken* by pre-given linguistic structures, *thought* by ideologies, *dreamed* by myths, *gendered* by patriarchal sexual norms, *bounded* by affective obligations, *cultured* by mentalities and acted by history's script. None of these ideas is, in origin, absurd and some rest upon substantial additions to knowledge. But all slip, at a certain point, from sense to absurdity and, in their sum, all arise at a common terminus of unfreedom. Structuralism (this terminus of the absurd) is the ultimate product of self-alienated reason—'reflecting' the common sense of the times—in which all human projects, endeavours, institutions and even culture itself, appear to stand *outside* of men, to stand *against* men, as objective things. In the old days, the Other was then named 'God' or Fate. Today it has been christened anew as Structure."

ANTHONY BRAXTON

From Planet to Planet

●

JOHN CORBETT. *Could you talk a bit about your quartet? How does it fit into the current music scene?*

ANTHONY BRAXTON. I feel that present-day strategies in the neoclassic continuum have sought to erect an identity based on initiations from New Orleans to the bebop continuum, and at that point to contain the identity of the music. But my work in the past twenty-five years has sought to erect a trans-idiomatic context for exploration, and along with that context to create a tri-metric architectonic unit that could serve as a basis for recognition in the postnuclear continuum. I feel the quartet is an excellent example of a postnuclear, tri-metric unit that demonstrates stable logic information, mutable logic information, and synthesis logic information in one time-space, where there is one individual having extended open improvisation and in that same space there is a logic containing two musicians working together—maybe in a pulse-track or whatever—and at the same time a stable logic component involving totally notated music. All these kind of interrelated partials now operate *freely* in the quartet, to create another context for experiencing and exploration.

I'd like to get into the music for your recent concert in Victoriaville, what music was selected for it, what the procedures were that went into choosing it. I know that there was a really interesting circumstance surrounding your score in relation to the other three musicians' scores, which I had the sense made it that much fresher . . .

Are you referring to my saxophone almost breaking? [guffaws] What a moment! [hilarious laughter]

That was wild, but I also understood that you were busy rewriting your parts beforehand.

That's right. I arrived and to my surprise I did not have my quartet book. It was sitting up in my living room nice and protected. I couldn't believe it. So I decided to write some new music, and I spent the morning trying to compose new music. And when we started to play [Composition] 159, suddenly, to my horror, I discovered that the main screw in my saxophone that holds the bottom part on was right at the point where it was about to come out. For about ten minutes I ran off stage and came back on and was able to put the screw back in without the horn breaking. So that was another major dynamic connected to the performance.

As far as the material that we played for the concert, that material comes from the quartet book of interrelated coordinate musics. At this point the quartet has moved into the solar system repetitive logic structures that establish independent repetitive cycles for each individual inside of the space, as a way to create a multiple logic state of identities based on independent cycles. In the same way that we talk of Saturn as a planet that has a ring going around it, that ring is connected to our understanding of that identity, and components of the ring come from the body of the planet itself. The concept of solar system repetitive signature logics could be viewed in that context.

I want to go back and make sure that I understand. The idea of solar system individual identities, is that linked to the idea of having a signature or set of signature musical attributes as an individual within the group, so that the group has an identity and then within the group there are things that, say, Marilyn has that one would think of as hers? Am I getting in the right direction?

By signature logic, in this context I'm referring to those secondary identities which are a part of a greater concept space, for instance a traditional composition that when approached—just as if we were in a rocket ship going to Mars, we'd get close to the planet then we'd go into the orbit of the planet, and after entering into the orbit of the planet we'd really move in sync. Solar system, in this context, being if we looked at the solar system's twelve different planet energies going around one point of definition, the sun. With some of those energies, as in the planet Mercury, a revolution goes by much quicker. Signature logic, in this context, would be, for instance, a phrase like "dee, do do da," then improvisation, then improvisation, "dee, do do da . . . bdiddl bmbm bop, tchtchbababa . . . dee, do do da." That "dee, do do da" is a signature. For the compositions I've been working with in the last five years, a signature logic might be comprised of three or four different signatures of various time lengths, with improvisational spaces inside of that system. But the nature of the system would be like if Marilyn is playing Mercury, then her variables will repeat quicker than Gerry if Gerry is playing in the position of Venus or Mark who is playing in Jupiter or if I'm playing Pluto; by the time my signature material repeats, their material might have repeated several times. So that's what I mean by solar system logic.

But let me back up a little further. There is a phrase I hope for you to think about: navigation through form. And I would even go so far as to say: navigation through form (as a tri-partial phenomenon/experience). Maybe you won't be able to use that [chuckles], but that's life, eh? But I wanted to say that because navigation through form is a relevant way of talking about my system. Navigation through form *on the tri-plane* [gasps as he finds the right phrase] ah, on the tri-plane. For the individual, navigation through form involving notated materials, improvisational materials, or language materials or vocabularies, and synthesis materials (compositions which bring together different uses). But there's another aspect: there's navigation through form for the group, moving through different areas of space, different states of architecture, different regions of sonic unity and construction . . . and nonconstruction. *That's* what I was interested in. For me, the challenge of a next thousand years would be the new super-spaces which are now opening up in physics, the new spaces opening up in mathematics in terms of recognition in the superatomic space, involving not just dialectical relationships but also including correspondence logics, and what these could pose for better understanding relationships, better understanding spiritual dynamics and intention. And on the first plane, the last category would be navigation through the dream space and the ritual and ceremonial musics, in the sense of taking a different path, like a highway. If the analogy is a city/state analogy, like driving from New York to Cleveland.

Let's say for the concert we start off with Composition 159. Okay, we start off in the solar system state, with repetitive logics. From there we move into the open space of extended solos. Meanwhile, at various points stable logic material is entering into the music in the form of Composition 147, which Marilyn is playing. From there, we arrive at a defined point that brings in Composition 148, and once we enter into the world of '48, the logic in that space suddenly establishes 108a as a pulse track directive. This kind of thing, it's like a navigation through different form states, where the individual has his or her own directive separate from the group, where the individual and the group have common points of primary spaces in compositions to play together, and where the individual in groups has synthesis time-space directives that tell them what to do in different time spaces to create the logic of the space. This is another context, outside of the concept of "blow, baby, blow," if I could say it like that.

You mentioned dialectics. I'm interested whether the tri-metric concept is still linked to a dialectical logic, since you're talking about two systems, two modes— that is, loosely speaking, determinate and indeterminate or open and notated— and their synthesis, which would be the "sublation" in dialectics between the two. Do you still see that linked to dialectics?

Yes, but linked to dialectics as just one-third of the system, not the summation point of definition. But not necessarily *not* that either. Let me put it another way: the model that I seek to build will be designed in a way that says whatever individual comes into it can be respected within the twelve identity states of my music. And for the individual whose tendencies move towards dialectical summation information, that aspect is available in my system, too. In other words, my model doesn't seek to tell anyone *anything*, but rather to establish a state of relationships that will allow that individual to navigate to his or her own attractions, based on each individual's own relationships within how they look at and experience sound.

This notion of navigation through form sounds very much like something that Sun Ra might also talk about.

Very good point, sir. My response would be: yes, you are correct. I view the work of Sun Ra as an essential component that must be experienced as part of moving into the constructs of the next thousand years. I'm very grateful to Evidence Records, for instance, for the possibility to get some of the early releases. I feel that Mr. Ra's work has been profoundly not-understood, in terms of what it merits.

One of the interesting things about the way Ra works is that it can make a place for such different players, even new players who don't quite get what's going on yet. In your music there seems to be the same kind of tolerance and interest in developing a system that can accommodate individual players and let them navigate through form.

Well I agree with your observation; I think you're totally correct. For me, I see that aspect of Mr. Ra's work as consistent with the challenge of creative music in the Trans-African continuum and in the American continuum, and also I see his decision to keep the door open as part of what the next context will have to better understand. For instance, in this time period we talk of multiculturalism. This has become one of the terms in academia, anyway. But the beauty of creative music has *always* responded to the universal axis, and the challenge of the American musics, in my opinion, has been how those projections have sought to fulfill the concept of democracy that the early fathers put together in terms of their hope for what this country could be. We're not there yet, but I have great hope for the possibility of a dynamic universalism that respects all of our people, and I have tried to have that manifested in my model, and I see Sun Ra's work as a model for the future in that same way.

The difference between the current conception of multiculturalism and what you're talking about is the difference between creative music as we know it and what's being passed off by the record industry right now as "world music," where music has to wear its ethnicity on its sleeve.

I agree with you completely, and I talk with my students about this. There is the danger of teaching our young people to play a little African music, a little Japanese music, a little bebop. When I speak of the concept of multi-culturalism, I'm not speaking of a concept that says for me not to accept the *fact* of my limitations by virtue of my life experiences, to negate that and participate in the music like we're in a candy store. Rather, I believe that the underlying components of the universal path of our species can still be used in a way that can be relevant and that can address itself to many different areas inside of a person's art. But there must be some limitations backed by the fact that, as musicians wanting to be involved in something meaningful, we can't disrespect our own lives either. It's kind of like: find your place in the circle, but don't try to *be* the circle. [laughs]

I'd like to talk about the relationship between creative music—particularly improvisation—and the fixative properties of recording. How do you view this relationship?

For me, I have always been very interested in recording. I was very affected by the music I listened to when I was growing up [in Chicago], when I would go to Marty's on 58th Street. And even now, when possible, I try to listen a lot to music. In fact, I need that. As far as recording is concerned, I agree with Thelonious Monk's advice to Steve Lacy, that is, to document as much of your work as possible. I have had the good fortune of working with very small companies as well as some of the large companies . . . for a second! And in a strange kind of way, I must say, it's good to be in the underground. At a certain point it became clear there would be no real money in this, which might not be so bad anymore, I mean once you get used to it. My purposes then became very clear: I wanted to continue to evolve my music and document what I could of it, but what that would mean was the realization that I'm not interested in the golden performance or the ungolden performance. I'm not interested in some of the measurements that have become current in terms of how we view the music. I see the model that I am building as an evolving model, and I'm not interested in it ever arriving. It's the process of evolution and discovery that excites me, and what sound opens up to me in terms of the whole experience of trying to live. As such, I have tried to approach recording based on: I want diversity. If I have to listen to it, I want to make sure it covers more than one base, because I'm not interested in virtuosity, I'm not interested in long compositions, I'm not interested in short compositions, I'm not interested in rhythm or non-rhythm. I'm not interested in one context of creativity as a basis to spend my whole life in, but rather I feel it's important to take advantage of the dynamics that have opened up in this time-period, and in the documentation, wherever possible, try to commit some of it to record or CD. I have a concept of architecture and modeling that can be akin to having twelve pieces of clay that can be put together in any order, or like having a giant erector set. Recording in that context will mean maybe I can slip in little pieces of the opera, or slip in a piece of [Composition] 83 as a secondary structure that fulfills some point of the structure in the same way that we talk of the Trump Shuttle going from New York to Washington, D.C.—I try to have structures that satisfy the urgency of the moment.

You mention not having a "golden performance," which makes me think of some things that Derek Bailey has said about the relationship between composing, improvising, and recording. Do you see recording as being at all antithetical to some of the open processes you aspire to in your music?

The question is so difficult. For me, I'm as interested in looking at notated music as improvisation. I see no inherent complexity there at all. In the end, it's really what you like listening to and being involved with. I know this for myself, I was not so interested in listening to some context of total improvised music where the understanding is whatever happens is okay. That might have been interesting in the sixties and early seventies, and I understand that many people are still interested in that. I salute them. For myself, I'm interested in taking that breakthrough that occurred and connecting it with a broader understanding of fundamentals in a broader context, like a further defined interaction dynamics, architectural dynamics, philosophical dynamics, and ritual and ceremonial dynamics. The arguments of the free jazz people and the bebop people have become irrelevant to me.

Do you see those arguments converging at a certain point?

Is it jazz, is it not jazz? Does it swing? Is it black, is it white? Can a woman do it, can a man do it? These are the arguments that are looking *back* to the last thousand years. In the next thousand years we will begin to see new forms of musics, on greater time-space scales; we will begin to see the effects of dynamic technology. And of course we will see the new problems that arise because of this, but we will also see the new challenges open to the extended territories of these breakthroughs. I pick up *Down Beat* and everybody says: "Oh, Louis Armstrong and Duke Ellington." The jazz world has locked itself in a little vice and continues to simply misdefine the music in a way that does not help our young people begin to think about the fact that the cold war is over; it's possible now to start to think about the future; there are new challenges ahead. My hope is that the next administration will symbolically be about the possibility for our people to look ahead, as opposed to the past.

That's an optimistic outlook!

[profuse laughter] I believe that the best is still ahead for our species—as well as the worst. But physicality is an opportunity, and I'm very grateful to

Anthony Braxton
(photo: Nick White)

have an opportunity to experience this. I would like to hope to build a context that can help our children do their best in the next time-cycle.

How important was the work of Earle Brown to you?

Earle Brown? Oh, yes! His "Available Forms I & II" was very important to me. He was important for me in the early period, Feldman and Brown. But especially Brown, the trios on Mainstream, and the duo pieces. Later I would have a hard time keeping up with his work because he didn't document it.

I bring him up because, not only in the early music but now as well, you're talking about a period where a lot of the different ideas you've been working with are coming together and are being used simultaneously and you can deploy the different techniques and concepts in the same space of a musical performance. Some of that relates, in my head, to the whole idea of mobiles and having parts that interdigitate the way that he was working with.

In fact, Mr. Brown was one of the re-structural composers in the fifties who helped to give us a more expansive understanding of structural material. And this aspect of his work has gotten kind of lost, since in America we don't value our lineage of mastership. But yes, Mr. Brown's work . . . and don't forget Jimmy Giuffre. These guys, they're American heroes. Our country has so much talent, but at the same time we don't seem to take advantage of it. And in terms of geopolitical dynamics, this might not be something we can afford to do. Everything's changing now, and meanwhile Americans are confused about what's happened. The Europeans and Japanese, if you want to learn about American culture you have to go there!

You have to go to Japan to learn about soul music from the 1960s.

That's right. They have already studied the music very seriously, and we're lost in arguments like: "Is it jazz?" [crazed laughter, then resolute seriousness] I mean, Sun Ra is in a wheelchair now. When is he gonna be able to have a decent life? I don't think its' gonna happen on this earth. John Gilmore, he's sick. Time is going by. Jimmy Giuffre, he looks frail. Sal Mosca, one of our great masters, nobody knows about him. Even my Ph.D. students never heard of him. I mean, I love my country, but we sure feel we can waste a lot of talent and it's not gonna affect us.

Well, now we've succeeded in going from extreme optimism to extreme sadness.

No, I am extremely optimistic, because to be otherwise would be a slap in the face to everything I've experienced. I believe in this experience, and I'm grateful to have a chance to kick it about and try to do my work. My hope is that the work will make a difference. But there's nothing like having a chance to kick it about.

[on the phone between Chicago and Middletown,
Connecticut, December 1992]

The following is a list of music that Anthony Braxton suggests:

1. The Florida State University Marching Band School Theme
2. Sun Ra, "Brainville" (from *Sun Song*)
3. Sun Ra, "Bygone" (from *Mayan Temples*)
4. Paul Desmond (w/Brubeck) "You Go to My Head"
5. Frankie Lymon, "The ABCs of Love"
6. Ornette Coleman, "Peace" (from *The Shape of Jazz to Come*)
7. Alban Berg, *Lulu* (conducted by Pierre Boulez)
8. Richard Wagner, *Parsifal* and *The Ring*
9. Charlie Parker, "Donna Lee"
10. Lee Konitz/Warne Marsh, "Sax of a Kind"
11. Dinah Washington, "You Go to My Head"
12. William Grant Stills, *A Bayou Legend*
13. Cecil Taylor, *Akisakila*
14. Sal Mosca/Warne Marsh Quartet, "Steady As She Goes" (from *Live at the Village Vanguard, Vol. II*)
15. John Coltrane, "Central Park West"

ALTON ABRAHAM

Brother's Keeper

●

ALTON ABRAHAM. First of all, Sun Ra was introduced to me in . . . must have been 1951. Somewhere 'round that area. He was working out in
Calumet City; at that time they called it "sin city." They had a lot of bur-
lesque houses. At that time, they didn't allow black people in those places;
even the black musicians had to sit behind a curtain. I wasn't there, but I'm
just telling you what he told me and what the rest of the musicians who
played there said. Tommy Hunter, "Bugs," he was our drummer, he worked
with Sun Ra at that time because Sun Ra didn't have a band in Chicago at
that time, but he did have one in Birmingham when he was in high school
and when he got out of high school. I was introduced to him in my very
early teens, in that time period, and that's where they told me he was working making $10 a night, playing two, sometimes three times a night. We
found out that we had a lot of things in common, because at that time period
we were already doing ancient biblical research and research in astrology
and researching the origin of mankind—that means black, white, and everybody. Found out that all people came from one source, civilization had its
beginning in one particular area. Those that know know that that area is
either the area around the Tigris and Euphrates rivers, or it's in certain parts
of Africa in that area.

JOHN CORBETT. *Can I ask you about the context for some of that? Leon
Forrest has a book that has a character in it that speaks and prophesies in a way
that's strikingly similar to Sun Ra, and Forrest has mentioned that there were a
bunch of people on the South Side doing that kind of research.*

That might have been us, because we were the ones that bought a lot of
books. I have a library of over fifteen thousand books dealing on those
subjects. We knew that when you say something you have to be able to back
it up. So whatever I say, there are books to back it up. We used to talk about
subjects and then we would go, maybe within a few days or week, and find
the book that says the very thing that we were talking about. When I met
Sun Ra, I was doing internship at Provident Hospital, in my early teens. At
that time none of the guys were into playing with him. They called him
Sonny Blount *this* and Sonny Blount *that*. It was very hard for him to find

anyone to work with that wanted to play with him, because his chords were different, his structure, his way of playing so-called "pop tunes," standards, were different. And they didn't like the things that he was talking about. He was talking about the space age. We were talking about the space age [gestures at James Bryant]. We were talking about space travel and things like that. So we had something in common at that time.

When you say "we," who constituted the we?

That was the group that we had at the time. Some of the guys have died since. The fellow that introduced me to him was named Lawrence Allen; he's still alive. We had our own all-males club, a research organization that we research everything, scientific information.

That's the origin of Saturn "Research"?

"Research," that's right. That's how it came about.

Was there a guitar player named Israel involved?

No, he was not involved in this. No, he came along the scene, maybe about four, five years, six years . . .

BRYANT. Eight years.

. . . after that. He never was directly involved in El Saturn Research. There was only a few of us into that, because a lot of guys came around. We had a hell of a lot of people that came around to hear us talk. To be actually involved in it, they were not involved in it.

Did you have a public forum, a place where people could come and hear you?

Not in the beginning. Later on we did . . . [points at a document he's drawn from his briefcase] . . . see what that says, see the address?

4115 South Drexel.

That's right, that's where everything started from. That's our house. Sun Ra was very much an introvert. He would be very comfortable just sitting over in a corner playing by himself. Nobody wanted to play with him. His name was Herman Poole Blount, and nobody could recognize a name like that. We were talking about space, we were talking about the Creator and all that. So I said we gotta find another name. He told me: "The Creator said that I should call myself . . . [mumbles]" He was too shy to say. [he and Bryant laugh] I said: "What is it? Spell it out." He said: "Which one sounds better?" and wrote out La Sun Ra and Le Sun Ra, and it came out Le Sony'a Ra, and then Sun Ra. We were his family, you understand. He said that since I have some Blounts on my side we were probably cousins, 'cause in the South everybody's connected. But he said he had no family, and I didn't know that he had any family for forty-some-odd years. We conducted business from that address there. We did most of our pressing and recording at RCA. I always wanted to stay in the background. We started it up for him, for Sonny.

So we started El Saturn Research and we started the Sun Ra Arkestra . . .

we were already doing research on the origin of the races and things like that, and the purpose of mankind. The earth didn't just pop up like that. They're teaching in school that everything happened through evolution, but that's not correct. The Darwinian theory is not correct. Everybody began to find it out, but we found it out back then. Since nobody wanted to play with Sun Ra, I said start your own band. So we started getting jobs for him at the social club level around in the Chicago area, which was a lot of jobs. There was a lot of social clubs then.

'52, '53, I said, "Well let's enlarge the band." The first horn we hired was John Gilmore. We had another guy that we used to use, John Tinsley. Whatever year Gilmore got out of the Army, that was the year he started, and before that the guys we were using were Harold Ousley and John Tinsley, and other guys that didn't stay active in it. Then we had Robert Barry, then we had Richard Evans. Then we hired Pat Patrick, Marshall Allen, then came Arthur Hoyle, and then Jim Hearndon was in there. The other trumpet player was Dave Young. Then we used another player, Walter Strickland?—something like that. That was the set of the band, should be seven pieces. Then we brought it up to eleven pieces. Then we began to rehearse. Used to rehearse every day. And as the band got larger, then Sun Ra began to write the music at Club DeLisa for Walter Dyett . . . no, Sammy Dyer. Sammy Dyer was the choreographer for the dancers of the floor show at Club DeLisa. Walter Dyett was the director at Du Sable High School who John Gilmore came through, Pat Patrick came through, that group. I went to Du Sable, but I was not a musician. I was in the glee club, did a lot of things that way.

But we began to take jobs; at that time there was a place called the Grand Terrace Ballroom, back in '54. At that time we played at Robert's Show Lounge—you've heard of Robert's Hotel on the South Side? We used to play club dates there and play there every Sunday. In 1954 we also had our club at the Majestic Ballroom at 47th Street, right off of Lake Park. And we used to have a very large following there on the weekend. We played Birdland '54–'55. Birdland is at 64th and Cottage Grove. Pershing Lounge was right upstairs over that, and used to be that Ahmad Jamal used to play upstairs at the Pershing Lounge, and Jack McDuff. It was once called the El Grotto Club, before it was Birdland. We played in Birdland up until 1959, but [later] it was not called Birdland because Birdland in New York filed a lawsuit against Birdland in Chicago. So Sonny asked Cadillac Bob—Cadillac Bob was the owner—he told him to change it to "Budland." We played with phonetics, and when you play around you find out there's a lot of information in the use of permutation. The first gig we had as a trio was a Shep's Playhouse, on 43rd and Lake Park. There was Crown Propeller Lounge, Railroad Worker's Hall, and Appomatox Club on King Drive. I'm talking about the earliest, '52 into

'55, '56. It was called the Appomatox Club, then Ambassador Club, then Princeton Club. These were the principal places we played at until '55. Then including the Trionad Ballroom, which was on 62nd and Cottage Grove. Then we began to get college dates at University of Chicago, Mandel Hall, and at Northwestern University. That was the main circuit at first. As time moved on we began to use up to seventeen pieces. Basically, our main working force was eleven pieces. Most things were recorded with eleven pieces.

The main purpose of this organization, from the very beginning, before we even had any musicians, we wanted to do some things to prove to the world that black people could do something worthwhile, that they could create things, they could do things that other nations . . . like we studied composers like Beethoven, and we read the books of Schopenhauer, Nietzsche. We decided that we had some things that nobody else had, and that's why this all started, to prove to the world and also primarily to America. We knew at that time that America was endowed by the Creator to be the leader of the world, believe it or not. And the leaders of America, meaning the president, must always act in a way that is conducive of what the Creator wants mankind to behave like. We talked about space travel, we talked about how the new world would be in the space age that was comin' up on us. We had studied the prophecies of the pyramids, the prophecies of Nostradamus. There are a lot of other minor prophets, but they were not seemingly as accurate as the prophecies of the pyramids and the prophecies of Nostradamus. Okay, the prophecies of the pyramids ran out in the early 1930s. That indicated that the earth should stop right there, there's nothing to take place after 1930. None of the great minds knew what would happen after that. Nostradamus's prophecies stop at the year 2000. In other words, none of the other great prophets: nothin' else. According to the prophecy of the pyramids, the earth stopped back in the thirties, 'round 1933, I think. After the year 2000: "It's after the end of the world [we all chant together] *don't you know that yet?*" This would explain why the spirit of the people is in disarray, because the leaders haven't taught them properly. Our great colleges and universities, preachers and priests, they're teaching the so-called "wisdom of past ages." They're teaching from *tradition*. They're teaching things that took place way back when, when some men were swinging on ropes with apes and some were walking on four, some were walking on two, and neither one knew where they were going.

My point is this, mankind really is on borrowed time. That's why we said "space is the place." We tried to tell the people to get ready to take a trip to Saturn; why go to the moon? We were talking about moon and space travel way before the Russians launched the first Sputnik. We tried to wake them up that Russia—we even said this, America don't look out, Russia is gonna surpass them, and they almost did. We knew that America should take a better stand to move its citizens forward, that there are no such things as black people and white people. People are people, that's what the Creator want America to act on. You're s'posed to see hearts and minds when you see people. Don't be so quick to judge people, because you might be discarding your next saviour. Look at George Washington Carver, look at Percy Julian, you see. These are black people. Everybody knows, there are dogs in every group. You see, the powers that be in this country have to reorganize everything and do it from their hearts. If they don't have hearts, they have to find someone that does, and try to learn to at not like a man, try to learn to act the way they would think a higher power, a god, a Creator—because they are. Those forces are all around, they're right here now, they're right here with me. When you see me, you see a representative of what the Creator and what the higher powers are about. We don't have time to think about petty things about prejudice and hate. We don't hate anybody. We don't have time to hate. If mankind would take the time to think of what the plan is from the intergalactic standpoint, you don't have time to hate. You don't have time to even catch a disease or anything like that. We started Sun Ra, because he was content to sit back in one room, nine-by-twelve room, he was content to stay there with his piano and his little pull-out couch, with all that stuff piled up on his bed and all that stuff piled up on his piano. He was disgruntled with the world. We started this 'cause the world needed it, you see. We were already researching, reading the books, putting out papers.

What kind of papers were those?

We used to type out information that we would research, cut stencils in them, and mimeograph them off, and give them to people in our group. And somehow some of the newsmen got ahold of them.

BRYANT. A lot of those groups were born from reading those papers.

Elijah Muhammad was around. I didn't know him. I was in my early teens, and they were doing what they were doing. We used to meet out in Washington Park. I used to live a half a block from Washington Park. We used to meet out on 54th and Washington Park near King Drive. We had our own tree that we used to stand by. People came to our tree. Meeting out in Washington Park, we became known as the crazy men, those guys from space, they make all kinds of noise. The Christians and Muslims were out there, and some other groups. And we had hundreds of people around us. The Christians and Muslims got together and started heckling us, talking about us. Ex-congressman Gus Savage used to be in the crowd, he used to come out there. One day, it was bright and sunny, not a cloud in the sky, very beautiful. We were talking, and people were attacking us. "How do you know we're gonna go to the moon? How do you know so and so?" We would answer the question. "I guess next you'll call yourselves gods!" I said: "We *are* gods." And we said: "We're all gods!" And that just made everybody angry. Then all of a sudden a wind storm came up, a cloud came out of no-where, the sky turned black, the trees start "shhhhh" wind blowing through it. And people got scared and took off. There's always been a power, I couldn't get away from this. It always made me come right back to it.

How many people were in the group?

About twenty, 'cause some of the musicians used to come out. Sun Ra was right there. I made him change his name, took him down to City Hall. Then I started helping him financially, pay his rent, because he was not making any money. This is back in '51, '52.

How old were you at the time?

I was around fourteen years old. I was working part time and going to school. Hey, you could do a lot with $10. I had help from my family at that time period. It was easy, $10 here, $20 here, $50 here, you could do a heck of a lot with that. I started helping him with rent, food, bathin', and buying clothes for him. And buying books. I would pick him up every evening, and when I wasn't there we would talk on the telephone. That's how we dis-cussed different things about a point of view, like: Who was Schopenhauer? Who was the Aryan race? Who was known as the "spiritual man"? What was the "spiritual man"? What was the origin of those terminologies? What was the purpose of the so-called sermon on the mount? What was the pyramid, what was the purpose of the pyramid, what is the circumference of the pyramid? That's so much research right there. The words we didn't under-stand we looked up and made a dictionary from them, and then we made another dictionary through the permutation process. Then we used numeri-cal codes that we developed. It went into spirit of the numbers; every num-ber has an intelligence behind it, every number has a spirit behind it. Every-thing has a spirit. A grain of sand has an intelligence. From that standpoint it has a code also. You heard of the word "molecular," the word "atomic," the word "subatomic," the word "neutrinos," but the code comes in in the word "atomic" and "molecular." The intelligence of a grain of sand has a mind all its own. That grain of sand will tell you it has enough sense to say: "I'm not gonna try to be anything but a grain of sand." You never seen a grain of sand say: "I'm God, I'm gonna go jump on the back of that horse." What he does, he's smart enough to wait until he gets on somebody's shoe or cuff and jump up on that horse. Or he wait until the swift wind comes by and take a blow up there. See, he's got more sense than mankind. Some people don't have the sense of a grain of sand. Maybe a grain of salt, but the grain of sand outlasts the grain of salt. Salt dissolves.

I had an opportunity to hear Sun Ra explain some of the numeric and per-mutation process, in terms of "earth" as a permutation of the "third" planet from the sun, and "dirt" as a permutation of "earth," and a number of other permutations of "earth."

[to Bryant, who is giggling] He's been studying a little more than he lets on. You know about some of the things I'm talking about. Back in the thirties, after ragtime was out, then there was supposed to be bop. Then our music was supposed to come in, because the music is the driving force behind the development of the rise and fall or the stagnation of a civilization or of a world or of a country. Now, our country moves forward because of the music. It's a driving force behind the stimulation of certain of the so-called "senses" and spiritual points within our subconscious. Our psychologists can only touch at it lightly, but there are ways that you can *ring* and open up certain minds. Within you there are billions and billions of worlds. Within the people that we call retarded, there's an area in everybody that can be reached. Back in 1954, I did some musical therapy with *Cosmic Tones of Mental Therapy* [sic] and several more albums at that time period and tapes, at Mount Sinai Hospital, California and 15th Street. Some patients were in a catatonic seize. I said: "Let me try some music." I helped set up the X-Ray department at that hospital at that time.

You're a radiologist, is that true?

[fumbles a bit, avoiding the question] I taught. My point is this, I said "Let me try some of our music." One of the catatonic patients came up and said "You call that *music*? You call that *music*? That's not music!" She talked for the first time. There used to be a dirty guy, lived out in the park. One day he came up with a clean shirt, necktie. We said: "What happened?" He said he listened to what we were saying and it encouraged him to go back to his family and start facing responsibilities. We talked about self-determination. The Creator wanted this planet, primarily the Americans, to stand on their own two feet, do something worthwhile, to make this a better planet. To start teaching, helping, subsidizing the arts.

The radio stations didn't give us the push. They called us crazy for talking about space travel and goin' to the moon, but now we can see who's really crazy, can't we? We told the musicians that they had better learn to play more than one instrument, because in the future one instrument will take the place of a whole orchestra. And that's what keyboards do now. And guitar sounds like a saxophone. You can do tremendous things with a synthesizer. The synthesizer was developed as a result of Sonny. There was a guy named Moog. This guy invited Sonny over to his house, and he designed the first synthesizer for Sonny. He made a lot of money off of that. That was another prophecy. We were trying to tell people what the Creator wanted us to do, and people were calling us crazy. The newspapers wouldn't give us any good write-ups. *Down Beat* never would give us a write-up.

It is said that Sun Ra once played some music for John Coltrane that really impressed him, changed him deeply. What was that music?

Well I'm not gonna tell you what it was. What happened was that Coltrane was staying at the Sutherland Hotel in 1956, and Sonny and I went to visit him. At that time Coltrane was recording for Atlantic Records, but Coltrane agreed to come over on Saturn. Pat Patrick was showing Coltrane some of our codes, you see, and you're not supposed to show to people until they're with us. It's like your frat; you don't get the codes unless you're a frat brother or sister. You'll notice that Coltrane's music began to change after 1956, he began to try to reach out. He got a new birth. He thought he'd done everything, but Pat showed him some new things, some stylin' that Sonny had taught Pat. Also some verbal things, it goes together. That's all I can say at this time. Atlantic Records—the guy's name was Neshui Ehrtegen—when they heard about it they renewed his contract, gave him a pretty good sum of money, I was told.

You must have a huge archive, not only tapes but music and papers.

We have research that we did back in that time period that I'm presently putting together. We've got more poetry that hadn't been put together. We've got music, and regardless of what anyone says, I own the name "Sun Ra," and Ihnfinity Incorporated owns the music.

Well just because you own the piece of paper that changed his name doesn't mean you own the name, does it?

It could, if it was just that.

BRYANT. A name is somewhat like a company. And the company belongs to Ihnfinity Incorporated.

We were his family. Who edited the first thirty-some-odd albums? Who funded things? Who did everything? I did. And there are musicians around who know this.

Did Sun Ra do things that weren't signed by you, that didn't go through Ihnfinity?

Occasionally, he got a little greedy. I never contacted him on it.

What was the relationship with Danny Thompson? He was managing the Saturn releases in Philadelphia, wasn't he?

Yes, but he never was an officer in El Saturn Research and Ihnfinity. He acted in that capacity at that time, because we had to do it that way.

I have a single of the Cosmic Rays. Sun Ra told me that there were two doo-wop groups, the Cosmic Rays and the Cosmic Echoes.

New Sounds, Roland Williams and the New Sounds. I'm trying to get some of their tapes together. There was the Qualities and there was the

Clock Stoppers. There's a forty-five out on the Clock Stoppers, the Qualities, nothing out on the New Sounds. We always put out a small amount because that was what we could afford.

The Cosmic Echoes?

Nothing happened with that group. [pulls an album out of his briefcase] You've heard of this fellow, haven't you?

Nope.

Lacy Gibson. He's one of ours, a blues singer. We had another label called Repeato. Lacy was on Repeato. Richard Abrams, Muhal—I recorded him on Repeato. We helped a lot of people while we were coming up.

When Sun Ra left, ultimately to New York, you maintained a close relationship?

We sent him there! He went to Montreal to play some gigs.

BRYANT. There was continuous care sent every week or two weeks the whole time he was in New York. Money was sent for hotel bills and airplane tickets.

When he moved to New York, it almost sounds like he started to do what he threatened to do when he was here: not go out, keep the Arkestra only as a rehearsal band, play the low profile. Was that because he didn't have you there pushing him to get out?

Well I was told by Richard [Evans] that when he was in New York, he was the same way. If you look at the early pictures, he's in the back.

Edward O. Bland's movie, too.

Then Richard said: "Sonny, why you sittin' way in the back? I'm gonna put this piano up front." That's when he put the piano where it should be, up front to the side. He was very much an introvert. That constant influence we had, he missed that, people told me. The spiritual side of it lessened. I was constantly making him keep talking spiritual things while he performed. "Talk about the Creator, talk about the Creator." In every one of those albums, there's a message; in every one of those poems there's a code. Unfortunately we never could get the financial support to really go after this. But the ground work is there. Phase two of what we were trying to do is to get it out there on a very wide form. It's not wide enough. Before he got sick, he was ready to take some of the shows like Johnny Carson, some of the MTV shows, to give him much wider publicity.

I understand some of the band is trying to set up an Arkestra "Foundation" now that Sun Ra is gone. What do you think about that?

They're trying to do that for themselves. Those people were never given the codes. They can get up and play, but the feeling's not gonna be genuine because they don't have the code. James Jackson don't have the spirit and code to go out and do what he's doing, because you have to go out and earn it. John Gilmore earned it; Marshall Allen earned it. I can give the code. I can train you, train him, train any of them and they'll sound it. You have to be given the code. The only people who knew what this was supposed to be was me and Sun Ra. Why? Because we were the ones who started it up, we researched it in the beginning. Then later he came on the scene [nods at Bryant].

What year did you get involved?

BRYANT. About 1953. I met Sun Ra in Washington Park, and we were talking about space. I was telling him about some of my encounters with actual spaceships. That's how we became close, because nobody else was talking like that. Then we all started to work together. I shared any information that I had gained in space encounters.

ABRAHAM. Remember, the purpose of this was to help black people and to give concerts for black people, to wake them up, wake them up. We found out that we could not do things only for black people. White people came to the concerts. We couldn't throw them out; why should we? We had to be cordial. Here we are talking about representing the Creator, and we're not gonna make it for white people too? But we got no help from nobody, white or black. All these records, I got them to him so he could sell them at the concerts and pay the bills. Everything that got pressed up, the money came from this end and went to that end. There are a lot of things that went wrong, misgivings. His earthbound side came out also sometimes. That's another story. A lot of illegal albums came out, but they'll be stopped. They have to deal properly with us. We're looking for a place here in Chicago to reopen a theater, show-club where we can teach this philosophy and keep the music going. Because I can write the music, the space music. Part of our corporation, something it says in our corporation contract, that we do what the Creator wills us to do to the best of our ability. That's what Ihnfinity is about, making it better for all mankind. Not just for himself, but everybody. The wrong impression was given when the Creator asked Cain "Where's Abel?" Cain said that he's not his brother's keeper. But mankind is each other's keeper—you are your brother's keeper. And your brothers are of many colors.

[Chicago, June 1993]

Free Retirement Plan

●

JOHN CORBETT. *Could you talk a little about the relationship between playing as an improvisor and your work as a commercial musician?*

DEREK BAILEY. This touches on something that has become rather more obvious to me lately. Some of the characteristics that I find attractive in the area of free playing are similar to things that I liked about the band business, years ago. I mean I started playing in the forties, late forties. And everything was fine for me until, I suppose, the very early sixties or even by the late fifties. Essentially, what happened was the rock and roll change. When rock and roll came along, for a working musician, particularly playing guitar, everything was transformed. There were certain things that that meant. First, you had to stand up all the fucking time. But in a more general way, the essential difference was that before the change people who listened to music, popular music—the most accessible music, regular music—weren't schooled to listen to recorded music. They didn't expect to be totally familiar with it. If you were playing in a dance hall in 1952, you could play for most of the evening and you might be playing all kinds of rubbish, but it was *your rubbish* to some degree. You weren't being asked to play other people's rubbish. You might to some extent, but that would only be a small part of what you were doing. A lot of the time you were playing a type of musical wallpaper. If you fulfilled the function that you were there for, which in a dance hall would be for people to dance to or in a night club it would be for people to get drunk to and make sexual alliances, then it didn't really matter too much, in detail, what you played, as long as it was in general what they expected. The main thing was that it fulfill its function. You were part of the pleasuredrome, you were part of the services offered by this business.

Ten years later, if you were working in a dance hall or nightclub, everything had changed drastically. Everything you played had to be totally familiar to the people *not listening* to it, if you see what I mean. You're still wallpaper, but you had to be exactly the kind of wallpaper which these people surrounded with themselves at home. Recorded music had taken over popular music entirely. So if you played any kind of tune, it had to be in a form that they were familiar with before *you* played it. Not just a song that they were familiar with. So suddenly you were no longer a musician working in a public situation and being responsible for what you did. You were a kind of surrogate. As a working musician in popular music you were a surrogate for recorded music, and that was all. Before this change from unfamiliar wallpaper to totally familiar wallpaper came about you had really quite a lot of freedom. It might be that you were in a nightclub or dance hall situation where you could in fact play exactly what you wanted. Now, what I wanted then was not what I want to play at this particular point in time, in 1992. But what I wanted to play, my musical appetites, could be satisfied in that world as a working musician in the 1950s in a way that they couldn't be satisfied later. And it was to do with this change in demand for what you have to do. It became a much more regimented job, perhaps a job more like an orchestral musician. Anyway, by that point I was working in the studios, which I recognized was absolutely nothing to do with what I wanted to do. But at that point, I was fortunate enough to bump into this stuff [improvised music]. And I went along with it.

So I'd say there are many connections between what I do now and what I used to do. I think that what I do now is what I set out to do when I started to play music. I never wanted to do anything other than play the guitar, but there was never anything I specifically wanted to play. I suppose when I was very young, I mean seventeen to twenty-two, I was obsessed with jazz. But that very quickly passed, almost instantaneously, when I recognized all kinds of things. I became more interested in, let's say, a generalized sort of playing at some point. It coincided with me finding that you couldn't make a living in England playing jazz on the guitar. I found out the hard way. So I went to things like learning to read music and all this shit and I just became a working musician. And in fact I spent the next few years working in as many different situations as I could find. That was the attraction to me; if I couldn't do it then I'd find out how to do it. All this had a looseness about it. One of the things I felt about jazz was the fact that it got very specific. Playing in a jazz club had all kinds of stereotyped requirements which you wouldn't necessarily meet playing in a dance hall, strangely enough. If you were playing in a small group you could do all kinds of things which were not acceptable working in a jazz club. Things were very rigid, or they were in those days. And now, what I know if it, it seems to be even more rigid.

Can you maybe briefly mention a few of the specific things which you might be able to do, say, in a given dance hall situation?

Yeah, I can as a matter of fact. I used to like to change the sequence from chorus to chorus, which is something I could do working with compatible musicians in a nightclub. When I say change the sequence, I mean change the substitutes, so the second chorus you wouldn't play the same substitutes

Derek Bailey
(photo: Caroline Forbes)

that you had earlier and you wouldn't necessarily play the same voicings. The general feel and the taste of the piece you were playing might change from chorus to chorus, because you were substituting substitutes and maybe changing voicings. And also I was quite interested in imitating different people from chorus to chorus. Something like that you could not do in a jazz club. For harmony voicings, playing the guitar, you followed the pianist, even if there was no pianist. So for instance, in November you might be playing the chords as Horace Silver played them. But the previous month you'd been playing them as Wynton Kelly played them. And then shortly after that we were all playing them as Bill Evans played them. You know it was a total fashion thing, within a very strict, limited area. There were a lot of stylistic limitations, stylistic prescriptions. So you just did it. In those years I played often in jazz clubs. I used to play regularly two or three nights a week in a jazz club after I'd finished work in the dance halls, which was not so unusual, lots of people did that. And I used to do what was expected, largely. The word "freedom" was not a word associated with jazz at all, but it is a word I would associate with working in the band business. I'd find that kind of openness in many working situations, even, strangely enough, in the studios more than in the jazz club.

Another similarity between then and now is the possibility to play with lots of different people. I do like to play with new people. It seems to me that if you're working in this field, freely improvised music, it's one of the sources of replenishment. It is for me, anyway. I'm so bereft of ideas of my own, perhaps, that I need to feed off other people. And I've always looked to other people. In this music, that's almost part of your material, what other people play. I used to like that when I played in the band business. I hated touring because you were playing with the same band all the time, so I would change, I don't know, my average would be three, four regular jobs a year. I was always changing jobs. I changed cities three, four times a year during those years. I found the business of movin' into a new band great. Getting out of it what you could, then looking for another situation which had something you could get something out of. I have to say, I feel the same about playing now, that its stimulus comes to a large extent from the people you play with. For instance, in this particular time in England—being heavily superstitious I don't want to put the blight on anything but it does seem to be quite a purple patch: it's either the beginning of something or the middle of something or maybe it's just finished. But for the last year or so, I think it's been very fertile. You get it now and again, sometimes it disappears, sometimes it comes up. But London seems to me to be okay at the moment. The main thing, of course, is this plethora of new players. They come from all different directions. I mean, half of them aren't players, but they're in this scene. I see that as being really useful.

What you said about jazz reminds me of what Adorno said about jazz. He said that there was a sort of rhetoric of liberation associated with it, with the dancing and the musical figures that went along, but that it was incredibly strict, binding in an absolute sort of way, with this veneer of being loose.

I think that's true. But I always assumed that I never really knew what jazz was, simply because of where I was looking at it from. To be precise, South Yorkshire. That's one of the things that made me change. By the time I was twenty-one or twenty-two, I realized that if I wanted to play like Charlie Christian I should have started at a different time, and *definitely* in a different place, and maybe in a different race. And I have to say, nothing I've experienced since that time has made me change my mind. I never got to say what I wanted to say, I think, except around the edges, playing jazz. I could feel happy about what I was doing only when it was completely eccentric in that context, then somehow I might be getting towards it. And of course it's only in recent times that I've felt that what I play kinda suits what I want to play, in that sense, that expressive sense, which I'm not sure means much anyway. My experience is that jazz in Europe and certainly in England . . . I mean England's a very special kind of country, for fuck's sake. If you're gonna be a jazzman you'd better not start in England. And English music, come on . . . So it's always seemed to me like a fantasy. You go to a jazz club in London—and this applies now as much as it did, say, forty years ago—you can see guys dressed for a night's fantasy. I'm talking about the musicians, these guys live a fantasy life. It is 52nd Street, in 1945, as far as they're concerned—between the hours of 8:00 and 10:30, which are the hours you're allowed to play under our licensing law, anyway. This doesn't mean to say there are no good players. There are some excellent players. But I have to say, there are always those kind of quotes 'round them, you know?

What you're talking about was a spatial fantasy forty years ago—Europeans looking at African-American jazz—and now it's a spatial and temporal fantasy, as well. The same thing's true in the States, though. It's a hard kind of nostalgia.

I get the impression that in the U.S.A., finally, you've all turned into Europeans as far as jazz is concerned. Without going into voluminous, tedious length, it's not possible for me to describe what it was like to experience jazz forty, fifty years ago. It was the only thing in the life of some teenager, growing up in Northern Britain, that had any magic about it. And the other thing that was also fantastic was also American, which was the cinema. Coming from my background, a working class background, all culture that meant anything to me was American culture. All the rest of it, which I had stuffed down my throat to a certain degree, was completely alienating. For instance, because at school I was a kind of music pupil I used to have to attend Saturday morning rehearsals of the Hallé Orchestra. This was during the war. Now, I don't know how widely known this is, but during the war they didn't play German music in this country. Because of the situation, these people were no longer immortal, timeless geniuses, they were part of the enemy. So you didn't hear Bach and Beethoven, what you got instead was Sibelius. And ever since then I can't hear a note of Sibelius without slumping into catatonic boredom, which is what I associate with my musical education such as it was. *Except* when I got away from it, went home and listened to my uncle's records or him playing the guitar or the radio. That was different. This is probably a common story of musicians of that time, but this was magic music. *Now* it doesn't seem like magic music; it seems formalized, it almost seems like Sibelius, some of it.

It used to be like a volcano, jazz. It spewed out all these amazing musicians, one after the other. Forty-five years ago, say, all the great jazzmen were alive. Even the ones that died young. There are always many who die young—we are talking about *the* romantic music. But forty years ago all the great jazz players were alive, some of them were at the beginning of their careers. I mean how many are left? This is an extinct volcano, it just throws off a few sparks now and again. But at one time there was this constant flow of new people coming along. That's something I associated with jazz when I was young. It was like: what's happening next? It was always: have you heard the new guy? There were always these new people coming up.

Which connects with what you were saying about constantly playing with new people.

Right, it offered that. The boundaries were always being pushed back. *Somebody* was doing *something*. And nobody, as far as I'm aware, presented himself as a great imitator or a guardian-of-the-tradition. That was left to Europeans and their obsession with older art forms.

How did contemporary European classical music figure into it for you?

I knew nothing about it. One of the things that distinguished my musical identity when I was young was ignorance. Man, there was so much I didn't know. Possibly I don't realize the extent of my own ignorance now—but at the time it was ridiculous. I had no idea who John Cage was until I met Gavin Bryars and Tony Oxley, by which time I was thirty-two, thirty-three years old. But then again, I'd never been interested in music in that way. To me, it was always a personal thing. I could almost say that the whole of new music was invented for me by Gavin Bryars and Tony Oxley, and later, by people like John Tilbury and Evan Parker. These were the people who were the encyclopedias that I robbed. So all my knowledge, so far as I have any, is second hand. I can only work that way, I think. The people I work with, I can fleece them rotten, but abstract knowledge is something that I have a real problem with. I mean I still have no record collection as such. And as far as it goes, it's full of Incus records. [laughs] And I never listen to them.

I can't imbibe music as a general force through, how can I explain it, through some abstract procedure like studying it. So, to mention Gavin again, who, when we used to play together, used to get all these scores and records of Messiaen and so on. And he'd say listen to this, and I'd say fantastic. But for me it's always been a practical thing, that's just a limitation. It seems to be the only way I can work, the only way I can imbibe stuff is from people I know . . . or want to know.

I'm playing with a couple of guys at the moment, very interesting characters. They both play what I'd have to describe as live electronics. They're into more current activities like sampling and scratching.

Must be Pat Thomas.

Well, there are two of them. That's one. And the other's a guy called Matt Wand. Now they both work with computers and patches and all the rest of it—again, something I know nothing about. But recently I've found it very enlivening playing with these two guys. They're an interesting couple because, while you could say that they both do the same thing (although Pat has a keyboard), they're completely different people. For instance, Pat is a very fine pianist, a really accomplished piano player. Matt is not a musician, he's a filmmaker, and he got into manipulating sounds for his own ends— film soundtracks and stuff. But he's actually a really good instrumentalist. These things are about reactions, tolerances, and all kinds of things you know, whether you can stand yourself doing something twice, or whether you can't. Or whether it doesn't matter. You know all kinds of funny things come into it. But to hear these two play duo is fantastic. When we play a gig, I always get them to do a duo. They're so different, but they come to this same point where they're using this machinery. Technology, they both come from different directions and yet they can both humanize it in a very interesting way. To find a way of playing with them is, well, currently a very absorbing thing for me. Now, how did *they* get in here? I don't remember how we got onto them.

It connects somehow. We'll realize it retrospectively.

I'm sure. And if we don't, it fits in with the music we play, because with those guys it's sometimes absolutely no connections. And yet what connects, what ties them together, very often, is some . . . I don't know, I'd have to use some useless word like "commitment." These guys are so agile. We did a concert recently in Germany with Tony Oxley. I'm negotiating with the radio (it was on the radio) to put it out on Incus. I really like it quite a lot. At the moment it's got that neutral quality, where it doesn't bring a lot of associations. That's quite interesting. I mean, a lot of the music they play is old bits and pieces of music, but to me it doesn't have the associations that the music had. So there's a certain sound, for instance, which is produced by a saxophone player when his soul is being stirred, which to me freezes the balls, it stops everything in its tracks. When they do that, when they play a bit of tape, it doesn't have that effect on me. And it's the same way with the resonant bass, that kind of goes *ghoommm* and you know already somebody knows what the music should sound like. But the sound on tape doesn't locate in the same way, doesn't bring with it all those clichéd associations. The context is different, of course, because it's probably following some woman screaming in childbirth or something, or some noise. They can do the opposite, they can dehumanize these overhumanized sounds.

Which is interesting because it takes the whole question of recording, which was the springboard that you were talking about for getting you out of commercial music and into improvising freely, and reincorporates it.

That's the great thing about improvisation. Or *playing*—"improvisation" has got that heavy sound to it. Playing is really subversive of virtually everything. So you clamp it down, like the industry's clamped down on it. I mean they don't want improvisation, naturally. You can't make money out of this shit where you don't know what's gonna happen from one minute to another. So, the process has been, of course, to nail it all down. But then the subversiveness gets into the technology, so even a guy doing a mix, you can't nail him down. There are guys improvising remixing a record. And that's where the life is in music. It always seems like it's the vein, the conduit for life in the music. That appetite seems to me to be always to do with changing things, which is often to do with fucking things up.

Which, in itself, has to do with analyzing what's going on, because if you aren't paying attention to what's going on you can't know what you have to fuck up.

Right. And then when somebody comes out and says, "I've got it, this is what it is!" you say, "No it isn't, *this* is what it is." Because you do something else. Which is the great thing about some fool writing a book about improvisation. You know that nobody's going to agree with it, and by the time the thing comes out, the music's gonna be different. If it stays alive. And that's the nice thing about something like the London Musicians' Collective, which has been up and down in its long history. The tendency of an organization like that is to nail it down, even though I suppose they all know what we're talking about. And this word "documentation" always comes up. Yet, it's really just generating activity, which is sort of essential. And you can leave it to the people involved to fuck the whole thing up, to change it.

It works by shifting perspectives and shifting levels. Once you've pinned it down in one place, it will shift to another level. I think there are, for instance, lots of dangers in writing about it, pinning it down in language. But one can always take solace in the fact that at a certain level it's gonna do what it's gonna do, regardless. I think the much more dangerous things are when a widespread understanding of improvisation becomes something fixed. And then, at that level, maybe it's important to discard the term. What happens is that you have a small group of people who think they "know" what improvised music is and are convinced that they're interested in improvised music, when quite often what it is that they're interested in doesn't have anything to do with that. I think the perspective from within the mainstream or even alternative press in the U.S., in my opinion, is very much more focused on fixing. I mean, it's all about fixing what something is so you can talk about it long enough so that you can sell it to someone. Even in the limited sense, not only on a huge scale.

I've got a lot of faith in this activity, whatever we're gonna call it. Its resistance to naming is a sign of its volatility. I mean they've never found a name for it. You know, at one time it used to be referred to as "free." Just "free." The whole area was the "free" area. I always rather liked that because it was so fucking meaningless. It was one of those four letter words, like "rock" or "jazz," which doesn't have any meaning. Maybe somewhere those have got some kind of sociological-sexual connotation. But "free"? And everybody used to say, "But it's not free, is it?" And you'd say, "No, it's definitely not free." But then that word fell out of use. Anyway, maybe we'll come up with some other four letter word. Four letter words are good for music, it seems to me, if you want to nail something onto it. But I think it'd be very nice if they don't find one. People say funny things about it. Somebody said, "Improvised music, what is that?" And improvised music is a description; improvised music is music that is improvised. It seems strange that a description is inadequate, whereas a name is meaningful. Of course, this is the whole business of naming, something to do with our species and symbols. If you give it a name, then you "know." You can identify it, preferably by some short, easily remembered name, and then you're okay. Your set of reactions and opinions know what to relate to. No lasting name, in music, that I know of, has been imposed, has it? The early jazz players didn't like the name "jazz." In the early days of rock, it didn't have that self-congratulatory ring to it: "rock forever!" and so on. Nobody invented it. Where did it come from? All these names come with the music.

Then again, some interesting names have been invented—like "rhythm and blues." It's said that Jerry Wexler coined the term to replace "race records" on the charts, though he later said that he'd rather it was "rhythm and gospel." But I interviewed Texas blues pianist Whistlin' Alex Moore, who claims that it was derived from "rhythmin' blues"—that is, taking the blues and "rhythming" them. Beautiful, I thought. But these things are about setting up borders for profit, mostly. I mean, what you've said about playing in bands reminds me of the American scene, too. There were musicians who were playing what we'd now call free jazz in the context of R&B bands—Big Jay McNeely made his entire act playing what might now be associated with Coltrane or Ayler. It seemed that border hadn't yet been built when you were working in British dance bands.

You notice a lot of these things were economic. It was an industry, of course. The band business was an easy business to work in. There was a lot of work. If you can imagine that a town like the one I grew up in with half-a-million people in it had—it'll sound like an exaggeration—every night, maybe fifty places that had live music. In the same town, you couldn't find six live music events in the course of a week *now*, or if you did they'd all be visiting events. The music was gruesome music sometimes, but then again sometimes it wasn't. If you walked from where I lived into town, which was like a mile, and you passed fifteen, twenty pubs, most of them would have some live music in them. Usually from a solo performer to a quartet, but given that situation, if you're any good at all, if you can provide what's needed, it's a worker's market. So you can get away with murder. And a certain eccentricity wasn't thought of as being necessarily . . . unexpected. During that period, I knew some extraordinary musicians, I must say. Some of the most inventive musicians I've ever met, including the people I've worked with since. And also some of the most peculiar.

There was a guy I knew who was playing in a quartet in a dance hall. When he heard that Charlie Parker played with his back to the audience, *he* decided to play with his back to the audience. But he played the *drums*. He set up his drums for the first set every night with his back to the audience. This guy was a great player, in a generalized music sense. He was a very, very fine drummer. I think he must be one of the two or three best drummers I've played with. He was a very good singer, he was very funny. I mean, they were never gonna fire him, and this guy was notorious for things like setting the band room on fire, all this kind of behavior that is semi-expected of certain "characters," as they used to call them. But this guy was a really extraordinary, very, very fine musician. He played guitar really very nicely. And funnily enough—it was a complete bluff, but it was such a good bluff—you've heard Han Bennink play the piano, how Han can make himself *sound* like a free piano player—well this guy could make himself *sound* like a bebop piano player, which is a different kind of thing. He had oddities, like he always wanted to play in D. But people could get away with things. This freedom arose in that time because of the market. If they didn't like you, you could go down the road and get another job. Later on it started getting harder, but initially, when I first started, work was quite easy. I suppose I wouldn't have gotten into it otherwise.

What was the drummer's name?

Jeff Todd. A great musician. Jeff was quite a man. He's been dead for many years. He died when he was thirty-eight, which was a good age for a guy like that to reach.

What did the transition period between commercial music and free improvising look like to you?

It was so gradual, it wasn't any decision at all. For me, it was being fortunate enough to meet these guys and tag on with them. There is this background of the work I did gradually disappearing, this life as a working musician—which suited me fine. If you could freeze a time, that time wouldn't be a bad time for me. It suited me, but it changed. And it was obvious that it was changing. It was a very funny period. This was the early sixties: '61, '62, '63, '64. I had experiences where I was still changing jobs quite often, but by this time I'd set up this regular connection with Tony and Gavin, so we were already working in this area. They were also working in these [commercial] situations, though they were young guys who'd just come to it. Gavin, in any case, was a student, but I met him playing in a nightclub. He was depping [substituting] for the bass player in this nightclub where Tony and I worked.

But there were funny things, because I'd lost interest in trying to make sense out of this working situation. I knew it wasn't going anywhere because I'd reached a stage where I'd got what were supposed to be the rewards of that kind of world, and I knew it was nothing to do with what I wanted. I was working in the studios at the time, making quite a lot of money. During that time, over the sixties altogether, even after I moved back to London and started playing with John [Stevens], Paul Rutherford, and Evan [Parker], I was still doing studio work. I could work one day and easily get a week's money. It was an easy way to make a living and also do what I wanted to do. But I sorta hated it, and I'd never hated any musical work I'd done before. I'd disliked some of the music, but I had never hated the job. I came to find working in the studios unpleasant, I didn't like many of the people I worked with. Conversation was primarily around bathrooms and carburetors, which I'm sure are arresting subjects, but they weren't the ones I wanted. I still was inclined to talk about music, which was looked upon as some kind of dreadful social gaff in that world. So I was looking for a way out. I'd finished with the other world, but I was looking for a way to continue *feeling* as a musician as I'd felt before. And I found it working with these people.

Another funny thing that happened at that time was the rise of Britain's particular branch of rock and roll. I was offered quite a lot of jobs which later turned out to be with household names. It was a very peculiar period. For instance, every year they have this thing in London called the Royal Command Performance. And this is a huge variety show, they invite famous Americans, it goes on for hours and hours, the Royal family come and it's at a famous theater. It's a big gala occasion and you get a silver program with it. And I got booked to play on this thing, in the pit. This was at a time when I was working with the Spontaneous Music Ensemble. (I was never sure if I was *in* the Spontaneous Music Ensemble or a fellow traveler, but that's another story.) This Royal Command Performance went on all day, the same day the Spontaneous Music Ensemble got a gig in Brighton or somewhere outside London. So I turned this Royal Command Performance down. I said to the fixer: "I'm sorry I can't do this, I've got another gig." And he says: "You've got another gig? This is the best 'gig' of the year." And what he meant was the money, I guess. The relative money was, I suppose, sixty times what I was getting for the SME gig. So it was unknown for someone to put a dep in for this. You couldn't put a dep in for this gig. And I couldn't put a dep in for the SME, because there was nobody else playing this kind of music, at that time. So I was stuck with these two jobs. There was no confusion about which one I wanted to do, but I had to do the other one where—almost by law—you can't put a dep in. You can't put a dep in when the Queen's coming. So that was that. I did this, and the other guys went to Brighton.

I got offered this job in a restaurant. I hardly ever worked as a bandleader, but on this occasion I did. And this was in a place on a small island off the coast of France called Jersey—I guess you might call it "Old Jersey." It's a tourist place. And this was earlier in the same period. I'd worked on this island a couple of times, at different times. I liked to go there, it was quite a good musical scene in a general way, very good for work and a lot of good musicians. Anyway, I wasn't sure about this; it was for six months and I thought: "That's a long time to play this shit." So I got a contract out of this guy where we were supposed to play jazz. He was the son of the man who owned the hotel, his first year in hotel management. I don't think he ever got past his first year, possibly because of our adventures. I said to him: "I've got to have a contract, Digby, in which it says that I am the musical director and the choice of music played is entirely mine." He said "I don't mind, you can play what you like. We're very easy here and I'm a jazz fan, you know." So what we settled for was a contract which said we could play jazz in this restaurant six nights a week for six months. I took a trio: vibes, bass, and guitar. Gavin Bryars was on bass. And for dinner music, we used to play things like John Coltrane's "Alabama," which sounds a bit odd played by vibes, guitar, and bass, anyway. "After the Rain," things like that. We were, in that period, playing a lot of Coltrane tunes, for some reason which eludes me at the moment, although I suppose it was because we were playing modally a lot. Kind of before we were playing free—which is not free, of course. But I mean we were doing a lot of modal pieces, and we'd got a lot of stuff we'd written ourselves at the time. We needed somebody who could play piano for the absolutely berserk shit on Saturday night, 'cause that is inevitable. Regardless of contract somebody's gonna want you to play a certain kind of dance and if you don't play it you're gonna get punched on the nose. So you'd better play it. But virtually all the time we used to play other things.

At that time we would play Scott LaFaro tunes in 7/11, and all those things. We were in a rather technical phase. It was all right, we kind of got around it. The people just couldn't stand us. But we got away with it. We didn't leave until I walked out for something totally different. I had an argument with the head waiter and packed up my instrument on the dance floor. But it was not a musical argument. We could play what we liked. It's not an ideal situation, but then again it's extraordinary what you can do if you fulfill your function. I mean, people *can* drink soup to John Coltrane. During the day we ran a little jazz club. And that was verging on the free things. So there were oddities like that; the demands of being a working musician and stumbling into the free playing at the same time led to certain odd situations. And certain strains. It came to the point where, for the first time for me, I couldn't play—on the job, while I was working—the music I wanted to play. By that, I mean I couldn't at some time during the evening. So for instance at one point I got very interested in some things that I thought Coltrane was doing in his improvising. I always thought Coltrane was interested in serialism, for instance. There are certain sections of his solos where he plays phrases backwards and forwards. Nobody seems to have picked up on that, too much. And I would be sitting in a nightclub with a quartet or something—I can remember this happening in Manchester—and we'd be playing some standard tune. This quartet's sitting there in evening dress and the guitar player's playing about three times as fast as he's technically equipped to do, running these phrases backwards and forwards on some tune like "Over the Rainbow." Before that, I'd always been able to accommodate what I wanted to do, at least at times, within the work. And that seemed to me to be a natural way of working. It was when I realized that the music that I wanted to play had got to a point where I couldn't accommodate it in a working situation, that's when the break came. That's when I just stopped working as a musician and did some studio work, and I did a bit of teaching (which I preferred to the studio work). Until I somehow started making a living doing this stuff. But the natural way of working things out, for me was working it out in a practical situation. I'm an obsessive practicer at home, but I don't think anything happens for me as regards development or pick-ing up new habits or whatever you want to call it, except in the playing situation. And it's always from other people, I think.

The prescriptions on behavior that you've talked about—having to stand up to play rock and roll, having to dress and act a certain way to play jazz—do you think that there has come a period, or maybe come and passed, where the music called free improvisation has been subject to that kind of thing?

[nods] I think it's suffered from, at different times, everything that any other music's suffered from. There's as much posturing in it, there's as much formalized music. Perhaps not *as much* in some of these cases, but all these besetting sins of all the musics that we're complaining about, yeah, sure, they appear in freely improvised music for different kinds of reasons, I think. They come to it not because it's an open space, but because they think there's some structure there they can use for their musical ends. So they're likely to take whatever they think is useful for their purposes. It's inevitable, and I don't think it matters. In a way, archetypal improvisors wouldn't get anywhere in any other music.

I like to think of myself as someone who's interested, like you, in new players, in newer things going on. But at this festival [LMC's Festival of Experimental Music] I must admit, the things that have been most satisfying have mainly been older . . .

Yes. Maybe you should have come to Company Week instead. That is all about playing, which I suspect is what you are interested in. Something described as a "Festival of Experimental Music" can cover all kinds of things. Some of these people taking part think of themselves as artists, I would guess. "Playing," which although undefined is a better word, I think, than "improvising" for what, say, John Stevens and I were doing on that festival probably has very little to do with what some of the people operating in this area are concerned with. For instance, for this year's Company Week, I invited David Shea, whose turntable playing I like very much. He's a player. He makes it work *with other players*. Reminds me of the way Teitelbaum uses electronics when he's playing with other people. They both bring something to the music—to the playing—which is somehow beyond their individual performances. Now, Christian Marclay, I would guess, is not interested in playing, as such. He's an artist, a good one, probably, and is primarily inter-ested in presenting his conceptions. See, artists like to present their ideas, don't they? "This is what I've thought of/discovered. What do you think of it? Great, isn't it?" Playing is not really about that. It can include that but it also includes many other things, too, and important among them is working with other people. It's not only about your own ideas.

But it's a mistake to think that the newer people are not interested in playing. Most of them are, I think. They weren't well represented on this festival, though. In this country, there's a whole bunch of newer people: Oren Marshall, Alex Ward, Steve Noble—a very significant figure in this music now, I would say—Vanessa Mackness, Matt and Pat, a group called the Honkies—very lively—Conspiracy; all these people and quite a few more are all players who have turned up in recent times. But the LMC, while it includes players, has always been prey to artists.

Another problem is simply the form—a festival. Festivals are primarily social occasions; old friends get together to give a succession of party pieces. They exist because it's a format that suits promoters. Essentially, they are antimusical. Company Week is sometimes mistakenly referred to as a festival. In fact, it's the opposite. On Company Week people are invited for a period of five or six days in which they make music together with other players, most or all of whom they won't have met before. There is no time or use for preconceptions or reputations. The precise opposite of a festival which is built on both. A festival is a flower show; exotic blooms carefully presented. Company Week is a muddy ditch; it's where things can grow.

[Here we break for lunch, after which we resume, talking about more up-to-date stuff.]

I never have had, and I don't have, any long-term strategies. Of course, at my age that's a suitable posture, I think. It's kind of staggering on from one thing to another. But in recent years it's been quite busy for me. I got involved in television programs, which were based on the first edition of the book. And then the subsequent re-edition of the book, based on the television programs. All this involved me in all kinds of peripheral rubbish. Although, a lot of it was very instructive. As it always has been, that kind of digging around in the improvisational aspects of other musics. If we have to include these dirty words, I think of it as being a "tradition" of what I do, people messing around with music, manipulating music, whatever kind of music. And as I've said I think it's quite virile in this town right now, which makes it, for someone like me, a possible life-support machine, in a way. And there's a strange mixture—the older players seem to me to be both very active and playing very well . . . I mean, take John Stevens, who's been in and out of freely improvised music. I've played with him two or three times in the last year, first time for a very long time, and he seems to me to be playing very beautifully. But also Tony, we've recently done this recording with these two samplers, Matt and Pat. And there seems to be possibilities in all directions. You can't calculate these sorts of things.

The book and the films have been little more than a distraction. I don't consider them central to what I'm interested in doing. But it's related to playing, and this area's funny in that anything that's related to playing is part of it in a way. Like organizing gigs, Company Week, for instance, which I organize. And whenever there's an Incus thing, I organize it. I don't see that as extra-musical. It seems to me to be, in a sense, musical, because that's the way we are—we have to do it. That's what's encouraging about a lot of the newer people, they seem to automatically accept this thing that part of playing this music is putting it on yourself. And it's not just because nobody else will put it on. There does seem to be a kind of compatibility between the cottage industry philosophy and a music that's made, to a large extent, from scratch, starting from nothing. The fact that there are no structures you can hook into seems to me quite appropriate. It means that if you don't put some time into organizing the music, you're slightly missing the point of the music. I don't know of anybody in this music who's done it over a long period of time who hasn't done any organizing, sometimes in a central, serious way. People who now maybe don't, somebody like Han . . . I mean Han, when the phone rings he goes out and plays the gig, whatever it is, and I don't think he does any organizing at all. He does a lot of painting. But in the past he's done an enormous amount of work. And if he can do it, it seems to me that anybody can do it—and you can take that how you like.

I have to say, the only side of promotion that bothers me is that we don't get much effective promotion. I've always taken the American attitude as being admirable towards promotion. When I spent some time in New York, everybody seemed to be hustling all the time. I don't see anything wrong with that. I much prefer that, as a kind of adjunct to what you do, to flat-out romanticism.

Except when you have to deal with it all the time, so that it starts to eclipse what else is going on—like the music, for instance.

Well in that case you're not doing it right, are you? It can't swamp the music of course. But I assume that that's something that you know about. If you don't want to do it, it's easy not to do it. But I don't find any stigma in it. I prefer hustling to somebody who goes on the bottle because they're not getting any gigs. It's also a very dirty game, hustling. It's dirtier than carrying CD boxes up and down stairs. And these dirty aspects of playing are, to some extent, a corrective to make sure you don't entertain the illusions associated with the music business and all the poisonous fucking gloss that goes with that. That's responsible for all the short-termism in music. The fact that most musical careers are very short, even very well known musical careers. I mean, if this stuff is what you want to do with your life, then you'd better make sure it lasts a lifetime. And one of the ways, it seems to me, is to avoid delusions about what it is about. Music is a very efficient vehicle, perhaps the most efficient vehicle, for bullshit.

I mean, who the fuck do we think we are? There is so much garbage associated with the public face of music. It seems most people in music believe that you can only survive on a tidal wave of hyperbole and bullshit. And maybe that's so, but if you're gonna believe in it you're in trouble. One of the ways of rectifying any delusions is to carry a few boxes up and down stairs, or to have somebody on the telephone: "We'll ring you back." Such as some overpaid, underknowledged arts administrator.

It also puts you more in touch with what you're doing, doesn't it? It gives you more control over it, maybe how people perceive it.

It's a bit difficult there, John, that side of it, because I have to say I don't know what the public (so far as we can call our small audience the public), how they perceive us. Because of this barrage of rubbish which normally surrounds the presentation of music. If you don't use all that rubbish, who knows? That's the chance you have to take, that people will actually see that what you see is what you get. One of the advantages of all this cottage industry aspect of it is that it keeps you in touch with the more grisly aspects of making a life out of playing this music that virtually nobody wants to listen to. But how it strikes other people, I wouldn't like to speculate because they're fed constantly on this other stuff. And it might be that that is why, to a lot of people, they can't even recognize it as musical activity.

I just think it's a kind of personal thing, that if you can't maintain some kind of realistic assessment about this activity vis-à-vis general music activity, and even beyond that (because music itself is such a minority activity, of course), then you're in trouble. My expectations were never that I'd have the opportunity to do some of the things that I've done. As regards the way people look at us, I can't figure it out because I'm still in contact with people who thought I was some sort of licensed lunatic when I played *regular* music. I'm talking about my family. That kind of thing, that defensiveness towards those people has always been part of my life, and I don't feel anything odd about people disliking what I do. I still feel relief to be doing it, but I don't expect it to match, in any important respect, music as I read about it in magazines. [smiles]

When you guys were making those records, in the late sixties, for Island, Deutsche Grammophone, and RCA, I wonder whether you thought that those opportunities would turn into anything on a big scale?

It was possible to get them then, which it's not now. Stevens was quite good at doing that, and Tony was quite good at it. I don't know why. I had no idea where they came from. To me it was like Paul Rutherford ringing up and saying: "Deutsche Grammophone are putting out a triple box record of free improvisations and we've gotta go to Berlin and record some music for it." I said: "Well, that's amazing." But I didn't assume there was a career going to blossom out of that, no. If I thought anything other than *what a nice gig*, I assumed they'd made some kind of mistake. I know that sounds a little bit contrived, but I think that's as far as I'd push it at that time. Although funny things went on, after all you're talking about the sixties when people made fortunes overnight. I taught guitar to millionaires.

See, I was no longer young, even then. [laughs] It was something I'd gradually come into, but all the other guys that I worked with at that time were quite young, so it was really their first music. Tony was in the jazz world, but people like Rutherford and Evan, they'd knocked around for a year or two, but they were quite young, early twenties, and they hadn't worked as musicians. They were remarkable players, a revelation to me. But maybe they did have some expectation of it just getting bigger and bigger. I mean, they'd grown up with free jazz, and new music, and it was very fashionable. People like Cage and Albert Ayler were far better known then than they are now. And maybe they thought we were on to something. What I thought was, well, this will do. I was looking to retire, and I retired into this, which turned out to go on a lot longer than the thing I'd retired from. I can't say I thought of it as a potential ladder to fame and fortune. At best it was an indication that maybe I could carry on behaving in a totally irresponsible manner. To me, this music is a hideaway, and still is in a sense. I can do what I wanna do, and that seems successful. That's the success I was looking for.

Four years ago, I remember talking to you about Cecil Taylor, specifically about how you said you thought he'd missed his chance to play with and be challenged by some of the most innovative European free improvisors—like yourself, Han Bennink, Evan Parker, and Tony Oxley. Two years later, in Berlin, he had a chance to work with all of you.

I thought it proved what I was saying.

Maybe with Evan, that was true—I thought it had its moments. Certainly I didn't think the encounter with Han was what it would have been in the early seventies, say. But with Tony Oxley and especially with you, I thought it worked extraordinarily well.

Yeah, it was a great gig for me. We had a good time. I've played with him a couple of times since, but with the trio with William Parker and Tony Oxley. I must say, I'd much rather play with him in duo than with the trio. The language gets much more, I don't know, oriented towards some sort of beat when he's playing in the trio. Whereas his language is much more open otherwise. But the last time we played together there was something sorta cracking in the trio that was really quite interesting. You know, he's not a loud player. One of the interesting things that you find with him, and it came as a surprise to me, is how quiet he plays. Of course, he always takes a lot of trouble with the PA, so he's always well miked. But he plays quietly.

And he's such a liquid player. I don't like playing with piano, usually, although it is one of my favorite listening instruments. But the fucking thing is too big, it seems to me. And the only free player that I've ever played with who's got over this mechanical thing is Cecil. He has a definite . . . it's not a glissing thing, but it's liquid. I guess it's technique in pedalling, 'cause his pedalling is fantastic. He really moves around in the middle of the instrument beautifully.

When I turned up for the sound-check, he said, "Do you want to talk about the music?" And I said, "Well, I'd prefer if we don't." He said, "Okay." I said, "But I would like to play the acoustic guitar for a bit, if you don't mind." And he said, "Anything." And I said, "I might not play it on the mike." "Anything." So I just walked around playing the acoustic guitar, which in that hall was really resonant. Every time I've played with him I've liked it. The trio was much more restricting, but then again it's nice. I feel like I'm Tiny Grimes to his Fats Waller, rhythm in the background. I found that the most satisfying way of playing until somehow the last set in Manchester it all cracked open. And it promised all kinds of other possibilities. But there's been no chance to pursue them since then. He's remarkable. When you consider the social and musical environment in which he's had to work, his achievement is extraordinary. And continuing.

[London, May 1992]

PETER BRÖTZMANN

Machine Gun Etiquette

●

Sitting on a park bench up above the dock of the bay at
Vancouver harbor, German saxophonist Peter Brötzmann
and I spent about an hour tossing some words into the wind
on a blustery afternoon in June 1992. The night before, as part of the du Maurier
International Jazz Festival, Brötzmann had played a powerful duet with percussionist
Hamid Drake, a recent partner whose masterful tabla, traps, and frame drumming draw
out the reedman's more rhythmic tendencies. That night, after our interview, Drake and
Brötzmann were joined by pianist Marilyn Crispell for a trio that—after a few introduc-
tory kluges—was utterly breathtaking. The following night, the trio moved on to record a
CD in Toronto, but on that bench we reviewed the state of things old and new, and how the
notorious noisemaker is looking to attend to his sweeter aspect. Unprovoked, Herr Brötz
led.

PETER BRÖTZMANN. I am fucking tired of jokes in music.
JOHN CORBETT. *What about somebody like Han Bennink?*
For an audience, it's always a new thing. But if you work with such a guy
for years and years, you know it all. Then you have the feeling, standing in
the corner—"Oh, *this* again. And *that* again. Okay."
But you can't go out on the road and play something absolutely fresh every
time you perform.
No, of course. That is impossible. Nobody does that. The only thing you
have to try to do is to keep yourself together, try to get some communication
with the guys you're playing with, and from time to time get things over to
the audience. Misha is the perfect partner for Han because Misha takes
nothing very seriously. He is sitting there, smoking, drinking a little brandy,
sometimes even he is playing, but on the other hand he lets Han do his
things. But even in that duo—they know each other for thirty years nowadays, I think—I saw them two years ago, and for me it was the same thing. I
knew all the stuff. But Misha is always able to surprise me. Because he
[doesn't] give a shit.
Maybe it's a very special Dutch attitude. Willem, for example. As much as
I like him as a person, as a player, even as a composer. But I think his fucking

tentet is so boring. If you have heard it twice, it is enough. And the same is going on with Han. The few times I have seen him since we split, he does always the same things. He is doing them perfect, because he can. If he plays the brushes with a little swing beat, or the shuffle or whatever . . . yeah, fantastic. But I must say, for me it's not enough. I don't know if I'm able to do things in another direction, but I'm *trying*. I don't like to sit down and live from my last twenty-five years. There was one of the reasons I joined [Last] Exit and I enjoyed it. People can say whatever they want, we played good concerts, we played bad concerts. Of course, that's the way it goes. But it always was a kind of challenge for all four of us. I liked that situation much more than being perfect.

You know, sometimes I wonder where the audience for the music is going to come from. For a while I thought it was going to come from the young rock listeners.

It was a nice experience doing a couple of tours with my son. Of course we played different places than I usually play, with different people. These young people, between fourteen and twenty, they were surprised. "What is this old man doing? What kind of shit is that?" They didn't know anything about it, but they liked it. What is happening in the rock field is mostly rubbish, too. That was the same experience playing with Exit. We had really a very mixed audience, people coming from all kinds of music experience, which was really nice.

It seemed like Last Exit might break in a big way for a little while. I don't think anyone with any sense thought so, but . . .

Yeah, that was quite an illusion. When I showed up with Exit for the first time in Europe, people came to me "Oh, Brötzmann, now you're making big money." And let me tell you, the numbers we sold of Exit records, in half a year I sell more solo records.

That's what Steve Beresford said. He got a gig doing something commercial, and suddenly all of the improvisors he was playing with thought he was a millionaire.

It's still a pity. Maybe it was the right time to stop it, but it was quite some fun. Musically, sometimes. Not all the time. And these people are a little bit difficult to handle, too. But I like to play with Sonny and especially Shannon.

It would be a nice trio. I'm not fond of Laswell.

No, he's not a fantastic bass player, but I think he's a good guy to keep things together, musically. As I told you before, we had lousy concerts, but we had some good ones. I don't like, for example, the last record we did, *Iron Bars* on Virgin. It's bullshit. But, I didn't have any kind of control on that. It was that kind of studio production that I *hate*. You show up in the night, play a couple of up and downs, and somebody's mixing after that. Exit was really a live band. These Americans, they make things so difficult. Not the music, but the things around. This kind of image problem they all have.

Machismo bullshit.

Yeah. I don't know, maybe I'm real German in taking things too serious, sometimes. But I don't like very much what is going on in jazz and improvised music. Forget about the bebop revival people, but even people like Lester Bowie or David Murray, they're just going the easiest way. Of course, European audiences like that—maybe audiences everywhere. I think so. But it doesn't take you anywhere. I'm always ready to make mistakes. I like to get some challenge, some strange situations. I know what I can play. I know that I am, if I want to be, one of the loudest saxophone players in the world, nowadays. But that doesn't make me any happier. [laughs] Now I want something else, I want some tension.

Something occurred to me last night while listening to you play. On the early octet records where you and Evan are playing together, it's always clear who's who. But you had certain things in common. Then each of you went in your own directions. And now last night I heard some things that sound more like Evan to me in some ways.

Oh, I mean, that might be that Evan is a guy I like very much. I love his music. I like his way of just going his way, playing the way he is playing. He is unique. He is working hard. We don't see each other so often, but when we do we talk quite a lot—about nonsense or about music or whatever. We know that we went different ways, but I think that we know that everybody did the right thing for himself. You don't find very many people with this very straight concentration on the horn, on the music. And you have to think about the world. Coming back to *Machine Gun*, '68. Of course we came out of the same musical backgrounds: trying things, getting fed up with the American hard bop, things like that. But it was a kind of political thing, too. Nowadays you miss the political side of the thing anyway. Everybody's just hunting gigs, which is necessary. Everybody has to survive. But, especially if I look at most of my black American comrades, they mostly play and earn money in Europe and Japan. They just do their thing, but there is not very much mind behind it. Or if they still think about their situation in the States, they don't show it anymore.

Politically, you're talking about.

Yes.

I know what the political circumstances were, but my recollection of asking you about '68, say vis-à-vis the student riots, was that they weren't something you were involved in.

In Germany and France—England is and always was an island which was not so very much touched—but it was the feeling, the very naive feeling that we could take a little part in changing the world, the society. To make it, maybe, kind of better. It was very naive, but it was true. Of course, I had to do with people like [Ulrike] Meinhof. We were sitting in the same bars, talking, sometimes playing. Got drunk, mostly, later in the night, of course. I wouldn't say there was an ideology behind the music in that very straight way, but it was really a very common feeling.

It is something that I think a lot of people are really averse to remembering. Someone like Derek constantly disavows there being anything political about what he does, when just the politics of getting a gig doing this kind of music . . . this is politics, could there be anything more backstabbing and sleazy than that?

Yeah, that's true.

I've never really seen a good history on you. How did you get involved in playing saxophone in the first place? You were a painter, right?

Yes. I got to art school in Wuppertal. At that time my main interest was in painting. I was always playing clarinets. Very soon, then, saxophone. My first experience with all the gallery situation was an art market. It was so disgusting, and I hated the people. If you go nowadays to an opening, you look around yourself, go out and vomit. Twenty-five or thirty years ago, exactly the same shit. So I worked with some semiprofessional [musicians]. That was much more exciting. I went on with painting, but I never was so ambitious to do exhibitions anymore.

This must have been early sixties.

Early, early sixties.

You were playing in what kind of band?

At that time it was a kind of swing/bebop band. All the other guys studied music at a very famous school in Essen, and they knew everything. I was really the only amateur. But then the band split up. I went over to Wuppertal, studied this art business, and played around with local cats. Somebody told me there was this young guy trying to play the bass, who was Mr. Kowald, at that time seventeen years old.

You were older?

[proudly] Yeah, nineteen. Much older. Peter lived with his parents. I had my little studio, so he was always hanging out at my place. But he had to be at home at 10:00, he was drinking milk. But we changed that, very soon. His parents were always very angry about me, because he never showed up at home anymore, he dropped studies of ancient languages, Greek and all that.

You're the corrupter.

Yes. Then, with different drummers, Peter and I were the main thing. We worked nearly every night in a kind of club, it was just a hole somewhere, some cellar. '62, '63.

What were you playing at the time?

Some Mingus, some early Ornette Coleman. Of course we listened to Coltrane. And early Miles Davis things. We had a time we played all the Mingus things, tried.

So listening to American music was largely inspiration.

That was one side of it. But, because I was involved in the art business, I met people like Stockhausen and especially Nam June Paik. I listened to [David] Tudor and John Cage. They all worked in Cologne a lot. With Paik, I'm still good friends. I was working for him, just fumbling around with his machines and things. He stayed quite a long time in Wuppertal; there was a very good gallery that took all the early Paik things, early Beuys, and these kind of things. So I learned from this side that I shouldn't give so much about the bars and the harmonies, just trying to find out what is possible.

I saw a reference to a group of yours on a poster for a Fluxus festival. I didn't know the Paik connection, but I always thought about the Fluxus connection with Han and Misha.

I met Misha in the early sixties not because he was playing in some jazz club in Amsterdam with Monk tunes, but I met him first through Fluxus activities. Some years later, I met Han and Willem Breuker. But that was already '66. In '64 to '66 I had my first contacts to American musicians, like Don Cherry, Steve Lacy. Steve Lacy was very, very helpful. Carla Bley, we did this funny tour, which was fucking useless. But the connections to Steve and Don Cherry were very helpful. The German guys, like Alex Schlippenbach, Manfred Schoof, whenever we showed up at some little festival or in a club, they just laughed their asses off. At that time, they played the Horace Silver style thing, and when we started they just shook their heads and joked. Then I was working with Carla and I was working in Paris with Don in a good old quintet with Gato Barbieri, Karl Berger, J-F Jenny [Clark], and Aldo Romano. And Don invited me to come to Paris, which was really a good experience for me. Coming back to Germany, of course the other comrades *did* know that Brötzmann played with Don Cherry in Paris, so that was the beginning of a kind of relationship with Schlippenbach and Schoof.

The foot in the door.

I met Sven-Ake [Johansson] in Brussels, and he didn't know where to live or where to go. So Peter and I and Freddy [van Hove] set up a concert in Antwerp and then we took Sven-Ake to Wuppertal. That was the first trio thing. And out of the first trio thing and the Schoof/Schlippenbach Quintet—Gerd Dudek was in it, Bushi [Niebergall], Jaki Liebezeit was the drummer—out of that combination was formed the first Globe Unity.

How longstanding was the trio with Sven and Peter?

Until I got a little bit closer to Han and Willem. After *Machine Gun* the trio was loosening up a little bit.

So that was well after recording For Adophe Sax, *which you recorded in 1967, and put out on your own, independently.*

Yeah. I got some money, because at that time I was doing some advertisement work to survive with the family. I already had a family, two kids, so I had to do something. I got some money, so I put out the first record on my own. *Machine Gun* was the second, in 1968. And then '69, FMP was happening.

But those records didn't get put out again until several years later. At some time you stopped working with Sven as much.

Sven moved to Berlin and I tried to find out what was happening with these Dutch guys. We formed a trio for a short time with Willem, Han, and myself, which was really nice. Then, I introduced Han to Fred, because I knew Fred already since the mid-sixties. So, the trio [with Bennink and van Hove] just was there.

That trio lasted up till about . . .

Middle of eighties, I would say. Then the duo [with Han] went on some other four years. Then, being so often in Holland, I met Harry [Miller]. I think Han had the same feeling that we should finish it, so the other trio [with Harry Miller and Louis Moholo] was there.

That trio was formed prior to you and Han stopping, right? Because The Nearer the Bone, the Sweeter the Meat *was late seventies, right?*

Yeah? Don't ask me. Maybe it's in some books, some Germans must know. There are some very wise people writing really big books about it.

There's a cliché about the German scene being interested in violence and energy. Do you find those things to be offensive clichés, or do you think they're on to something?

I think clichés always are wrong. Over here, Kowald and myself are the most well-known German people in this field of music. Of course, I like to *play,* yeah. Especially in those times, I really enjoyed it—playing loud and just, "Shit, lets go!" But, on the other hand there are a lot of German musicians doing really different stuff, really quite good things. I mean, Albert [Mangelsdorff], for example, never was a really violent player. This was a really fine gentleman. So I think this cliché is not true. I remember one big article, it must have been the mid-seventies, in the *Guardian,* showed my face with a kind of viking helmet on. Oh my god, so stupid. At that time, there it was quite a British attitude.

But then there are a number of clichés about British playing, too. That it's only little tiny things.

Yeah, I always call it English sickness. I mean, as much as I like English musicians, and I think they are the best-skilled musicians in Europe, I think the only one, or maybe two who get out of that, are Evan and Tony Oxley.

Not Paul Rutherford?

[pause] Yeah, maybe I am talking now in clichés, too. Maybe there's some more people. But I've played with a lot of younger English musicians, like Beresford and guys like that. It's always this fumbling around, and don't come to some point where you can say "Yes, that's it." It goes on and on. And Derek is a really special figure in the whole thing over there. He knows what he's doing, he has his philosophy in his bag, and I appreciate that very much. I mean I played duo concerts with Derek, and he was fucking steaming like hell. Or he played duos with Han, and it was amazing. But then, recently, in Wuppertal he was sitting there, doing this and that, fumbling around, let the electronic guys doing some things. Tony was sitting there, really looking very bored. And the German audiences have real trouble with this.

Last night you were mentioning some changes that are going on in your music that maybe relate to changes that are going on personally.

Yeah, I mean it goes hand in hand. I think this sort of, let's say, *steaming* life—looking for a lot of alcohol, a lot of women, and playing as loud as possible or raving around—it doesn't seem so interesting anymore. I mean, I do my little secrets, of course. [laughs] No, I still like women and I like drinks, but much more with distance. And that's the same way I'm looking at the music these days. I'm trying to find out what way I'm looking for in myself and in the playing. But as you mentioned last night, the last solo thing [*No Nothing*] is already a step in this direction. And working, for example, with Hamid makes certain things really possible, because he is so open. I'm still interested in tension and in getting things really *together.* But it can just be a breath, it doesn't have to be screaming all the time. Maybe I'm slow, it took me a long time to realize that. But if you listen to some of the good old records, like the ones with Mangelsdorff, you can realize that that was always there. But what the press and the media made out of me was always: "Oh, there is this screaming ugly German."

Did you ever feel like that influenced your self-image, in terms of how you played?

No. When I was really young and when the first things showed up in the papers, I was reading them. But that is really a long time ago. And now I am quite happy when they write my name correctly. Recently, there was an article about my son and me in the *Zeit.* This guy interviewed us, he came two nights. We talked, in the afternoon we talked. Of course, we had a bottle of rum on the table, and of course after four hours we got drunk. And he forgot about what we said when we were still sober. He was just taking all the things that we said in a happy mood. What can you do with this kind of

Peter Brötzmann
(photo: Laurence M. Svirchev)

journalism? So I don't give a shit. There's so few people who know about it, and even my old friend Bert Noglik, he always was too kind to me. He was always too friendly. Even if I knew I was playing shit, he was writing "Oh, that was beautiful." I can't stand that either. So this side of the business is very unimportant for me. What sometimes annoys me is that the whole work that FMP is doing since 1969—and it really is a unique work in this field of music—I find the media and the radio stations just don't know about it. I'm angry about that sometimes. Not really for myself, but for FMP and Jost [Gebers]. That's really a shame. I have contacts to some artists, famous artists. I played for the Bienalle, and all these writers show up, TV, and they say, "Oh, that is fantastic! I've never heard things like that." I mean I'm working on the shit at least twenty-five years! The only thing press is still important for getting gigs. That thing with my son in the *Zeit* arrived when I was on tour in Africa and all of a sudden Goethe directors were saying, "Oh, he's in the *Zeit*, Brötzmann's in the *Zeit*."

It's a shame, because the press is kind of set up so that it can only accommodate clichés and sound-bites. And I think your music is a great example of that. I mean, I have always tried to resist that notion that you were just interested in energy. I see your music as being multidimensional. I hear the kinds of lyrical things that you're now working on and that we heard a lot more of last night, were always there in different form, relating to a certain kind of very hard to talk about emotion that you were trying to evoke. You started having more contact with American free jazz musicians, not the very first ones, but people like Frank Wright and Bobby Few, somewhat later. I think I read Kowald talking about how this second generation really opened his eyes to how important it was to maintain an ongoing relationship with the African-American community. He's gone on to make that a priority for himself. How do you feel about that?

I think the most important thing I learned from people like Frank, Bobby, was just being aware of what you're doing. If you're on stage you have to work your ass off whatever happens. There was a thing I was always trying to do, but it was good to see that other people were thinking the same line, in a way. Of course, after fifteen, twenty years I see it a little bit different, but at that time it was important for us to have that connection. I think that trio with Louis and Harry could still be going on, if Harry would be alive still. I'm always fond of drummers, the most important guys for me in the band. That was a reason I had really great times with Andrew [Cyrille], of course with Milford [Graves]. I don't know, I thought and am still thinking that some of the Afro-American drummers, if you want it like that, they have a different kind of feeling from most of the Europeans. Han knows everything, he can play everything, but it is different, it is very European. I think Tony is the only European drummer who has this touch of being relaxed and playing still strong. Beside Louis and Tony and Han there are not very many good drummers in Europe. Of course you could mention Johnny Stevens or Willi Kellers. But Johnny is not playing at all. He just can't sit at home and wait for somebody to call.

It's neat to see you with Hamid, because I think it brings out certain totally different things. He accents a very specific kind of metrical thing that I don't hear in other cases.

Uh huh, that's true.

It has a power and tension, but he's a different kind of percussionist than other ones I've heard you with, with the tabla, the African percussion. Together, you could almost smell of "world music."

[laughs] Yes. I don't think he cares, and neither do I. We didn't play very often together, but I would compare playing with him a little with the good old times with Bennink in the very early years.

Somebody told me that when you practice you play Lester Young tunes, is that true?

I try my best, [but] of course I can't. At home I play standards. For some reason, I still have a lot to do with the normal jazz tradition. I don't listen to avant-garde things at home. During the last times I listened to some good old European classical music much more than to jazz. I have my little favorites. The more you are working yourself, the less listening is important. But it's changing, I have time—coffee, breakfast, some Sonny Rollins; finishing the night, some rum and coke, Lester Young or Billie Holiday.

We were talking about Braxton earlier and you were saying that you liked the quartet but there was always something missing in Anthony's playing. I remember an interview with you in Cadence *some years ago where you were talking about that in terms of technique, that his interest was a little too technical. That always struck me as funny, because what you do is technical too.*

Sure. And Evan is another good example. He developed his way of getting the sounds, especially out of the soprano. You have to have some kind of technique to get to the point you want to, or get close to it, actually. But, of course technique is always the *second* question. The question is what you have in your head, or even how you grow up and are taught playing. Anthony is a very, very classical, very Europe-orientated man. I sometimes prefer to go into some blues bar in New York and listen to very simple, normal blues saxophone player or whatever. Some years ago we had a little festival in Wuppertal, and I was playing with Andrew [Cyrille] and Peter [Kowald]. Anthony was there, so we decided to make a short duo, which I have on tape at home. It's funny, I just listened to it recently. It's very nice. That's four, five, six years ago. And we said we should do some kind of duo thing. I would still like to do it, because he is so completely different in his attitudes. It could be quite interesting.

It seems very interesting. Here you have a European coming out of being very interested in black American music and a black American who has a European attitude. Very different sensibilities about the horn—his from a somewhat slicker kind of place.

I don't know, maybe it has to do with being black, being very intelligent, being a great artist, and always looking with one eye over to Europe, to the Contemporary Music scene. You have seen his scores: big, big books. I mean, fucking hell! I'm sorry, for me it's quite nonsense. People in France like Anthony very much, because he's the right mixture, between being black and being very intellectual, too. Always nice, in France, if you're a black artist—not a guy from Algiers, definitely not. But this kind of Sidney Bechet tradition. Behaving. Eating with a knife and fork.

I always wondered if that fucked up attitude was a trans-European attitude or if it was just something found in France.

It's very special Paris-style.

I saw a poster in Paris that said "The Evolution of Jazz," with a picture of Charlie Parker as a Neanderthal.

[solemn pause] Yeah, it's not funny, but they have a really certain attitude.

There's such a cliché about the French love of jazz, but it comes across as a kind of patronizing thing.

Another example is Frank Wright. They loved him in Paris, they loved him because—especially with the quartet when the quartet was steaming—yeah, okay, that is jazz, that is some fucked up black guys breaking something up. And Anthony was the other side, behaving, dressed very good, drinking champagne, talking nicely.

Do you think there's a connection between the black American experience and postwar musicians who were youngsters just after the war? What was it that made that music strike a chord in you?

Really hard to find an answer to. I don't know why. My father always listened to Tchaikovsky, Beethoven, and the good old German and European classics. Maybe I was running away from that. I always was attracted by jazz music, Kid Ory, Armstrong, Bix Beiderbecke, things like that. I don't know why, but maybe even as a kind of protest, getting away from all that family shit, which I did quite early.

Did that family shit also have to do with a certain rejection of European history? Was it a rejection of this long history of great art in Europe, too?

No, I wouldn't go so far. No. Especially at that time I didn't think about those things. But I had long discussions with my father about the war, prewar times, after-war times. He, luckily, was just a normal soldier. He was not in some kind of position, but his brother was quite a high-ranked officer in the army. The funny thing was I could argue with him much better than with my father. My father, I always had the feeling he wanted to forget what was happening, because he was not the man carrying the rifle. With my uncle, I had really big fights going on through all the night. Which was interesting. I started to try to realize and to know what was going on quite early in my life. I was reading all the Brecht things and the French things, like Sartre, Camus, and others. And I grew up in a very upper-middle-class family, so I always was running away. So the lucky thing was that I got this clarinet from the school. I always went out in the night and played with these much older guys. Not being home, coming home early in the morning completely drunk, and then going to school two hours later and falling asleep.

So that had more to do with the "jazz life" than any kind of political protest.

Yes, I think so. The first girls, the first alcohol, things like that. Very important. To come back to nowadays, my feelings about what is happening as I look around, I don't see very much happening. You always have times where it's really happening, and then you have valleys. I think we're in quite a valley at the moment. You can take the Europeans or you can take the New York guys. I recently saw Elliott Sharp with his Carbon band in Wuppertal. Everything is so commercialized. From the beginning to the end, you know what to expect. If you look at all the John Zorn projects, at the end it's always the same, you know already what is happening. Sometimes, of course you find good players in the bands. But I think there are very few people who know what direction they have to go, or what point they could reach. I see the field of music at the moment just as we are sitting here, watching what is going on there [points far off in one direction] and there [points another direction], with much more distance than I did some years ago.

If you found it dissatisfying enough, do you feel like you could leave it?

[very long pause] That is a question which shows up more often during the last two years. And sometimes I could imagine that at least I would take a longer break. But for some reasons that is not possible. One is very realistic: I have to survive somehow, pay my rent and phone. And on the other hand, which is more important: if I don't do it, I get nervous. I'm cooler than I was years ago, when I would say [nervously] "Okay, where's the next gig? When is it happening? Four weeks, fucking hell!" I was really getting nuts. But now I can sit at home and paint a little bit. But that has to do with the money too. As it looks, I am quite busy for rest of the year, and even for next year, so I can't complain. I don't know how Evan thinks about it, or Han, but sometimes I must admit I'm getting tired of certain things. I'm getting tired of that modern life, anyway. It's just such a lot of bullshit. And that makes me feel stronger about doing the music, because that sets a point to do things different.

That's good. Then it's not something that makes you feel apathetic about playing.

No, no. If it was that then I really would sell the horns.

HAN BENNINK

Swing Softly and Play with

a Big Stick

●

HAN BENNINK. Have you heard from Peter Brötzmann lately?

JOHN CORBETT. *Right here. We did an interview
down the street, this time last year. He's doing very well, and his playing is
fantastic. I think it has gotten somewhat clearer lately.*

Yeah, yeah, yeah. More basic, more concrete. I think that for myself, too.
At least, that's what I'm working on.

You're working on clarifying your work?

Clarity. A clear story, no bullshit. When I like to rattle around, I can do
that. I don't need any more enormous drum kit or bells or gongs or whatever
sort of shit. I find something here and there behind stage. Canadian stages
are very clean, so there's nothing to find, but yesterday I found some strings,
a cardboard box, and a piece of wood. They are more interesting to me
sound-wise than many other things because sounds are everywhere and it
depends on what context you put them in. When I play on something, it's
still playing with two sticks, so I just let the audience hear the difference
between how the drum kit sounds or a garbage can, piece of junk, or whatever. That's the idea.

You can make anything swing and be interesting.

It's not true. I have to work myself up to a sort of level into a concert
where I feel free to do that. It's not like: Now I'm gonna do this or that. It has
to come in a sort of way, it has to come spontaneous to me. There has to be a
hole that I can think "Wow! Oh yeah . . ." There must be sort of tension.
Yeah, I can pick up some sticks and play with them, but that sort of opening
or hole is not always there for other material, you know? To speak about
music is always very difficult, because if I could say in words what I am
playing, then I'd rather write a book. But it's music, so you have to do it each
time again.

*I've seen references associating you and Misha Mengelberg with Fluxus,
though it's not widely talked about. I think it's interesting because I see real
connections between what you do and that whole milieu and sensibility.*

Absolutely true. I never was in Fluxus, though Misha was. He's older than
me, seven years older. So he was in Fluxus, but I was in third class of art

school. But I was already very interested in dada: Kurt Schwitters, Marcel Duchamp, Max Ernst, Picabia, Man Ray, all those guys. I still am. When I work and when I exhibition—this year I had an exhibition in a very good gallery in Amsterdam. I'm not selling a lot, but I got appreciation all over now. Very famous people come in and say they like it. But my work has reflections from Fluxus. I know an artist living in Berlin, Thomas Schmidt, a Fluxus artist. And I know [Wolf] Vostell, I've seen Nam June Paik, all those guys. But at that particular period, with the happenings, I was too young in fact.

You were in art school?

For four years in Amsterdam.

How did you get involved in jazz?

I was already, because my father was percussion player in symphony orchestra. For his hobby he played clarinet in the Benny Goodman style and tenor saxophone in the Coleman Hawkins style. And he really could play very, very well. I used to do gigs with my dad when I was about seventeen. My father could play all instruments; he played violin, accordion, everything. He could read fantastic, and he always forced me to go and try to read music. I can't read a note. I was so surprised to see Tom Rainey, Joey Baron, Gerry Hemingway, they really can read like ravens. I'm not interested at all. I shut my eyes and let myself go—I like to play each tune different. I gigged with my dad's dance bands; we played with acrobats, we did shows for the army. [lowers his voice to a near-whisper] I never went in the army. By a certain age, seventeen, eighteen, there is a certain music, like my son, he's into rap music now. He's seventeen. And I was into jazz music, 'cause jazz music, West Coast style, was very "in" in Holland. My first record was *Dave Brubeck Goes to College*. But then I heard a record of Charlie Parker and Charlie Parker played "Kim." That record, Jesus Christ! I was buying everything, following everything, as best I could. I went to America in 1960, playing on a boat of the Holland-America line. I played with a trio and a singer, just to go and see New York in 1960. [in rapid-fire succession] I went to the old Five Spot at Cooper Square, I saw Ornette, I went to Bleecker Street where John Coltrane played "My Favorite Things," I saw Aretha Franklin just herself playing piano with a drummer, I went to Café Ruffio on Bleecker Street, I saw Billy Higgins, saw Sonny Clark playing with Lacy, I went to the Half Note, I saw Bob Cunningham and all sort of guys. Really, I was there very early.

You have an amazing memory of it.

Oh yes.

How long were you there?

I was there with the ship for ten days there. On the ship we had a sort of jazz trio. We were the specialty, and there was also another band for real entertainment like waltzes. My drumming completely changed. I saw Elvin [Jones] and . . . Misha Mengelberg is always saying "When you went to New York you learned so much, seeing those guys." And it's of course true, 'cause we were aping, in a way, listening to the records. And the first time I saw Art Blakey, I fell off my chair, man. And I caught Kenny Clarke in 1957, in [the] Concertgebouw, with Phineas Newborn, piano player, and Oscar Pettiford. And later on I saw Lucky Thompson, Oscar Pettiford, and Kenny Clarke—I still have recordings from that. Oscar Pettiford was playing with a broken hand because he had a car accident in Vienna. He was always pissed; he used to fall asleep on the toilets, Oscar. Great rhythm section, though. Fantastic! Watching those guys helps a lot, when you're young.

I think you mentioned once that your favorite rhythm section was Kenny Clarke and Ray Brown.

Well yeah, that's my favorite. The first Modern Jazz Quartet, that's my favorite rhythm section. Of course, famous rhythm section are Philly [Joe Jones] and Paul Chambers, and I like also Louis Hayes and Sam Jones very, very much. And I like also the rhythm sections that Erroll Garner used to play with, like Harold "Doc" West and Eddie Calhoun. Vernell Fourier and Israel Crosby playing with Ahmad Jamal. Those rhythm sections are *so* tight.

What is it about those rhythm sections that makes them so great?

It's the swing and how tight and how precise the bass and drums are playing. It has to walk. Some rhythm sections are so sloppy you could put a whole elephant in the holes. I like it real tight. Nowadays I don't play too often with bass players; I play with Ernst Reijseger now. With ICP Orchestra we play with Ernst Glerum, he's *very* good, can play fantastic bowed chords. He was also in the Amsterdam String Trio.

Do you feel like you've had bass players to have that kind of tight rhythm section with?

Oh, I think I can play very, very well and I once did with Dave Holland. I love playing with him; it would be nice, man. And I recently did a duo with Jaamaladeen Tacuma in Amsterdam, and all the hip bass players are talking about him. I like how he plays four-on-the-beat, really tight, really heavy into it. We played a fantastic duet. He was so surprised, very funny. Great guy. Cornell Rochester I also like. [a sparrow comes up to Han's foot] Oh, a young one, nice one. Cornell was watching me the whole afternoon, we are very close. I was also very close with Ed Blackwell. He was one of my heroes. I miss him very, very, very much. Beautiful person, beautiful player.

I want to ask some general questions about your philosophy and approach to the use of humor in music.

The humor thing is very delicate. It's a particular humor; it's another frame. People laugh already when you come onstage with shorts on. I think that's really normal because I sweat my ass off. It's the way you do it. When they laugh, I go further on. With Paul Plimley and Myra [Melford], I have more or less chance to come off the kit, for example, than with others. That's the musical context. Of course I can sit beside Paul and play a bit on the floor, but I got a different response from him than from the others. When he's immediately playing on the floor with me there's no counterpoint. So I fuck off then; I go in another direction. When I do something and the others in the Clusone Trio are just going on, that makes a real strange tension. I can work with that. I do it to make room in the music, and I do it for myself, because I actually come from that art school. It's not only the musical input, you can do more. Like Claes Oldenberg did, for example. You can play with an enormous drumstick, two very longs ones, but *really try* to play with them, not only show them. What I often do is play very fast, break a stick, grab another stick—and I know what I'm doing—I grab a big Aboriginal stick, hold it, you see the difference, and I throw it away. That might be very funny, but it's just to let them see the difference. Or sometimes I go with that big stick and simply play with it. That's a very delicate point: if it was *only* humor, that would disturb the music. And I *play* what I am and I *do* what I am because I am like that, and it never disturbs the music, it helps the music. Otherwise I couldn't do it that long, you know? Sometimes when there are holes into the music you can hear people laugh, they are into the whole context, they fill that with their laugh like an opera. But how it exactly works? That is pure shamanism. I really don't know. It's daily life, all differences, and all rules, and you can fight with the rules at the same time.

Do you see it as being related to vaudeville?

Yeah, of course. But I learned that from my dad. I was playing parties when I was seventeen. And a drummer always had chances to play with a cuckoo whistle or a whip—that belonged to the drum material, so it already was in that sound-effect world. I've seen Gene Krupa live on Broadway in *Metropole,* or there's a movie with Big Sid Catlett and Jo Jones, *Jammin' the Blues.* It's one of my favorite movies, fucking unbelievable, and they play just snare drum and when they have a rim shot eyebrows are going high. I think that it was there already, and of course it's vaudeville. Of course when Misha and me are playing in Italy, they understand it because they understand *commedia dell'arte.* It's instant composing. You sit there, you do the music, you improvise, and that's what it is. It's very basic, very clear.

I got thinking about this issue because one of the evenings that I saw you in Switzerland a few months ago, it seemed that some of the tricks weren't falling right.

Yeah, yeah, right.

Han Bennink
(photo: Nick White)

What happens then? I mean, those tricks seem like they can be a way of kick-starting things.

When they don't fall, it's like the music sometimes; you hit here and there and it doesn't fall either. And then you have to improvise yourself out of that in order to come into the right context. But it belongs to my musical baggage and my musical language, and that's all I can say about it. And of course not each concert is the same concert, and I'm glad. Otherwise I'd give up. I still have the urge to do it better and more intense and so on, and that keeps me up all the time. I do my best and that's all I can.

Well, things fall right a phenomenal amount of the time.

I know, I know. [laughs] I've been playing and a stick has broken and flew and took the cigarette out of Misha's mouth, just the ashes. A broken stick flew into a lady's eye in Fiorenza and broke her glasses. I had to pay 60,000 lira in order to repair the glasses, but she was not hurt, thank goodness. They were all falling right, in a way. Yesterday I was sort of Houdini; I was bound in strings and I tried to play with that. I saw the strings the other night; it was there for two days and I didn't use it till yesterday. Why, I don't know.

Once, when you played in Providence, Rhode Island, you did something incredible. You put your foot on the snare drum like you sometimes do, to change its pitch, and someone in the audience laughed. You knew that would happen again, put your foot on the snare again, someone laughed, and you stopped cold, marched angrily out of the theater, and came back in dragging a huge cardboard foot, which you'd obviously seen earlier backstage. Incredibly quick connection. It was clear at that point that the humor has a conceptual base as well.

That was a nice example. That steps into the right context. [pause] On the other hand sometimes it also bothers me, because I like to be taken very, very seriously. And as soon as the word "humor" comes, everybody gets a sort of strange idea. But I like to be taken very seriously. It has that feeling: "Oh, that guy Bennink is a bit crazy, and for that reason they give him attention as a drummer." They've been writing about how I look and what faces I make, I have books full of that. [laughter]

You have a magical way of taking things that could easily become shtick and making them not shtick. It seems to be a question of taking sounds and putting them into different contexts, sometimes in a very decal sort of way. I think of your visual art, where you take a little rubber stamp. It's like taking a little patch of this and put it here, and see what it's like.

Yeah, that comes by.

But there is also a lot of variation in terms of the way you can interact with any kind of other players or ensembles.

I would like to play with as much variety in my life as I can. I'm not interested to play with heavy metal bands, but I did play with a punk band, just for one night. And they asked me to play a solo concert in a punk club. In the last year there are things I've been doing that are weird. I played with Art Hodes, who is dead now. Then I had four gigs with Percy Sledge. And I did a record with Cecil Taylor. [laughter]

How did you feel the encounter with Cecil worked out?

I like to *do it* with Cecil very much, rather than listen back to it. I know Cecil since '67, because there was a bandleader Boy Edgar, who brought Cecil for a whole week to Amsterdam. And Willem Breuker and myself, we were playing with Cecil. He was in Hilversem, in the radio station, and I was living in the place where I still live. I went on my bicycle to the studio, knocked on the door, and there was Cecil. I asked if I could listen because I was very interested in his way of practicing in '66. He said all right, so I was sitting there, and the next day I was already playing with him. Since that time we know each other very, very well. I think there happened something that fell wrong since Berlin, because I got a phone call from a very important black man from the *Village Voice* or whatever even more important paper from New York, and he was bringing it to me like now I'd finally played with the *guru*. And I think Cecil is a great fucking player, no doubt about that, but when they go in that sort of direction, I'm not interested in that shit. I like to be as basic as normal—you are already crazy enough in this life. So I was maybe giving him a bit funny answers, and that may have fallen wrong by Cecil. I don't know, and I don't care at all, actually. I like to play music, no gossip stuff, no bullshit stuff. He's fine, he's very funny, and he has lots of energy. We did seventy-five minutes at that kind of level in Berlin, and also the encores. I liked the encores better with Cecil, I don't know why. [laughs] I've seen Cecil play with Max [Roach], who broke his foot pedal. They couldn't find each other for sixty minutes, then they played an encore for shorter than a minute—it was gorgeous, one of the best musics I've ever heard in my life. Maybe it's necessary to do all that other stuff in order to reach that encore. You never know. I have the feeling that when I play with Cecil I find myself playing more and more conventional in order not to co-op with him but to counterpoint with him. I think Tony Oxley just gets along with Cecil all the time, you know? Like swimming *with* him. I like to *bite* here and there, it's good for the music. When it's all going too good I don't believe in it. It's going too smooth. We also had our moments on this tour, with Clusone Trio, where somebody breaks up and suddenly the context is not fitting. You have these disconnections, but it's good for the music 'cause the next day you play much better.

That keeps the music fresh.

Sure, sure. When it's not like that, forget it. Then you're telling the same story each time. I like it as fresh as I can, as fresh as the Bread Garden. [looks at the restaurant that we're sitting in front of]

Could you just describe your practice routine?

My practicing is sort of ridiculous now, 'cause I have sticks all the time on my bed and I come in the hotel, switch the television on as a cusion, and I start practicing doing something. It's not a particular roll or a single stroke. It's all there, I just let my fingers move, the sticks move, and train all the time. I knocked this off playing on strange drum kits. [points at a scab on his hand] I train like a maniac. I like it. And when I'm not training I write in my diary, I write letters home, I bike.

How about practicing at home?

I have a houseboat on a small dike in a gorgeous neighborhood twenty kilometers from Amsterdam, and I have a stable for myself, in a meadow where I go. It's really dark, there's no light, I have a bit of electricity but it's very dark. For painting it's bad. But it's enormously quiet. My only neighbors are cows, and they love music. When I go in the meadow and practice—because I play a bit of saxophone, but since I play with Michael [Moore] who's so fucking good, I more or less gave up! I've fucked around on lots of instruments; I had a trombone, a violin—Ernst gave me a really beautiful violin from France. When I play in the meadow, the cows come and make a half a circle and they listen. Very, very nice.

Do they have bells?

No, our cows have no bells. And they stink terrible because the shit in Holland is not what it was. Holland is beautiful, but it's too small. We stand shoulder on shoulder till our heels are in cow shit and we can't get rid of it. Lots of pollution.

How do you find things in the music now, both in terms of the infrastructure—money, places to play—and in terms of new players?

First of all, I am glad that I still am able to play and that people appreciate it. The situation in Holland is not that bad at all. I more or less play for the same salary as a new member of the BIM [the BIM is a co-op of musicians]. That's just the money we get from the government and we like to spread it as good as we can, so we give everybody a chance. But it doesn't help me financial-wise, so I have to go out. In order to go out of Holland, they have to ask me, or there must be a need for the music. I worked for fifteen years very intensely with Peter in Germany. And Germany is much bigger; they have more relations, for example, with Japan, so I went to Japan. Now I work all over the world except the United States. They don't want me there; they don't give me a work permit when we come—you have to play for the door. South America, I haven't been. But for the rest, I've been playing almost everywhere, most of it in Europe itself. For instance, we have to do the Clusone Festival, because we took the name Clusone Trio. So they gave me carte blanche. This year, we're gonna be the Clusone Trio plus Bill Frisell (sounds not bad to me), and there's a young tenor player, Tobias Delius. He's my dearest friend; we have a quartet with Larry Fishkind, and Tristan Honsinger. Tobias is also playing in Michael's band. The first guest we asked was Jaki Byard, but he couldn't make it. Then yesterday I heard this trumpet player I would have asked immediately if I'd known him before.

Dave Douglas.

What a bright sound of the trumpet and incredible player. First chance I have for a trumpet player, I'll call him. But I never had a band myself. There never was a Han Bennink Trio or Quartet. It was Misha and Han, or Willem Breuker and Han Bennink.

Do you think there ever will be?

No, no. I like to carry on like it is.

You're in the tradition of rhythm section accompanists.

Yeah, I like to keep it like that and try to play with everybody.

Are there any drummers around these days that really knock your socks off?

Absolutely. You can learn from everybody, also how *not* to play. I heard a record Gerry Hemingway played with a blues singer or something like that, and he was playing on the off-beat all the time, so the high came on the one and the three . . . and he was still swinging! Those sort of things knock me off. There are incredible drummers around—I've heard some drummers from Burundi recently. I'm scared of that shit, absolutely. Very good. And I've seen a Scottish drummer, John McPatrick, he's playing the shit out of the snare drum. There are many good players, man. Elvin. I saw Roy Haynes on a good night in the BIMhuis, Jesus Christ!

There are a lot of drummers who are visual artists.

Yes, weird, that is. Tony Oxley, Daniel Humair—he's actually getting more money from painting than from playing.

Sven-Ake Johansson, you.

Jamie Muir. I met my old school colleague, Rob van der Broek, he's playing with the European Jazz Quartet. He was with me in art school. Phil Minton came from the art school. There was a particular time in England that many of the improvisors came more from the art school than music schools. Maybe the art schools were more open than the music schools or conservatories. There is Wim Janssen, brother of Guus Janssen, he is a drummer and a painter. It's very weird.

I wonder if it has to do with some sensibility about space.

Probably. I met a drummer in Montreal, he's also a painter. It's so open in Canada, such big space. I'm jealous of that, I must say. I'm gonna miss that as soon as I'm in Europe. But I love to go back to Amsterdam. [chuckles to himself knowingly] The speciality, the humor is all there. It's a very, very open mentality, that's what I like.

How important was organizing and running the record company, ICP Records, with Misha? I was talking to Derek about this . . .

Compared to Derek, Misha and I are amateurs. Compared to FMP, compared to Incus, we are amateurs, and we like to keep it that way. First of all, Misha and me, we are no businessmen. We do the music and make a choice what to do, which is most of the time our own material because we are too poor to pay the others. Then I have to make the cover—always very cheap. One time through the presses, not two colors. And that's not good when you want to do business. The record business, well you really have to make a hit or it's not interesting. It's just for you guys [critics] and the people we play for, but money-wise it's nothing. We were losing money all the time. It was sucking time, that's all. And my time's too short. I like to practice for myself and do something for myself, and leave that for someone else.

[Vancouver, July 1993]

THE EX

Live Free . . . Or Try

●

*Three simple words: do it yourself. Punk-motto/free-im-
proving principle. Perhaps this is the molecule of language that best represents punk and free, two musics in
which the notion of "independence" is still something of an ideal, two musics that revolve around accountability and self-determination, two musics whose common catalyst
should outweigh any idiomatic dissimilarities.*

*Fact is, they have crossed paths more than once along the way. Saxophonist Lol
Coxhill played on the Damned's second record; the Pop Group (all of whom, save Mark
Stewart, wanted to be jazzers anyway) invited cellist Tristan Honsinger to sit in on "We
Are All Prostitutes"; ATV leader Mark Perry's groups The Door and The Window and the
Good Missionaries both explored some of the possibilities of improvising; the Minutemen
and Saccharine Trust both flirted with free music. In Slan, reedman John Zorn and
guitarist Elliott Sharp meet vocalist Yamatsuka Eye of the Boredoms and drummer Ted
Epstein of Blind Idiot God; improvising percussionist Roger Turner played with the
Noseflutes and the Fall's original guitarist Dave Barker has recently been working in a
trio with Turner and trombonist Alan Tomlinson. So it wasn't exactly a new idea when a
Dutch band started to do it. But then again that certainly didn't mean it couldn't sound
fresh, as Terrie, Kat, Luc, GW Sok—collectively, the Ex—went on to demonstrate.*

*Anyone with an ear to the ground already knew about the Ex in 1990, when they re-
leased* Joggers and Smoggers, *their first collaboration with improvisors. Since that
time, the anarchist punk band has forged a working relationship with cellist Tom Cora
and has played with a cross section of the improvising world. I caught up with guitarist
Terrie and drummer Katrin in the fall of 1991 at the October Meeting, a ten-day-long festival of improvised music in Amsterdam. There, at the BIMhuis (Amsterdam's out-music
emporium) the Ex was a main attraction one night, playing with drummer Han Bennink,
saxophonist Ab Baars, trumpeter Claude Deppa, trombonist Wolter Wierbos, singer
Greetja Bimja, and keyboardist/live electrician/trumpeter Steve Beresford. With the
latter, the group's two guitarists also played a short, intriguing trio. Heads down, guitars
hanging droopily and at times touching the floor, the two of them appeared to be digging.
Afterwards, Beresford said that it was like playing with a couple of improvising badgers.*

CORBETT. *How did you get involved with the BIMhuis crowd?*
TERRIE. Luc, the bass player, knew Han Bennink from years and years

and years of seeing him. His friend was really interested in that kind of music. And then suddenly we saw Han Bennink play—the first time was a three-hour solo gig—so fantastic, so energetic, so new, so powerful in noise and everything that you felt it related to things we were doing. In behavior, in attitude, in improvising. So then we saw Ab Baars playing. We were busy recording the *Joggers and Smoggers* record. He sounded so fantastic. So we asked Ab could he play on the record, cause we didn't know who he was or anything. We read an interview a few months earlier when Wolter won a prize, saying "I'd really like to be involved in other kinds of music, like the Mekons."

This is Wolter Wierbos?

T: Yeah. So we remembered his name and that he was open to it. So we asked him, too. And Ab was completely open to everything, really supported us and asked if we could play here [at BIMhuis]. So that's how we got here.

You've been based in Amsterdam since you started, when was that, 1980?

KATRIN. '79, August.

T: We live out of Amsterdam, in a little village.

K: It's twenty kilometers from here. We live in a squatted house.

From a distance, that connects you with the English Crass scene. Was that inspirational?

T: [hesitantly] Yeah . . . they were the first band who really had strong ideas about putting out your own music and doing exactly the things you wanted to do, putting out records cheap, with information, leaflets, organize gigs. Yeah, inspiring in the beginning. Naturally, it was a bit small-minded. The whole scene around them became small-minded. It was more the fans who ruined the whole thing.

It's said that the Crass scene was sort of like hippies who cut their hair, which is funny because there was this image that punk had to be something that was antisocial, aggressive, noncommunal. And the Crass thing seemed to really go against that in very communal, antiestablishment but not antisocial ways.

T: Yeah, that's what we were also about. Not to do with any . . .

K: . . . unsocial things. We took over the ideas that you can do what you want, that you can start a band without all these techniques and stuff, but can just take your instrument and play. That was one idea of punk. And also that you can play very dynamic and you don't pay mind to all these nice melodies. You just go your own way and see what happens. We took that idea, but for the rest we didn't take any of those ideas: asocial, drinking, drugs. That was not what we wanted. We wanted to be positive.

T: First is also the way we live, the squat scene, doing benefits for things, that whole attitude.

That's not something we're very familiar with in the States. Can you explain a little about the politics of squatting.

T: It came out of a lot of empty houses and a shortage of places for people to live. So it was quite logical to take them and make the best of it, rebuild it. That was a whole kind of subculture here, at one point ten years ago. It was a big scene. More than 10,000 squatted houses. Around that came a lot of shops, little workshops, restaurants, places to do gigs and it was really self-made. We come from that.

K: It also happened because lots of normal people supported it. I hear quite often in other countries that when people squat a house the neighbors come around and want to kick you out. That didn't happen here. A lot of people saw that the squatters wanted to make good things with it, and start projects in those houses.

In the U.S., I think it's an aspect of the continuing paranoia about socialism. Have you played in Eastern Europe?

T: Everywhere, except for Romania. Poland, Czechoslovakia, Hungary, Yugoslavia, Russia.

How were you received there?

T: It was quite different from country to country. It's a good thing to see that it's not the "East bloc" you might think it is, but is really different countries. Like in Poland you felt that the youth is really rebellious against the shit there. Fantastic. Czechoslovakia was even more. It was completely forbidden to do gigs.

K: So we did illegal gigs.

T: Fantastic. The second time we wanted to play there we couldn't get in, we were locked up at the border for seventeen hours.

Why was that?

K: We had some political stuff with us, posters. And they thought we would do something illegal in the country. We told them that we'll stay in that hotel and we're only driving through the country. But I guess they didn't believe it. And we had to wait for so long because they had to inform their bosses and they had to drive two hours to come to the border and they took typewriters and they have to get the whole story.

T: It was like from a cheap spy film. They came in such a Russian limousine, guys in hats came to interrogate Luc with a lamp. Really scary. [laughs] Crazy.

You're very internationally minded, involved with musicians from a lot of different places. How do you keep in touch with things going on with liberation movements?

T: Amsterdam is a really international city. You meet people from everywhere. So it's not very difficult to start contacts. It's quite natural, you're never looking for people very far away. You simply meet them.

The connection between you and BIMhuis *seemed really natural to me. I mean I've been listening to improvised music for years and years and I've been listening to you guys since about 1985. To see Wierbos and Baars on your record made perfect sense, in a certain way. But then again, institutionally they seem like they're very far away.*

T: Yeah, that's why it's really important for those things to come together sometimes.

Is it really different playing at a place like this?

K: Different audience.

T: Yeah, For us it's a challenge. And I think it's good for the BIM, 'cause it's a real institution and people come every week and you hardly see new people here. I find it really nice when people who normally come to see us see Han Bennink for the first time. It works out from both sides.

Politically, how does the band operate? How do you toss ideas around between members of the band and how do you generate ideas for what is a good thing to be singing about? Is there a lot of debate?

T: Well, we see each other nearly every day. We work with the record distribution we do. And we talk about things. But we never have really heavy political debates or something. It comes more from the social feeling. Like, you meet some Kurdish people, you hear them play, you think about it and you see all the misinformation you get here and it's so different from what you hear from themselves. It's nice to put out things that will support them in that way. With the band you can really spread information and get money. That's two things that can help a lot of people, which is very important for us.

Have you ever had disagreements about benefit gigs or something? Or is it pretty obvious to all of you what you should . . .

K: It's pretty obvious. I think we've got all the same attitude and the same look on life. And the same feeling for what we'd like to do and what we don't like to do.

T: We're lucky that way. It comes naturally, we're all good friends.

Aside from Crass, what other groups were inspirational for getting you started in the DIY *music scene? I'm thinking of the Pop Group.*

T: Yeah. We did our first gig with a PA with the Pop Group. Our fourth gig in our life. When we started there were a lot of new bands and a lot of exciting groups between Amsterdam . . .

K: We were not the only ones who started it. There were lots of people who formed a band and played. There were lots of evenings where there were three or four bands and people came to them and enjoyed themselves. And then, through the years it just went down. I think it was a bit the same in all these other countries.

Less and less.

K: I have the feeling it was everywhere like that. There was a sort of wave.

Which is funny, because in the press you get the impression that the alternative music industry is doing so well, everything's so hunky dory. But it's become institutionalized.

K: There are so many people meanwhile who want to make money out of the whole development of this scene. But you have to be careful. There are many bands who work together with these people. There are not many bands left like us, who never work with those people.

T: A lot of bands seem to be independent because they can't get a record contract, not from the idea that it's important to do it yourself. It's really weird, in a way, that there's nothing very new coming out.

K: I mean, I can also understand that when a band starts and plays for years and years, there comes a point they want to make a step forward, they want to maybe play at bigger places and have more possibilities. But that doesn't mean always that you have to work together with record companies. I think it's a pity that many people can't imagine another way.

T: It should always start with the music, if you like that. Of course we sometimes play in big clubs, but we also play for ten people. It depends on how it's organized and who will come. Something is never too small or too silly. A big place can be horrible and a small place can be horrible. It's completely to do with other things.

It's a gradual thing that happens. Bands get sucked into the idea that they can simply say "Okay, yes we have to compromise on this. But if we compromise on this we'll be reaching so many more people. And we won't have compromised everything, so a little bit of us will get out into that." If you calculate that wrong, you're really in trouble.

T: We have also calculated sometimes and thought: "Whew, stop here. Never again."

Like what?

T: Like you're asked to play and suddenly it's completely out of hand and they used you because you're a bit famous, used you for the amount of beer they can sell and they come up with a nice story that it's a benefit. There was a Dutch alternative broadcasting organization, the most alternative one. They say, "We want to put out a CD so that we can promote our station." I thought maybe it's not so bad, we did some live sessions that were pretty good. But when we came to pick up the CD at this sort of record party with all these horrible people in suits it was put out and distributed by a major record company. And they didn't say nothing about that. There's nothing on the CD about the broadcasting company. It made me feel: "mmm, yeah." Cause they come up with the nice line: it's for a benefit. Then you feel used a bit.

What are the other projects you're working on?

T: We're really busy with the six singles project. We're on the fourth.

Just the Ex, or with guests?

K: Guests.

T: Next will be with Belgian comedians.

Always a surprise. Next with comedians. Next one with trapeze artists?

T: No. The comedians have a lot in common with us. One is a really big fan of ours, that's how it started. We did some gigs with them. And it was quite natural. They are very famous in Belgium, never heard of here.

Seems really rare for a rock band to be so open as you. The autonomy that you maintain lets you make all of the decisions, be mobile, wide-thinking . . . and quick. The other thing I was thinking was that it really made sense for you to be playing with improvisors at a festival like this because as a band it seems like you work fast and there isn't that lag time. When you have really big record contracts and it's like a year and a half later you get what somebody's been working on back then.

K: That's developed over years. We're lucky that we have this subculture that we can work with, like Dolf with the studio, and lots of other people. We work together, and we are really lucky that we have these possibilities.

Are there plans to put out the old Ex things on CD?

T: Yeah. The problem is mainly money. 'Cause we put out so many new things all the time that we need money for that. But as soon as we have some more money we'll start putting out old things, like *Blueprints for a Blackout.* Two-record set that fits on a single CD.

Did you guys ever play opposite a band called Jackdaw with Crowbar?

T: Yeah. Fantastic.

They're not around anymore, huh?

T: I have the feeling they're always falling to bits and then coming back up. I've seen them with seven members, two, five. It's mainly the singer and the guy who writes the songs, the guitarist.

I was really sad that a lot of the bands on Ron Johnson are gone. That was another thing promising in the world—the Ex and a lot of the things on Ron Johnson . . .

K: Shrubs.

T: Big Flame. Have you ever seen them?

No. I've heard they were great. It seems that a network is a really important part of what you all do.

T: Yeah, and that's what De Konkurrent Distribution does. All over the world there are these little mail-orders. That's really important to keep that going.

K: It's definitely growing, this whole network thing.

How did you meet Tom Cora?

T: It started with the band Orthotonics. They were more or less stranded in Amsterdam, and they stayed in a squat that was also a music hall and restaurant we ran. We had a tour with Chumbawamba from England at that time. Orthotonics didn't have any gigs because everything was disastrous, so we teamed up together with the three bands. And Pippin [Barnett], their drummer, is a good friend of Tom, and he told about it. Then Tom came to the CBGBS gig when we played in New York, and he was real into it from the start and had a fight with the PA man who switched us off when we played one minute too long. It was a good start. And then we rehearsed a bit, did some gigs. He was really into it. 'Cause for him it was such a strange experience to play with people who are technically hopeless, like we.

The Hair of the Dog

●

JOHN CORBETT. *You started the Parliaments when you were fourteen?*

GEORGE CLINTON. Thirteen, I think. Matter of fact, I still talk to one of the guys who was in the group then, he's in prison. He reminds me of things I forget. But we used to sing in grade school. We was in like sixth, seventh grade when we started the group. And all through junior high school we sang together.

You started calling it the Parliaments right away?

Right away.

And that was cigarette reference?

Pack of cigarettes, yeah. There was those groups the Chesterfields, the Kits, every kind of group you could think of. There was cars and cigarettes.

And birds.

And birds, right. Birds, that's it. [laughs] Cars, cigarettes, and birds. So we were the Parliaments. Made our first record in '57, I think, '57/'58.

"Party Boys"?

"Party Boys" and "Poor Willie." APT Records, part of Paramount. But we recorded for a production company, her name was Bea Kessler, and she did Shepherd and the Limelights, the Heartbeats, the Pastels, the Monotones— you know, "Who Wrote the Book of Love?" They were from my neighborhood.

Were the Parliaments designed to be a recording group, or where did you perform?

Oh we performed all around town, dances, cabarets, and things like that.

Around the same time you did hair at the Uptown Tonsorial Parlor?

Damn, you got some good information! Uptown Tonsorial Parlor. [savors the name] That's where we all used to work. And I had one called the Silk Palace. Uptown was Calvin, Grady, myself, used to work there, in Newark. That was the thing to do was to do hair.

I just recently put that together, how that's carried over to the present, with your incredible hairdos. Style is obviously really important to you.

To me, when the rappers first hit the scene they was the corniest lookin'

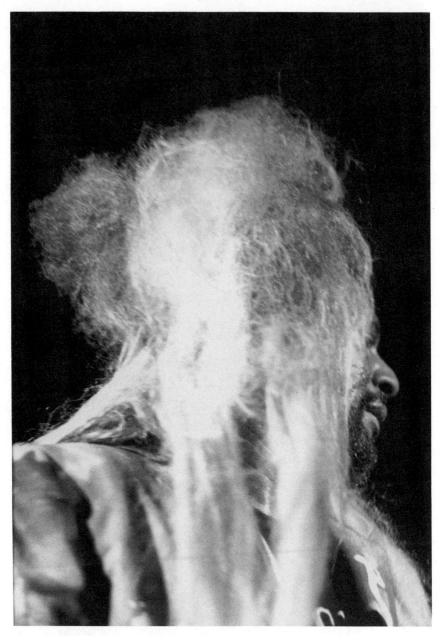

George Clinton
(photo: David Corio)

things I ever seen 'cause they all looked like suburbia black people, or either white people, you know the body language, the hand thing. [cocks his hand] All that came from the fifties, you know, dude walkin' 'round holdin' his crotch and everything. But it was so nonchalant and casual that you never really *noticed* it. Most of 'em started out holdin' their pockets. Then gradually [creeps his hand down to his crotch]. But then after a while it was like *both hands,* like your shit is really heavy! [Steph groans] I was like "Damn, this look really silly!" But all the sudden, now all the younger rappers that's around now look cool to me. Naughty by Nature, Kriss-Kross, TLC, ABC. All them look like the fifties when everybody was cool with it. Lot of the heavy rappers *now* look cool doin' it, but the ones first came out, Run 'n' them, I used to say "Boy, don't move! Don't move, please!" And then you see Arsenio Hall try to copy that, and I was like "Holy shit! Don't y'all promote that shit!" Public Enemy, Flavor had a cool groove on him. Everybody else had that hand thing. Oh man, put your hands in your pocket. I mean, I loved the raps. Rakim's still my favorite rapper, but he say he don't dance or smile, so that's how it was. Cool was like that. It was like Sir Nose: I don't dance, I don't sweat, I don't fuck. If you gonna be cool, it's got to be to the nth degree. Like Rakim, you gotta be cool . . . and still bad. And he's the only one I know out there whose got that vibe on him. He say: "I don't dance and I don't smile." And he'll peel your cap if you want to start testin' your rap out on him. That's [like] my son, I said: "Do anybody ever challenge Rakim?" He looked at me like I was *crazy!* "Don't even think of nobody challenging him!" I know *I* ain't heard nobody could do nothin' with him. But I just thought, since they like to dis each other so much, did anyone have the heart to do that. He said: "You ain't even s'posed to *think* like that. Nobody dare think of dissing him!"

What did you think when Digital Underground started copping a lot of your riffs?

Well, I knew their brothers and things before that record ever came out. The Uhuru Maggot, [Dr.] Illinstein, all those guys from Berkeley that do public radio at Berkeley. They had given me tapes of those guys when they were real young. They're a band, they're a real band, and they was trying to do the band thing at first. So when they came out I pretty much knew about them. The ones that got me, though, was De La Soul. A lot of people had already sampled us, but we didn't know they was gettin' paid for it till they sampled *One Nation.* And since I own *One Nation,* Warners had to direct them to me, and then we realized "Oh, you're s'posed to get paid for this shit." See, the record companies gettin' paid all the while.

I want to ask you about your philosophy of sampling.

I want to make some money off it! [laughs] No, we're putting out a five-disc set of samples, one's out already. Live samples and from the studio and everything. The idea is to make it easier for them to sample, because first of all they don't catalog black music. It'll pop back up years later in somebody's private collection if it's any good. And if there's nothing good they'll just keep auctioning it around to different people. So it don't really get cataloged. So when samples started coming out, I just realized that, hey, this is a good way to be on the radio anyway. And by having that attitude, I was able to realize that if I made it easy for 'em to get it, I could still make some money off this stuff. And consequentally, it got so popular that now the companies have to deal us owning the stuff. See, ordinarily the stuff be outta print so long that everybody just take for granted that you ain't s'posed to get paid for it no more. They'll tell you that the debt's got interest. And the debt is not a loan, that's not the way the shit works. It's not a loan, but they treat it like a loan and start applying interest to it. That's illegal, too.

How do you feel about rap in general?

I don't understand the whole hip-hop scene or rap scene down on chicks the way they are. Not themselves, but the environment that they're in that makes that possible. I'm thinkin' they ain't but seventeen, eighteen, nineteen years old, they ain't been around long enough to have their heart broke, to know anything about "Bitch, bitch, bitch, bitch, bitch, bitch, bitch." But it's a combination of the old pimp school of thought, guys used to screw 'round talkin' shit with each other and it was a joke, but then you add that to the misunderstanding of the family life of, say, Muslims, the male and female's relationship to each other. . . . You get a bunch of young kids that don't understand the cultural difference there, and you add a pimp style of rap to that and you get so [strains his voice in disbelief] *the bitch ain't shit for real.* I mean they all forgot that they mother's a woman! Not the guys that are rappin', but whoever they're talkin' *about,* whoever they heard saying these things. I think that they got mixed up between the old pimp school and a custom of somebody else, and you put the two together with somebody's only fifteen years old or thirteen or twelve, they don't know the difference. Right away, when they say "Bitch, get my money!" it's not a joke no more, it's not just clownin' in the barbershop. 'Cause, I mean, the girls could do it just as good as you could if it was just on that level. But when you get that custom or religious aspect added to it and everybody think they got to go for it.

To me that's in the same category as drive-by shooting. A drive-by shooter's got to be the punkest motherfucker in the world. I mean when I was growin' up the coolest thing you could do was take an ass whoopin'. If you took it in good faith, hey you a cool motherfucker. "Hey, I took it." I mean, even your woman could pick your coat up and "Okay." That was the coolest thing you could do. But to run by and shoot somebody out the window while you drivin' ninety miles an hour and shoot everybody but the person you're shootin' at, it's got to be a punk. But they so young, they don't know nothin' about punk or not. Just that they fired the gun is enough for them, that they're grown or they done some'n. And the media immediately report it. I mean, you can't say they shouldn't report it, but people have to understand that everything that you hear and see ain't the gospel because it's on television and the newspaper. So you get all of that, we take all that into consideration. Even though we do the same kind of songs, I want people to know that we doin' it 'cause it's out here, this is what people say. And I put it on Sir Nose if it's too bad. We did a whole bunch of those things on a song, but we used Sir Nose as tryin' to infiltrate rap to cause race riots, men against women, pro and anti-abortion, gay and straight. I mean, we put him in there to cause conflict between everybody, 'cause that's his gig. And you put it on him and people say, even though the song sound funny or cool and everything, we know that everything Sir Nose do gonna *sound* good but it ain't shit, it don't mean shit. I mean, there's a bigger enemy out here than fuckin' 'round with the sucker MC, now. Who the fuck wanna kick his ass anymore? I mean, do you get much pleasure out of beatin' up a *chick?* You use your AK-47 on a *chick?* I mean, there's a bigger motherfucker out here, there's a new world order out here that really needs somebody . . .

. . . to fuck with it.

To fuck with it. I ain't into no revolution or no whole lotta organization, 'cause you start an organization and they infiltrate it and make you look like shit. Which is what I think happened with the stupid guy in Waco, Texas. Anytime I see the government, the opponent is up fifty points with me. I don't care how bad they look. And the heavier the government bring out stuff, the more points the other side get. [laughs] The fact that that just wasn't the FBI and the police let me know something just wasn't kosher with what they doin'. I mean, "cult" is a really funny word. When you hear mufucker come in with "cult," he's already guilty, the government's already guilty of *somethin'*. I don't know what the fuck they done did, but the fact that they have to keep remindin' us that it's a "cult"—I mean we could figure that out for ourself. And sure enough, as soon as I find out it ain't that little of a cult, it's part of a *big organization*. It's just a fraction of that. And there's a lot of people that fit in the same category who think that these are the last days. And ain't no people got no shit that burn like that. That's the same shit that burned down MOVE's place, that's the same shit that burned down the SLA. That kinda shit will burn underwater. Whatever that shit was. Their terrorist point is their point of view. The whole disassociation with the establishment is more scary to the government than if you rob banks or if you a communist. They were more afraid of hippies than they were communists.

I read an interview where you were talking about playing the fool or the jester as a way of being able to say anything you want.

Yeah, 'cause I ain't gonna be no preacher, ain't gonna be no guru. But I think we should trade information. Bein' in the media with this much attention, we have an obligation to at least say *somethin'* every now and then. That's why I have to agree with Sinead O'Connor. I wish things wasn't like they were in this world! We have to really listen to some things that're said that we don't wanna hear. 'Cause some people know these things; if they don't speak up on 'em, I don't care how big or important they are, they have an obligation. Like the Baghwan, they chased him outta Utah. I didn't know he was dead—he was dead soon as he got out here. And they was right behind him tellin' nobody to listen to him. Anybody that has that information and don't tell it is *fucked!* I heard him say somethin' about Mother Teresa and I think that's pretty harsh, but you have to kinda like listen to that. If you know that information and don't say *somethin'* . . . or at least tell somebody where they can find out some other information than what they know. That's basically what I do, 'cause if you preach whatever you preachin' anyway it's gonna change before they can understand what you're talkin' about. You know, if you join an organization or a cult, they gonna get it infiltrated and make you look like shit before you can get out there. And ain't nobody got no definite answers anyway, so my thing is just: "Think." You got to think, even though they cut schools out. To me, the most important person in the world is a teacher. They should be paid more than anybody in the fuckin' world. But if we don't have no better sense than to let the lottery in. They promise it will go to the schools and then they don't give nothing to them, and at the same time they take the money and people still go out and buy tickets. Why you gonna go out and buy ticket if they didn't give money to schools like they was s'posed to? Why don't we all stop buyin' the fuckin' tickets? If you don't stop buying the tickets, you ain't got nothin' to say to nobody who sells crack. 'Cause everybody's tryin' to get a dollar, and you gonna tell 'em that, okay, drugs kill. You got to think about that, cause I'm out here with a *whole bunch* of druggies, and I ain't seen nobody die from the drug. [lowers his voice] But they do die from guns and robbery. And they done made "drug-related" the same things as *drugs.* And they're different. Drug-related relates more to the fact that money's involved. It relates more that if it was legal, you probably wouldn't get these deaths.

That's true, what kind of world would it be if we said it was a "money-related" death? I mean, what wouldn't be?

[laughs] Wouldn't it sound funny! That's right. Money-related death, but that's what the fuck it is! And they work that one so good this time. You take a aspirin, it's a drug-related death. They need some statistics for "drug-

related" so they can get allocations for more money to fight drugs. Not gonna fight no drugs, though. They ain't hardly tryin' to fight drugs, 'cause they fight drugs they won't have no job. And people are so fickle with that one, I mean lay people who grew up with the sixties would know that one. "These crackheads" . . . But no, if y'all stop agreein' with the fact that that's what's doin' it, you gonna tell me that these little black mufuckers with Adidases on got no trillion-dollar business. They say drugs a trillion-dollar business, but they got a little bitty Mercedes, or Taurus or Ford or somethin' look like a Mercedes with spoilers on, they got no money. You believe that they *really* got the dope money? The money's on the boats and planes. Those mothers got little cracks with something that's hinted with coke, I mean its *hinted*. And they get the most time, 'cause people believe what they see on television. I mean even the dealers themselves believe it. They really do believe it themselves, because the promotion on it is so good and there's so much money made from fightin'. We got a song called "Dope Dogs," goes: "There's more profit in pretendin' that you're stopping it than selling it." I mean, news had to make a fortune off drug-related stories. *48-Hours* on "Crack Avenue" have all these sponsors. Next week: "Maybe we was wrong about the *48-Hours,* maybe it's not that bad"—same sponsors. And rehab? You s'posed to pee and bring $25. They got so many customers, just bring the $25, we'll find you the pee. I got a friend, he's a guy and they told him: "If this you're pee, you pregnant!" Rehab's a joke! A lot of people need the time off, 'cause that's about the best you'll get out of rehab is time off. Once you get it off, you have to do it for yourself, 'cause believe me they gonna take up that space far as your addiction. "Forget all that, be hooked to us." 'Cause you pay. It's all money-related. That whole concept of drug society . . .

"CIA *I owe!*"

"CIA I owe." You heard the song already, huh? It's called "U.S. Customs Dope Dogs." That'll be out pretty soon, too. That's on One Nation Records, our own label. I had to do one record my own way 'cause all the sudden they tell me what to do and I'm listening to all these records out here, everybody sayin' everything they wanna say: "Foot up the bitch's ass!" "Killed the mutherfucker!" and this and that. And everything we bring in, they be like: "You can't say this." Wait a minute, what the fuck is that?!! I mean I know we don't say nothin' *that* deep, but it must be *how* we say whatever we say. Yeah, but I keep it tongue in cheek, 'cause I ain't into preachin' and anything people got to get they got to be able to get it and be able to think about it, they can't get it, jump up and go do nothin' about it other than think, 'cause the minute you start to go crazy, they prepared to tear this country up. They don't care nothin' 'bout this country. The people that's in charge is a very small number of bankers, federal reserve, secret organizations and shit like that. They don't care which country stand and which country go. They could care the fuck less about that. Matter of fact there's more money, cause they usually have a bank financin' both sides of any war. That's all it is. So, it's a waste of hip-hop or rap or kid's energy to be pissed at a cop. Cop is a broke motherfucker! My thang is, I ain't gonna be mad at no mother broke as me. Know what I'm sayin'? Ain't no broke motherfucker got business being mad at another broke motherfucker. There's always somebody pullin' strings in black and white situation. If you could follow both people's lives, you find out mutherfucker in Aryan Nation, probably his father lost his farm and they told him: "All them blacks on welfare took up all the money, and that's why dadadada, dabadabadi . . ." And [poor blacks say]: "All white people get a better break than you, and . . ." And it's just that easy. Now you got abortion/anti-abortion with the same kind of intensity, and neither one of them right, thoroughly! And neither one of 'em wrong, thoroughly. But you got somebody else who will make *this one* right this time, *this one* right that time.

Gay/straight, too, you were mentioning.

Same thing! Same thing!

It's interesting, I was thinking about the lyrics to "Jimmy's Got a Little Bit of Bitch in Him."

That was a friend of mine at the record store. And the dude was just findin' out *himself.* And we were like "Who gives a *fuck!*" And so far he was asexual, he hadn't done nothin'. I said shit, the worst motherfucker is the one who don't do nothin'. Mufucker that's got that shit packed up. We used to joke with him about that. That's funny, he thought we were the lightest ones on him. We said the harshest shit, but he said we were easier on him than his family was. We was like "So what! *I* ain't gonna sleep with you." It ain't no big thing, it just ain't no big *thing.* But I look at the television the other day: they gonna accept Bill Clinton's thing 'bout gays in the army *if* they wouldn't come out the closet. Now they just said, "If they got some secrets we could get 'em and blackmail 'em." They wouldn't be able to do that unless they hide it. You make 'em hide it, that's only reason it would be valuable that way. If nobody gives a fuck, it's no value. Who gonna blackmail you if nobody care to hear it? So what? Who gonna pay the ransom then? If he ain't got to be ashamed of it, he can't be blackmailed. Whoe, you *want* it to be fucked up! That's where that shit's at.

You mentioned something earlier that I wanted to ask you about. You talked about Muslim families, and I wanted to ask about the relationship between One Nation under a Groove and the idea of nationalism, black nationalism.

It's a planet. I could justify, if I wanted to say black, 'cause if you all came from one lady, they done proved that genetically. That we all came from one woman somewhere in Africa. We got different pigmentation, we all still from that same piece of life. But I'm talkin' 'bout a planet 'cause I think since then there's probably some aliens here that ain't from this planet. I'm sayin' anything that's here. That's what I'm sayin', cause the other shit is too fragmentized. Sure you can pair off all kinds of ways, but I think you're really short-changin' yourself in *this* era, trying to do *that* one. For whatever reason it's gonna start changin', genetically it's gonna start changin'. That's just too weak of a concept: black or white or gay or straight or pro-this or pro-that. I think that's too shallow to lean on. And I don't even think that Islam as a nation even now believes that anymore. For the most part the system is run by Europeans around the world pretty much now so they gonna get the number one vote if it's gonna be somebody. But we all know better than that: when the slaves came here, somebody had to go catch 'em and bring 'em to the Europeans—they were other black people. It's human nature, good and bad in all of it. And we're probably one of the most popular groups *with* the Nation of Islam. And I been hearin' a lot of white groups even is down with the concept, 'specially when they been to jail and learned the information, they ain't talkin' 'bout no white *person* . . . it's a *mentality,* a *frame of reference* which is basically European, and if you want to break it down anymore, it's bankers. It's motherfuckers with money. Secret organizations and things.

Of course, when it comes to music it's the white musicians playing black music who make all the dough. Eric Clapton syndrome.

He gave it a little respect. I have to let him, 'cause see, he taught me something about black music that I didn't even know. See, 'cause I was down on blues and shit. I thought it was some old shit, until I heard "Spoonful" and all those records. And he knew so much about the people that I was ashamed. So when we start doin' funk, we started makin' sure that we was understandin' what we was talkin' about. Then there's other people, like what's his name, Pat Boone. Like his version of "I'll Be Home . . ." He covered every black hit record that was out there, and he got a bigger record. That's the deal we made with the [Red Hot Chili] Peppers. Said if y'all gonna get there first, make sure you acknowledge the funk. And they did. We trade off, 'cause when they got the Grammys, that's the only way I would go. I have to have my own agenda for goin', I have my own reason to be going not just because they say "come." So we got there and it was all cool. [Nods at Babblin' Kabbabie] And I told them the best way to do it, since they gonna need a white funker; I told them I will give it to 'em, give 'em the hardest core funk I can, the silliest mugs in the world—I have to hold his hand while he do it, but you cannot say that he ain't got it! And there's a million mufuckers that wish they was up there and be like: "How the fuck did he do *that?*" He don't have clue! But in the industry, you have to learn. 'Cause once they get you not to *be* black, the industry will take black music and you'll see it on television selling a Ford. I hear Jimi Hendrix music on television now, Motown music all over tha place. And they usually wait till they get all of the people who's involved with it out. Believe me, when they first started to try to get a good pop-funk band, Thomas Dolby and myself was talkin' 'bout it. He says: "Well, you know as soon as I get in . . ." I said, "They ain't gonna let you in! If that's what you up to, you ain't gettin' in." Peppers, too. I told 'em the same thing. Accident'ly, after the first record, and they got a lot of funk fans, and then they went off and did their own thing. And then they came *back* and did it again, and nobody wasn't ready for it. And it was so fuckin' funky that it was like, "Oh, *shit!*"

One thing I noticed about your strategy for your own music is that in concert you do little bits of your current songs repeatedly in between older ones.

When we got a new song that we want to put out, "Rhythm and rhyme, rhythm and rhyme, rhythm and mutherfuckin' rhyme . . ." That's on the new album. When we do that, when we got a chant that we wanna sell, you might hear that every song that we do! "Party people pumpin' their fist like this, party people . . ." That's another one.

"Whacha gonna do, George?"

Yeah, that's "Dope Dog." So all that shit is popular; ain't no record out yet! I'm tryin' to tell the record company "Y'all don't know . . ." I try to give it to 'em, but they . . . Okay, I'll do this the way I used to do it. We used to pump the chants all night long, and then the record come out and people be waitin' like "When'll we hear that record's got that *chant* in it. *Ohh*, here it is!"

We did that with "Yank My Doodle." Saw you do it live back in '89, then didn't hear it again till Trey's record.

That's deep, man! He's in the band now, Tracey is. This new one, they ain't gonna be able to get around it, 'cause "Rhythm and Rhyme" is on that motherfucker. People say they buyin' every record they see just to see if that's on it.

So you started doing that chant stuff with Funkadelic, "Wo ha, hey," chants like that?

Oh those was popular way 'fore the records came out. "I Got a Thang," "Wo ha hey," "Yeah, yeah, yeah." All those was like a couple of years before we put 'em out. We was doin' 'em on the road.

Tell me a little about the genesis of the outer space DJ on Mothership Con-nection.

I'd noticed that disc jockeys was off radios, beginnin' to be FM now, so it was like [lowers his voice, cool and seductive], "Good afternoon, ladies and gentlemen." No more [louder, more hyperactively] "Hey, everybody! Hip-pity op, go out an op, you I'm the joke." All that was missin', so I just put it in my own record. And that was *Mothership Connection*. That one worked 'cause we used the funkin' thing, the costuming thing was beginning to be different. It was Parliament, again, so we gonna go back to costumes we got to go back way deeper, couldn't come back lookin' like Earth, Wind & Fire. Couldn't come back lookin' like Ohio Players. None of that. So when we come back, we got to come back lookin' like we *steppin'*. We took all of the money from the hit record, half of band left 'cause they thought we had been workin' all that hard to get a house and a car. I said, "You get the house or the car. Can't get 'em both cause we gotta get a spaceship." So most of 'em got Sevilles, and after the novelty wore off of it they was pissed! [laughs] So a lot of 'em didn't make it to the *Funkentelechy* album, even though they back 'round now. That was a hassle, but if it's gonna be about glitter, then it's got to be glitter of the highest order. 'Cause to me that's all what show business is about. Once the novelty's worn off somebody, it's hard to entertain 'em. And once they know you, it's hard to entertain 'em. So they never really *knew* nobody 'cept the names of the groups. When Parliament came back, it was like a brand new group. And we wore that out for a couple of albums, and they was surprised when *One Nation* came out. They was like "What the Hell?" It was like bouncing back and forth to each group. Parliament was the glitter. When we got the spaceship, I spent the rest of the money on publicity, 'cause then you have to *tell* somebody that you spent this much money on somethin'. Money begets money, and it's a crap, but it wasn't too bad 'cause we got *Time, People, Newsweek*. We got 'em all. One guy came to do an interview, and he said, "Now I know this is a whole bunch of *shit*, but I guess you paid for it." [laughs] I liked him! Everybody scared me 'bout him, said when he interviews you he gonna wear your ass out. I said, "I paid for it, nobody else paid for it." He said "I like you more. At least the record company didn't pay for it, you paid for it out yer own pocket. You know how this shit work, don't you?" I said, "I hoped it worked like this."

[in awe] You paid for the whole Mothership Connection Earth Tour?

We didn't even get money from the record company, we told 'em to keep it. And it didn't work till the third album. It didn't work for *Mothership Connection* 'cause it was old by the time we got the money. *Clones*, they shot straight for a pop record on *Clones*. If they had put "Funkenstein" like they should have done . . . if they'd shot straight for the black radio again, "Dr. Funkenstein" probably would have been better. But they went for the pop, "Do That Stuff," 'cause we had just come off of "Tear the Roof Off." So it was a pop record, tryin' to get radio. It was Neil. Right away, set us back. But "Flashlight," after the live album. And after everybody had seen the show, the rap: "You didn't see them when they came through? See them next time!" So the live album was out, and when *Funkentelechy* came out, "Flashlight" was right on time. All three of those years was put right together in one year. That's when *everybody* saw the spaceship. People who didn't see it the first time missed the second time, but with the hit record the third time we was like all the way over.

How do you feel about those late Parliament records now, looking back at them? Gloryhallistoopid *and* Trombipulation. *Critically, they're the ones that get the hardest time.*

And they're the most popular! But only because *now* we been away from that sound for so long that you can appreciate it. I started appreciating it when Humpty and them showed up, and Ice Cube. 'Cause that's *all* they sampled, those records. That's their favorite two. We might have been movin' too fast at the time. For *Gloryhallistoopid,* I really thought it was time for us to go sit down. So I just put some songs together that I liked. Like I say, when I think we're in trouble we make the best records. I said, "I think we'd had too may hit records, they gonna shaft us upside the head for this motherfucker, no matter *what* the record sounds like." 'Cause you know, our planned obsolescence period come into effect. I don't care how good it is, it's like get the fuck *outta* here! And I thought *Gloryhallistoopid* shoulda been that one. But when it came out, people really, actually liked [sings] "My name is the one . . ." It was one of those records I made up at the microphone in about two minutes. And it was like really fuckin' happenin'! And the other one I never would have thought that anybody would ever *think* about buyin' "The Agony of Defeet"! I never imagined in a million years, anything but the concept. I figured the concept. That's where I gave Sir Nose his lead; you know he won for a minute. He's back there tryin' to find his ancestors and shit. And it was time for me to go sit down.

Your approach to studio work seems to see it as being part of a team, which is something that a lot of people in your position don't think. They think "I know better than anybody."

Oh, no! I don't want the job, I don't need that much work! That's what's so funny, I see people come in the studio and literally tell everybody what to do. Then you only need you. And I'm glad to come in here and sit right down here and walk upstairs every two hours and see how they're comin' along. I have fresh ears, then, and I can make a choice. But if I'm sitting right there, I'm gonna get creative every five minutes, and that shit ain't gonna never get up there. In the old days we used to use twenty-four hours to get a drum sound. Get the drum sound just to find out that all the rest of the shit won't fit 'cause the drums is too wide! You know? Fuck all this shit! [laughs] Let an engineer do it, and then you can say this, that, that, and that. Much easier to me. I mean, some people know beforehand. Sly, Prince: they got to know beforehand. But that's like practicing your spontaneity for me. I don't want to practice spontaneity.

That seems like a very jazz attitude.

That's why it's called "funk"! Funk is a jazz term. It's like, do the best you can and when in doubt, vamp. You head straight for the vamp so it's like, "You don't know where you're at?" [hits the table] "E!" But everybody really wants to *know,* and they don't want to admit that they *don't* know. Or they think they have to *know* to justify their jobs. That's what it really come from, most people think they have to know to justify their job. To me, producing is just gettin' all the ingredients and let them . . . I don't even have to know what Bernie's doin' or Bootsy's doin'! I just know it's Bernie or Bootsy, so I know it ain't gonna be nothin' not right correct-time-wise, key-wise.

You mentioned that funk is a jazz term.

Improvising is like: we played the song now let's see how far we can go out, still relate loosely, meet ya back here at the coda. And blues same way. Blues guy say, "What key's this on?" And just *play.* But then you get real cute, and get all these new groups: "They don't know our arrangement." You ain't *that* fuckin' deep that they can't figure it out if they're a musician. That attitude helps you mentally more than anything. You don't *have* to be correct, you don't *have* to be right. And that's what blows most people out, when they're worried or sad that it ain't workin' or don't sound right. And you can't *get it* right if you act like that, if that's the way you feel. You up on stage, the people think you right all the time. Ain't nothin' we can do they don't think we mean to do. And you'll get it right if you just pretend that you don't mean to do it.

I have a list of names and I'd like to throw them at you and have a short response about each one. Ready? MC5.

White niggers.

Wayne Shorter.

Oh, he used to live 'round the corner from me in Jersey. Him and Larry Young. We used to think that Larry was testin' his organ and we used to think Wayne was testin' his horns when they would practice. We didn't know he was playing music, we didn't know what jazz was yet. I told Miles the same thing, you know. [makes sputtering, half-intoned noises] Wayne Shorter, yeah he's a bad motherfucker!

Chuck-D.

That's my man, that's my man, that's my motherfuckin' man, when it comes to tone and shit in rap. It's between him and Rakim. Chuck-D, yeah that's my boy.

Ice-T.

Homeboy, he's from Newark. I like his attitude and I like his tone of voice, now. But I hated that fuckin' "Reckless" when it first came out.

Prince.

Bad motherfucker. Badder than most people know about. Badder than most people will ever know about. I mean if he start releasing some of that stuff he got in the can . . . maybe he will now that he supposedly retired. That may be a good idea that he retire so that he can get some of that shit out the catalog that he's got that's bad. Yeah, he's one of the baddest.

James Brown.

I don't know how the fuck that motherfucker got away with "Uh, good God!" back in the old days, but now I know that that is so much pure dope in that music that I'm glad he didn't have to *say* nothin', 'cause if he'd said somethin' we probably would have all od'd. Cause that "Uh, good God!" is dopey enough.

Trey Lewd.

He's gonna be the next bad motherfucker around. He wrote most of the songs on my album now. That's my son, he's gonna be a bad motherfucker!

Miles Davis after Bitches Brew.

Well, Miles Davis any time was nervy. I've always admired his ability to change styles and not care what his contemporaries say or think. Even when the musicians around him thought he shouldn't have did it, he was his own person, he could do whatever he wanna do. He's *that* motherfucker. And he got *ear,* too, man. He could tell no matter what the new sound was, he wasn't afraid to go fuck with it.

Sun Ra.

[giggles] He's all out, daddy. You know what, I didn't find out about him 'fore six, seven years ago. Maybe a little longer. I knew the name and everything, but I didn't know anything about him. Now I met a lot of musicians that's with him, and the calibre of people that's with him . . . no wonder he could play around so much. I mean, it's kind of like what we do, too—you're able to play a lot when people are that brilliant as musicians. He could write the shit out right there for 'em, like a letter.

Coleman Hawkins said that Sun Ra wrote the only chart that he could not play.

Ouch. That's some deep shit there, ain't it?

Bob Marley.

That's funny, I used to tease him a lot when I first met him. I wasn't that hip on reggae, we all gettin' high, smokin' spliffs, and he used to be always talkin' about Haile Selassie. And I say: "I wanna get high, too." I mean I never could understand him. He be tryin' to explain to me, and I say: "Man, cut it out! You was born in Maryland!" [laughs] To me, Bob was like Sam Cooke in a political type setting. You know, Sam Cooke was like Jesus to black people for a long time, before he became "You Send Me," before all those songs, when he was with Soul Stirrers. What the Beatles or Jimi Hendrix was to psychedelic, Bob Marley in that era was like that for whatever the political situation was in Jamaica and all around the world. And he wanted all sides to be together. The spirit was with him. You know that spirit comes through you. He would probably just like to have played music and have fun, but when that spirit comes through you, you chosen.

Do you know a producer named Lee "Scratch" Perry? No? Ed Hazel.

Mr. Maggot Brain. His music will be here forever. His was a ball of sensitivity. He just felt everything. He'll be here for a *long* time.

Bootsy Collins.

Funkiest motherfucker in the world on a bass! Told him: "Don't play no bass-lines on no keyboards, though." Bootsy's got some other kind of rhythm, him and his brother, too, Catfish. There ain't too much more rhythm outside of Bootsy.

Bernie Worrell.

Wow. You can't say that in no little bit of words. [Steph sighs] There ain't no *lot* of words you're gonna be able to say that in. Bernie is all of it, anything that you need to be in music, Bernie's it. He's anything he need to be.

Smokey Robinson.

He's my idol. Lyrics? That's my idol. That's what made me put so many puns in songs, 'cause Smokey used to pun songs to death and I think that when I left Motown it was about, let's see how many different ways I can make the same concept come to light, some synonyms or antonyms. Smokey wrote the book on that shit. He's my favorite songwriter.

Sly Stone.

Probably my favorite artist, period. I'd hate to even think of what would have happened if he'd gotten out . . . we probably couldn't stand no more of his stuff. We'd probably OD'd, like I said about James Brown. When he said "I'll be gone for a while," the upper spirit take care of that stuff. He's all of it, like Bernie. Add lyrics to that kind of thing. Sly can write songs that sound like he's talkin' to everybody; everybody thought Sly was talkin' to them. And he's still a *street* person. He's a for real all-that-shit-at-once.

The Beatles.

You name the good ones, Sly, the Beatles. Them, too. Put the four of them together and I think of them like I think of Motown, Sly, Jimi Hendrix. All of them was creators of something special. The Beatles caught the wave too for a minute. Some of us are clever. Stevie had to be what he is, he grew up in it with all those singers, he was talented at eleven years old, he had a thing right from the beginning. But then he went to college, so he s'posed to be as great as he is. Myself, I s'posed to be able to do it, too, cause I was around enough music enough different places that I was supposed to be able to do this. I just call that clever. But some people catch onto a thang, and to me the Beatles caught onto it. Cause you can't do that shit later. Circumstance ain't the same, it can't be done. For whatever reason, Sly don't do it; for whatever reason Motown can't do it. When that thang come through, it just come through and everything you do is right.

[Detroit, May 1993]

NICOLAS COLLINS

Trombipulation

●

Nicolas Collins's medium is mediation itself. In this case,
"mediation" is not only technological (sampling, electronics, radio, records), but encompasses musician initiative
and interaction—the im-media-cy of live performance. Thus in the notes to his four
contributions to the 1982 Lovely Music release Going Out with Slow Smoke he explains
that the pieces are "concerned with the social interaction of electronics and performers,"
and he elaborates further: "as no part or participant has total control of the situation,
they move from accidental coordination to intentional manipulation of the sound produced."

Concocting scenarios in which to act out these power relations is Collins's compositional method. For this, he combines the roles of conceptual artist and engineer/pro-
grammer. He is not unique in this—one need look no further than the MIT Sound Lab to
find similar concerns. Yet it is the broad-minded intelligence with which he approaches
such issues that sets him apart; even admitting that power relations are involved goes
beyond the highbrow aestheticizing of much of the intermedia crowd.

Most recently, Collins's situations have included him as a performer. Using a computer
mounted on the body of an old trombone, he plays duets with improvisors in which he
samples and regurgitates their music, usually recasting it—sped up, slowed down,
treated, modulated, etc. In some cases, this lets them accompany themselves; in others it
allows Collins to shift attention to the minutia of their gestures.

In one such performance with guitarist Tim Brady, at Victoriaville's Festival Musique
Actuelle (1989), I found Collins's music to use (and elucidate) the smorgasbord of implications laid out by new-media technology and its relationship with people as the
agents of its employment. The next day, over Greek food, we hashed out some of this junk
in a most enjoyable hash.

JOHN CORBETT. *I was thinking yesterday while watching you play about
the various things you do by manipulating other people's work while you're on
stage with them and the various levels and degrees of doing that. I wonder if you
could talk about what you see as options in that situation and what the motivation to be working like that with another improvisor and manipulating their
work in a live setting, what the implications are for you.*

NICOLAS COLLINS. Right. It's kind of a big question, because it's kind of like, "What the hell am I doing up there?" There are a few things that come to mind. First is that one of the reasons I stayed away from the improvisational music circuit for a long time is that not only do I have very few ideas about notes, I mean my music's never been about pitch and sort of consciously determined set of notes and harmonies and that kind of stuff, but I also find the whole idea of a lot of notes to be very disturbing. As a result, I had certain aesthetic problems with it, probably a lot having to do with coming out of a rather minimalist background. When I started to work with this instrument in an improvisational setting my thought was that by constantly holding back up information that a player had just put out, two things would happen. One: it makes the player think a second time about something that he or she thought was transitory, you know, once it was out it was gone. Very often I'll make two or three minutes of variation out of one two-second phrase. What it tends to do is just slow down the whole musical process a fair amount. When it generates what I would call a good interactive improvisational situation, it does sort of change the pace of musical development in a way that I find very conducive to my own aesthetic; where one tends to pay more attention to timbre, one is more conscious about each sound one makes, rather than making sort of general sonic gestures. So my feeling is that it creates a situation where potentially you can reflect more on the sound material than you would under other circumstances. In that way it ties the pieces I do that are solos that work with either prepared source material or something like radio: generally speaking, out of a large mass of material that's potentially moving by, either on tape or coming off the air, what I tend to take is a small piece of it and do variations on a small section. Variations more in the sense of different ways of viewing one thing rather than permutations of it; in other words, I don't do a lot of, "now it's on this note, now it's on this note, now it's on this note, now it's on this note . . ." It's more a question of, "This is what it is—here's a little piece of it, here's another little piece of it." That's the principal point. And there's a secondary issue, which just comes down to the fact that most of my interest in ensemble work—I suppose solo work as well, though it's a bit more difficult there—is to keep the situation rather dangerous, keep it risky, unpredictable insofar as possible, insofar as one can still remain commercially viable under those circumstances. When I've worked on sort of pseudo-notated or composed works with instructions for players, it's always been based on interactive instructions, where a player really doesn't know what he or she is going to do until the circumstance arises, and then one has to follow an instruction that is conditional. There's a nice risk factor in this, which is that I can't make my sounds under normal circumstances with that instrument. I mean

I can have some source tapes and stuff like that in behind. But most of the time when I work in an improvisational setting the only input I work with is the player, or at least at the beginning. So if we both sit there waiting to start, it's one of those stupid zen clichés.

One hand . . .

. . . one hand, yeah. One hand on each side of the stage, and no chance of colliding. So there's an element of just putting me at the mercy of the player.

Ironically, it might seem at first glance that the player is at your mercy, but it's reciprocal.

Well, it's a subtle power relationship because I've often been sort of sensitive to the question: what if what I happen to catch and draw out for two minutes is something the player didn't really mean, like it was a mistake or it was not his favorite part, or something like that? You know, very often what I'll do is literally catch the person as they click the keys or tune or something at the very beginning, and that will remain an element I'll work with for the beginning of the piece. So, yeah there's a two-way power struggle that goes on. I don't try to intentionally screw people over, but it's just that very often what I find interesting in what someone does is not what they find interesting in what they do. So that's exactly what comes out in a kind of stealing situation.

But what's interesting about that is that if you take the consideration that we're in an age where recorded music is the common currency, and interpretation of recorded music is perhaps different from interpretation of live music, what it seems to do is cloud that issue in a very nice way.

Yeah, that's actually a nice observation. I hadn't thought about it in those terms. I tend to think about it in old-fashioned ideas about, "This is now, and the record is a musical instrument, and the radio is a musical instrument." You know Cage told us that fifty years ago. It makes you aware that there's all this consumer instrumentation, in a manner of speaking, available to us. But you're right, the bigger issue, the one that has more to do with music is that there are two forms of interpretation now, and it gets clouded when you have certain forms of even commercial music that work with, say, backing tapes, or the phenomenon that I remember from the late sixties going into the seventies, where concert performances for pop bands had to start being more and more accurate reflections of records. It was sort of pushing the limits of, for example, PA technology, beyond what it could do. So there were always those two kinds of bands: the ones you loved to hear live and the ones you wanted to hear on record. You know remix is a bit like that, except that a lot of remix remained a sort of closet phenomenon. I mean it was generating radio tapes or it was dance floor. There were very few DJs who actually did concert performances. Like Christian Marclay. But what

I'm talking about is six years ago, when remix started as a dance music phenomenon, it still took a back seat as far as performance goes.

I'm interested in the historical implications of your music. I mean you can take the observation that some philosophers and historians have made that with recorded culture one's history catches up with one. So there's this increasingly small distance between when something happens and when it becomes histor-icized. What was interesting was watching the possibility of having someone play something and then regurgitating it or working with that material in almost a historical sense. Since history has to do with interpretation, and it's you interpreting and changing the shape of what they've just played. And then them again having a chance at it.

Right. And what's also interesting when you mention history is that there's another element of sort of standard historical theory which probably comes into play, which is that notion of "commentary." The idea that early books were commentaries on and analyses of the "natural world" and then you get a second generation of texts that were analyses and commentaries on the texts. Sometimes when I'm working on these pieces that are very much about a specific thing, like the Shirelles' tune or the one with Peruvian brass band music, the image that pops up in front of my eye is the academic texts that you would sometimes have for something like Shakespeare or Chaucer or Milton, where you'd have the text on the right side of the page and the other side would just be a constant running commentary of notes, alterna-tive versions, things like that. And it's like my source material is the text on the right side of the page and what's actually coming out of the trombone is on the left. The idea that, just as you have two notions of text—one looking at nature and one looking at the other text—we're obviously in an age where that's happening in music, where there are those people who are making music directly (that might be the commentary on nature) and then there's someone like myself who's standing next to them doing a commentary on their music, which is a second thing.

Seems to me that this is very different from a common attitude in the improvis-ing community in which there is a goal of absolute egalitarianism, one that in its most utopian form doesn't recognize the fact of the inherent power relationships it creates. There's no guise of equanimity in a certain respect in your music, though when someone comes to it they know what's at stake. They know what they're getting into, and the power relation is two-way, but manifest.

As they say: "Separate, but equal." But very definitely separate. It's such a clear-cut distinction that there's no way you could confuse one instrument and its role with the other. It's a little as if, in some very strict form like, you know, Schubert lieder, like the accompanist suddenly took a break. It wouldn't fit, you know? The roles are so tightly defined. Yeah, it's interesting the whole idea of political modeling in music, because it's something that I think all of us in our generation have thought about in one form or other. I don't think we're unique in that, but it's been a very conscious issue in a lot of different parts of the music scene. You get stuff all the way from Christian Wolff, whose music started out as being about the politics of the ensemble with that beautiful notational system for coordination and everything, and then became overtly political in terms of text. Cardew is another good case.

Cornelius Cardew.

Yeah. But you know, obviously those Zorn task and game pieces, all the way up through something like "Cobra" are very much about dynamics of ensemble as a model for other kinds of social interaction. These things succeed or fail to differing degrees, but nobody's really sat down and looked at the nature of that failure and what it means for the appropriateness of thinking about musical structure in those terms. It remains a sort of "holy Grail" for composers to do "politically responsible music" that's that way from lyric-content, production value, all the way down to the way the instruments are built. It's an interesting question.

It's funny, because it seems to me that a lot of people when they get involved at a more manifest level, lose track of the fact that there's a reversibility all the time. So especially when you start making didactic music aimed at "the working class" and start attempting to figure out what they are going to be able to "understand," and then making "simple" didactic music based on some idea of what their "folk" origin is, that that can ultimately be seen as an incredibly conservative thing.

Yeah, it does seem like things are always reversible. I think that's true.

JON ROSE

The Violable Tradition

●

Few musicians maintain a scope that is at once as narrow
and as all-encompassing as violinist Jon Rose. His work is
exclusively about the violin. Everything in the world, that
is, as seen through the violin. With this four- (or in his case sometimes more) stringed
cipher, and fictitious characters like Australian unsung hero Jo "Doc" Rosenberg—about
whom Rose has just edited a volume of essays called The Pink Violin—*the violinist spins*
a tangled tale, a disinformational mythology of Western musical culture. As an instru-
mentalist, Rose is a virtuosic improvisor, but he's an improv-subversive (even by im-
provisors' standards), out to overturn expectations, to mercilessly upset conventions
wherever he hears them.

In October 1990, on the day after he recorded live with German quartet Slawterhaus,
Rose and I sat down in the restaurant of Victoriaville, Quebec's Hotel Colibri, for an
involved chat and a cup of much-needed coffee—apropos, given the impending release of
his culinary adventure Violin Music for Restaurants. *Between sips, we discussed a vast*
diapason of topics, from his historical radio plays on Paganini, Beethoven, and Mozart to
rebop, postmodernism, technology, and the politics of consumerism.

JOHN CORBETT. *I want to ask you about radio and things like that, the stuff*
you're doing now, but I want to start by going back and getting some history.

JON ROSE. Dangerous. Complicated. Doesn't make any sense unless you
know it all. I've played the violin from the age of seven, and I'm nearly forty.
It's an instrument that's central to everything I do, whether it's in radio,
playing live, or whatever. It's a story between me and the violin. Classical
education with scholarships and all that kind of stuff, the usual thing—
rebellion and joining rock bands and jazz groups.

Was this in Australia?

No, no, it was in England. I was born in England. A whole bunch of
different things, anything from playing with flamenco guitarists to studying
sitar to studying electronic music to composition like Berio to playing in a
swing group to playing in cafés to playing in strip clubs to playing in session
orchestra, writing pieces for big-band, jazz notation and stuff. Extreme
background. Many different things, none of which, of course, satisfied in
any particular way. [laughs] And then about fifteen years ago I suddenly

found "the way" to make sense out of the whole thing, and that was to build—in German its *Gesamtkunstwerk*, "total art work"—around the instrument. Once I finally figured out how to get these abilities focused, then it all fell into place.

So the violin became this *Gesamtkunstwerk*. And that involved working out an improvised music language on the instrument. That's the most important thing to do. Then to actually rearrange the instrument itself, completely rebuild it. I've done over twenty different kinds of violins—violins with extra necks, more strings, joined together like Siamese twins, controlled by wind or by wheels like steam train pistons with two bows on the end. Plus interfacing with electronics, building electronics into the instrument, microamplification systems, stuff like that. Then there's taking the violin into new situations. I did a lot of concerts of improvisations that were outside—in the desert, sea, at supermarkets, on freeways, whatever. The other major thing then was to make radio and film about it—it sounds very pretentious, but to actually rewrite the history of the instrument.

I was the kind of obnoxious kid that would never accept anything that I was told. And the violin, it's all very clear what's supposed to happen; it's the most rigid education that exists in music. So I wanted always to make up my own history. That's really why I started to write things about it, make films about it.

So your Beethoven piece is based around the violin?

The way much of that material was recorded was using an ultrasound method where I play the violin and the movement of the bow and the movement of my body control a midi system. So while I'm playing the violin I can also be improvising with or controlling or colliding with or being a bit antagonistic with a whole bunch of programs which I employ and modify. And this is sort of the major thing I've been working on for the past two years. It's like bringing the violin into some sort of virtual reality coming directly from the technique of playing the violin, being a violinist on stage. Most of the Beethoven material was recorded like that. The idea was to make up a fiction that Beethoven visited this town, which he never did, and wrote all this music and like archaeologists we "discovered" a whole bunch of it. That's part of many historical projects I'm now involved in. I just did Mozart last month. You know it's his anniversary next year, so I figured there's this supermarket that is recycling Mozart like crazy. In German-speaking countries at this moment, Mozart is everywhere. It's ridiculous, like Coca-Cola over here. Out of control, just an industry. This is one of the reasons that I like working in radio, I can exercise my kind of satire.

In radio, there are also possibilities for dissemination.

Yeah. The kind of work that I make in the studio in radio, which is very complicated and requires a lot of work, I want to be able to do it live. That's my ultimate thing, but the amount of memory required to do that is enormous, totally impractical in terms of a touring musician, which I am. So the system I tour with is minute, two sound boxes.

You do all your own programming?

No, the software that is the interface between the ultrasound and the midi is written by a guy at STEIM studio in Amsterdam. But his job is really the easiest, because the hardest job is to make sense of this in terms of a synthesizer you can buy in the shop. For months I couldn't get it to do anything. Very interesting. Just finding the grey areas in this technology, which is very cheap and accessible. Finding the bits that they never figured. In all these machines and all these black boxes there's these grey areas that no one really knows about.

It seems like the problem of finding the "edge" of things is central to your work, in terms of the violin itself and maybe in the history of the violin, trying to find the edges of its history.

Well that's it, I mean the history that's set there is awesome. The violin is the perfect instrument for any kind of political or musical-political attack. It's *the* icon in Western music. Nobody wants to play a two-hundred-year-old trumpet. It's green and things are growing in it.

It seems that and the piano are the two . . .

Yeah, but the piano's not an icon in the same way that a violin is.

Because you can't pick it up and hold it?

You can't possess a piano. You can *possess* a violin, pick it up and hold it, and you know it's worth a lot of money. Actually David Prentice sent me a great ad in one of these home buyer magazines that America invented, unbelievable ad saying something to the effect of, "Improve your self-esteem and show your good taste to your friends—buy this demonstration violin." You could put it beside your armchair, it was made of gold with gold strings. It wasn't a proper instrument anyway. The whole ad was to improve your taste. About the most tasteless thing I've ever seen. Really incredible. But you can do that with a violin. Everybody understands what a violin is; you go on the street and ask anybody and they'll have a clear idea what it is. There's not many things you can do that with.

You also find violins or bowed instruments in virtually every musical culture.

Sure. Before the violin, everything was much more interesting. It put an end to interesting string instruments in Europe, actually. They came up with this one, simplified thing that was supposed to do it all, but really couldn't. The situation before the violin was much more varied, with no set rules about how to tune it, what it should look like or even how to play it. So it was much freer. And then there's this connection with the Islamic tradition, of course, which is really important. Anyway, that's a side I've really explored with the string instruments, but now I'm more interested in the electronic cultural aspect of it. The situation we're living in is quite ridiculous. I mean it's very hard to take seriously sometimes.

As the end of your Paganini hörspiel *makes pretty clear.*

Right. The Reverend Ike is cleaning up the United States from the evil influence of violins. "We're gonna burn every one of them satanic instruments! It's the voice of the devil." It's about the violin, but the violin as a representative of a other things, too. It actually sort of predicted the present demise of the National Endowment for the Arts, with good old anti-porn shit and all.

Have you ever played with George Lewis's computer?

Yes. I did a violin fest in Berlin beginning of 1989, a whole four days just devoted to the violin. I didn't ask George to bring a violin, but I asked him to bring his computer system. So I did a piece with that, and we tried it out in Amsterdam when he was there. What he's working on is really quite advanced stuff. I mean he's been on this for ten years now, and it's extraordinary. George is interesting, 'cause he's totally obsessed with the language of what it can do, but he's uninterested in what it sounds like. Which is . . . well, we all have our zones of activity and forget other ones; otherwise you go crazy. But it's very interesting.

That's what he says about video, he's interested in the process *of doing it.*

Of course, that's his thing. And he says, "I already play the trombone." That's his music thing and he's got them in two completely distinct boxes. I try to let things cross over when they can. I don't have a "set" way of working. And the other thing is that I was involved with composition as a method of making music in the mid-seventies, but then I gave it up. I thought, "This is just not working out." I wanted to be an improvisor, and everything I've done since then has come out of the basic aesthetics of an improvisor. Oddly enough, with this electronic music stuff, I'm composing all the sounds, every single one of them. In a much more concrete and direct manner than I ever did when I was writing dots on paper. So, there I am back composing again. I swore I'd never do it!

It's tough to call choosing samples "improvising."

Well, also the way in which the whole thing is connected. I mean, what I'm doing with the space violin project has connected me more extremely with pre-composition or pre-structuring of an event, and with the business of live [music], of surviving out there, you know? On stage, with it all going on, that's the improvisor. It's as extreme a musical experience as I could ever have with an improvising group, that's for sure.

In part, I ask about George's computer because Derek Bailey made an interest-

ing *comment about George's computer, that playing with it is a lot like playing with George, that he's programmed the computer in ways that really reflect what his mode of improvising is.*

Of course. Totally, totally. I mean he's trying to say that it's not, that he's making this thing that is somehow . . . but everything you touch is loaded. Yes, exactly.

The space violin piece seems like something very specifically tailored for you.

Yes. I doubt very much if anyone else could play with it, mainly because they don't know what it can do. Sometimes when I perform at electronic music fests, there's all these guys who come on stage who know much more about this shit than I do. And they say, "Where's *this,* and where's *that?*" They don't know what's going on. And this is an off-the-shelf, $500 synthesizer and one program, one bit of software. So, to me that shows that within this area of activity, a lot of people aren't working very hard, and their heads have basically been bought by the industry. The industry says, "In order to move that ashtray from over there you need to go buy a 533P6 which will move it from there to there. And if you want to move that ashtray from there to there via there, you have to go get a 543P26567B," or something. And everybody says, "Oh right" and goes and does it. But for example in this thing I use, people start hearing things that they think are sequences and say, "Where's the sequencer?" There is no sequencer. One of the first rules of electronic music is that you can modify one wave form with another wave form. That's all it is. But it's like, "That's not written in the book."

Stockhausen seems important in terms of rethinking electronics without the high-tech.

Well, I last made a program in Cologne, and Stockhausen was just arriving and he was going to take over the studio for a year. [pauses and laughs] "I vould like ze studio for ze year!"

Did he ride in on a horse, with his son blaring trumpet?

Yeah. My aesthetic is basically junk. It always has been. I did actually once have quite a very good violin, but it was stolen within months. Then I got another one which was also quite good, and that was also stolen. And now I have one which was not so bad, and it was broken, too. Misha Mengelberg dropped me off at a set of traffic lights on the only day it snowed in Amsterdam about seven years ago, and I slipped. I'd only got the violin two days before. I just figure I don't have much luck. So now I only play on cheap instruments.

That must be a strong point of connection for you and Chadbourne.

Definitely. Yes, Eugene understands me there. [laughs]

He likes playing on the crappiest instrument he can get someone to bring to the concert. How did you get hooked up with Chadbourne?

I invited him to Australia. We knew of each other. I had a series of projects going in Australia called the Relative Band, which was like the international improvising connection. I invited him in '85.

That was the one with Jim Denley and Gillian McGregor?

Yeah. And then after that every year it seemed we'd do a tour and it was on a different continent.

So for you does Slawterhaus also revolve around the violin? You play so much synth with them.

It's strange because the first three years with Slawterhaus I played cello which had a lot of strings. It was fun, but to me it was quite clear once [Peter] Hollinger's playing full out, an instrument with that kind of subtlety of sound and frequency range just doesn't cut it. Everybody disagreed with me, but every tape I ever heard of the band I could have put on a vacuum cleaner or something. You couldn't hear anything. So one day I turned up with a whole bunch of sounds I'd worked up for Slawterhaus on a synthesizer, and everybody freaked out . . . "What!??" And they very soon agreed. But it also meant I played more violin, which is one reason I did it, 'cause I wasn't playing that much violin.

Synthesizer fills out some sort of mid-range?

I feel much better about the balance of what I do in the group. It's quite clear that if I just played the violin or cello, it lacks some sort of bottom end, in a way. So when the band's really blowing it's brains out . . .

What's the history of Slawterhaus?

When I was first living in Berlin full-time, which was '86–'87, DDR was still going and Johannes Bauer had a concert like they always had with Dietmar [Diesner] and Peter. Somebody was going to play bass but couldn't make it, and they asked me to fill in. We did four concerts, and it was a band. We've never discussed the music, really. Now and then someone might say something. We have the chemistry; everybody feels totally they can do exactly what they like.

Seems like you and Peter really connect in that group.

Well, I'm an old rock and roller! The group has played in very different circumstances. There've been gigs where we've been invited to do the music for a video and Peter's played a plastic mug and wastepaper bin and everybody else played acoustic. But it's still a group. Music often comes down to personalities, unfortunately and fortunately. I mean, there are bands that would just never work, not because of the *players* but the *people*. So if the people trust each other and there's a connection.

It also lets you take some risks that you couldn't otherwise take.

Sometimes we get unbelievably theatrical on stage, especially D.D. and me. And Johannes is completely untheatrical, just goes and has a cup of tea or something.

Although, that's kind of theatrical in itself.

Yeah, yeah, he's got his own way of dealing with it.

It was interesting yesterday there was a lot less quotation than I've heard in your music on record. There was one reference . . . or there were probably lots, but they were submerged enough that I didn't catch them.

It depends how I'm feeling, I must say. Though I'm actually thinking at the moment—because I'm doing in the radio work so much stuff that's directly tied into a certain period or style or person—that when I actually get on stage I just want to play my own stuff.

Of course, that brings up the question of what your own stuff is and whether that stuff isn't yours too.

I'm quite clear when it's my language. To a lot of people, they probably can't tell. But to me it's obvious.

When did you move to Australia?

In the mid-seventies.

Was it there that you started to improvise?

It was there that the most important ideas started to emerge. I never go to England, except to see my parents. I had to get away from that thing so I could expand.

Which in a sense is funny, because there was so much important improvising going on in Britain at that time.

Sure. But it had nothing to do with me. I was totally in another space.

Is there a strong scene in Australia?

Not as strong as it was. Up until about '83 I was thinking that the scene in Australia was about as good as anywhere, better than most. There are some problems specific to Australia. First, to make any kind of events which involve anybody from overseas, you're gonna have to have government funding, it's just too expensive. And in the seventies there was a big boom to get things happening. And then in about 1984–85, there was this whole political debate where the Australian Opera Company, which was already taking 87 percent of all government money for all artistic activity of any kind, wanted another $2 million. And they went directly to the government, and got it. And that money came from all the fringe and interesting activities. On the economic front, a town like Sydney has been totally gutted in the last ten years. All the places where there used to be to play, they don't exist anymore. The streets don't exist. They're changing it into a banking and insurance place, where all the money from Hong Kong and Japan will come.

Now you're living in Holland, where the situation has historically been opposite, with the government being more supportive.

It's changed there. I must say, Berlin is my town in Europe. In Amsterdam, there's clearly a scene around the BIMhuis. This is actually quite a closed little scene. If you're visiting, it's not so bad, but if you actually decided to go and live there and do your work there, you wouldn't be looked at. Whereas, in Berlin it's a town of immigrant population all the time, and it's expected that everybody's from outside. It's more open, I find. This closed scene was something I couldn't understand, 'cause in Australia everybody is immediately interested in anybody who pops up. But it can work both ways. It depends on the political formulation of the situation. If you're a famous black American jazz musician and you come from New York, that's definitely a positive selling point, a lot of Europeans would use that as a favorable thing in terms of marketing anything having to do with jazz or improvised music. It depends on individual situations. I can say there are situations—I'm not gonna mention any fucking names—but that person is there, and that person is getting work purely by nature of the fact that he is coming from the right country and is the right color. And it's really shit, it's unbelievably bad. That's not a common thing, but I have seen it work. Of course. But that's nothing peculiar to music, it's like the whole of our economy—I call it the "age of shopping"—postcommunism, postcapitalism, it's the shopping age. It's just nonstop "sell sell." And there's a natural European aesthetic, I suppose, which is against that.

But it seems like there's a strong fascination with it as well. I mean it's the difference between a place where even the most fragmented thing is grounded in tradition to a place where there's a Woolworth mentality.

That is a tradition. That tradition of selling and packaging, that's not a young tradition now, it's more than forty-five years old. It's not something that sprang up yesterday. It's sort of weird. Personally, I don't have a "side." I'm an immigrant wherever I go. Australia is somehow even more strange than Europe or America because it has a sense that they have to compensate for the fact that they're not in Europe. This alarmed me when I was first in Australia. The place had everything going for it, so to import this static bullshit was unbelievable. To voluntarily give everything to an opera company! We worked it out and it would be cheaper to send each of the people who go to the opera on holiday first class to Italy for three months of the year and take in like thirty operas. Australia is like a place that is neither America or Europe, big American influence, big Japanese influence. It's an element of belief. That's what's interesting about American culture. There's a belief syndrome here, people watch the television and there's a big enough percentage to keep the whole thing working. In Europe it's very hard to get

10 percent of any group of people to believe anything. We've been blown apart by two world wars and God knows what. You don't accept, can't go along with that sort of thing. So that's one sort of fascination. And that's the big plus for American culture in Eastern Europe.

They're hearing the "ching" of cash registers.

Yeah. They're doing a lot of self-inflicted damage. Hungary, for example. Disgusting. I must say, the whole thing with America and its cultural side, it's really interesting, particularly now. I mean, all these old games with East/West confrontation, all the reasoning behind why a lot of the economy has been set up is gone. So it's like, what are you gonna replace it with?

Seems like they quick-fixed it with the Middle East.

But the Arabs are too foreign, too far away.

Still, it seems like the Soviets were constituted as distant in the old system.

We're also in this postculture age, in the sense that every empire that there ever was—the American one or the British or the French or the Romans or the Greeks—in terms of the idea of dominating other parts of the world, it always meant military presence and economic presence, but above all, to sell your way of life, and your way of thinking, and your music and your art, to introduce that wherever you were. That's really changed with the Japanese. It's the first time that guys who are really hell-bent on dominating come along and say, "You just keep doing what you're doing. It's fine, we're just gonna take the money . . . and *own* it." This thing with Sony now, it's unbelievable—one company can own what we record it on and what we play it on. They own the Berlin Philharmonic. And they're not saying, "We want you to change." They don't want a *Japanese* Berlin Philharmonic or a *Japanese* Miles Davis. This is new, I think. I don't know any other empires where they had that. I mean, I can't understand it.

One thing that I find appealing about your work is the ability you have to go back and forth between different kinds of projects, from doing the radio plays to doing, say, "straight" improvising gigs with Joelle Leandre. Is that flexibility important to you?

I could never be a polished performer in the way that some people are. I would get too nervous about it. I have to have this built-in *failure risk*. The idea of perfection, something finished or 100 percent—anything with these fixed measures I just don't like. I have a natural chemical reaction against it. Even on big radio productions, I use a lot of material the quality and techniques of which are really non-studio.

It seems that that kind of "unfinished business" attitude seems to come out of dadaism. Do you see it that way?

Yeah, naturally. I think the whole notion of dadaism is the most important thing that happened in art in this century. It's critical, I think. If you don't realize it, if you don't see it then . . . my God, life is just unbearable! It's like this whole thing with postmodernism now. These twenty-year-old bebop players, they stand up there and pretend they're jazz players, you know? How can they do that? I mean, how can anybody with a brain believe that what they're doing is not just total reiteration of the past without any awareness of what it means *now*? Of course, these younger people were invented for the jazz industry. For me, a really good musician from now is somebody who's really aware of where they are in time and history. You can see it in the way they use musical genre, musical language, their own language, or in the way they divide it or mix it. Within a minute, you can see all these things that are going on with somebody while they're playing.

SUN RA

●

In June 1986 Sun Ra and the Jet Set Arkestra visited Providence, Rhode Island's (now sadly defunct) Lupo's Heart-
break Hotel, for a whirlwind tour of his music from tight
arrangements of Jimmie Lunceford, Fletcher Henderson, and Duke Ellington through to
the cosmic classics of his own pen, like "Space Is the Place," and "Have You Heard the
Latest News from Neptune?" and a hefty amount of just-plain-space. The show was
remarkable for several reasons. The day before, Ra and John Cage had shared a bill
reciting their poems in New York. Billy Bang had just sat in with the band two nights
before and was (wrongly) rumored to be "on his way to the gig." Regardless, it was a
fantastic performance, June Tyson belting out the space anthems aside John Gilmore's
palpable crooked-man tenor solos and Marshall Allen's alto explosions.

I took the occasion to organize an interview, accompanied by my pal Jim Macnie (now
a reporter for the Boston Phoenix, Musician, etc.) and a reporter from the WBRU news
staff (who knew—and I suspect cared—little about Sun Ra, and who summarily shang-
haied the interview in search of a sensational story with irritating, somewhat condescending questions, hence his pseudonym). We had the wonderful opportunity of dipping
momentarily into the enigmatic and disarmingly personable and humorous wellspring of
a man who remains bigger than life.

IRRITATING REPORTER. *Just an incredible show . . . wow, I've never seen
you before. [turns to me] Do you want to start the interview?*

JOHN CORBETT. *Sure. Well, first I just want to say that it's great to have you
back in the area. You haven't been here in . . .*

SUN RA. . . . quite some time. Since then I've been to Europe several times
and all that. It gets so that I don't know what time it is, or what date it is.
Over in the music so much that I don't know about years or nothin', because
I'm dedicated to it and I'm sincere about it. Whenever you're like that, you
don't even know your on the planet. 'Cause you're so involved in your art,
you see. And you can play better for people when you're like that. If you're
thinking about trivialities and things like that, you can't really be an artist
enough to be yourself and project what you feel.

IR: *What are you trying to get at with your music? I mean what do you want
your audience to feel? Is there a certain something?*

SR: I want them to feel happiness because the things they think are happiness, that's not the kind of happiness that is eternal, you might say. They should have this happy feeling that anywhere they're going out in the universe or omniverse, they will be in tune.

IR: *So you see music as an eternal happiness, in a way?*

SR: It's a bridge to happiness. With music you can express any emotion. And you can paint pictures. Therefore, a musician actually feels about space, outer space—he can really take people out there—because he expresses that feeling, and the vibrations of it will just put them over in the sound and the sound becomes like a spaceship and lift 'em on out there, you see. And they're there. And when they get that feeling, they're getting prepared for goin' out there. They have to be prepared, you know. And the music can prepare them for space. It can prepare them for timelessness, you see. Like, multiplicities of time, therefore it's not any particular time, and that makes this timeless music. You got that. So when you do that, you put all these different times together—they can't be separated and identified as times. And you know, you got 'em all clashing together, you got 'em in the cracks an' all that, and it's just like you've got twelve notes, twelve sounds in Western music, but there are many more sounds. Maybe they just got the four/four and the three/four, but there are many, many different rhythms. All these rhythms, I'd really have to teach the earth musician how to play them. But they can't be taught. They have to feel it.

But what I'm doin' is so profound . . . so simple, that the people can catch it before the musicians. It's the first time this ever happened on this planet, that the people can catch what I'm doin' and feel what I'm doin' quicker than musicians who are well schooled. And I will take a musician and it will take some time for them to even hear—even though they might be in the band— it's some time before they can really hear what I am doin'. But the public, they might not even know any music, but they can feel what I am doing. That's the situation. Because the earth musician hasn't been anywhere but here. So it's kind of difficult to say "look, let's play space, you know." Then you write it, and they might play the notes, but then it might be some time before they could really play the feeling. On the other hand, people who are not musicians, they're not restricted to say "well, this got to be right" or "this got to be wrong." All they know is how they feel. A schooled musician is really in trouble with me, because they have these limitations, they're be- hind these bars in music. It's the same thing as jail, to get behind these bars and the measure thing, you know. But I've risen up outside the bars. I'm not in the bars. I'm playing according to how I feel. And that's just like when you talk, you don't talk in "one, two, three, four, one, two, three." You express yourself by certain words, and you don't really know how you're going to say them. But you can't study that. You say them according to what you need to express yourself. And that's the way music should be, it should be what the musician is expressing, and not worry about the rules and all that, as long as he can express himself and people hear and feel it, that's the answer.

JC: *Can a person be a good musician and not be a schooled musician?*

SR: Yeah, that can happen quite often. But in this kind of music it's gonna be a challenge for the schooled and the unschooled, because I'm expressing something I've experienced on psychic planes. If they haven't experienced that they might be doubtful or they can't reach that point yet. For instance, some of this music, if you're playing it on your phonograph and somebody comes in the room that's not really your friend (but supposed to be), the music will get really soft. You'll have to strain. But if somebody comes in, a really true friend of yours, the music will be amplified and get louder.

IR: *You're talking about psychic planes. What are you talking about? These experiences, what have they been like?*

SR: Well, one experience I went to Jupiter, you know? And that's why I'm always singing about Jupiter: I actually was there looking at this planet. So I been there. Now people might not believe it, but I went there and I know I went there. I didn't stay there too long . . . I had a guide. I couldn't see him—he was standing off behind my left shoulder. Something like a shadow. He was there, he took me there.

IR: *Has going to different planets really broadened your music? How has it affected it?*

SR: It's affected me in a way where it made me be *me*, instead of being what somebody else's image was of what I should be; it made me really be true to myself instead of being programmed or oriented to something else . . . the way man's world is—which is shaking and just about gone—I didn't become a part of that. Fortunately I didn't. And because I didn't, I can help others to not be part of the program-thing. Because they're facing liquidation. And I mean real liquidation, 'cause that's what the meltdown is. It's liquidation. They always talk about Russia liquidates people, this time they really did it. Some psychics told me that some of the people near that nuclear reactor melted in their boots. I mean bones and all. It was so hot, they didn't have time to burn. It was so hot they actually melted, liquidated, meltdown in their boots. Now, that hasn't been told to the general public 'cause it's terrifying enough as it is, but it was a meltdown. Therefore, I've been singing about space for a long time, about the space age. And this time it's staring every person in the face.

IR: *So you've sort of broken out of the "conventional" types of things that people are singing about and writing about and sort of been a vanguard in your own sense?*

SR: Well it's more than avant-garde, because the "avant-garde" refers to, I suppose, advanced earth music, but this is *not* earth music. It has nothing to do with it. Music that's from a celestial plane, it's not part of this planet. The things they have on this planet, you judge a tree by the fruit. You see the conditions. Those are the things that people think are right. And this wisdom has brought them to the edge of anarchy and the edge of destruction. So, therefore, I won't deal with those things. I'm talking about something that's so impossible . . . it can't possibly be true. But it's the only way the world's gonna survive, this impossible thing. I'm talking about impossibilities. So I have to play things that are impossible. I have to get to a piano and hit some notes on there that aren't on there. And I'm doin' it all the time. Some piano players are watching my hand, and they say "it's not on the piano." Of course it's not on the piano. That's the way I feel about things, so when I hit the piano, it's going to sound what's in my mind. I don't think of the piano as a piano, I think of it as an instrument. And I want the drummers—don't think about playing drums, think about playing instruments. I don't want them to play saxophones, I want them to play instruments. And actually when they play instruments, then they make other instruments vibrate. And those other instruments are *people themselves*. They are instruments, you know? They got two harps: they got one here [points to one ear] and one there [points to the other]. Now, they don't know that their ears are harps, got strings in 'em. And that's the way they hear, you see. So say, for instance, they haven't heard but maybe about four strings in their head vibrated. All the rest of the strings up there all these years—nothing happening. Now, suppose I play some new sounds, it's gonna make some strings in their ear vibrate. It might hurt their head at first, but then that's 'cause they haven't used their ears! They haven't heard these sounds. But the instant that string vibrates, then that's another string that's alive. Let's pull all these strings, hit a chord and make them all vibrate. Then the person will be more alive than they've ever been.

See, on the earth plane they got nerve-gas and all that. Well actually I've got some nerve-music. I play my nerve-music and get these folks on this planet in order. Actually, I could stop a war by gettin' up above with a spaceship and playing some of my music. And they'll stop fightin'. They have to. Because people are made a certain way and from a scientific point of view, certain sounds will stop them from fighting. A whole army would stop if they heard a sound that frightened them. They would flee for cover. And that's all you need. Sounds! You get up above them, you play these sounds: everybody stops fighting. You know man is very superstitious. If he hears a sound he can't *explain,* he'll stop everything—and flee for cover. So will animals in the forest. They hear everything—the bees and the birds. But suppose a strange sound happened. Every animal in the forest will stop eating grass and they'll get in the wind. And then maybe they get on the mountainside and say: "What was that?" Because the sound would make them run. So, that's what I'm talkin' about, *in music.* Strange sounds can make people turn another way.

IR: *Has this sort of philosophy been with you ever since the beginning, ever since the [Fletcher] Henderson band?*

SR: Philosophy is a conjecture. I'm dealing with equations. That's different from philosophy. Philosophy is something like religion, it's a theory. It could be true or not true. But I'm not dealing with theories, I'm dealing with equations. And these equations are very important for people to know. If people on this planet had one thing to hold on to that they know is true, they'd have something to work with. But they don't have any equations, you see—except how to make a nuclear reactor. But I'm talking about other, simple equations. Like if I ask some teenager: "What's the number of this planet?" They couldn't tell me. Everybody ought to know the number of this planet. They need to know. Why's it called "earth"? Now that's very simple, but they're not teachin' it in school. And it's the first thing they should know. Why is this planet called "earth?"

JC: *Why?*

SR: You don't know?

JC: *No.*

SR: Earth is the third planet from the sun, right? Number three. If you take "third" and permutate it, you might have "dirht." Do you have dirt here? Okay, well you got third planet, number "three." Take that and permutate it: "ereth." What does that spell? Earth. Well that's why it's called earth. The letter for this planet is "g." See, somebody took the "g," which in Greek is number three, in Hebrew it's number three, somebody took that "g" away and put a "c." Now "c" represents the water. So they took the "g," which stands for the earth, and it's perfectly all right. This planet's number three, so: alpha, beta, gamma. And you can prove that it's true with the word "g-eography"—talking about the earth—and "g-eology"—talking about the earth. So they should put that "g" back up there where it belongs. And not put the "c" up there where the water is in place of the earth. So, they might say: "This whole thing is like magic." People: no such thing as a man and a woman. That's over with. That was abolished. So they are really gods. Everybody on this planet is a god. You see, so they've got to find out what's the code, the rule for gods. Because, if they try to follow the manlike thing, they're *passe* before they begin. Man has no fate but to die and to be in a box. So then they have to realize that they are gods. And when you're a god, you've got no "ten commandments of god." You got another kind of code.

And you have to, what I call "evolute E-V-E-R." You move on to eternal things, and not be just *passe,* back there in the past. But, you know they got certain symbols and things that you've got to be aware of. And if you were teaching that in school, there wouldn't be any trouble with teenagers. Because it would balance. All they need is something that they know is true. And then they would settle down. But they don't have anything to hold on to. We're in the space age. Mom and pop can't tell them anything. They know more than mom and poppa, in one sense. They have to really stop calling them "children." They're not children; no such thing as children on this planet any more. They come in knowing things.

IR: *What do all the elaborate costumes symbolize?*

SR: Well, in the early days in every nation, everyone had their costume. 'Cause they identified the nation. Like everyone today got their flags and things. That represents the nation. And that's the colors. If you're out fighting a battle, they say: "Fly your colors. You got to have your colors." And so every night I'm fighting a different kind of battle, so I have to change according to that night. Tonight I wore this because it fits in with the black background. Now if it had been another kind of background I would have worn my other stuff. It has to blend. If the background was a certain way and I put on my other stuff it wouldn't look right. But this looked all right, 'cause this is black and shiny, and this fits with the purple, and that's music too, you see. Costumes are music. Colors throw out musical sounds, too. Every color throws out vibrations of life. And every statue throws out vibrations of life. That's for you people who call it "heathen worship," like some people got this Buddhist statue. This statues throwin' out some *sounds!* You can prove it scientifically, 'cause the wind comes by [whistles], and makes a sound. And if you stand before it, you'll be oriented by the sound. And if everybody worshiped Buddhah, went and stood before Buddhah, they gonna be brainwashed and programmed by the sound comin' from Buddhah. It's just as if he's alive. Any other statue you face is definitely alive. The wind makes a sound. There's a movie called *Unheard Sounds*—I saw it; it was in the New York Library, but it didn't get much publicity. But they demonstrated you can hear sounds from statues. So I'm dealing with things on a very meticulous basis, because my job is very difficult—impossible. My job is to change five billion people to something else. Totally impossible. And that's why I've played the low profile. Because it can't be done, but I have to do it. I'm told by superior forces: "It has to be done, and you can do it." So who am I to doubt it? Everyone else can do the possible things, why should I waste my time with that? Everything that's possible's been done by man; I have to deal with the impossible. And when I deal with the impossible and am successful, it makes me feel good because I know that I'm not bullshittin'.

JM: *How did it feel to read your poetry yesterday?*

SR: You mean in New York? Oh that felt nice, you know, that something is happening because some folks have brought us together, John Cage and I. And that, to some people, seemed totally impossible. It was. But John Cage felt that what I'm doin', well that's it, and what he's doin', that's it. And we're both talking about the same thing, in one sense, about happiness. And that people don't have to be what they are and do what they're doin'. He's talking about that. Of course, he's talkin' about the "love thing"—that's his department. But I'm not talkin' about that. As far as love is concerned, I got a song that says: "The men love me, and the women love me, little children love me, 'cause one of my names is Sin. And everybody loves me." I didn't do that one tonight. But it really gets strange reactions, 'cause one time I did that in Baltimore and a man was sittin' there, and at that part he jumped up and hugged me and said "yes, I love you. I always been lovin' you." I couldn't get away from him. So I said I better not sing that too often. [laughs]

But, yes, I'm dealin' with equations. And they're gonna be put out there. It actually will change the planet. And people need to know the truth, and religions need to know the truth. They have to know that what they're doin' has brought this planet to the edge of anarchy and destruction. You judge a tree by the fruit. Whatever they're doin', even if it's right, it's killin' people. And that's what I'm talking about. There 'ain't nothing they can say. In fact, they're killing each other in religions. But today we've reached the end of the road. There are superior forces. Of course, they worship a *supreme* being. I'm talking about a *superior* being. A supreme being is all right, but a superior being is much better because "superior" can always get better and better and better. "Supreme": it's finished. It can't go no further. But superior can keep on movin', keep on movin', because it gets more superior every day. And I like that word. It's an active word. "Supreme" is an adjective, but "superior"—it moves over into something else, now doesn't it. You might say it's a verb, because it's so active. So I'm dealing with activity. Action speaks louder than words, they say. And of course, as I said, I've been playing the low profile, because it really will get to teenagers. I know that. In Germany, a woman said to me, "This music is gonna reach teenagers, and it's going to reach them all over the world. And they all are going to listen." At that time I told her, "Well I won't ever be around then because as far as I'm concerned they're all chips off the old block, and the old blocks ain't no good." But increasingly, like in Europe, more and more they're showin' up. It even made a London newspaper that punk rockers, all them showed up this time. Right up there on stage, John [Gilmore] said: "You know, I believe it's going to happen." I said: "I know it is, John." Because they got to have something to hold on to. And dope is not gonna do it—you get tired of that. Religion's not

Sun Ra
(photo: David Corio)

gonna do it. Education's not gonna do it. Actually, this whole thing about space, because the year 2000 is right around the corner, you know. And if you've got a kid five years old, he'll be twenty in the year 2000. Now they got to have something to hold on to. The French government seems to be aware of that, because they've offered me to come over there and take over all the arts. And this way, create, and while I'm creating the dancers are there, the poets are there, the novelists are there, in this one place. And as I create, they create. No government has ever thought of that. In other words: all the arts move together. 'Cause they'll be hearing the music. And then they create dances according to what they hear. And they'll be dealing with creativity then. And that's a good idea. Now they say they're going to do it. In fact, I'm going to Germany and the French government has asked me to invite some of their dignitaries to come up there so that they can talk about it.

JM: *Does it surprise you that they asked you to do that?*

SR: Well, no. I like challenges. Of course I'm a Gemini, so that means I'd be quite pleased to do the impossible.

IR: *How did you get the name Sun Ra? What does that signify?*

SR: You see, on this planet everybody who came here tryin' to help the planet, they couldn't do it because they didn't have the authority to do it. So what I did, I went and registered Sun Ra as a business. So then I put down what my business is. So if I want to go out and help people, it ain't nobody's business if I do! Sun Ra is not a person, it's a business name. And on the certificate, it's a business certificate which was gotten in New York City; they didn't notice that I didn't have down there what my business was. They stamped it, notarized it, and they filed it. So therefore, it's a business name, and my business is changin' the planet. So I have legality behind me. If Jesus had done that, gone and gotten himself a business certificate, he'd have had the right and he wouldn't have had to go up there on the cross. But then, he didn't have no legality, and he didn't have any authority behind him what-soever. All these other people have been trying to help the world, they don't have the authority to do it. And at least you should respect man enough to go to his coach and say I'm gonna do this and I'm gonna do that, and make him sign it. He can't do nothing. So Sun Ra is a business name. So if they say that my name is this-that-and-the-other, just remember, it's a business name. And business is not family, nothin'. They just happen. A business just hap-pens, it's not born. It just happens. And corporations are like that, they just happen. And they're eternal, too. You get a corporation, it's eternal.

[At this point the reporter began asking Sun Ra to do a station ID for the jazz show, but Sun Ra was not finished . . .]

SR: Of course my individual name on my passport is Le Sony'r Ra. That's what the United States government stamped. And Egypt stamped it. And

Germany stamped it. And England stamped it. And France stamped it. And Finland stamped it. All these nations stamped that my name is Le Sony'r Ra, and if it wasn't, it is now. [laughs] It is now. 'Cause they stamped it. And therefore, I've got the approval of man that that's my name. And I don't have any other identification. Sometimes I use Sun Ra on musician's cards as my professional name, but actually it's a business name. So I have the business of changing a planet. I have my legality and everything, and I have my right and authority to change the planet. Every nation on the planet, to change it for the betterment, because they don't know what to do themselves. So I do it for them. Not from a religious point of view; from a business point of view. You see, because this planet belongs to someone else, and the landlord sent me here. The tenants here are not treating the property good. So we have to either evict them, or get them to change. And if they get evicted, where are they goin'? No other landlord gonna let them come on their planet. So I'm tellin': "look, this is not your planet. You're staying here. It belongs to somebody, the landlord." Some people say it belongs to Satan. Well then they really ought to be scared. Yeah, they really ought to be frightened. Now, what did you want me to say about the station . . . ?

Fred Anderson   Anderson tends bar regularly at the Velvet
Lounge, which keeps him from being very active as a recording
artist. His few records are all worth seeking, however. For a
sample of his work as a founding member of Chicago's AACM, see Joseph Jarman's mid-sixties
Delmark record *Song For.* As a leader, Anderson recorded several LPs for small labels between
1977 and 1983; the most readily available of these are *Another Place* on Moers Music (quintet
with George Lewis on trombone, always a treat) and *The Missing Link* on Nessa, both of which
showcase his marvelous, husky tone and rich sense of melody.

Derek Bailey   One of the great joys of listening to Derek Bailey's work is that so often it
introduces you to other musicians you've never heard of, like teenage reed wonderchild Alex
Ward, who plays with percussionist Steve Noble on *Ya Boo, Reel, & Rumble,* released on Bailey's
Incus label. That said, Bailey's solo guitar improvising is mandatory listening for anyone
interested in guitar, improvisation, or both. Two solo discs mark twenty years of solo development; the first, recorded in 1971 (reissued with extra tracks), is beautiful and extremely noisy,
while the latter disc (rather poorly recorded) dates from 1991, with seven elegant pieces
recorded sequentially in two sittings on one day. Earlier solo records include *Aida* (which
many Bailey fans swear is the best), *Lot 74, Domestic and Public Pieces, In Whose Tradition?,
Improvisation,* and my personal pick of the pack, *Notes.* With his fledgling improvising ensembles, there are excellent records available: *The Music Improvisation Company 1968–1971* has just
been reissued on CD; the same group's self-named ECM release is often seen at used stores.
Emanem records recently put out a couple of early Spontaneous Music Ensemble records,
though most releases by this group are very hard to find (despite many years of scouring
stores, I have a bunch yet to scare up). SME leader John Stevens drums fantastically on his 1993
duo disc with Bailey, *Playing.* Drummer Tony Oxley has a couple of impossible-to-obtain
records that include Bailey from the late sixties on RCA (Oxley's later Incus record sans
guitarist, *February Papers,* is utterly gorgeous). Iskra 1903, a trio which used to include Derek
(now violinist Phil Wachsmann), alongside trombonist Paul Rutherford and bassist Barry
Guy, has an excellent double record set on Incus. Bailey's work as a duo partner has produced
many fine records—with Evan Parker, some of the most sensitive duo improvising you'll find
anywhere: check out their *London Concert* and *Compatibles.* With Anthony Braxton, Bailey
made several excellent recordings (*Royal, Duo 1 & 2,* and *Moment Précieux*). To hear Bailey,
Braxton, and Parker in mix 'n' match sessions, *Company 2* documents the second meeting of
Bailey's nonfestival (all Company releases are full of interesting music; some, like *Once,* also
include some duller moments—such is the risk that improvised music takes to reach for peaks
of unforseen intensity). I highly recommend two unusual Company recordings: *Fables* and
Fictions. More recent Bailey records include a duet CD with bassist Barre Phillips (*Figuring*), a
trio disc with South African drummer Louis Moholo and African percussionist Thebe Lipere

(*Village Life*), and a splendiforous duet with Brazilian percussionist Cyro Baptista (*Cyro*). If you like Bailey's approach, don't miss his outing with clarinetist Tony Coe (*Time*), his duet with percussionist Jamie Muir (*Dark Drug*), and his encounter with Americans George Lewis and John Zorn (*Yankees*). And, for goodness sake don't forget to obtain Bailey's earth-stopping 1988 tête-à-tête with pianist Cecil Taylor, *Pleistozaen mit Wasser.* Naturally, every time I pick up a 1960s record with an English studio band on it, I check for Bailey's name; guitarist Davey Williams told me that Derek once admitted to having played on a Dinah Shore record, a factoid that Bailey now denies.

Han Bennink   Though I am an advocate and big fan of improvised music on record, I must admit that Han Bennink is best experienced in the flesh. It's just impossible for vinyl or disc to suggest the spatial and conceptual provocations that Bennink throws at an audience, his slapstick humor (often visually cued), and his impeccable timing. Plus, when he does record, more often than not the sound is less than stellar. Still, his records are not to be passed over, as several outings with Derek Bailey indicate: *Derek Bailey & Han Bennink* (1972), *The Topography of the Lungs* (a 1970 trio classic with Derek and Evan Parker), and *Han* (1986). Bennink's ongoing duo with pianist Misha Mengelberg should be sought out; you can start with their rhythm section work on Eric Dolphy's *Last Date* record from 1964 and proceed to their insane SAJ record *Einepartietischtennis*, or, if you get very lucky in a European flea market, some of the records on their own Instant Composers Pool (ICP) label. An alternate *Last Date* was issued on ICP, notable for the record's flip side, which is a duet between Mengelberg and his parrot, Eeko, who chewed up the master tape heard on side A. Bennink also drums with Mengelberg's ICP Orchestra—check out two volumes of *Bospaadje Konijehol (Forest path rabbithole)*. With Dutch saxophonist Willem Breuker, Bennink has made two bonzo records as the New Acoustic Swing Duo, and an excellent old record on Horo, *A European Proposal* puts Mengelberg and Bennink in the ring with British trombonist Paul Rutherford and Italian saxist Mario Schiano. His recent *Clusone Trio,* with clarinetist Michael Moore and cellist Ernst Reijseger, is simply a killer. Bennink has a couple of solo records, too; I like the clear sound of *Tempo Comodo* best. Over the last few years, Bennink has recorded in less out-there contexts as well, featuring the music of Herbie Nichols and Thelonious Monk on *Regeneration, Change of Season,* and *Dutch Masters*. His propulsive kit also drives Harry Miller's buoyant, South African-tinged *Down South*. For Bennink's important collaborations with Peter Brötzmann, see below. Bennink's favorite record, if you're wondering, is New Orleans drum genius Baby Dodds's solo 10-inch on Folkways.

Steve Beresford   Beresford has been described as a musical chameleon, and indeed his discography reflects the breadth of his interests and activities. For Beresford the pianist, definitely check out *Directly to Pyjamas*, his duet with hero Han Bennink (released, as is much of his work of recent vintage, on the hard-to-get Nato label from France). His noisier improvised side is audible on *Imitation of Life*, with Tristan Honsinger, Toshinori Kondo, and David Toop, and also on his wonderful solo LP, *The Bath of Surprise*. The group Alterations made several fine records, of which I prefer *My Favourite Animals*. For Beresford's bizarro-camp-pop stuff, there's plenty to choose from: Vic Reeves's *I Will Cure You* beats all; Beresford made a tape with General Strike for Touch called *Danger in Paradise* and with John Zorn he concocted the dangerously hip *Deadly Weapons*. All the Melody Four records are equally bonkers and fab, as are his dedications to Doris Day, Charles Trénet, and Brigitte Bardot. Beresford plays with the Frank Chickens on two records, on the Flying Lizards' eponymous

LP, on a bootleg Slits record from 1979 (*Typical Girls*), on a dub reggae record by Prince Far-I (*Cry Tuff Dub Encounter Chapter III*), and various other Adrian Sherwood projects (most notably with the inextinguishable beat of African Head Charge).

Anthony Braxton   The specific concert referred to in our interview was released as *Quartet (Victoriaville) 1992* on Victo Records; incidentally, the section during which Braxton jerry-rigged his sax was edited out. The magnitude of Braxton's recorded output since the mid-sixties is truly stupifying, both in sheer quantity and range of approaches. And his records often include Braxton's own charming, neologism-packed notes (which always serve to piss off critics) and quasi-scientific graphic composition titles (which have recently started to include stick figures and landscapes!). From the early years, two Delmark records are mandatory listening: the breakthrough solo record *For Alto* and little-instruments oriented quartet session *3 Compositions of New Jazz*. Similarly AACM-influenced records on Actuel (*Anthony Braxton* and *This Time . . .*), from when Braxton disgustedly left the U.S. for Paris in the late sixties, have yet to be disc-ed; however, *Town Hall (Trio & Quintet) 1972*, a rare live record has recently been reissued on CD. Other fine solo records are available on New Albion, Inner City, and hat ART. Braxton mentions his "minute" with a major label—he recorded some incredible music for Arista in the mid-seventies, including a duet with Muhal Richard Abrams and a criminally overlooked record with two different trios, *For Trio*. Arista also released two large ensemble recordings, one three-record set for three orchestras (which includes notes with plans for a piece to be completed by the year 2000 that will utilize galaxies rather than orchestras—shades of Mr. Ra) and the magnificent *Creative Orchestra Music 1976*. Recent large-ensemble works have been issued as *Eugene (1989)* (more jazzy), *Composition No. 165 (for 18 Instruments)* (very Stockhausen-ish), and the gorgeous *2 Compositions (Ensemble) 1989/1991* (more Webern-esque). Other highly recommended odds and ends include a trio disc with percussionist Tony Oxley, an encounter with Rova Saxophone Quartet, duets with Marilyn Crispell and Peter Niklas Wilson, an overlooked classical record with the Robert Schumann String Quartet, and a quartet record with David Rosenboom playing piano rather than Crispell. Braxton's variously celebrated and despised standards records are hit or miss; I like the two *In the Tradition* records on Inner City, but don't much care for the two on Magenta. A Monk date with pianist Mal Waldron is excellent, as is the Lennie Tristano disc with Rova's baritonist Jon Raskin and piano prodigy Dred Scott. I once heard Braxton complain that record companies only wanted to record his quartet music, to which he responded by assembling one of the best quartets in modern jazz history—with Crispell, bassist Mark Dresser, and drummer Gerry Hemingway—destined to go down alongside Coltrane and Coleman's classic four-somes. There are many excellent quartet records, including three two-disc sets on Leo, but for the best (and a fine way into the music of Anthony Braxton), I propose a large investment right off the bat, with the four-disc set *Willisau (Quartet) 1991*, a brilliant half-live/half-studio hat ART box.

Peter Brötzmann   For the bulk of his career, Brötzmann has worked hand-in-hand with Free Music Productions (FMP), the record company for whom he has created much of his best work, and whose style of graphics he, in turn, deeply impacted. Early records, as of yet unreissued on digital format, include 1967's Albert Ayler-esque *For Adolphe Sax* (great trio with Kowald and Johannson) and 1969's *Nipples*, one half of which is quartet (classic Brötz/van Hove/Bennink plus bassist Bushi Niebergall) and the other side adds Evan Parker and Derek Bailey. The essential record from this period is Peter Brötzmann Octet's *Machine Gun*, a tremendous statement of energy and love for powerful sound; the CD reissue has a fascinating alternate take of the title cut, which is an aural adventure that culminates in an unprecedented orgy of free jazz and rhythm and blues. A rare mid-seventies LP called *Hot Lotta* brings Brötz and Kowald together with Finnish free musicians Edward Vesala (percussion) and Juhani Aaltonen (tenor, flute), and on various Globe Unity Orchestra records Brötzmann is heard to great advantage (listen to side one of *The Living Music* by Alexander von Schlippenbach for a taste of his most ferocious blowing). Brötzmann's commitment to trio format is in evidence in more great music with Bennink and van Hove (*Balls, Outspan No. 1* and *No. 2, Tschüs,* and *Brötzmann*), with bassist Harry Miller and drummer Louis Moholo (*The Nearer the Bone, The Sweeter the Meat* and *Opened, But Hardly Touched*) and with Bennink and pianist Misha Mengelberg (*3 Points and a Mountain*). A 1971 concert brought trombonist Albert Mangelsdorff together with the Bennink/van Hove trio, resulting in a three-record set that's now available on CD (*Elements/Couscouss de la Mauresque/The End*). And, if you're down for what he calls a "very special" record, don't miss Brötzmann/Bennink's outdoor record *Scwartzwaldfahrt,* recorded on the trees and rocks and in the babbling brooks of the Black Forest. Since the disbanding of his regular trios, Brötzmann has worked in a smattering of different, variously successful ensembles. His adventures with Last Exit won him few points in the improvising community, but may have introduced him to more rock fans; I prefer their first, self-named record to any of their subsequent releases (though I wouldn't trade one note of *Machine Gun* for a month of *Last Exits*). Likewise, a disc with his son, guitarist Caspar Brötzmann, *Last Home,* drew him into an alternative rock context, as did his surprisingly enjoyable bass-saxophone-only encounter with bassist Bill Laswell, *Low Life.* Perhaps the best way to listen to Peter B., however, is alone. His second solo record (of three), *14 Love Poems,* is sublime; Brötzmann's version of the Ornette Coleman free jazz standard "Lonely Woman" is simply one of the greatest five-and-a-half minutes of passion in recorded music.

John Cage   An accepted line of thinking maintains that Cage was a great philosopher of art, but that his music is better thought about than listened to. I wholeheartedly disagree. Cage's music remains a paradigm for artistic experimentation; the experience of sitting down and listening to Cage remains a genuine, potentially transformative one. For the unmoved, listen to *Indeterminacy,* his self-narrated "new aspect of form in instrumental and electronic music," recorded with David Tudor in the late fifties and recently reissued on Smithsonian/Folkways. Then slip on a slice of his early piano music on *John Cage* (Tomato), *The Perilous Night/Four Walls* (New Albion), and the early percussion compositions masterfully interpreted by Quatuor Helios on *Works for Percussion* (Wergo). For an intriguing pairing of old and new, volume 2 of Arditti String Quartet's *Complete String Quartets* includes one from 1949–50 and one from 1989. Several labels have specialized in Cage's music: Wergo has an authorized "Edition John Cage," hat ART has released excellent Cage material since the late eighties, and the small, pleasingly packaged mode label has a "Music of John Cage" series that features some of his least-recorded late work. Some of the most beautiful Cage recordings were made for the misnamed Mainstream label back in the 1960s—his "Cartridge Music" and "Aria with Fontana Mix" are classics (compare the former with a new version on mode's fantastic *Music for Merce Cunningham;* compare the latter, which originally had Cathy Berberian singing "Aria," with Eberhard Blum's new version on hat ART). The Italian Cramps label has a sampler simply called *John Cage,* with pieces from 1947 to 1971, including an edited version of "62 Mesostics Re Merce Cunningham" (for a full-length version of this harsh piece, Eberhard Blum does a heavy version on a hat ART two-CD set). Believe it or not, there are a couple of recordings of Cage's "4'33"," the silent piece, perfect for digital technology.

George Clinton   Starting with Parliament, I'm going to give you the plan to put the P in your life. Get *First Thangs* first. Then, in this order, get all the Casablanca Parliament records—*Mothership Connection, Funkentelechy, Chocolate City, The Clones of Dr. Funkenstein, Up for the Down Stroke, Parliament Live* (go to a used record store and get the LP, which, if yer lucky, will contain a poster and T-shirt iron-on); after a break to get some Funkadelic stuff (see below) get *Motor Booty Affair, Trombipulation,* and *Gloryhallastoopid.* If you want it, the recent compilation *Tear the Roof Off 1974–1980* is good and contains great notes by the funkiest critic on the planet, Greg Tate, but it ain't all you need, dig? P-Funk Allstars have a live one and the studio monster *Urban Dancefloor Guerrilla.* The Brides of Funkenstein made two glitzy records for Atlantic, while Parlet's tough-to-find three on Casablanca are a bit better; Bootsy Collins's spinoff records are all a little goofy and cute, but they're awful funky, too. Collins's own three-woman production, *Godmama,* is a rarely seen bomb (that's good, in P-Speak). Bernie Worrell has a bunch of cool dates; check out his newest, *Blacktronic Science,* which has ample P-Funk sound and lots of Clinton's dulcet tones. Other bits and pieces include Clinton-produced records by Eddie Hazel, Philippe Wynne, Fred Wesley, and the Horny Horns (check the super-tuff one called *Say Blow by Blow Backwards*), Incorporated Thang Band, Trey Lewd, and the less-advisable Jimmy G. and the Tackheads. Clinton's solo records have been somewhat critically short-sheeted, though like the late Parliament records they were very popular dance-inducers. Of course, get *Computer Games* for "Atomic Dog" and much more; Clinton's Paisley Park debut, *The Cinderella Theory,* has lots of great material and a touch of drek (it's worth it). *Hey Man, Smell My Finger* has just hit the shelves, and you need it bad. Otherwise, you can count on getting your fill of stinky funk on the original Westbound Funkadelic records, all of which have been reissued and all of which are worth owning. The later Funkadelic records, including the classic *One Nation under a Groove,* have just been reissued on disc by Charly, though Pedro Bell's intricate record covers are easier on the eyes at 12 inches. Avoid at all costs the Clinton-less *Who's a Funkadelic* and the Funkadelic single "By Way of the Drum" (ruined by producer Jeff Lorber) . . . P-yew! Westbound's singles collection is essential to the well-stocked house, with kickin' photos and an outstanding historical liner-book that you need a magnifying glass to read. For the *Family Series,* I like the second volume best, but I eagerly await the last two installments. Finally, to hear the very earliest, if you can find it there's a bootleg on Sta-Tite Records that goes from the doo-wop of the Parliaments' 1958 "Party Boys" to the acid-funk of Funkadelic's "Vital Juices," the B-side guitar solo to their 1975 single "Red Hot Mama."

Nicolas Collins   Collins's experiments with remix, which he took into a vanguard nondance context, culminated in *Devil's Music,* a nonstop radio samples LP that needs to be reissued on disc. His two currently available CDs are both highly recommended. *100 of the World's Most Beautiful Melodies* features Collins using his trombone-computer to sample, hold, and edit improvisations by a cool cast of characters like Davey Williams, Peter Cusack, Shelley Hirsch, Zeena Parkins, George Lewis, Ned Rothenberg, and John Zorn. *It Was a Dark and Stormy Night* contains three intriguing compositions: one solo for trombone-propelled electronics, one for modified, skipping CD machine and string quartet, and a semiotic shaggy-dog story that gives the disc its name.

The Ex   Many of the Ex's best songs are on small-batch 7-inch singles, like the four-record set *Dignity of Labor,* "Enough Is Enough," "War Is Over/Dust/New Wars II," an installment-plan set of six singles called *The Ex 6,* and "1936" (which is packaged as two singles sandwiching a book of photos from the Spanish Revolution). The group is vehemently against record-collector elitism, though, and has done its best to make its work widely available at a reasonable price, and their packaging usually includes posters, newspapers, postcards, and other tasty agit-prop surprises. For a taste of earlier, slightly rawer days, *Hands Up! You're Free* is taken from three separate sessions they recorded for John Peel's radio program, and look for the group's 1981 record *History Is What's Happening,* one of the all-time great post-punk records. *Blueprints for a Blackout* has been reissued on disc, as has the two-record *Joggers and Smoggers,* a fantastic value on one CD. The group's exciting encounter with improvising cellist Tom Cora is available on *Scrabbling at the Lock,* which also contains vocals by Catherine Jauniaux.

Fluxus An excellent collection, *Fluxus Anthology/Recorthings* brings together assorted Fluxus sound materials old and new, including work by John Cage, Joseph Beuys, Yoko Ono, Nam June Paik, Milan Knizak, Ben Vautier, Wolf Vostell, and others. Vostell's own *Dé-coll/age* is a tough-to-find noisy gem, and records and discs are available by Beuys and Paik (piano duets by nonpianists), Takehisa Kosugi (violin solos and improvised trios with Peter Kowald and Danny Davis), Alison Knowles, and other Flux-folks. For a bird's-ear on additional "expanded arts" sonic exploration, check out the compilations *Futurism and Dada Reviewed* and *Dada for Now.* Kurt Schwitters *Ursonate* (performed by Eberhard Blum for hat ART or Jaap Blonk for BVHAAST) is a must-hear, and if possible you should try to find a copy of Jean Dubuffet's early-sixties sound recordings, collected on Finnidar Records as *Musical Experiences.*

Von Freeman For such a tireless musician, Vonski has made far too few records. His earliest work went largely undocumented, and the 1972 big-break record with Atlantic, *Doin' It Right Now,* remains a fairly obscure object for used-bin searches. Several outings for Nessa in the seventies are pretty good, but not indicative of his live punch. *Freeman and Freeman* unites him with son Chico to good effect (and includes the beautiful piano of Muhal Richard Abrams), and a record for the tiny Southport label, *Walkin' Tuff!,* is also strong. Recently, I caught him recording live at Chicago's Green Mill (best of all possible jazz lounges) with trumpeter Brad Goode for Delmark Records; this may well be the disc that catches up with Mr. V.

Milford Graves Regrettably, Milford Graves has not made a solo drum record, though he has come close. A mid-sixties ESP record makes a "percussion ensemble" out of a duet between Graves and Sunny Morgan (of course, Graves is an ensemble in himself); his two records of duets with pianist Don Pullen, *Nommo* (vols. 1 and 2), are free music underground classics and in spots they indicate the astounding sound of Graves by himself. He also appears on pianist Paul Bley's *Barrage* (with a rare non-Arkestra appearance from saxist Marshall Allen) and a couple of Giusseppi Logan records, all on ESP. Graves's recordings with the New York Art Quartet are also great—the self-titled NYAQ record with LeRoi Jones reading "Black Dada Nihilismus" is particularly hardcore, though Graves is better recorded on Fontana Records' *Mohawk.* Graves's work with Albert Ayler is available on *Love Cry,* and his slightly later recordings include a great record with guitarist Sonny Sharrock (*Black Woman*) and his own ridiculously overdriven trio with reedmen Arthur Doyle and Hugh Glover on *Babi.* Graves applies his polyrhythmic approach to the piano with success on an obscure Japanese record, *Meditation among Us,* which includes plenty of Graves's drumwork and playing by excellent Japanese improvisors like the late saxophonist Kaoru Abe and trumpet mad-hatter Toshinori Kondo. Last time I saw Graves live he was playing in a drum-quartet project with Andrew Cyrille, Famoudou Don Moye, and bop-giant Kenny "Klook" Clarke, just before Clarke died (this project produced the record *Pieces of Time*). Over the last few years, Graves has played occasionally in a trio with saxophonist Peter Brötzmann and bassist William Parker—we could only be so lucky that this group would make a record.

Barry Guy   Guy's solo records *Statements V–XI* and *Assist* are both marvy, but they don't pack the blow of his newest lone venture, *Fizzles*, released on Maya Records. Maya—Guy's own label—has two other great discs, the double double-bass of *Arcus* (with bassist Barre Phillips) and the sextet *Elsie Jo*. For a very different bass duo, hear *Paintings* with Peter Kowald. I've also found John Stevens's *No Fear* to be a burning trio with Stevens and Trevor Watts, from 1977; more diffuse, *Endgame* adds pianist Howard Riley, with whom Guy made a number of very rare early trio albums. Guy personally recommends a trio record with Riley and violinist Phil Wachsmann, called *Improvisations Are Forever Now*. LJCO's first two "phases" are documented on rare records: the double-LP *Ode* from 1972 is amazing; SAJ's *Stringer* sports a two-drum ensemble (Tony Oxley and John Stevens) from 1980, with Brötzmann and Kowald in the fray as well. LJCO has made its five best for the Swiss Intakt label; *Zurich Concerts* (with Anthony Braxton), *Double Trouble, Theoria* (with Irene Schweizer), and the two-disc *Portraits* are all excellent, though the band's most consummate disc is *Harmos*, a sparkling recording that can serve as a smart way to ease a neophyte into the pleasures of improvised music and satisfy the appetites of devoted free fans as well. Guy's partnership with Evan Parker has produced a couple of deep duo records as well as the trios detailed below.

Jackdaw with Crowbar   All the Jackdaw records mentioned in "Free, Single, and Disengaged" are hearty listening, though they're way out-of-print. An unexpected new record, *Hanging in the Balance*, from 1992, lacks some of the quirky strengths of the earlier batch, though it has slowly grown on me. Other great bands that recorded for Ron Johnson include Big Flame (who have a complete-works disc due out), Splat!, the Noseflutes, and Twang; one further group deserves special mention—the Shrubs were one of the great bands of the eighties, and their two records, *Take Me aside for a Midnight Harrangue* and *Vessels of the Heart*, and two EPs, *Full Steam into the Brainstorm* and *Blackmailer*, are lost treasures. For a sturdy sampler of unreleased Ron Johnson material, get *The First after Epiphany*, which includes the Ex's outstanding "Knock."

Catherine Jauniaux   Jauniaux has been a bit-part musician for much of her recorded life. Catch a passing sliver of her voice on the Ex's *Scrabbling at the Lock*, with Third Person on *The Bends*, and with Tim Hodgkinson on *Fluvial*. With Aqsak Maboul, she appears most extensively on the essential *Un Peu de l'ame des bandits*, and her singing uplifts the Work's great *Slow Crimes*.

Franz Koglmann   Finding early Koglmann is a more or less hopeless task; each copy of his rewarding LP *Opium/For Franz* (with Bill Dixon) comes in a lovely one-of-a-kind hand-painted cover. You might try to hunt down a copy of *Good Night* by Trio Kokoko (with Koglmann, bassist Klaus Koch, and reedman Eckard Koltermann), an introspective date on the Swiss Creative Works label. The Pipetett's *Schlaf Schlemmer, Schlaf Magritte* has now been reissued on hat ART, the label for which most of Koglmann's mature work has been recorded. Various first-rate ensembles work through his intricate charts on *Orte der Geometrie, Ich*, and *The Use of Memory*, all recommended. A quintet featuring soprano saxophonist Steve Lacy, *About Yesterday's Ezzthetics* is fabulous, especially given the outrageously tight drumwork of Fritz Hauser (check out his mini versions of Sonny Rollins's "St. Thomas"). Koglmann's *A*

White Line is a fine record, full of cut-and-pasted takes on West Coast (American) jazz, European improvised music, and dodecophony; its liner notes, by Koglmann, are very problematic, however, as they attempt to distinguish between black jazz's "emotional immediacy" and white jazz's "rational/geometric lucidity." "You must understand," he explained in his own defense, "I never thought white people are the thinkers and black people are just living in feelings. If you get this impression from the text, I must say the impression comes from overstatement. With the distance of time, here is a kind of overstatement." I find Koglmann's best trumpet and flugelhorn work on *L'Heure blue,* which also includes nutty piano from Misha Mengelberg and great clarinet from Tony Coe (who took the original tenor sax solo on Henry Mancini's "Pink Panther"). With pianist Paul Bley and bassist Gary Peacock, Koglmann turned in strong an all-Annette Peacock session appropriately called *Annette.*

Ikue Mori   Of course, you must own *No New York*—for the Contortions, for DNA, for Teenage Jesus and the Jerks, for Mars, for all of it. John Zorn's Avant label has issued a great live DNA record. As for Mori's later recordings, there are some bright moments by Toh Ban Djan on *Rodan* by shamisen player Michihiro Sato (or Sato Michihiro, if you prefer). Her total drum machine concept is best heard on Zeena Parkins's *Ursa's Door* and on Jim Staley's *Don Giovanni,* and the duo record between Mori and Jauniaux, *vibraslaps* on Recommended Records.

Sainkho Namtchylak   A sampler called *Out of Tuva* (Crammed Discs) collects Sainkho's work between 1986 and 1993, including adventures with the folk ensemble, a cut with Tri-O, a number of pieces with a Moscow orchestra, and a couple of pop cuts. Her best, most varied, and in places frightening improvised work is on her solo CD, *Lost Rivers,* on FMP. The quartet FMP disc is less interesting—for ensemble-Sainkho, I would stick to Leo Records' *Letters,* which sets her up for solos and interesting encounters (a couple even composed) with Swedes Mats Gustafsson and Sten Sandell, the Swiss group Kieloor Entartet, and French bassist Joelle Leandre. She also appears on an unusual miniopera, *Tunguska-Guska,* along with free jazz drum pioneer Sunny Murray.

Evan Parker   Dazzle your friends, amaze guests, and contemplate the limits of unitary subjectivity: Evan Parker's solo soprano records are perfect for parlor room get-togethers and headphone meditation alike. The lot of them was collected in a very limited edition box, but if you see them individually snatch them up. As Evan suggests, each one is unique and substantially different from the others: my own taster's choices would be: *The Snake Decides, At the Finger Palace, Saxophone Solos,* and the new *Conic Sections.* Don't get *Process and Reality* (Parker's overdub disc) or *Hall of Mirrors* (his meeting with electronics expert Walter Prati) until you've heard one of the unadulterated horn recordings. Parker's duo selections are plentiful. With Barry Guy, he has *Incision* on SAJ and *Tai Kyoku* on the Japanese jazz & NOW label. There are also strong duo records with pianist Greg Goodman and trombonist George Lewis. The saxophonist's longstanding duo with percussionist Paul Lytton has resulted in a couple of keepers, and with drummer John Stevens he recorded two volumes of *The Longest Night* in one evening. For his records with Derek Bailey, see above, and he also plays on many early records by the Spontaneous Music Ensemble, Tony Oxley, Company, and Music Improvisation Company. Don't miss his long soprano solo against a patchwork of other players on London Jazz Composers Orchestra's *Portraits.* Parker was a long-term member of South African pianist Chris McGregor's luscious Brotherhood of Breath, whose records on the Ogun label often feature his tenor solos. I'm not crazy about Parker's meeting with Cecil Taylor and Tristan Honsinger on FMP, but he works regularly with two trios that have been together for the long haul (Parker works very well with ensembles that have established a "voice" of their own). With Barry Guy and Paul Lytton, you can't go wrong; their *Atlanta* disc is gorgeous, as is their Incus record (with guest George Lewis), *Hook, Drift, & Shuffle.* The Alexander von Schlippenbach Trio, with Parker, pianist Schlippenbach, and drum genius Paul Lovens, have made some of the best trio free improvised recordings available. Parker's own preference, when I inquired in 1985, was the group's *Pakistani Pomade* (yet to be CD-ed by FMP), though that was before the stupendous *Elf Bagatellen* hit the shelves. After that studio date, with its lucid-dream communication, the trio recorded a more free-jazz-like live disc, *Physics* (both FMP).

Pinetop Perkins   At this ripe age, Perkins is busy making some of his best music. *On Top* is a terrific release, as is *After Hours,* and Perkins plays superbly on Zora Young's *Travellin' Light.* From the mid-seventies, *Boogie-Woogie King* and Luther Johnson's *Luther's Blues* are fine no-frills sessions. In general, I would avoid the Legendary Blues Band's material, much of which has a staid sense about it. Instead, get Perkins with Muddy Waters himself, on *Blues Sky* and on Chess Records' *Muddy Waters* three-disc box. It's available, so you have no excuse not to own Earl Hooker's fantastic *Two Bugs and a Roach,* and for a listen to Pine Top Smith's original "Pine Top's Boogie Woogie," along with nineteen other great late-twenties tracks, Magpie Records' *The Piano Blues: Vocalion 1928–1930* is just waiting to be had.

Lee Perry   An in-depth Lee Perry discography closes the chapter "Tabula Rasta," but a few additional releases are also worth mentioning. Heartbeat continues to amaze with its most exciting Scratch release yet, *Soundzs from the Hot Line,* featuring seventies Black Ark recordings that include the outrageous "Bionic Rat" (here taken directly from tape, as opposed to Trojan's *Open the Gate,* where it was obviously mastered from a clean record) and a thirteen-minute masterpiece called "Free up the Prisoners." *Soundzs* also contains "Ashes and Dust," an old track with new vocals that are a good example of his more extravagant rambling. *Excaliburman,* the first CD release on Seven Leaves that I've run across, is taken from the same period; also fantastic, it includes an edited version of "Free up the Prisoners." On the French Lagoon Records (which I am convinced is simply bootlegging its recordings) and its associated label, Crocodisc, we find both indispensable and utterly wretched releases bearing Lee Perry's name, if not his seal of approval. *Revolution Dub* is a boot-stomper, laying back on unbelievably big beats and brilliant mixes in much the same manner as the equally fine *Black Ark in Dub. Stay Red* is credited to "Lee Perry and Friends," and Perry is cited as executive producer, though Aisha Morrison is named as producer and the mixes—while based on Scratch backing tracks—don't sound much like Lee to me. Even more unfortunate is *Lee Perry Meets Mafia and Fluxy in Jamaica,* which claims to have been recorded in 1976–1977, but features dull, synth-droopy dance-hall beats not in use until at least ten years later. Finally, Lagoon provides a true jewel with *The Good, the Bad, & the Upsetters.* Though it contains no useful liner information (and fails to mention Lee Perry anywhere), the music on this disc tells all—late-sixties vintage instrumentals from the leanest and meanest; get this one and—zow! —groove to the psychotic drum break on "Straight to the Head."

REM   One reason I chose to focus on REM is that, while their records perfectly exemplify the simulation or recuperation of the local-mode music object, the group also made some very strong music; in other words, they're not as easily dismissed as some of the other groups that have gone through this process. Of course, I prefer REM's early work. There, on the *Chronic Town* EP (now available on the CD compilation *Dead Letter Office*) and *Murmur,* the songs retain a mysterious quality, and a murky, dub-ish mix blankets the steady beats. By the time of *Green* and 1991's Grammy-grabbin' *Out of Time,* the group has transformed into the model alternative rock group, with a well-coiffed image, MTV rock-u-mentaries, clear lyrics, and their own patented sound. There is a funny sort of reciprocity that changes the sound of a group like REM, though—as their signature guitar-jangle became the hegemonic rock sound, that very jangle (even on their early records) started to sound mainstream.

Jon Rose   The *Slawterhaus* record suffers from a drum-heavy mix, though the playing is gripping improvised music with a monster rock beat. Rose's historical *hörspiel* are available as *Die Beethoven Konversationen* (Extraplatte) and *Paganini's Last Testimony* (Konnex). Another pastiche-oriented project that incorporates a number of great improvisors (starting with a great spoken-word piece from Derek Bailey) is *Violin Music for Restaurants* (ReR Records). More straight-up improvisations can be heard on *The Relative Band '85* (very nice, loopy playing with flautist Jim Denley, vocalist Gillian McGregor, guitarist Eugene Chadbourne, percussionist David Moss, and saxophonist Steve Moore), on pianist Greg Goodman's *The Construction of Ruins* (duets with Goodman and trios with Goodman and guitarist Henry Kaiser), and on duet records with vocalist Shelley Hirsch, bassist Joelle Leandre, and Chadbourne. His violin work can be heard—along with a snippet of his alter ego, Jo "Doc" Rosenberg—in a hodge-podge of mixed settings (with Barry Guy, Evan Parker, Elliott Sharp, Fred Frith, Luc Houtkamp, etc.) on *Forward of Short Leg,* though the record apparently made him a host of enemies, as he didn't ask many of the other twenty-one participants for permission to release the recordings.

Hal Russell   Hal told me that his first recording session was with Woody Herman for Decca Records, in about 1943, and he recalled that it was called *10 Day Furlough*—though I've never found it nor seen it listed anywhere. Joe Daley Trio's only record, *Newport '63,* is a sought-after rarity, and rightly so. It demonstrates what a personal concept of free-play, quite apart from Ornette's ideas, the Daley Trio was working with. Russell's recording legacy as a leader is not so extensive but virtually all worth listening to. With the NRG Ensemble, pre-ECM records include *NRG Ensemble, Conserving NRG,* and *Generation* (with saxophonist Charles Tyler), all of which include undeservingly obscure saxist Chuck Burdelik. The band also made and distributed cassette tapes; my collection includes *The Sound of Music, Fred,* and the bombastic/fantastic *Hal on Earth. Eftsoons* is a delightfully clamorous duo LP by Hal and Mars. Hal also recorded with the rock band Coctails on their *Long Sound* CD just before he died. But what will hopefully keep Hal Russell in stores near you are the three records he made on ECM—the first, *The Finnish/Swiss Tour,* is a straightforward set, not unlike one you might have seen at a festival; *Hal's Bells* is a solo record on which Hal plays all instruments and uses overdub to make himself an ensemble (I asked if he knew Sidney Bechet's similarly produced sides from the forties, and Hal replied: "No, wow, I'd love to hear those!"); finally, *The Hal Russell Story* is a narrated trip taken by the NRG Ensemble through Hal's life, a weirdly retrospective last work (as if he knew), and something that gets me in the gut.

Sun Ra   There is now a safe and effective way for the newcomer to get into Sun Ra's unfathomably large musical omniverse. Evidence Records, a small label from Conshohocken, Pennsylvania, has been reissuing Ra records at quite a clip. Two ways in: either move chronologically, testing waters with early, more traditionally orchestrated big-band sounds of *Sound Sun Pleasure, Jazz in Silhouette, Supersonic Jazz,* and my favorite *Sun Ra Visits Planet Earth/ Interstellar Low Ways,* with a detour for the disc of showy standards called *Holiday for Soul*

Dance and space-chanting on *We Travel the Spaceways/Bad & Beautiful,* then proceeding on to deeper waters with *Cosmic Tones for Mental Therapy/Art Forms of Dimensions Tomorrow, My Brother the Wind, Vol. II,* and the wild solo disc *Monorails and Satellites.* Or, you could just dive right in and learn to swim with *Other Planes of There,* from 1964, which contains extensive synthesizer insania. Of course, all Saturn records are now in the collectible domain and should be snatched up whenever seen—*Discipline 27-II* desperately needs to be reissued, if only for its chant: "Have you heard the latest new from Neptune, Neptune, Neptune, Neptune?" For a long while, until Evidence came along, *Sun Song* and *Sound of Joy* were the only readily available early-Ra, and they remain excellent records (both bought by Delmark from Transition). ESP has reissued their three very adventurous mid-sixties Ra records on CD; Shandar's two volumes of *Nuits de la Fondation Maeght* and Actuel's *Solar Myth Approach* have also been disc-ed, though MPS's essential *It's after the End of the World* has yet to be treated to disc upgrade. Live dates on Leo, DIW, Rounder, and hat ART are generally good, though I would steer clear of *Friendly Galaxy* (Leo) and *Destination Unknown* (enja), both of which were recorded as Ra's tight grip on the band loosened. Three later Black Saint releases are fine, mixing more standards in with Ra originals; ditto on the quality of two A&M discs, one of which (*Purple Night*) features trumpeter Don Cherry, the other (*Blue Delight*) includes drummer Billy Higgins. One great, obscure record that I've found is a full-length LP of *Nuclear War,* which contains excellent Arkestra work, roller-rinkish organ, Duke Ellington's "Drop Me Off in Harlem," and the great title rap ("It's a motherfucker, don't you know, if they push that button, your ass gotta go . . . whatcha gonna do, without your ass?!"), an update to Charles Mingus's 1961 "Oh Lord Don't Let Them Drop That Atomic Bomb on Me." Finally, for dabblers only, a decent collection came out on the Blast First label—*Out There a Minute* includes cuts excised from various Saturn releases. Personally, I like 'em better in context.

Swedish Improvised Music   The collection that Hal Rammel taped for me is called *Sounds: Contemporary Swedish Improvised Music,* on Blue Tower Records, and it contains an exhaustive booklet with info on the scene and players. Elder piano-statesman Per Henrik Wallin carries a slightly Thelonious Monk-ish sensibility into open territory with drummer Kjell Nordeson and wonderful young reed player Mats Gustafsson on their outstanding Dragon release *Dolphins, Dolphins, Dolphins* (yes, it was digitally recorded, digitally mastered, and appears on disc: DDD). Gustafsson is heard also in a duet with my favorite drummer of all (really) Paul Lovens on *Nothing to Read,* and he is a member of the brilliant trio Gush, whose debut is called *From Things to Sounds.* Gush's keyboardist, Sten Sandell, has a varied disc of his own (*Music from a Waterhole*) and a trio with fellow keyboardists Kristine Scholz and Mats Persson (*Strings and Hammers for Fingers and Nails*), both available on the beautifully packaged Alice Music Production label. That company has also put out a disc with Gush-percussionist Raymond Strid in duets with clarinetist Paul Pignon, and a lovely release by Lokomotiv Konkret of free improvisations accompanying Jewish folk melodies. Finally, Rammel's own instrumentalism is audible on a cassette with Swedish multi-instrumentalist Johannes Bergmark called *Where Saws Sing and Fiddles Bloom.*

Throbbing Gristle/Psychic TV   Though there is a huge amount of TG material available, I think that three records make a sufficient collection: their first release—reissued as *The Second Annual Report*—is abrasive and essential, laying the groundwork for years of industrial music to come; *Greatest Hits (Entertainment through Pain)* is more song-oriented (and includes "Hamburger Lady," surely one of the most unsettling songs of all time); it paves the dance floor for the pre-PTV *20 Jazz Funk Greats.* With PTV, you'll either get completely into them and need everything or be turned off at the doorway—one listen to *Towards Thee Infinite Beat* should let you know your psychick persuasion. Incidentally, if the idea of simulation and sophistic resistance is appealing to you but Psychic TV is just too boring to abide by (as I find them), you might take a listen to the music of Nurse with Wound, HNAS, or any other records on Steven Stapleton's United Dairies label.

Ed Wilkerson, Jr.   As a saxophonist, Wilkerson's best work on record is with the Ethnic Heritage Ensemble. Their records *Impressions, Welcome, Three Gentlemen from Chikago,* and *Ancestral Song* are all excellent, though their best is their big-label breakthrough *Dance with the Ancestors,* on Chameleon (a division of Elektra). If you can find it, Douglas Ewart's Clarinet Choir cassette *Red Hills* is a strong, reedy date. Eight Bold Souls' two records are both solid, showing off Wilkerson's writing style (try the newer *Side Show* for its better soloing), but the big-band Shadow Vignettes' *Birth of a Notion* is very uneven and begs for a better follow-up.

INDEX

●

John Corbett is a regular contributor to such
magazines as *Down Beat, Option, The Wire,* and *New
Art Examiner,* and his scholarly work has appeared
in *October, Stanford Humanities Review,* and
Semiotext(e). He teaches at the School of the Art
Institute of Chicago and hosts two weekly radio
programs.

Library of Congress Cataloging-in-Publication Data
Corbett, John, 1963–
Extended play: sounding off from John Cage to Dr.
Funkenstein / John Corbett.
Discography: p.
Includes index.
ISBN 0-8223-1456-8 (cl). — ISBN 0-8223-1473-8 (pa)
1. Avant-garde (Music)   2. Music—20th century—
History and criticism.   3. Improvisation (Music)
I. Title.
ML197.C768   1994
780'.9'04—dc20   93-43239 CIP